Praise for *Maintaining and Evolving Successful Commercial Web Sites*

If you run a Web site, own a Web site, or are merely responsible for the success of a Web site, this is the book you need. Big picture philosophy and detailed practicality make *Maintaining and Evolving Successful Commercial Web Sites* the appropriate practicum for progressive Web professionals.

—Jim Sterne
Author, Speaker, Consultant, Target Marketing of Santa Barbara

Ashley Friedlein takes four very complex but important subjects and boils them down for you to their essentials. With an abundance of practical examples and a strong feeling for what common sense dictates, he leads you to the heart of what it takes to keep a big site running and improving.

—Bob Boiko
Author, *The Content Management Bible* (Hungry Minds, Inc.)
and President, Metatorial Services Inc.

Ashley Friedlein makes a much-needed contribution to the (often neglected) area of Web site management. Using clear language and straightforward case studies, Friedlein masterfully tackles the "post-launch" phase of Web development. This book will be sought after by all Web site managers.

—Hurol Inan
Author, *Measuring the Success of Your Website* (Longman)
and Consultant

Maintaining & Evolving Successful Commercial Web Sites

Managing Change, Content, Customer Relationships, and Site Measurement

Maintaining & Evolving Successful Commercial Web Sites

Managing Change, Content, Customer Relationships, and Site Measurement

Ashley Friedlein

MORGAN KAUFMANN PUBLISHERS

AN IMPRINT OF ELSEVIER SCIENCE

AMSTERDAM   BOSTON   LONDON   NEW YORK
OXFORD   PARIS   SAN DIEGO   SAN FRANCISCO
SINGAPORE   SYDNEY   TOKYO

Senior Editor   Tim Cox
Publishing Services Manager   Edward Wade
Editorial Coordinator   Stacie Pierce
Project Management   Matrix Productions Inc.
Cover Design   Yvo Riezebos Design
Cover Image   Getty Images/David Gould
Text Design   Side by Side Studios
Composition   Omegatype Typography, Inc.
Copyeditor   Frank Hubert
Proofreader   Toni Zuccarini Ackley
Indexer   Helios Productions
Interior Printer   The Maple-Vail Book Manufacturing Group
Cover Printer   Phoenix Color Corp.

Morgan Kaufmann Publishers
An Imprint of Elsevier Science
340 Pine Street, Sixth Floor
San Francisco, CA 94104-3205
www.mkp.com

07   06   05   04   03   5   4   3   2   1

Library of Congress Control Number: 2002110022
ISBN: 1-55860-830-3

This book is printed on acid-free paper.

Contents

Preface

So you've got a Web site. Now what?

Now it needs to be maintained. Now the pressure is on to maximize the returns on the investment made in the site. Senior management wants reliable information on how the site is performing, customers need to be better serviced, and it is time to go to the next phase to stay competitive. Internal and customer expectations continue to rise.

As an industry, we have had a bit of time to build experience and learn what works and what does not. We are more confident in the basics. But now we are expected not only to squeeze as much performance and value as possible out of existing Web sites, but also tackle more advanced and complex issues such as content management, site measurement, personalization, and integration of the Web site into core business processes and objectives. The challenge is to increase quality and competitive advantage and yet be as cost efficient as possible to ensure profitability.

This challenge is all the more daunting because we must confront the following realities:

▶ *Designing and launching a Web site are just the tip of the iceberg.* Once the site goes live, it needs constant attention and nurturing to flourish. Site users and project stakeholders are unforgiving and fickle creatures who expect only the best and quickly get frustrated if the site does not deliver. The content must always be relevant and up to date, the site must be easy to use and contain no errors, and customer service must be fast and effective. It turns out that maintaining and evolving the site are bigger commitments than launching it.

▶ *It is becoming impossible to manage the information overload.* When the site was small and only a limited number of people had access and an interest in it, it was just about possible to manage content updates to meet customer and business requirements. Now things are going multilingual, multiserver, multiplatform, and everyone wants to be involved. Real-time, dynamic, syndicated, outsourced, personalized. How are we going to tame the information beast?

▶ *It is no longer acceptable for Web sites to be unaccountable.* Once upon a time, Web site investment was a no-brainer. Despite the fact that the Internet was always touted as the most accountable medium, proper measurement, analysis, and reporting were afterthoughts. Not so any longer. Now solutions must be accountable. Yet more information, processes, and technical complexity must be confronted.

▶ *Web site development requires integration with the whole business.* The industry has learned that great Web sites do not exist in a digital silo. They are just one weapon among many in the battle to acquire and retain customers. They must be integrated with the core business and deliver value to it. A Web site touches all parts of the organization and requires a complex mix of skills and input to deliver, maintain, and evolve. With increasing companywide integration and higher levels of decentralized control and ownership, it is becoming very complicated to see and manage the big picture.

To grapple with and overcome these challenges, we need to understand the problems and the needs both of the business and its customers, and we need tools, processes, and approaches to break the challenges down into manageable chunks. It is important to understand the relevant theories and concepts, but above all, we need to have knowledge that can be put into practice.

As the industry enters adolescence, I hope this book helps ease some of the growing pains that we are all facing.

How This Book Can Help You

As the title suggests, this book will help you maintain and evolve successful commercial Web sites. Although the book assumes that you already have a Web site, most of it is also highly relevant to the building of a new Web site or the complete redevelopment of an existing site. For example, the transition to a full content management system typically occurs at the same time as a site redesign and relaunch.

This book is the second that I have written. The first, *Web Project Management: Delivering Successful Commercial Web Sites*, concentrates on the A–Z of launching a new site from nothing. It also covers the principles and practices of project management for the online environment. If you are looking for a Web development method or want to find out more about the discipline of Web project management, managing a Web project team, managing budgets, time lines, tasks, deliverables, milestones, testing, prototyping, and documentation, then you should refer to my first book.

This second book accompanies the first and goes into a lot more detail on the specific challenges of maintaining and evolving Web sites, which are the final two stages of the Web development method proposed in the first book. This book is less about providing a single A–Z process and more about providing the knowledge, tools, approaches, and processes to manage the key site maintenance and evolution projects that you are likely to face.

At the time of writing, there are only a few books on the market that address the management challenges of, say, Web content management or Web site measurement. There are, as ever, plenty of business and marketing management books that talk about concepts such as electronic customer relationship management (eCRM) but few that really help with the realities of delivering on these strategies. This book aims to convey the necessary thinking and concepts as clearly as possible but concentrates on the practicalities. It covers the key areas of site maintenance and evolution to be as comprehensive a manual as possible in supporting ongoing Web projects.

Much of my own experience is in working with larger scale commercial Web sites, and the content of this book certainly applies to those. However, this book is about best practices, techniques, and approaches, and they can be used to the benefit of projects of all sizes. The budgets and resources may vary, but the end goals, processes, and concepts are the same.

Although the book refers to Web sites and customers in a way that would suggest this is for business-to-consumer public Web sites, all of the issues tackled have just as much relevance to business-to-business sites, virtual private networks, intranets, extranets, or any other Web-enabled, networked environment. They all need to manage content, report on performance, manage users, and manage change. There may be differences in the goals of each site, in the technology, and in the business processes, but the maintenance and evolution challenges are the same. Although other digital channels, such as interactive TV, mobile phones, or networked kiosks, have some specific challenges, they too face the same issues. The platform for delivering these digital propositions is increasingly being centralized, not necessarily physically but in a common networked environment, in an effort to improve the consistency and quality of experience that the customer gets and to ease the pain and cost of multisite maintenance.

This book will help you answer the following questions and others like them:

▶ How can I better manage changes to the Web site?
▶ How can I scale up to allow more contributions to the site and more content and still maintain quality and control?
▶ How can I deliver Web site personalization?
▶ What is content management and how do I go about it?
▶ How can I improve the customers' experience on the site?
▶ How do I measure and report on how well the site is doing?
▶ How do I maximize the value the site creates?
▶ What is eCRM and what does this actually mean for the site?
▶ How do I ensure that what we do now is the best platform for the future?

Audience

Whatever the job name or description, this book is for people who are involved with managing projects of all sizes related to Web site maintenance and evolution. The book is written assuming that the projects are being done in house, but all of the principles, practices, and processes are the same if you are a freelance consultant, a Web agency, or any other contracted third party.

The following sorts of roles will find the book relevant:

▶ *Production:* project managers, producers, Web managers, Webmasters, production managers, quality control, testers, developers, designers
▶ *Editorial:* editors, copywriters, content contributors/administrators
▶ *Commercial and marketing:* e-commerce managers, marketing managers, business analysts, market researchers
▶ *Customer service:* eCRM/customer service managers
▶ *Specialists:* usability engineers, information architects, management information services specialists, data analysts

This book is aimed at both the generalists who need to understand, tackle, and manage a range of specific issues and at the specialists who want to understand how their areas of expertise fit into the wider picture and what else is going on around them.

Content

The book is structured into four main parts plus a resources section at the end. You can read any of the four parts of the book, Change Management, Content Management, Customer Relationship Management, or Site Measurement, as stand-alone sections for greater insight into each of these areas. There is an introduction and conclusion for each part that summarizes the key learning points.

You may also choose to read the entire book from start to end. I begin with Change Management because this will help you introduce control to the way in which your site is maintained. This is followed by Content Management and Customer Relationship Management so that you can then focus on improving the way you manage the two most fundamental and important elements of your site: its users and its content. Finally, the part on Site Measurement will ensure you properly understand what is going on with your site, how it is delivering business value, and how you might improve it.

Throughout the book, you will come across tips, notes, case studies, and cross-references to support the text and help you get the most from it.

Acknowledgments

My greatest thanks and love to my wife, Annabel. It is very hard to write unless you can get the space and time to concentrate and focus. She helped in the unenviable task of proofreading, and she pushed me on if I looked like I was flagging, but most of all, she took care of so many things that would otherwise have distracted me. This is all the greater a sacrifice on her part as my resulting ability to focus on the book meant I spent longer periods of time less focused on her. Now that she is writing a play, we will see how well I do with roles reversed.

I was happy to stick with the publishers of my first book, Morgan Kaufmann, and they have continued to provide excellent support and commitment throughout the process of writing this second book. Thanks in particular to Tim Cox, my Editor, not only for his expert editorial guidance but also his flexibility and support in the contractual negotiations. Stacie Pierce has been wonderfully efficient and reliable in managing the whole process, in particular the reader review feedback, which is always invaluable but takes a lot of work to make happen. At the time of writing, the book is just being delivered into the safe hands of Edward Wade, Publishing Services Manager, who I must thank for turning my assorted digital files into a book that I am proud to see on the shelves.

One of the most important things in Web development is to work collaboratively with a team of experts and to continually iterate and improve your site. With a book, you can do this at least until the point of printing, and I would like to thank my reviewers, clients, and those who supplied case study material for working with me to provide their insight and expertise, which certainly improved this book. My reviewers were Dave Robertson, Steve Caudill, Mike Stone, Morgan Everett, Katie Clapp, Cherelyn Were, Amanda Taylor, and Terrance Crow. For the case studies, thanks to Nick Andrews of WHSmith Online, Jeremy Tapp of Magicalia, Jonathan Hilton of Wheel, Julian Everett and Gordon Maynard of Teletext, Elin Parry of Channel 5, Dave Robertson of Autoglass, Linda McDougall of Nedstat, Andrew Mayer of Netpoll, Paul Coombs of Channel 4, and Andrew Davies of FirstDirect.

I also owe a debt of gratitude to all the other authors out there, some of whom I know personally but all of whom have helped develop the industry, furthered the debate, and shared their expertise, knowledge, and passion. The many books that I have read have helped develop my own ideas as well as give me new ones. In particular, I would thank the authors of the books I recommend in the final part of this book for their outstanding efforts.

A special thank you to Matthew O'Riordan, the cofounder of e-consultancy, not only for giving so much of his valuable time to support my personal projects, such as the online companion material for this book, but also for teaching me so much about how best to implement all those vital behind the scenes elements of Web sites—content management systems, information architectures, measurement, data exchange, and so on. Web development is at its best when working closely with a team of people you trust and respect, and I have greatly enjoyed my partnership with Matthew.

Finally, my thanks to the Internet for making it possible for this book to be written in France by a U.K. author for a U.S. publisher for a global market.

CHANGE
MANAGEMENT

I t is well recognized that effectively managing change is one of the hardest things to do successfully in Web development projects. Not only do scope and requirements often change, but the underlying technologies and medium are continually evolving. Furthermore, the markets have seen roller coaster change that has often dramatically affected business models, budgets, or project remits.

Change is endemic to the Web, so rather than fight it we have to get used to working with it. This requires finding the right balance between proper planning and specifications, on the one hand, which provide structure, control, and confidence, and hyper-reactive, accelerated development, which provides speed and flexibility, on the other. The particular blend of the two extremes that you use in your own approach will depend on a number of things: the nature of the project itself, the heritage of working practices within the organization, and the type of people involved, among others. External factors, such as market conditions, also play a strong part: In the heyday of the Internet bubble, process was very much sacrificed at the altar of speed, whereas we have seen quality and accountability come back into favor, demanding more rigorous project processes and documentation.

This part of the book focuses on how to manage day-to-day change when a site is being maintained and is evolving. This is change that is often happening outside a specific project. Not only is there lots of this change, as everyone has their corner of the site that they want to see updated, but it is usually the kind of change that is least planned for, least predictable, and least structured. As the frenetic activity of project delivery gives way to the more mundane nature of daily site updates, it soon becomes clear that unless you can manage both planned and unplanned changes to the site, things can soon dissolve into a disorder that ultimately affects the overall quality of the site, with inconsistencies and errors creeping in. You will no doubt appreciate that the people and processes of Web development are much harder to master than the technology itself, and it is precisely people and processes, not technology, that must be conquered to efficiently maintain a Web site from day to day.

The greatest amount of change occurs in updating site content. Thus, you might think that this section belongs in Part II on Content Management. However, not all sites use a full content management system nor are they ever likely to do so. Equally, even those that will migrate toward full content management in the longer term will need to go through a stage of more ad hoc content management on the way. Good quality change management, as outlined here, helps address much of the pain that is typically felt by site maintenance teams. In some cases, such teams think a content management system (CMS) is the answer to their woes when in fact better change management is all that is required. In any case, a CMS is a tool to facilitate processes, but it cannot define them for you. The work that you do in analyzing and introducing change processes is very similar to the work that you have to do in defining workflow for a CMS so nothing is wasted. Therefore, before you spend a lot of money on a CMS, it makes sense as a first step to ensure your change management processes are up to scratch.

Key Areas We Will Cover in Part I

▶ The importance of regular meetings to communicate progress to the project team and stakeholders. What meetings should you hold and what should be covered?

▶ The role and contents of management summaries, progress reports, and risks and issues registers in effectively managing and reporting on Web site maintenance projects.

▶ The role and importance of documentation. What documents do you need to effectively maintain a Web site and manage changes to it?

▶ How to effectively manage changes and additions to Web sites by categorizing change and designing change processes, schedules, and documentation to suit sites at different stages of evolution.

Reviewing and Reporting Progress

Before we look at how you might create a framework and processes for managing less structured change, it is worth noting that even though the main development project may be finished, it still makes sense to have a process for reviewing and reporting on progress during the maintenance phase of a Web site. This has several benefits:

▶ *Regular contact with the project sponsors.* It is likely that during the main development phase of the project you had regular progress and status meetings with project sponsors and other senior management. Ideally, you will have had a regular slot in their calendars. Rather than let this slip, if you can continue to meet, even if only briefly, it helps make sure that attention does not drift away from the project. These senior sponsors will have been through a lot and seen everything that went on to launch the project and so will be more committed to ensuring its continued success. They will have the clout to maintain organizational focus, galvanize resources, and tackle risks and issues. As new ideas and new projects arise, they also will provide the best platform for deciding how best to take these forward.

▶ *Continued structure and discipline.* When you are working to a well-defined and carefully wrought project plan with any number of interdependencies, it is easy for the project team, and its individual members, to remain focused and motivated. The project plan should be something that everyone gave their input to and thus tacitly agreed to be bound by: a contract of mutual, negotiated responsibilities. However, once you enter the maintenance phase and the team perhaps feels tired and deflated, lacking the adrenaline rush induced by challenging deadlines, you need to make a real effort to maintain commitment and focus. If you continue to review and report progress, this forces the team to be accountable, to be assessed against more measurable and specific targets. As suggested earlier, if these activities continue to be reported to the project sponsors, then impetus is easier to maintain.

▶ *A tool for managing smaller projects.* During the requirements gathering, design, and construction phases of any major Web project, many tasks must inevitably be put aside or are overlooked during the intense initial launch phase. These will be a mixture of work planned for subsequent phases of the project and any number of smaller projects necessary to complete tasks missed during the main development effort such as documentation, training, and integration work. Depending on the nature of these tasks, you may wish to add them as part of the next phase of the project, manage them through a series of individual change requests, or create a set of smaller "miniprojects." If the requirements are clear and the scale of the miniproject is small enough, it makes no sense to do extensive planning, specification, and documentation for each project. Instead, you can use the review and reporting framework as a tool for tracking the progress of these smaller projects.

The following three sections look at ways you can monitor and report on ongoing work.

1.1 Management Summary

Management summaries should be prepared for presentation and distribution to project sponsors and stakeholders as well as other senior management as required. These summaries should not be longer than a page or two and should only include top line information about the key performance indicators, progress, and decision points. It is better to do shorter, less highly polished summaries more often than to wait too long and try to produce exhaustive reports and analyses. If management wants to see more detail on a particular area, you can always do that as requested. Otherwise, the sooner issues, trends, or decision points can be highlighted and addressed, the better. Aim to produce management summaries at least monthly, but preferably weekly.

Figure 1.1 shows a simple example of what a management summary might contain with brief explanatory notes for each heading. Note in particular the

---

Management Summary

Date:	*The date the summary is completed*
Version:	*The version of the summary*
Author:	*Who created the summary*
Distribution:	*Who the summary is going to*
Contacts:	*Relevant contacts for this summary*

Overview: This Week

Comments from overall project leader on progress, including particular highlights and failures: the three-line summary of the summary. If there are particular hot spots that need addressing or decisions that really need to be made by management, flag them here.

Review: Last Week's Action Points

Give an update on the status of action points generated by the previous management summary.

Performance Metrics

This should include reporting on key performance metrics and success criteria. Detailed facts, stats, and figures are not required, only the "management dashboard" version. Further details can then be requested if desired. This information should be provided by the management information (MI) team responsible for Web performance measurement analysis and reporting. Refer to the part of this book on Site Measurement for more details.

Projects

Each significant project that is underway should have its own section here. The information should be supplied by the project manager responsible.

Project title:	*The name of the particular project*
Project description:	*A brief description of the aims of the project*
Start/complete date:	*The projected time span of the project*
Project manager:	*The name and contact details of the person responsible for managing the project*
Milestone summary:	*Based on the milestones defined in the project plan, an overview of milestones completed, missed, and those coming next*
Activities:	*If required to supplement the milestone summary, details of activities and tasks: those just completed and those coming next*
Budgetary control:	*Summary of how the project is performing against budget: variances with an explanation, revised estimates, schedule of costs, etc.*
Risks and issues:	*What risks are there and what issues are impacting the project? What steps have been taken in mitigation?*
Other:	*If there is anything that particularly needs pointing out or addressing.*

Figure 1.1 Sample management summary.

review of action points generated by previous management summaries. This is particularly important as it holds people accountable, including senior management, and gives a sense that progress is being made. It also allows everyone to see how much work is being requested, by whom, and of whom. Often during the maintenance phase, the bigger picture can be lost, and business groups only see what they are interested in, appreciating less the effort that is going in elsewhere.

1.2   Progress Report

Management summaries are not particularly helpful for day-to-day operational management of tasks and projects. With the mixture of projects and ad hoc work that is likely to be around during the site's ongoing maintenance, you need to capture, document, and manage all the individual tasks. Doing so provides the necessary levels of accountability and structure as well as creates an audit trail of work undertaken and completed. These progress reports provide the detail not present in the management summaries, which can be very useful for later reference.

Whereas management summaries are a "snapshot" view, progress reporting and reviewing the status of tasks are ongoing processes. Documentation is continually updated. The purpose of creating and updating the documentation is less to provide time-specific benchmarks and more to provide a tool that can be used as a starting and reference point for meetings and work management. Ideally, progress review meetings should be held weekly with all relevant project team members present.

TIP   **Progress Review Meetings**

Holding such meetings on a Monday afternoon is a good idea: You have the morning to update progress from the previous week and think through the activities and issues for the week ahead.

Figure 1.2 shows a simple format for reporting on progress: focusing on tasks. This works most naturally when created from a project plan that will contain all the relevant information, except perhaps the notes. Indeed, if you have a project plan and all your work is project focused, then you can use just

Progress Report

Date:	*The date the report is completed*
Version:	*The version of the report*
Author:	*Who created the report*
Distribution:	*Who the report is going to*
Contacts:	*Relevant contacts for this report*

Task ID	Task description	Task owner	Create date	Deadline	Priority	% Complete	Notes
An ID that helps when referring to task	*A description of the task*	*Who is responsible for ensuring that the task gets done?*	*When was the task created?*	*When does the task have to be completed?*	*What level priority is the task? High, medium, low? Can help to sort tasks by priority*	*How complete is the task?*	*Any relevant notes, remarks, comments*

Figure 1.2 Keeping track of task progress.

the project plan itself as the basis of review meetings. If the completion status of tasks is being kept up to date by the project manager consulting individual team members, the review meeting is a chance for the entire team to get together to understand the overall status. However, using a project plan for reporting progress may not always work. There may not be a project plan; there may be several project plans as well as individual tasks that need tracking; or some team members may not clearly understand the presentation format of the plan. Not everyone feels at home with Gantt charts, for example. Keeping a single, simple list of tasks and progress makes it easy for everyone to contribute and understand.

TIP   **Online Documentation**

If you can, you should try and move toward providing documentation online. In particular, you will benefit from having documents available online that need to be regularly referred to and updated by a variety of people. Management summaries may be too sensitive, with too small a distribution, or require too much specialized manipulation to be worth doing as HTML. However, progress reports, systems documentation, risk and issues registers, and training and guideline documentation are all ideally suited to being online. Benefits include:

▶ "Write once, read many," meaning the document is centrally maintained but can be accessed by many.

▶ Access can be remote, on the move, personalized, and adjusted to suit the permission level of the user.

▶ Form-based data capture ensures ease of formatting and quality of structure of data.

▶ Manipulation of data for specialized views or reports is much easier; for example, sorting and reporting by task owner or task priority.

▶ Amendments and notes can easily be added with the user and time of update logged.

▶ Any system or templates you devise can easily be replicated and distributed around the organization or used on new projects.

1.3 Risks and Issues

You may have kept a risk and issues register during the main development phase of your Web project. As with progress reporting, you should continue to maintain this and use it as one of your key management tools. The types of risks and issues will change, but the need to manage them and the way you manage them do not. A progress report and a risks and issues register are two cornerstone documents that can form the basis of weekly update and review meetings for the core operational team.

A risk is something that has not yet occurred but which might become an issue. An issue is the negative effect of a risk having occurred. Typically, you will have more risks than issues as, ideally, not all risks will turn into issues either because you manage to proactively prevent the issue occurring or because it just does not happen. It is better to put down every risk and troubling fear that you have than to store your concerns internally so as not to appear out of control. Sharing your perceived risks alleviates the burden on you and spreads the sense of responsibility.

A risk register is a tool for ensuring that identified risks are addressed and monitored. The earlier a risk can be identified, the greater the chance that it will never become an issue that adversely affects ongoing work. Table 1.1 describes typical risk elements that you would use in risk analysis and reporting.

Table 1.1 Risk elements.

Risk Element	Description
ID	An ID that can be used to reference specific risks.
Risk description	A description of the risk.
Severity/consequence rating	A numerical or descriptive rating of the severity and consequences of the risk becoming an issue.
Impact type	A description of the kind of impact the risk will have if it becomes an issue: business, contractual, operational, technical, financial, intangible (e.g., loss of confidence), threats to availability, threats to integrity (e.g., corruption of data), or threats to confidentiality like inadequate control of access privileges.
Impact description	A more detailed description of the impact of the risk becoming an issue.
Probability/vulnerability	A numerical or descriptive rating of the probability that the risk will become an issue. This is helpful in prioritizing which risks to address and for planning ahead how to deal with the issue.
Avoidance/control	A description of factors, actions, and other measures that can reduce the chance of the risk becoming an issue or that help control the extent of the risk.
Risk owner	The person responsible for managing and monitoring the risk.
Status	Is this risk new (yet to be reviewed), being monitored, closed, or has it become an issue? Again, useful for sorting risks and prioritizing actions.
Date created	The date the risk was created in the register.
Earliest occur date	The earliest date that the risk might become an issue. Perhaps the risk is immediate, ongoing, or could be a specific risk at some point in the future. For example, there might be a risk that an expected spike in traffic due to an event scheduled in 6 months time could bring the server down. This date is useful in ensuring the most pressing risks are prioritized.
Last updated	When was this risk last updated and by whom?
Date closed	The date that a particular risk is closed as no longer a threat.

Tables 1.2 through 1.4 give suggested rating mechanisms that can assign values to some of the foregoing risk elements. Assigning fixed numerical or letter values has the advantage of allowing easier sorting and reporting by value. However, descriptive text is also usually necessary in explaining the finer points and details. Values give a relative notion of scale, but they do not explain the reasons behind the rating, which are vital to understand so you can take actions to stop the risk from developing into an issue. Status is a

Table 1.2 Severity/consequence rating table.

Rating	Category	Meaning
1	Catastrophic	Business survival threatened
2	Intolerable	Serious damage to business
3	Undesirable	Significant damage
4	Tolerable	Minor damage
5	Inconsequential	Negligible impact

Table 1.3 Probability/vulnerability rating table.

Rating	Meaning
1	Probable (>80%)
2	Highly possible (>50% <80%)
3	Possible (>20% <50%)
4	Unlikely (>5% <20%)
5	Highly unlikely (<5%)

Table 1.4 Risk status codes.

Status	Meaning
R	Risk
I	Issue
NR	New risk—not yet reviewed
OR	Open risk—still being monitored
CR	Closed risk—no longer considered a risk

useful risk element to assign a fixed value to so that you can filter out closed risks and concentrate immediately on new and open risks.

What kinds of potential, or actual, problems are you likely to need to manage and track as risks and issues when maintaining a site? Here are a few examples that could be project specific or ongoing:

▶ *Downtime due to load.* The server crashes or the site becomes unacceptably slow due to surges in traffic resulting from advertising. A prime time TV advertisement, for example, is likely to cause a huge peak in traffic. Load projections and adequate system redundancy and load balancing would help keep this risk from becoming an issue.

▶ *Downtime caused by technical maintenance work.* Examples include a server being moved or servers being rebooted. Issue avoidance measures might involve contingency planning and backup systems.

▶ *Data backup fails.* Data backup and archiving might fail because of configuration changes, software failure, or full storage devices. The impact of having no backups is potentially enormous. Issue avoidance measures could involve routine maintenance processes, monitoring and alerting services, multiple backup systems, and disaster recovery planning.

▶ *Fall in site quality through insufficient testing.* If there are too many changes and updates being made to the site with insufficient resources and processes, the temptation may be to cut corners on testing. There is a very real risk here that quality will be compromised through inconsistencies and errors that adversely affect the user experience. Issue avoidance measures might include additional resources and mandatory release processes that include testing and sign-off from a quality assurance (QA) representative.

▶ *Advertising going out without the destination page existing.* For example, an advertisement might include a dedicated URL to which customers are referred. If that destination does not exist, someone will be in big trouble. Issues like this should be avoided by proper interdepartmental communications and proper authorization and testing processes.

▶ *Email fails or malfunctions.* If much of your site functionality relies on email, such as registration or order confirmations, then email failure is a serious problem. Nor do you want to find out too late that your email application has started mass mailing your customer database. This risk will be particularly pertinent if you are changing email systems or introducing new email features. System monitoring and alerts, standby systems, problem escalation, and fallback procedures help prevent this kind of risk from becoming an issue.

▶ *Security.* There are numerous potential security risks that unfortunately are not likely to go away. Issue avoidance is in the form of effective security policies, procedures, and reviews.

If you wish, you can have an issues log that is separate from the risk register. By creating a separate document, you can really draw focus and attention to the few issues that must be resolved. Risks can sometimes seem too vague or unlikely, whereas everyone recognizes an issue. That said, more documentation than is strictly necessary is rarely a good thing because it only increases administration time. If you assign and maintain the status value of R (risk) or

I (issue), then there is no reason risks and issues cannot be managed via the same document. As mentioned earlier, if this register can be maintained and accessed online, you will see further increases in efficiency as problems are flagged and dealt with more quickly by a team that can be more aware of what is happening.

2

Procedures for Managing Site Updates

In the preceding pages, I provided some basic tools that you can use to report and review progress as well as manage risks and issues. These tools represent good project management practice, and they are as applicable during the launch as they are in the subsequent maintenance and evolution phases of a Web site. But what about the specifics of managing updates, changes, amendments, and additions? There can be a lot of pain and frustration involved in managing these when there are no accepted processes in place. Rather than swimming against a constant tide of requests, you want a system that runs smoothly and efficiently.

This part of the book focuses on creating processes and using approaches and tools to manage changes to Web sites. The benefits come principally in the resulting administrative efficiencies and controlled consistency of quality. However, the changes themselves still largely have to be carried out manually. The next logical stage is for changes and working processes to be automated. This is addressed in Part II of the book, Content Management, where we look at automating workflows and creating dynamic, automated publishing systems.

As you will see in Part II, there are many concepts and practices that differ from traditional offline publishing. The following pages on more "manual" online publishing procedures, however, bear a very direct resemblance to traditional publishing practices. Although the actual content, plus some of the practices, formats, and technology, differ online, and the rate of change is much higher, the actual processes that you should use transfer very well between media. So called "brochureware" Web sites have been frowned on in the past and sometimes rightly so because the content is out of date or it is written in brochure style rather than for the Web. But there is much to be admired in the processes behind creating a good brochure: knowing what effect you want to achieve, understanding the target market, creating compelling copy and imagery, reviewing and fine-tuning drafts, testing mock-ups with readers, and approving and signing off on the final version before it goes to print. If you are used to publishing processes such as commissioning, scheduling, reviewing, and editing, then you can successfully apply the same kind of rigorous thinking and processes online.

NOTE   **The Difference between Traditional Publishing
and Content Management**

I will not go into all the differences and concepts here as this is covered more thoroughly in the next part of the book. However, think about how a magazine is published: Content is commissioned, created, edited, designed and laid out, and finally printed. The end product, the printed magazine, is fixed; it cannot change once it has gone out. It is like a single instance or snapshot of content elements that are combined in a very specific and unique way. A site that is using a content management system to its fullest, on the other hand, may commission content in a similar way. However, what that content is, the way in which it is submitted, the additional information that is required, and the way that content is stored, manipulated, retrieved, and displayed are very different. The content, and end publication, is far from fixed. The piece of content is an asset with all sorts of attributes that can be used to combine, recombine, and package that content with other pieces of content in any number of ways to create any number of publications on demand. This necessitates quite a new way of thinking and quite different processes and success criteria. There will be more about this later. ■

2.1 **Documentation**

Before we look at the process for managing Web site updates, there are a few basic building blocks that need to be in place. Documentation may not be the most exciting work, but it is vital. In an ideal world, you will have created good documentation when planning your Web projects and then updated the documentation as you go to reflect the actual state of the system. However, this ideal is seldom realized. Documentation typically starts well and then begins to falter as delivery pressures mount. It is then unable to keep pace with change through the development process, and what is finally delivered bears little resemblance to what exists of the documentation.

Assuming your documentation has fallen into a state of disuse and disrepair, one of the first priorities when entering the postlaunch maintenance phase should be to bring it up to date. Again, ideally, you should update the documentation prelaunch so you know exactly what you need to maintain. Realistically, it is often only after the launch that there is enough of a lull to catch up with lapsed documentation efforts. There are three very important reasons you need to bring your documentation up to date to effectively maintain and evolve your Web presence:

▶ *You know what you have actually done.* Whatever your initial project plans showed, it is very unlikely that this is what you have actually ended up with. Subsequent changes, iterations, phases, scope changes, and reprioritizations will no doubt have significantly altered the course of your original plans. This is not necessarily a bad thing; it just reflects the iterative and changing nature of Web projects. However, at some point, you do need to take another "snapshot" to understand in detail what you do have. Among other things, you need this to plan future work and perhaps to fill the gaps that you identify. Iteration is good, but now and again, you need to bring your team back to a single, solid reference point that can be used for reorientation and focusing ongoing efforts. Updating project documentation forces a process of audit and reconciliation that reins in and realigns the sometimes chaotic energies of change.

▶ *Without documentation you cannot measure change.* To have a clear notion of change, and what to do about the change, you need to understand what your reference points are. Change is an alteration of one state to a new state. But what are those states and what kind of alteration must occur?

Without any benchmarks, yardsticks, or agreed understanding on what "is," it is extremely hard to define what "should be" and how it will be different from what is. This may sound a little philosophical, but it becomes painfully real if you have ever spent time arguing over whether a site update was really a change or an addition, or how much of a change it was, or whether it should always have been there in the first place. Documentation forces consensus on what exists at a point in time. It is then infinitely easier to define and manage changes to that state thereafter.

▶ *You need to protect yourself going forward.* Although it is to some degree excusable, or at least understandable, that not every last detail is defined in a document in the run up to a site launch, all the loose ends must be tied up as soon as possible afterward. In particular, this applies to any documentation that has contractual or other legal implications, such as service-level agreements or intellectual property rights contracts. If you allow these elements to go undocumented, it is likely nobody will address the issue until it becomes a very sudden, and potentially very serious, problem. Look at the number of companies whose Web site development efforts have been severely thwarted by their Internet service provider or perhaps their Web agency where relationships have turned sour and the company finds itself stuck in a difficult legal position, unable to free itself and move on. You must ensure that all relevant documentation is up to date to protect your ongoing efforts.

NOTE   **The Importance of Documentation**

This book is about maintaining and evolving an existing Web site. However, I would like to point out just how important good documentation is in creating a site or in launching a large new section. See it less as the nasty, boring technical details and more as an implacable, unmoving taskmaster forcing you to clearly articulate what it actually is that you want to do. Documentation is painful, obstinate, and relentless in the way it forces you to answer the questions you do not want to confront but absolutely must for the project to succeed. Good documentation achieves the following:

▶ It reduces complexity of communication. Have you ever got so deep into a project that your brain is fizzing just holding all the little bits together? Where you have not had time to document and now you might as well do it yourself because it would take too long to explain? And you are working too hard and getting ill with the stress? Perhaps not quite to this extreme, but would it not be nice to just point everyone in the direction of the font of all knowledge, your most excellent documentation?

▶ It gives a holistic level of clarity. As you think up new ideas and add bits and pieces here and there, you risk losing control of what the totality now looks like and how it holds together. Documentation forces you to have a single place where the whole project can be examined.

▶ It forces consensus between project members. Verbal agreements, descriptions, and specifications are dangerously open to misinterpretation or can be conveniently discarded or refuted at a later stage. Documentation enforces the same kind of focus as a written contract. It flushes out any inconsistencies or differences of interpretation.

▶ It engenders commitment. It is so much easier to buy into something if you believe in it and you do not have those nagging questions at the back of your mind. Good documentation is like a good business plan to an investor: All the aspects are covered and there is no reason to believe that this will not be a winner.

▶ It saves you time and money and might just save your project. Imagine that everyone on your project *really* knew what they needed to do, when, and why because they had been forced to rigorously think it all through and understand it in advance. Just think how well things could go. Good documentation helps force you to do all those things you know you should but somehow do not quite happen in the real world. ∎

Following are examples of documentation that you are likely to need to maintain and evolve your Web site. Neither the list nor descriptions are exhaustive, and your documentation may go by other names, but these are the main areas that you must think about covering. It is perfectly possible that you created all these documents for your original project specification and now need only to update them. However, unless you were admirably diligent, it is more probable that some of these documents will exist and others will need creating for the first time.

2.1.1 Definition of Terms/Glossary

Good communication is vital to the success of Web projects. This is true of any project but perhaps more so for Web projects where there is still little standardization and things continue to change at a prodigious rate. To avoid misunderstandings and to improve the efficiency of communications, it is helpful to have definitions of terms, or a glossary, that everyone in the project can use as a reference. This is particularly helpful for new members of the team.

Some of the terms you should include are discussed in Section 2.3, Categorizing Types of Change. Part IV of the book, Site Measurement, also includes definitions of many Web metrics that are often the cause for confusion.

2.1.2   Site Map

This is a visual representation of the contents of the site by section and subsection shown as a hierarchy that usually reflects the site's navigation. You will no doubt have used site maps extensively during the project planning and definition stages, so it should just be a matter of updating your site map to reflect the current extent of the site.

If you are fortunate, you will have a software tool that can automate this for you. Many content management systems, or simpler site management tools such as various automated File Transfer Protocol (FTP) publishing tools, include a feature allowing you to create a site map.

2.1.3   Content and Functional Specifications

The content and functional specifications define what content is on the site and how it works from a user's perspective. This might be done as a single document or two documents with the functional specification concentrating on the what and how questions, usually including use case scenarios, and the content specification defining the content itself.

These documents describe most fully what the site is from a user's point of view. The majority of day-to-day changes to a site affect the user's experience and are thus changes to the content and functional elements of the site. These documents, above all, need to be periodically updated if you are to understand and manage change effectively. If you can bring them fully up to date just pre- or postsite launch, subsequent change control documentation should give you all you need to bring the documents up to date at a later stage.

2.1.4   Technical Specification

Along with the content and functional specifications, the technical specification is likely to be most in need of updating and require the most ongoing work to maintain. The technical specification contains details of the technical architecture, hardware and software, network environment, database schemas, languages and protocols used, file structures, templates, components, integration elements, and configuration details.

These details may change a little less frequently than the site content itself, but they are what makes everything work. With a bit of help, almost anyone can define the content and functionality of a site because they can see it and describe it. The technical details and documentation, however, require much more specialized skills to understand and maintain. This is not the kind of information that you can afford to lose because someone leaves the organization, so it is all the more important to keep documented.

2.1.5   Design and Brand Guidelines

Creating a set of agreed design and brand guidelines makes site updates run much more efficiently. As you may know, endless discussions and debates over often subjective design details such as typefaces and colors can waste large amounts of time. It is not that these details are not important, but if they can be codified, it avoids having the same debates over and over again. Team members and content contributors can work much more efficiently if they clearly understand the design and brand parameters they must work to.

Design and brand guidelines might contain the following elements:

- ▶ Brand framework (brand attributes, etc.)
- ▶ Core visual brand elements (logo, ID, etc.)
- ▶ Site structure and navigation scheme
- ▶ Templates
- ▶ Styles and formatting (typefaces, titling, style sheets, etc.)
- ▶ Page elements (boxes, icons, banners, charts, diagrams, tables, etc.)
- ▶ Colors
- ▶ Technical requirements (maximum file sizes, file formats, browser compatibility, supported languages, plug-ins, the specification of the user machine, etc.)

2.1.6   Policies

In particular, you should create or update your security and privacy policies following standards wherever possible. You may also need to review your

Terms and Conditions of site use, particularly as you begin to add new content, services, and features.

2.1.7   Publishing Procedures

How do things change on your site? How are they updated? The documentation that answers these questions constitutes your publishing procedures. We look at these processes in more detail in Section 2.4, Change Processes, and then again in the Content Management part of the book where the publishing itself becomes more automated but the processes of content collection and the editorial procedures surrounding managing the content through to publication require defining.

2.1.8   Service-Level Agreements (SLAs)

These are otherwise known as maintenance agreements, support agreements, or application management agreements. The purpose of a service-level agreement is to describe the performance objectives and standards agreed upon between various parties in relation to services as defined in the agreement. Service-level agreements typically contain the following: services provided, costs, contacts, problem classification, escalation procedures, change management processes, backup, security, archiving, support structures, risk management, responsibilities, warrantys, and levels of reporting. You will probably already have in place several standard service-level agreements—for example, with your Internet service provider—but as you focus more on site maintenance, there will be others that you need to draw up and agree to, such as arrangements with content providers.

2.1.9   Other Contracts and Agreements

In addition to SLAs, there will be other areas of your ongoing Web development work that need to be protected by contracts and agreements with third parties. You might need to enter into nondisclosure agreements (NDAs) to protect sensitive commercial information or negotiate intellectual property contracts so that you are clear about who has what rights over digital assets that are developed and become part of your site. This is the territory of lawyers, and you need specialist advice to help with contractual clauses that typically address the following important legal issues:

▶ Defining quality standards of work: What is "acceptable"?

▶ Subcontracting: Is it allowed?

▶ Ownership and risk: Who owns what and what is the risk exposure?

▶ Confidentiality and publicity: What must remain confidential?

▶ Copyright and other rights: Who owns what intellectual property rights?

▶ Customer information and data security: Who is responsible?

▶ Indemnity and liability: Who is exposed to what?

▶ Insurance: Is it required?

▶ Competition, exclusivity, and prior agreements: How does other business affect the agreement?

▶ Jurisdiction: What laws govern the agreement?

▶ Dispute resolution: What happens if things go wrong?

2.2 Contact Information

Maintaining contact information for the purposes of change management is a fundamental basic that is rarely done well. Ideally, you should provide a directory of contact information that is accessible online as well as printed and posted on walls. You should provide some brief accompanying notes about the process of who to contact in what situation and, if more control is needed, give designated contacts through which to channel interactions. There should be a team hierarchy and a list of names with job title, role and responsibility, and contact details. It is important that this information is available and up to date. People most often reach for the contact list when they have a problem that they cannot sort out themselves using normal channels, so phone numbers are probably the most useful information.

Beware of who has access to your contact information. Depending on the size of your organization and the nature of the project, you may wish to make the information available to the entire company or only the project team. Certainly, if you are going to be sharing the information with partners or, indeed, customers, then you are potentially opening yourself up to all sorts of support problems. Maintaining a high-volume or highly specialized support service or help-desk type function requires a lot more analysis and process design. The contact information required for updating the Web site is normally only for distribution to members of the project team.

2.3   Categorizing Types of Change

Before we look at update processes, there are two further basic building blocks that require attention: what you actually call the change you wish to make and how important the change is. If these two points can be properly codified rather than described in subjective terms, it makes processing change much more efficient.

2.3.1   Naming

What is in a name? An awful lot it would seem. How you label change elements and refer to them are much more important than might appear on the surface. What do you mean by a *change*? Is that a *bug* or an *error*? Is that an *amendment, update,* or *addition*? The differences are often semantically vague, but it is important to be clear about the nature of any change when updating a site. Why? Mostly because the classification of the change will then have a subsequent process attached to it that is designed to deal with that kind of change. Thus, an accurate classification is very important in ensuring that change is optimally managed. Often there will be cost and contractual implications as well. For example, service-level agreements need to refer to types of change and how they will be handled and paid for. Third-party agencies charging for maintenance work need to keep a record of what they have done and charge accordingly. They require some way of cataloging the sorts of tasks they have been doing.

The best way to ensure that everyone is talking the same language and has the same understanding of the impact of their words is to create a glossary. These glossaries may become standardized and accepted to the point that they are not needed anymore, but for the moment, it is very valuable to define exactly what is meant by the terms used. It is more important that the terms are used consistently and that a meaning is agreed on than that the definition itself is "correct." This is similar to the way in which legal documents usually have a clarification and definition of the terms used "for the avoidance of doubt." Before you begin designing change processes, define the linguistic building blocks that you will be using.

Table 2.1 gives some examples of types of change, how they might be referred to, and a suitable definition. Note, for example, that *amendment* or *update* are not part of this vocabulary: They would be classified as additions or changes as appropriate. If you have a lot of changes that need to be addressed by different people, you might want to create subcategories. For example, *change* may have subcategories of *legal change, functionality change, hardware change,* or *content change.*

2.3.2   Grading

In addition to naming change according to an agreed vocabulary, you should rate, or grade, change as well. Once you have your process in place, this grading will further instruct people how to treat the change as it moves through

Table 2.1 Change elements and definitions.

Change Type	Definition
Web site	All content, code, software, and hardware residing on the servers (name, network, and physical locations) that are used to deliver the Web site at the URL *www.website.com.*
Issue	Any outstanding action that must be addressed, such as reported errors or change requests.
Error (E)	Any aspect of the Web site that does not perform as per the agreed specification or any subsequently agreed additions or changes to that specification.
Fix	A modification to the Web site that eliminates an error.
Workaround	The temporary resolution of an issue. Workarounds provide a temporary fix to an issue that should be revisited to provide a complete fix.
Addition (A)	A modification or enhancement to the Web site that creates new content or functionality that is not in the original specification or any subsequently agreed additions or changes to that specification.
Change (C)	Any aspect of the Web site that is as specified but requires updating without additions. For example, content that is out of date or inaccurate. Archiving, removing, or deleting content or functionality classifies as a change.
Request	Any issue logged for action with the maintenance team.
Response	The actions taken by the maintenance team to act upon any request made of them. In providing a response, the maintenance team will attempt to diagnose the cause of any issue and give a provisional indication of the time and actions required to resolve it.
Support	Refers to errors and legal change requests only.

the process steps. There is no room for shades of gray when you have a rigid naming and grading system for change types. The process will treat the change according to its name and grade. Unfortunately, this does not make the system foolproof because a change may be intentionally or mistakenly misnamed or incorrectly graded. You cannot completely eradicate human error, but you should be able to trace it and, by substituting the gray shades of subjective interpretation for the black and white of a naming and grading system, you will realize significant communication and processing efficiencies.

You could use numbers or letters for grading. Numbers are perhaps preferable to distinguish grades from change types. The most common level of grade to assign is the level of urgency of the change. Table 2.2 gives some basic examples.

Another grade that you may wish to assign to changes is for sign-off. A big part of any process you develop will be the levels of review and sign-off that are required before changes can progress. The people running the process may change with new arrivals not knowing, or remembering, what changes, at which stage, need to be referred for sign-off and to whom. They will be greatly aided if they have a clear guide that details the people and processes associated with each sign-off grade. Table 2.3 gives some example sign-off grades.

You can see how you might combine urgency and sign-off grading:

1.1 = Urgent and must be signed off by the board director

2.4 = Must be implemented within 48 hours and signed off by the project manager

Table 2.2 Grading according to urgency of change.

Urgency Grade	Description
1	**Urgent.** Change must be implemented within 4 hours.
2	**Fast track.** Change must be implemented within 48 hours.
3	**Normal.** Change must be implemented within 1 week.
4	**Project.** Change must be implemented according to the project plan with which it is associated
5	**Date specific.** Change must be implemented before a specified date.
6	**Custom.** Change must be implemented as instructed in a separate brief.

Table 2.3 Sign-off grading.

Sign-Off Grade	Who Needs to Sign-Off Change
1	Board director
2	Department head
3	Senior manager
4	Project manager
5	Webmaster/Any project team member
6	Anyone in the company (name required)

If you further combine the change type lettering (see Table 2.1), you would get to:

A3.5 = An addition that needs to be completed within a week and signed off by the Webmaster or any project team member

C1.3 = A change that must go through within 4 hours and be signed off by a senior manager

And if you have further subclassified your changes, you would recognize the following as an express train coming at you full steam:

LC1.1 = A legal change (LC) that must occur within 4 hours and be signed off by a board director

You might be thinking that there is no way you are going to persuade people to assign codes and names to all their changes. Indeed, what has been described may be too process heavy for your current requirements. But as you reach the stage where things are beginning to get out of control, managing growth and change is becoming impossible, and different parts of the organization are working in different ways, then introducing these kinds of techniques can help you retain control and maintain quality. With people coming and going and with the growing pressure on Web sites and their managers to be accountable, stricter processes and conventions are increasingly required.

2.4 Change Processes

With the basics now in place, you can start to design, update, and change processes. These processes combine change control with workflow and scheduling. We look at workflow in more detail in Part II of the book, Content Management, but essentially it is the series of tasks, events, and triggers that govern how a piece of work, such as change to the Web site, "flows" through the organization. Any process design work you do will be very valuable if you do decide to implement a content management system further down the line. The CMS only facilitates processes. You still have to define them. In fact, if you have not defined your update processes, you are not ready to start building or buying a content management system.

2.4.1   Single Points of Contact

You will notice that the update process proposed in the coming pages involves two coordinators who act as linchpins facilitating communication between the business as a whole and the Web site maintenance team. You might quite fairly ask: But does this not mean everything relies on just two people, which apart from being risky creates exactly the kind of bottleneck for changes that we are trying to avoid? There are arguments both ways:

The reasons against having single points of contact are:

▶ The bottleneck effect causes requests to be delayed because they can only go through a single point at a certain speed.
▶ You become overly reliant on these points of contact: What happens if either is ill, leaves, or is otherwise unavailable? What happens if either is not very good at his or her job, frustrating the efforts of so many others?
▶ The overall view of what is going on—that is, the bigger picture of all the changes that are being made—risks existing only in the minds of two individuals.
▶ Using fixed single points for change management hardly makes for a dynamic, real-time, reactive environment.

The reasons for having single points of contact include:

▶ The process is simplified with far fewer interconnected relationships and dependencies.
▶ Lines of responsibility and accountability are clearly drawn.
▶ A higher degree of centralized control gives greater consistency and, ideally, quality.
▶ It is easier to integrate with external third parties, such as an agency, as there is a clear point at which to "bolt on," or sever, the relationship.

NOTE   **Required Project Management Skills**

The coordinators I refer to, the important single points of contact between the business and the Web maintenance team, have the following responsibilities:

► Understanding and representing the interests of those for whom they are acting as a conduit
► Designing and refining processes for ensuring the smooth flow of work through the organization
► Ensuring proper review and sign-offs occur as necessary
► Optimizing the efficiency of work while maintaining quality standards
► Reviewing requests that are submitted to ensure they meet agreed criteria
► Keeping necessary documentation up to date
► Creating and presenting status reports and analyses
► Briefing teams on work that needs doing
► Managing resources, deadlines, and budgets

As you can see, these are classic project management responsibilities. The coordinators must also have a good generalist understanding of all the areas they are representing, be good at managing people and their expectations, as well as being tough and disciplined. Again, this is the classic project manager. The business-side coordinator should know the business in and out as well as the key people within it. The Web site maintenance team's coordinator should have a thorough understanding of all areas of Web development. The two should work closely together with each learning more about the business and Web development, respectively. Ultimately, the process should be able to function perfectly well with one or the other if necessary. To avoid overreliance on these two project managers, each should ideally have an understudy who also knows the ropes and can step in if necessary. ■

Single points of contact are preferable for sites up to a certain stage in their evolution, beyond which more comprehensive and automated content management will be required. If we look more closely at the point between where a change is requested by the business and passed over to the Web site maintenance team, the following stages typically occur.

2.4.2   Evolving Stages of Web Site Maintenance

Stage 1

At stage 1, we typically find the following situation:

► The volume of change demands from the business are not that great.

▶ There is little filtering of the way that requests are made of the Web site maintenance team.

▶ The handover between business and site maintenance team is not clearly defined.

▶ The maintenance team itself is small, and there are no real processes to support the way changes are accepted or handled.

▶ The Web site itself is relatively small at this stage and is accessed only by the site maintenance team.

This situation is typical of a simple, or immature, site. Although the way updates are carried out is not perhaps ideal, the work load is manageable, so things probably get done well enough in the end. In this instance, the maintenance "team" is likely to be a single Webmaster, possibly even part time or working at an agency. The generalist skills of a Webmaster enable him or her to cope with a mixture of ill-defined work following an ill-defined process.

Stage 2

By stage 2, the following has occurred:

▶ The volume of demands from the business has grown, but these demands are coming from even more people in an even less organized manner.

▶ The lines of communication between the business and the maintenance team are becoming increasingly confused.

▶ The maintenance team has some extra resources, but it is still is not well structured.

▶ The Web site has grown considerably.

▶ The Web site can still only be updated by the maintenance team.

This is a situation where pain really begins to take root. Quality starts to slip, tempers become frayed, and frustration sets in. The maintenance team probably consists of the same Webmaster as in the previous situation "supported" by a few other ad hoc resources and the part-time commitment of a couple of members of the business who have had their job title and pay slightly adjusted to recognize their extra responsibilities.

The problem here is a lack of defined processes to ensure that work flows properly through the organization. Perhaps the problems the maintenance team is facing are not that they are underresourced but that their skills, and the way they have been working, no longer suit the situation. The Webmaster may be a good generalist, but now it is time to split out the process, managerial, and operational elements if he or she is not to become overwhelmed. Introducing a project manager with the clout and skills to set up a process to review, filter, and, if necessary, send back change requests before they even reach the Webmaster would alleviate the administrative "noise" and allow the Webmaster to be more efficient in making changes.

Stage 3

The situation is now as follows:

▶ The volume of demand from the business is still growing, but it is now being channeled through an update process to a single point of contact.
▶ The point of handover from business to Web site maintenance team is very clearly defined.
▶ The maintenance team has grown a little, but more important, it now receives requests in a focused and structured way.
▶ The Web site continues to grow.
▶ It is still the maintenance team that does all the site updates.

The impending chaos of the previous stage has been brought under some control by shaping the process. It is this stage of site evolution, and to some degree the next stage, that we are addressing in this part of the book before moving on to the more complex stage of full content management. Typically, the major disadvantage at this stage of site evolution is that the business wants to do much more than the Web site maintenance team can deliver. At this stage, the benefits of getting the process streamlined outweigh this disadvantage, but the clamor for a more dynamic and integrated Web site will be getting louder all the time.

Stage 4

At stage 4:

▶ The business begins to get its own direct access to the Web site, no longer having to rely on the Web site maintenance team to make updates and additions.
▶ The business demand and maintenance team have not grown substantially, but the Web site continues to grow with the additional, more direct, business involvement.

Now is the time to start handing the power back to the business to do its own updates and changes. People, processes, and systems start to be integrated so that the Web site feeds more directly from the business. Finally, it starts to become truly dynamic. This transition must be handled very carefully and deliberately if it is not to result in an even greater chaos than was threatening at Stage 2. With existing update processes in place, it is a matter of gradually rolling out new capabilities and processes to allow the business to make its own updates. Start with the easier elements (e.g., changes rather than additions) and the most trustworthy people.

Stage 5

In the final stage:

▶ E-business and business have become the same thing: The Web site envelops the business, and vice versa.
▶ Both the business and the maintenance team are dynamically woven into the fabric of the Web site allowing each to make changes as required.
▶ There is still a point-to-point relationship between the business and the maintenance team, but this now represents a work handover point that is project-specific rather than ongoing Web site updates.
▶ To achieve this stage, a content management system (CMS) will need to be in place.

For more on how sites evolve toward full content management, refer to Section 6.3, Evolving toward a CMS.

By this final stage, there is a complex network of relationships, interwoven processes, and dependencies in place. The Web site and the business have become fused into a living organism with both business and site feeding off one another. Maintaining all this without a content management system becomes very tricky. Chaos can once again reign as one thing goes wrong and the effects ripple though the system causing further problems. Finding the source of a problem becomes harder as so much is integrated. Stopping the entire system to do routine maintenance work or to address problems systematically becomes unrealistic because there are so many business-critical functions running. The focus becomes less on creating processes for managing updates and more on defining processes to optimize performance, in particular how to address and resolve problems when they do occur as quickly and efficiently as possible.

NOTE   **E-business Teams and Organizational Structure**

The stages just described suggest that the business and the Web site maintenance team are separate entities with separate people. This is not necessarily the case. In fact, in the earlier stages, it is unlikely to be the case. What I am trying to show is a separation of roles and responsibilities, not necessarily people or departments. I think it is important for the roles and responsibilities distinction to be clear if any process is to work. ■

The update process that we are about to look at would suit a site at Stage 3. The first two stages are self-evident enough and have no real processes to outline. Stages 4 and 5 are addressed in Part II of this book, Content Management.

2.4.3 Process Mapping

To design your update process, you should analyze and map out the way that changes are made and flow through the organization. Create a process chart that diagrammatically shows each logical step that occurs with possible outcomes depending on the decisions that are taken. Once you have this, take it to key members of the organization and project stakeholders for review.

The way things are currently done is not necessarily the best. Using your initial process map, review and refine it until you have something that people agree works. This should help flesh out the details of who wants to see what and sign it off at each stage. Typically, too many managers want to be too involved such that the process would take far too long for even the smallest of changes to be made. However, it is better to document all the requested steps at first and then cut back by common consent, or higher level edict, at a later stage when the full picture is in place.

Figure 2.1 shows an example process for site updates. The business generates requests that are filtered through a coordinator representing the business to a coordinator representing the Web site maintenance team. The requests are then further filtered and modified before being passed to the maintenance team for implementation.

NOTE **Development, Staging, and Live Servers**

In a typical development environment, you would have three versions of the site on three different servers, or server clusters. The hardware, software, and configuration of each server should be the same so that as far as possible what works on one will

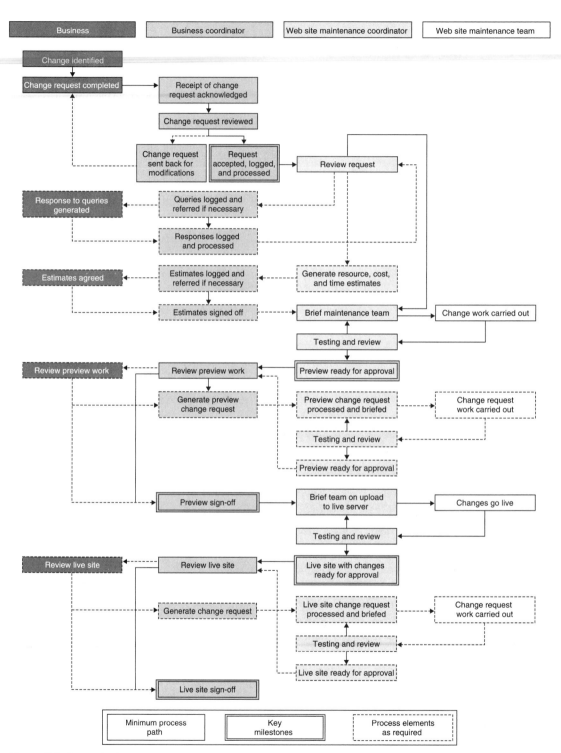

Figure 2.1 Example change process.

replicate seamlessly to the next. The development server is where all the initial development work occurs. This is the lowest risk environment. The staging server should ideally be a separate machine to the live server, although physically in the same place and with exactly the same configuration. For smaller sites with a lower budget, it is reasonable for the staging "server" to be simply a password-protected area on the live server. The staging server should be treated as though it were the live server: If things work on the staging server, the testing on the live server *should* be a formality. The staging server allows anyone with Web access and the right permissions to experience a replica of what will become the live site, so it is here that most testing is done. The live server is what the world at large sees. The live server is also often referred to as the production server.

Note the following about the process shown in Figure 2.1:

▶ This process shows two cycles of testing and review: one is a preview and the other is on the live server. In this case, the preview would most likely be on the staging server. Often there will be three review cycles: a preview on an internal development server, a second review and testing cycle on the staging server, and then a final cycle on the live server.

▶ Each of the two iterations shown here, preview and live, has a testing and review loop built into it that could also go through several iterations if required.

▶ This process could run quite quickly or it could be quite slow. The greatest lag would be caused by too many people having to review and sign off changes. The time taken in contacting these people and getting their approval, even if facilitated by a degree of automated workflow using emails triggered at each stage, would slow the process down considerably.

▶ One of the things that this process map does not show is any names or job functions attached to any of the stages. Clearly, the two coordinators have a lot to do, but you would also need to know who within the business or the Web site maintenance team to go to at each step. For example, the business sign-off steps at the preview and live cycles may be different people. It is better to abstract the process from the people as they are likely to change, whereas the process is designed to work irrespective of who is doing the work.

▶ Details of the actual change request and change log are on the following pages.

2.5 Change and Update Requests

The process just described gives an example of what happens, in what order, as a change makes its way to the live Web site. You should have a clearer idea of how these changes could be categorized, named, and graded. You may want to design alternate processes for each category of change to reflect urgency or sign-off variations. In these next two sections, we look in more detail at what might be contained in the change request itself and how to schedule the changes because the process has no timings attached to it currently.

It is important to have a standard change request document. Typically, this starts as a document with preset fields that can be filled out electronically. The document is then emailed as an attachment to the appropriate person. As a next step, you should turn the document into a Web-based form that works off a database. This has many advantages:

▶ You can use form validation to ensure the required data are correctly entered.

▶ The form is available to anyone, anywhere with a Web connection and access privileges.

▶ You can write the data to a central database rather than end up with a huge collection of separate documents. This facilitates sorting, filtering, analysis, and reporting.

▶ You can begin to automate the workflow around the request. For example, once a form is submitted, it could trigger an alert email notifying the relevant people, increasing efficiency.

▶ You can cut down the amount of information people have to fill in. If the user is logged in, details such as who has made the request and when can be automatically captured. Equally, if the request is a regular one, a previous version can be re-sent without being filled in again.

▶ You can easily change elements of your process without having to reeducate everyone. For example, if a document has to be emailed, the sender needs to know who to send it to. If the recipient changes, you must inform everyone of the changes and hope they remember. With a Web-based form, however, the sender does not have to know where it is going. The sender just clicks submit and you can then route the request wherever you wish.

▶ It is easier to include supporting information. Hyperlinking to additional information is particularly effective for including Help type information without cluttering up the screen with exhaustive instructional information. Power users have just the form, but novices can click "Example" or "Help with filling this out," which not only saves training time but again helps ensure the quality and consistency of data entry.

As a next stage, the request itself becomes a form of content update that is processed and even sent live automatically. But that is really the realm of content management, which we come onto in the next part of the book. At this stage, we must design a document or form that captures all the information we need to process the change efficiently. We will look at a document here, but you should easily be able to see how it would translate to a Web form.

Having to fill in a form to make a change is a burden that not everyone appreciates, in the same way that being forced through a rigid process is not always greatly appreciated. However, the benefits of having tangible change request information, rather than mere verbal requests, are significant:

▶ There is an audit trail. That is, there is trail of information that can be followed back if necessary. Most of the time, this will not be necessary, but when it is required, it is vital. Most often the information will need to be reviewed because there is some debate over what did or did not happen. Some Web sites have been sued for content they have carried that has since disappeared. How can you tell if it was ever there? You should be able to refer to your change requests. In some countries, companies are obliged by law to have a record of exactly what was on their sites at any given time in the past.

▶ People think twice before asking for a change. The danger with purely verbal requests is that they cannot be traced or confirmed, so people are tempted to make requests without really thinking them through. If they have to fill in a change request form, not only must they make an effort (so they must really want the change), but they also know that they will be held accountable for their request. Anyone could look through previous requests and see who has been asking for what. When there are budgets involved and bills to pay for changes, the request forms are not filled out so lightly.

▶ The contents of the form itself force the person filling it in to properly think through and define the request. The person cannot be sloppy or lazy in the request, as is the danger with verbal changes. If all the correct information is there in the correct format, this greatly improves the efficiency of implementation further down the process line. There is much less room for miscommunication or misinterpretation, which raises the levels of consistency and quality as well as minimizing rework.

Figure 2.2 gives an example of a change request form. Note the following:

▶ The form is very similar to a change control form you might use during the development phase of a project. If you already use such change control and have documentation, you should be able to reuse what you already have with some small tweaks.

▶ Do not forget that we are talking about changes or additions that are outside the scope of particular projects. This change request form works well for processing the many smaller changes and additions that occur from day to day, but it would not be sufficient, say, for the addition of a significant piece of functionality. That should be done as a stand-alone project with proper planning and specifications.

▶ There is a unique reference ID for each individual change request. You should have a standard way of forming these codes. In Figure 2.2, the ID is made up of the initials of the person who has commissioned the change and an incremental number for each additional change requested by that person.

▶ The change type field uses a code as discussed earlier. The example is for a change that must happen within the next 4 hours and can be signed off by the project manager. The completion dates and sign-off details are repeated for clarity and in case a textual explanation is needed to support the code. If auditing the requests at a later stage, the code will be more useful than ASAP.

According to the process defined earlier, this change request would be generated by the business and passed to the business coordinator and then to the Web site maintenance team coordinator for review and processing. Where it says "logged" in the process we looked at, this refers to a change log. Whereas change requests come through from all sorts of sources, the change log is a tool for keeping a central overview of all change requests and their status. This is essential for review and status meetings as well as for keeping a tally of the total amount of work that has been done, or is scheduled, allowing for improved resource and budgetary planning.

Change Request Form

Ref ID:	AF023
Change type:	C1.4
Date of request:	12.10.02
Date to be completed by:	ASAP
Commissioned by (name, dept., contact details):	Ashley Friedlein, e-commerce department (0123 456 789)
Request approved by:	John Doe, e-commerce department (0987 654 321)
Sign-off of change required by:	John Doe, e-commerce department (0987 654 321)

Description of change (text, graphical, navigational, pop-up, banner, or new section)

Text and link need updating

Reason for change

Link and text to partner site incorrect—we agreed to link directly to their XYZ product page, not their home page.

Impact of change on other areas/projects

Need to make sure this outbound link is tracked by our measurement system—but don't let this hold up making the change. We can always add tracking later.

URL(s) affected

If there is no existing URL(s), indicate that a new page is required, or if content appears in a pop-up window, please give the URL of the page the window comes from and how the window is generated

www.Website.com/products/index.html

Change to existing text

*Please copy text directly from the page and make your amendments here, highlighting changes in **bold italics***

Interested in ABC? We've arranged special prices for our members with XYZ, one of our partner organizations. To find out more about this offer, ***visit their site's ABC pages.***

Change to existing graphics

Please identify the graphic to be changed at the URL given above. If there are several graphics on this page, please describe which should be updated or, preferably, give the exact URL of the image itself (you can find this out by right clicking on the image and choosing Properties and noting the URL). Please also give the file path location of the new graphic.

Change to existing navigation or functionality

Please describe as precisely as possible what is currently there, or what currently happens, and what you would like to see it changed to.

Addition (new content or functionality)

If practical, you can paste new content into the space below. Otherwise, please give the filename(s) and path(s) that contain the content assets, specifications, or more detailed briefs as required.

Notes/comments/additional information

1. We must make sure that we are tracking this as an outbound link so we know what traffic we are sending through to our partner site.
2. This should come out of the marketing budget. If the cost is going to exceed $X, then let me know before proceeding.

Figure 2.2 Sample change request form.

Ref ID	Date of request	Date logged	Logged by	Last updated	Completion date	Status	Total labor-hours	Cost	Comments
How do I fill this in?	How do I fill this in?	How do I fill this in?	How do I fill this in?	How do I fill this in?	How do I fill this in?	How do I fill this in?	How do I fill this in?	How do I fill this in?	How do I fill this in?
AF023	10.10.02	10.10.02	JD	10.13.02	10.10.02	Complete	1	$100	Tracking not yet done. Created as separate request ID AF024.

Figure 2.3 Change log.

Figure 2.3 shows an example of a change log. Most of the fields are self-explanatory. Labor-hour and cost estimates are not always required, but in some cases (e.g., if you are working with a third-party agency that is charging you for updates), they are very important for budgeting and cost control. It helps if you have fixed status categories to aid sorting and filtering. If you are working with a spreadsheet or Web form, you can dynamically create drop-down menus from a central data source. Example status categories would be Under Review, In Development, Ready for Sign-Off, or Complete to suit your process.

As I have suggested with the "How do I fill this in?" links, you can also provide guides to entering data, such as date formats, to help promote consistency and save time if someone new is updating the log. How often you update your change log will depend on the volume of changes that you have coming through and your change process. However, if possible, you should update the log daily and then review it at a weekly status meeting.

2.6   Scheduling Changes

So you have a language of change, a process, the people, and the key documents to facilitate and log the changes. Finally, you require an agreed upon schedule that specifies when each step in the process will occur. This temporal structure helps manage everyone's expectations as to when a change will be visible on the site. Once the organization gets used to some kind of change rhythm, it will become more likely to submit changes on time to meet its own deadlines. Perhaps more important, the structured use of time improves quality and efficiency. The maintenance team is no longer snowed under with a thousand little requests from all directions but is able to have quality time to focus on development work during the allotted time and concentrate on making sure the critical uploads and go-live processes run smoothly. A more structured use of resource time also enables more accurate resource planning and budgeting.

The schedule needs to fit realistically with the process, and this may require some initial experimentation to find a comfortable balance between the demands for speed and control. Clearly, the urgency of a change is the factor that most affects the schedule it must run to. You may have alternate processes, or a short-cut version of a longer process, to handle really urgent changes. You should develop different schedules to match the processes.

Figure 2.4 gives an example weekly schedule to fit with the process that we looked at earlier. Typically, you might have emergency, weekly, and monthly schedules as standard. Each run of the schedule will process numerous individual change requests. Some weeks may be a lot busier than others, but on the whole, the maintenance team should be able to cope with slight peaks with some support.

As the number of requests goes up, you can expand the team to accommodate them, but when the volume gets past a certain point, you will be better off having two teams running in parallel, working closely together, with the schedule slipped by 2 days between the teams. For example, one team's weekly schedule starts and ends on a Tuesday, whereas the second team's schedule runs from Thursday to Thursday. Scaling this way any further is likely to break down, partly because too many different teams working on the same content and files become complicated and also because the coordinators will no longer be able to cope with acting as single points of contact for multiple teams. This would be the time to start looking at a content management solution, which we do in Part II of the book.

TIP   **Scheduling Major Updates**

It is advisable to construct your schedule so that major uploads and updates do not occur just before any period where support resources will not be available in the following hours and days. For example, Fridays are not a good choice if you have nobody available during the weekend. Not only can people be a little less attentive and committed on Fridays, with the lure of the weekend perhaps tempting them into cutting corners, but if something went wrong following the changes (and let's face it, things do go wrong now and again), you are left having to try and persuade people to come in to work to fix the problems over the weekend. Even if you can persuade your staff to do this, you may be reliant on other service providers to resolve the problem who are less enthusiastic. However, in some cases, the weekend is the best time to make updates, assuming you can get the resources required to make them, precisely because things are quiet and the site might not be used as much as during the week.

Weekly Changes Schedule		
Wednesday	AM	Web site maintenance coordinator receives processed change requests from business coordinator.
	PM	Web site maintenance coordinator reviews change requests and raises any queries with business coordinator.
		Business coordinator reviews queries and responds to Web site maintenance coordinator.
Thursday	AM	Web site maintenance coordinator develops briefs for maintenance team.
		Web site maintenance coordinator confirms resource requirements, timings, and costs as required.
	PM	Maintenance team is briefed on work.
		Development work begins.
Friday	AM	Development work in progress.
	PM	Development work in progress.
Monday	AM	Development work in progress.
		Testing and review by Web site maintenance team.
	PM	Preview ready for approval.
		Testing and review by business.
Tuesday	AM	Changes resulting from testing and review implemented.
		Preview signed off.
	PM	Changes go live.
		Web site maintenance team and business test and review changes on live site and make further changes if required.
		Live site sign-off.

Figure 2.4 Sample weekly changes schedule.

The schedule and process we have looked at are frameworks for managing multiple, smaller, unplanned changes. All those bits and pieces inevitably come through that need to be handled in a controlled way if they are not to get out of control or continually frustrate attempts at doing substantial new pieces of work. It is very likely that as well as these unplanned changes you will also have project work going on. Seasonal changes often account for a lot of work and a lot of requirement for changes. The advantage with seasonal or other project work, of course, is that it can be planned in advance. If you have a smooth-running process in place to manage your unplanned changes, it is significantly easier to concentrate on planning other work and ensuring the work streams are smoothly integrated.

In terms of scheduling work that you know is coming, there is no reason not to borrow directly from offline publishing practices. Just as you would create an editorial schedule showing what topics will be addressed when and by whom for forthcoming magazine editions, for example, you should create a master schedule showing all the planned work that is in the pipeline. A publishing schedule typically looks forward a full year even though details become increasingly sketchy the further into the future it goes. This is necessary to start commissioning the content, selling the advertising, and meeting print deadlines. Although the specifics of implementation may be different online, the need for planning is the same.

Your master schedule need not include your regular unplanned change process details but should include regular planned content update commitments such as monthly newsletters, quarterly reports, or annual financial presentations. The schedule does not need to include the details of the work to be carried out, as this should be contained in project-specific plans. It is a milestone summary of all the major site updates that will occur as far ahead as you can see. You might want to create the master schedule Gantt-chart style to show a sense of project durations and interdependencies, but perhaps the most effective medium is a simple wall chart calendar such as the ones sometimes posted in offices for teams to see when colleagues are away on vacation. A master schedule need be no more complicated than this. The simplicity means it is easy to see at a glance what is coming up and where the pressure points are likely to be. The openly visible, and physical, wall chart is more motivating for a team. The working year ahead is there for all to see. Implicitly, if you do not complain about the plan you see, you are buying into it and making some sort of contract to uphold it.

Summary

People often think that content management is the solution to the challenges they are facing in maintaining and updating their Web sites. This may be the case, but what is often required is simply improved change management. Two things we can say for sure about change management:

▶ If you need to bring more control and quality into the way Web site changes and updates are being managed, then you must look at change management. The problems are rarely ones that can be addressed with technology alone but are much more about people, processes, and documentation.

▶ If you think you need content management, address change management first. Not only do too many people rush headlong into expensive content management solutions that never deliver a return on their investment, but perhaps more important, it must be realized that effective content management is built on structures and processes. Content management technology is an enabler, but you still need good processes to make it effective. Like it or not, to do content management you will have to address change management in any case.

PART II

CONTENT MANAGEMENT

The processes and practices examined in Part I on change management are applicable to a Web site at any stage. They help introduce a rigour that ensures quality and efficiency. However, as Web sites continue to grow, even efficient change management cannot keep up with the volume and dynamism of change required. Nor does change management in itself give you the platform you need to dynamically match content to users across multiple platforms. Sooner or later, it is likely you will have to confront what has become known as *content management*. In some circles, this is refined to *Web content management,* but although we will be concentrating on Web sites, it would be wrong to think of content management as Web specific because its concepts, processes, and applications are valid across all channels and media.

To master content management, it is necessary to understand its concepts, its processes, and its practice. For this reason, this part of the book tries to balance a mixture of conceptual background information with real-life examples to show the theory in practice. There is also a section on how to tackle a content management project to help you understand the process of delivering a content management solution.

Key Areas We Will Cover in Part II

▶ What content management is and what it is not. Where does it come from? Why is it needed?

▶ A practical example of content management in action. To understand the higher level concepts, we start looking at the end product: a series of Web pages.

▶ The key concepts and building blocks of content management. These are the necessary foundation to understand content management. We cover the content model, the separation of content and presentation, templates, metadata, XML, the content life cycle, and workflow.

▶ Content management systems (CMSs): What are they and how do they work? Do you buy one or build your own? How do you select a CMS?

▶ Tackling a content management project. How do you put everything together to deliver a content management solution? What process should you follow? What are the tasks and deliverables?

3

Introducing Content Management

$$T$$he following few sections give a brief introduction into what content management means and how it relates to disciplines such as document management, information management and knowledge management. We then look at why content management is needed and, equally importantly, what it cannot achieve, before using a practical, real-life example to show content management in action in the next chapter.

3.1 What Is Content Management?

Content management as a discipline is the set of processes, technologies, concepts, and practices having to do with developing, collecting, managing, and publishing content.

This is not a definition as there is no accepted definition of content management yet. However, it is a working statement that is short enough to make sense and yet broad enough to encompass all the areas and aspects we will cover in this part of the book. If you come back to the statement after you have read all that follows, perhaps it will adequately sum up what you have learned.

Discussing "what is content management" in much more detail will probably only confuse the issue; however, it is worth briefly noting that it is a relatively new discipline that has evolved out of a series of others, some of which have long preceded it. Table 3.1 looks at some of those disciplines and how they relate to content management.

Table 3.1 Disciplines related to content management.

Discipline	Description and Relation to Content Management
Document management	Document management systems began to rise to prominence in the mid-1970s as a way to help large organizations manage a large number of files. They resemble a turbocharged file management system. They share many of the characteristics of a content management system inasmuch as they help store, retrieve, and provide access to content, but there are two important differences. First, document management systems focus on handling files of any type rather than content objects (more on what a content object is in Chapter 5, Key Concepts and Building Blocks). Second, a content management system is expected to create dynamic publications, whereas a document management system is only for managing and retrieving files efficiently. It should be noted that many of today's foremost content management vendors come from a document management heritage.
Information management	Information management is somewhat of a vague term that touches on many areas but tends to be focused on the processing of large amounts of data. This means that skills in processing, structuring, converting, formatting, collecting, and acquiring data and information are needed, and these are very similar to what is required in content management. Typically, some publishing is done, as in the form of reports. However, information management systems are not dynamic publishing systems. Nor are they customer facing in the way that content management systems usually are. Information management is more about batch processes, data warehouses, information processing routines, working with a small number of specialists, and large systems. Content management is about creating, managing, and publishing meaningful content and working with numerous distributed authors and an equally numerous and diverse audience.
Knowledge management	Knowledge management is about trying to understand and harness the power of the knowledge that an organization has. Knowledge management focuses on the tools and practices for discovering and squeezing out an organization's most valuable knowledge assets and making them available to the organization. The tools use technologies to search, index, mine, analyze, categorize, and synthesize vast amounts of data into useful knowledge. However, knowledge management is not about authoring and collecting content in the same way as content management. Nor are knowledge management systems typically as advanced in their management and publication capabilities as a full content management system. Whereas knowledge management focuses on addressing the almost intellectual challenge of identifying and distilling knowledge, content management is the infrastructure that makes it possible to store and distribute content. There is no reason a content management system should not be used to manage and publish the knowledge created by a knowledge management tool.

3.2   Why Is Content Management Needed?

It would be surprising if anyone involved in maintaining and evolving a successful commercial Web site did not recognize some of the following basic trends:

▶ The amount of information and functionality on the site is expanding rapidly.

▶ There are requirements for expanding the site to encompass new areas such as business-to-business relationships, multilingual sites, and integration with suppliers and partners.

▶ The content on the site needs to be more up to date and the process for updating site content needs to be more efficient. For example, the "Webmaster bottleneck" must be overcome.

▶ There are ever more content contributors to the site, many of whom have very different content authoring and delivery processes.

▶ Expectations for the reliability and quality of site performance are rapidly increasing. Broken links, missing images, and invalid email addresses are just not acceptable. Page load times must be minimized, and consistency of branding and presentation must be maintained.

▶ There is increasing demand for personalized content and functionality.

▶ There are growing requirements for content to be published not just to other digital channels but to offline channels such as print as well.

▶ There is a growing number of different types of media assets and content that have to be managed over and above basic text and imagery.

▶ There is increasing pressure for solutions to be accountable: Their performance must be measurable and auditable for a variety of commercial, legal, and other reasons.

Even if you have conquered one or two of these trends, it would be impressive indeed if you could confidently say that you can deliver precisely the right content, to the right person, at the right time, through the right channel, *and* have maximized the efficiencies of doing this by integrating and aligning your business processes with the ways in which you create, manage, and publish your content as well as maximizing the value of that content through its intelligent and dynamic reuse. That is both the challenge and reward of content management.

Section 6.3, Evolving toward a CMS, looks at the typical stages you might go through in evolving toward *full* content management using a content management system (CMS).

There is a difference between content management as an approach and as a content management system (CMS). Whereas the concepts, processes, and practices of content management can be applied at almost any stage and often for relatively little cost, a CMS is a costly piece of software to buy, install, and maintain. Total ownership costs are likely to run into hundreds of thousands of dollars, if not more, so this is a big investment decision.

The most likely indications that you need content management are as follows:

▶ You have lots of distributed content contributors and you are finding it very difficult to effectively manage how they contribute content and quality control of that content.

▶ You have lots of content contributors who do not have HTML-type skills and need an easy interface to submit content.

▶ Your somewhat informal processes for getting content onto and off the site are falling apart to the clear detriment of quality and at increasing costs to put right.

▶ Automation of content publishing to the site would save you a lot of time and money and improve the site users' experience and perception of the site.

▶ You have regulatory obligations to be able to store past versions of your site and re-create versions of the site from any point in the past.

▶ You would benefit from having greater control over the design of the site for branding consistency.

▶ You would like to deliver advanced levels of content personalization or advanced and accurate reporting and analytics about which users like what sorts of content.

▶ You have a need to publish different forms of the same content to multiple channels dynamically from a single source.

▶ You need to syndicate large volumes of content, either into your site or out from it.

3.3   What Web Content Management Cannot Achieve

Content management is a great way of improving efficiencies by shifting as much mundane processing work as possible to the dumb computer, which will work all night like a slave for no money. Unfortunately, the system is only as good as those who configure it: It can only do what it is told. So it is worth noting a few of the things that a CMS cannot do for you:

▶ It does not automatically organize your content for you. It certainly gives you the tools to help you structure and organize your content and will then happily manage and publish that content according to further instructions you give it, but it cannot work out the initial optimal architecture for your content. That is far too strategic a decision for a CMS to make.

▶ It does not create content; it only manages it. It will happily work with external content authoring tools and will create publications that are unique configurations of the content that it is managing, but a CMS alone does not originate content or design publications.

▶ It does not know what good content is. It does not even know the meaning of your content. It is, after all, just a dumb computer that will be quite happy to efficiently manage total nonsense.

▶ It does not process transactions. For that, you will still need a transactional system such as an e-commerce engine.

▶ On the whole, it is not that great at providing analytical information. It provides the necessary structure for a separate tool to do this job.

▶ It does not design for you.

▶ It does not know how to fix bad business processes.

Content Management in Action: A Practical Example

Before we look at the concepts and building blocks of content management and CMSs, I would like to introduce an example of content management in action. It can be difficult to grasp concepts without any concrete example of how the concepts eventually translate into something tangible. In this chapter, we start with something as concrete and simple as possible, a site's home page, and work out from the end result to examine what is going on behind the scenes. This will serve to introduce the concepts that we discuss in more detail in the following chapter.

Note that the example given is a real one. The Web site at *www.e-consultancy. com* provides online access to e-business information and advice. I am one of those who help run the site and contribute to it. Although the design will have changed by the time you read this, the underlying content management processes will have changed much less. Note also that this is deliberately quite a simple, and simplified, example of content management in action to get across the key ideas and practices. The site is run by a custom-built CMS rather than an off-the-shelf package that has been customized, but the technologies, processes, and practices are the same.

4.1   The Home Page

Figure 4.1 shows a copy of the e-consultancy home page as it would be seen by a registered user who was logged on to the site. Looking at this page

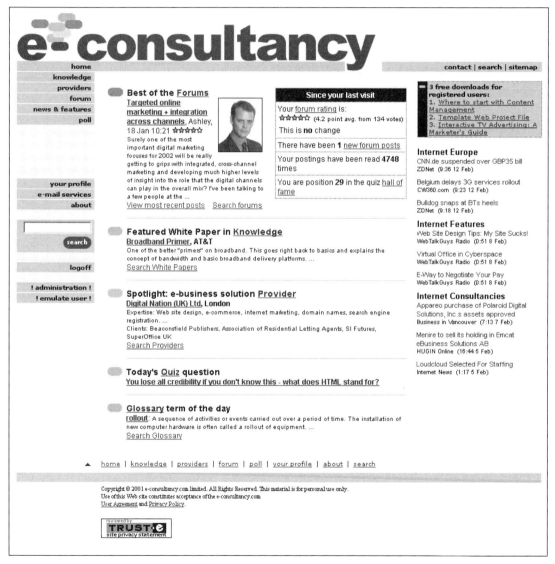

Figure 4.1   An example site home page: e-consultancy.

as a user (registered, in this case), you should be able to make out the following:

▶ The site's logo is at the top.
▶ There is standard footer information at the bottom.
▶ There is a left navigation column.
▶ There are general site tools (contact, search, site map) to the top right.
▶ There is a right column with a promotional box and news headlines.
▶ There is a personalized section giving information on what has happened since the user's last visit.
▶ The main window contains highlights of content selected from the site.

As a user, you probably do not think about how this page is constructed. You are there for a reason, and you will continue along your journey until you have accomplished what you came for. If content management is done well, the user should not notice how the system is stitching together content and creating pages dynamically. As far as the user is concerned, or cares, each page could be handcrafted in HTML. But we are interested in how the page has come to life, so what is going on behind the scenes?

The entire page is a template that brings content and design elements together to produce the final page. Indeed, the template contains subtemplates for controlling particular areas of the page. The content on the page can be broken down into content that is:

▶ *Fixed.* This is content that is hard-coded in HTML. It is directly referenced in a template file and pulled straight onto the page. This is content that does not need to change on the page. Once it has been loaded by the user's browser, it should be cached thereafter and so display very quickly.
▶ *Dynamically created but not done in real time.* There is some confusion around the word *dynamic.* Dynamic content does not need to be created on the fly as the user requests the page. Dynamic content is not fixed content as just described. It does not exist in a fixed form; rather, it is generated on demand from constituent elements according to rules. If you change the raw elements or the rules, you will change the end product. Why would you want to have dynamically created content that was done in real time? Mostly to reduce system load, to improve the speed of the site for users, and to reduce the likelihood of errors by "pre-preparing" your content.
▶ *Dynamically created in real time.* This is dynamic content that only comes into existence as the user requests the page.

Figure 4.2 shows a dotted line demarcating the content that is fixed. There is little reason to make the header and footer content dynamic as it does not change. However, as these elements are included in a template that appears on every page of the site, if you did want to make a change, then you need only do it once within the template file, and it would be done across the entire site.

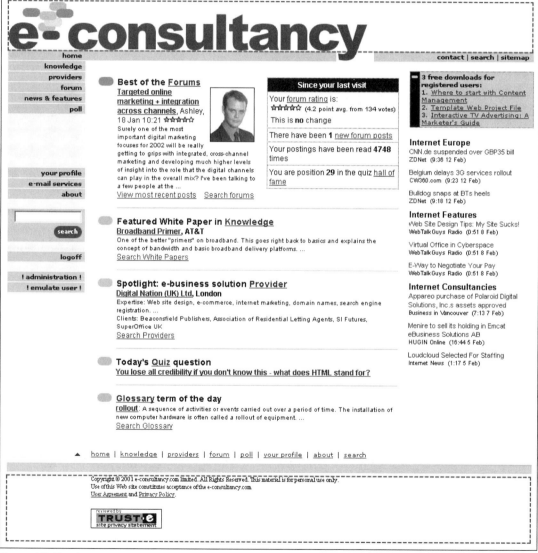

Figure 4.2 Fixed content.

Figure 4.3 shows the content that is dynamically created but not in real time. The content in the main window is generated automatically once a day according to a scheduled script. The news feeds in the right column are refreshed once an hour. Once generated, the content is then cached until the next refresh, which can be forced if required, to improve site speed and

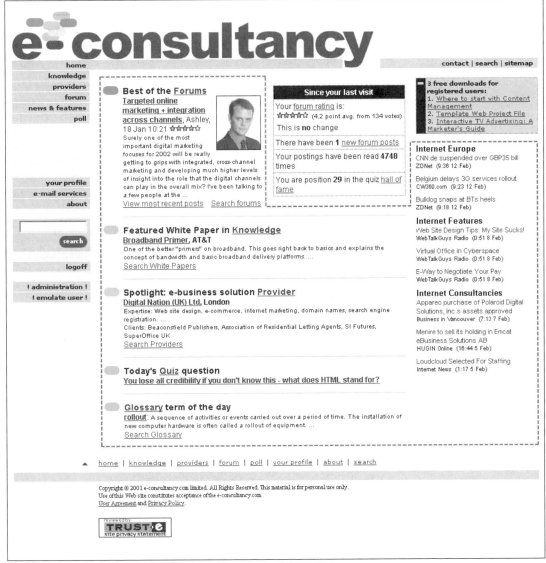

Figure 4.3 Dynamically generated content but not in real time.

performance. The frequency of dynamic update is a trade-off between what is acceptable for the users and the type of content (e.g., news needs to be updated more frequently) and what is best in terms of performance. At the point of dynamic update, the content is created as follows:

▶ *Best of the forums.* All posts to the forum are stored in a database with time stamps. Posts are also rated by users. A business rule in the template says that a forum post should be selected at random to be displayed on the home page, but the post must be rated at least three stars or higher on average and must have been made within the last 3 months. The elements of the post that are displayed are the title (which is also a link to the post), author, date, star rating, and the first 250 characters of the post itself.

▶ *Featured white paper.* The business rule here is simply to pick any white paper at random and display its title (which also becomes a link to the details of the white paper), the organization that created it, and the first 130 characters from its description.

▶ *Spotlight on an e-business solution provider.* This works very much like the featured white paper except the selected content elements are provider name, region, and then the first 80 characters of the Expertise and Clients fields.

▶ *Quiz and glossary.* It should be clear that for the quiz simply a question is displayed at random, while for the glossary an example term and the first 130 characters of the definition are shown.

▶ *News feeds.* These are imported into a relational database from an external site as an eXtensible Markup Language (XML) feed. These updates occur automatically every hour. The page template then pulls the content from the database and formats it, choosing to display only a certain number of elements in a way that fits in with the rest of the site.

The rest of the content on the page is dynamically generated as the user requests the page. Obviously, the personalization contained within the "Since your last visit" box has to be generated on the fly because the site cannot know who the user is until he or she logs on. In the example page given, the user is already logged on (automatically using a cookie or by entering a username and password), so the system can check against the user's profile to display the relevant information.

The navigation is also dynamically generated in real time from a central XML file that defines the site's navigational hierarchy. As you go further into the site, there is a "breadcrumb" navigational device along the top gray strip to allow you to see where in the site's hierarchy you are and to enable navigation up and across the site's navigational structure. This is defined by the XML file and rendered automatically to the page so that changing the site's structure and navigation does not require changing file directory structures or navigation elements but merely an update to the XML file. The site map is likewise generated automatically from this XML file, meaning it never needs updating; it is never out of synch with the actual site contents, and there are never any broken links.

You might think that the navigation could be automatically generated once a day, say, and then cached as with the main body content. However, the navigation is personalized to the user, so different categories of users see different navigation. In this case, the navigation is personalized based on the permission level of the user. The user logged on for this example is an Administrator-level site user, and you can see at the bottom of the left navigation that there are two additional items of navigation ("administration" and "emulate user") that give the user access to special areas of the site.

Finally, the promotional box at the top of the right column needs to be generated on the fly as it changes often and is controlled by "go live" and "expire" parameters that the promotion is given through an administration interface. For example, a promotion can be added at any time and set to stay live on the site until a particular date. Equally, the administration interface allows the user to get rid of a particular promotion by setting an expire date that is before the current date. As the page is requested, the system checks to see if there are any valid promotions to display and then renders them according to the template file governing that part of the page.

4.2   Content Collection, Management, and Publishing

We are now going to zoom in to the featured "white paper" on the home page. We have discussed the simple logic that the template uses to display what the user sees on the home page. But what goes on before that content ever makes it to the home page? How is that content created, captured, managed, and then published?

The content in the example is relatively straightforward to create and manage. It is text only, and it can all be easily entered through a Web form directly to the content repository—the database that manages all the site's content. Figure 4.4 shows in simple terms what is happening. You will notice

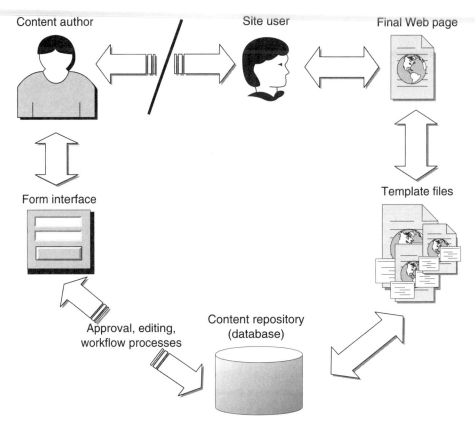

Figure 4.4 Collecting, managing, and publishing content.

that although the content author is creating content with an end user in mind, the relationship between the two is not direct.

Figure 4.5 shows what the form interface for adding and editing e-consultancy's white papers looks like. Note the following about this screen:

▶ Content is created and added directly to the database via this Web form, which is on the site itself. There are no sign-off stages involved in setting the content live: Once it has been entered, it is eligible for display on the site.

▶ The content is split into content that the user will see on the site (display data) and content that will be used to help manage and maximize the value of this piece of content (management metadata).

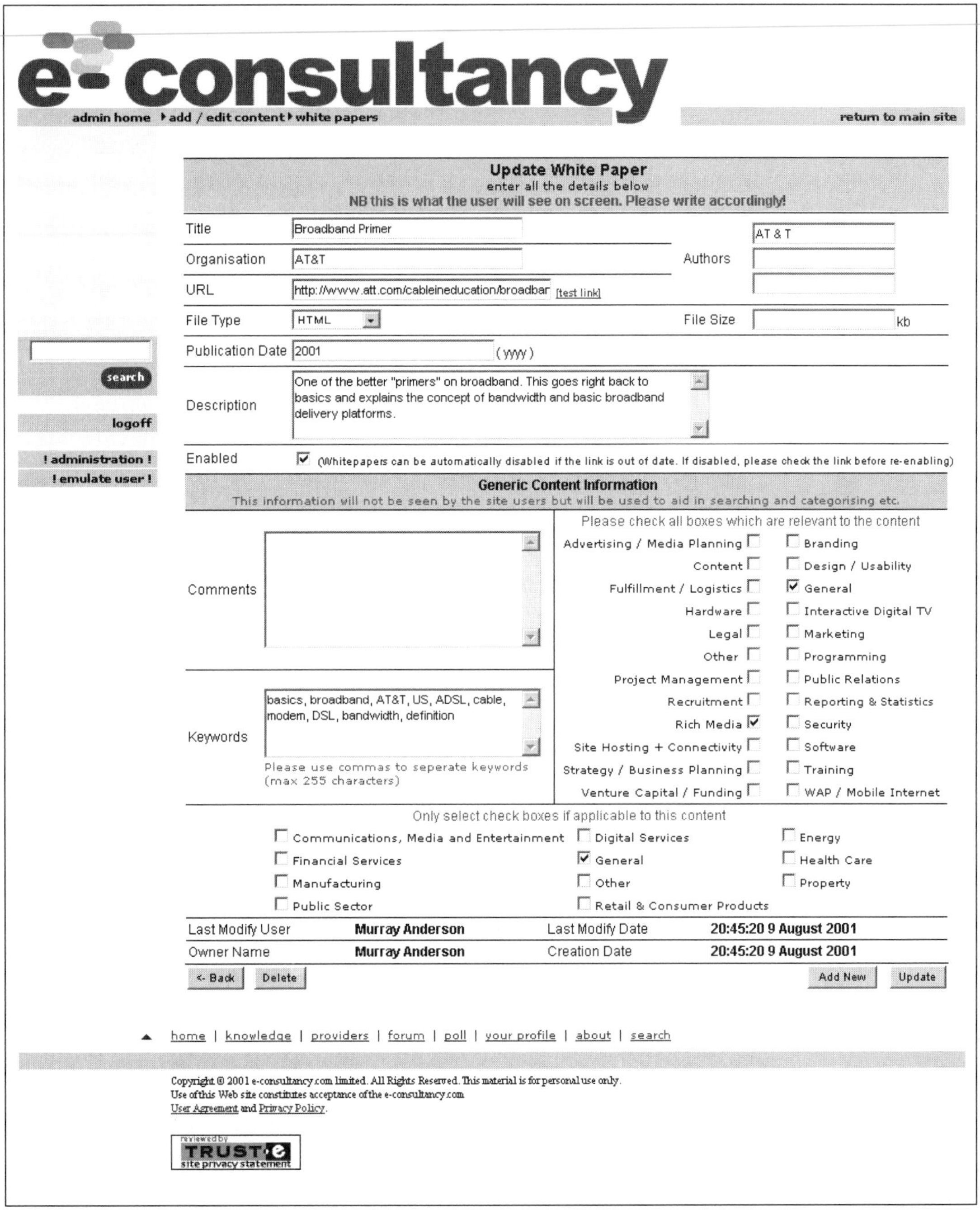

Figure 4.5 Form interface for adding white papers to the e-consultancy site.

► The Generic Content Information section of this content capture form adds four extra layers of information to the basic white paper information. First, there are comments, which are simply notes to help any future editor. Second, there are keywords, which are used to help improve the quality of the site's search results when searching on terms relevant to this piece of content. Third, there are 24 content categories representing topics such as marketing, design, interactive advertising, and so on. Fourth, there are 11 industry sectors, one or more of which may be relevant to the content.

► There is information about who created and last updated the piece of content, which is automatically logged, and basic details are shown at the bottom of the content editor's screen.

► Both the generic content information and the logging of who has updated what and when are common to *every* piece of content that is added to the site via Web forms such as this. This makes it possible to understand, track, and serve the content not only by its content section (e.g., white papers or providers) but also by topic (e.g., show me all project management content we have) or by industry sector (e.g., show me everything we have to do with the financial services sector). As you can imagine, having this additional data, or metadata as it is known, makes it possible to combine and serve the site's content in ways that suit the user relatively easily.

► There are some link management features associated with this piece of content. You can test the URL for the white paper directly from the form to see if it works. More powerful than that, however, is a link checking function, which runs three times a day to automatically check that the link is valid. If the link fails three times in a row, then that white paper is automatically disabled so it no longer shows on the site. The content editor is sent an email with a link to that white paper's form interface so he or she can check the details and try and fix the link. Once it is fixed, the content editor reenables the piece of content by checking the check box in the form, and it will appear on the site again. Obviously, this helps ensure site users experience as few broken links as possible and the site's content is as up to date as possible.

4.3 **Workflow**

We look at workflow in more detail in the following section as one of the key concepts behind content management. For the moment, let us look at the series of tasks and task triggers that represent the workflow surrounding how an e-business solution provider is added to the e-consultancy database and how it can subsequently be edited.

The providers database is a directory of more than 2000 United Kingdom new media agencies. To ensure the information stays current and that as much in-depth information on each agency is available as possible, the agencies themselves are encouraged to add and update their own listing's details. The process works as follows:

1. The agency requests, via the e-consultancy site, to be added to the providers database.
2. An email with the agency's request is sent to the e-consultancy content team.
3. Their request is reviewed, and if accepted, their details are added.
4. The agency is sent an email confirming their listing and giving further details on how they can edit their own listing in the future.
5. Someone at the agency applies to edit the agency's listing.
6. An email is sent to e-consultancy alerting the content team to the agency's application.
7. The application is reviewed, and if accepted, edit permissions are granted to the applicant.
8. An email is sent to the agency applicant confirming permission to edit the agency's listing and giving an encoded link that enables its edit ability.
9. The agency can then edit their listing via the site whenever they wish.
10. The site tracks and reports on who has edited what and when, storing previous versions, as well as tracking at what stage each edit application is and the status of each applicant user.

So what does this process look like in reality? Figure 4.6 shows the page that any site user can go to in order to suggest their own, or another, company for inclusion in the database.

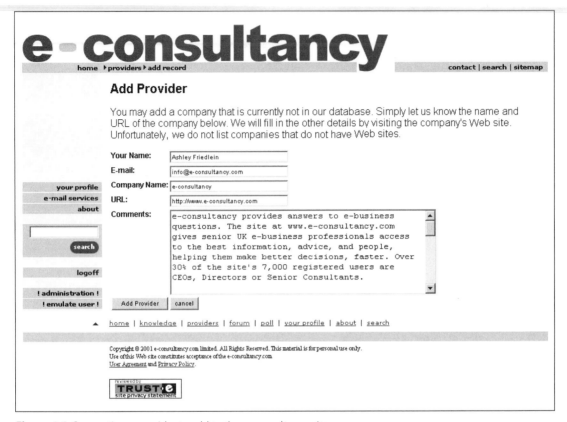

Figure 4.6 Suggesting a provider to add to the e-consultancy site.

Once the request to be added has been submitted, an email is sent to the e-consultancy content team who then go to a form interface that they use to fill in the agency's details gathered from the agency's Web site. Note that the content team does not see the middle section of the form as shown in Figure 4.7. This is only visible to the agency once they have permission to edit their listing as the information it contains (typical project budget, annual turnover, etc.) can only really come directly from the agency.

Once the agency is added, they are sent an email confirming their listing and giving instructions on how to edit their own listing. Assuming the agency applies for edit permissions, an email is sent to the e-consultancy content

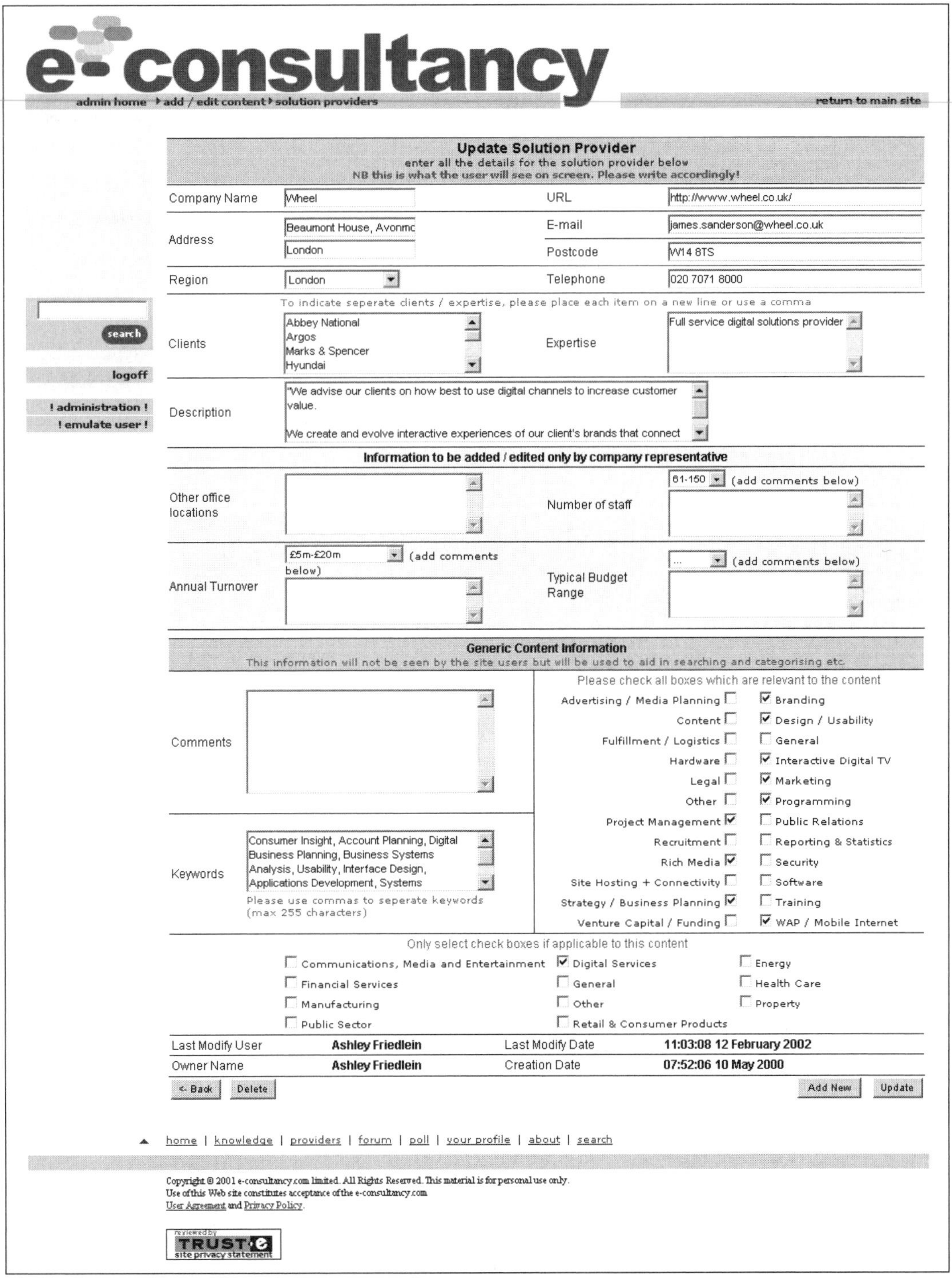

Figure 4.7 Adding a provider's details.

team with a link leading to the page shown in Figure 4.8, which shows the application that has been made and allows the content team then to review it and grant or deny the application.

If the agency applicant is granted listing edit rights she then follows a link back to the site that enables her editing ability. Figure 4.9 shows the interface that the agency uses to modify their listing. As you will notice, this is not the same interface that the e-consultancy content team sees. Not only is the agency's interface somewhat more user-friendly (it looks like a regular Web form), but it also excludes all the additional metadata fields that the content team can view and edit. However, the agency can see, add, and edit sensitive information regarding their size and financials.

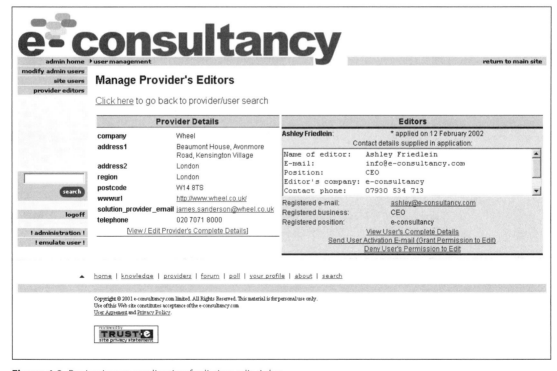

Figure 4.8 Reviewing an application for listing edit rights.

e-consultancy

home ▸ providers ▸ edit record   contact | search | sitemap

Edit Provider

Below are the details associated with the company name you selected. Please note:

- these details are taken live from the database. As soon as **you update the records they will go live**
- e-consultancy keeps a log of who edits which records for reference and security purposes. However, we do not keep a record of previous versions. If you **overwrite** a record which you then want to retrieve, the only way to do so is to re-enter the original information.

We are very keen to maintain data quality standards in our database. Consistency in the data formats is clearly important. If you are unsure as to how you should enter / update your information, please refer to our Editor's guide.

There is some key data which many users look for that e-consultancy is unable to add or update, either because it changes too often or because it is commercially sensitive. You, however, can enter / update this information in order to help attract the right kind of people to your company. These fields are: **Other office locations, Number of staff, Annual Turnover, Typical Project Budget Range.**

your profile
e-mail services
about

search

logoff

! administration !
! emulate user !

Company	Wheel
URL	http://www.wheel.co.uk/
E-mail	james.sanderson@wheel.co.uk
Address	Beaumont House, Avonmore Road, Kensington Village
	London

Region   London

Postcode   W14 8TS

Telephone   020 7071 8000

Other office locations

Number of staff   61-150   (add comments below)

Annual Turnover   £5m-£20m   (add comments below)

Typical Budget Range   ...   (add comments below)

Clients
Abbey National
Argos
Marks & Spencer
Hyundai
Safeway
National Savings

Expertise
Full service digital solutions provider

Description
"We advise our clients on how best to use digital channels to increase customer value.

We create and evolve interactive experiences of our client's brands that connect their customers with their products and services."

Record Last Updated 12 February 2002

Update Provider   Cancel

▲   home | knowledge | providers | forum | poll | your profile | about | search

Copyright © 2001 e-consultancy.com limited. All Rights Reserved. This material is for personal use only.
Use of this Web site constitutes acceptance of the e-consultancy.com
User Agreement and Privacy Policy

TRUST e
site privacy statement

Figure 4.9 Editing the provider listing on the site.

Key Concepts and Building Blocks

T his chapter picks out the most important concepts and building blocks that make up content management. If you understand these, then you pretty much understand content management. We focus here on what these key concepts are and why they are important rather than how to implement them or how to embrace them as part of a content management project. Ideally, the practical example in the previous chapter will help you understand the concepts discussed here more easily.

For all the various concepts and building blocks that we are about to address, content management can be boiled down to a focus on two things: structure and process. If you cannot remember the details of what follows, you should at least be clear on the overall importance and benefits of structure and process that a content management approach delivers. The need for content management in the first place is usually driven from a loss of control. Structure and process are about reintroducing control as much as possible without sacrificing the ability to be flexible, reactive, dynamic, and innovative. Ultimately, there has to be some balancing act and trade-off between control and flexibility. Introducing content management principles and systems to your Web site

The practical project process elements are covered in Chapter 7, Tackling a Content Management Project.

because it has grown too large to manage effectively is very similar to introducing more structure and processes to a business that has expanded beyond a certain point and needs better controls to keep running effectively.

5.1   Structuring Content

We have to structure things to manage and understand them effectively. Consider the following wide range of scenarios:

▶ You are the curator of an art gallery and want to mount a special exhibition. Is your exhibition based on the works of a particular artist? Or works from a particular period? Or works from a particular artistic movement? Or works according to a particular theme? Or works from a particular country? Your exhibition has a purpose and meaning once you have decided how to structure your choice of works to display.

▶ You are about to undertake a Web content management project. How should you structure the project? By phases? By business unit? By particular work streams? You have to decide how you are going to approach the project to have any hope of managing it effectively.

▶ You are creating a site with a restaurant reviews section. How will users want to find and compare restaurant reviews? By restaurant name? By location? By price? By type of cuisine? By chef? By restaurant star rating? The way you structure your restaurant review content is going to make any or none of these possible.

Structure is vital to managing most things, and content is certainly no exception. Well-structured content is easy to manage and configure in different ways to suit the desired end result. Structure is what enables reuse and repackaging of content to maximize its value. And because we are dealing with dumb computers, *content structure must be made explicit if it is to be understood by a content management system.* That might seem obvious, but do not forget that we humans can infer structure in ways that a computer cannot, or at best can very poorly: A highly designed book cover or film poster may have a structure (title, author/director, reviews, etc.) that is evident to us through the design but would mean little to a computer without some extra help.

How do you categorize structure? As you can see from the few example scenarios given earlier, there are any number of ways to structure things. Other common structures might include product line, job position, gender, age, nationality, color, size, or topic. The right way to structure your content will depend on what you need it to do and how you plan to manage the structure.

Structures themselves are frameworks with different axes, but the only way that we can understand structure is by naming the elements of the structure and defining the relationship between the named elements. Names usually need to be descriptive to carry meaning for humans, but computers just need names to be applied consistently and uniquely and then be told how to understand and interpret those names to get a handle on the overall structure.

If you look back at the e-consultancy example from Chapter 4, you will note various structures at work: an overall generic content information structure with its various fixed categories that are applied to all pieces of content as well as structures that are internal to specific types of content, such as the data elements that go together to make up a piece of white paper content. You will have noted also how the templates can then apply business rules and logic to use those structures to manage and publish the content as Web pages. The structures as you have seen them on a Web page should make sense to a human because of the names given to each element. These same names may or may not be used by the computer, but as long as the relationship between what the human understands and what the content management system understands remains consistent, the structures will stay intact and can be efficiently managed.

So what does *not* have structure in terms of content? A single video clip file has no structure. What can you do with it except reference it directly? As you begin to add information such as video clip duration, format, topic, category, and user groups it is suitable for, you are wrapping the single file up with information that allows it to be used and reused as part of a structure.

5.2 The Content Model

The content model is also sometimes referred to as a content taxonomy or content schema. It is at the heart of what is more broadly referred to as information architecture. The content model is the underlying structure of your content, so connotations of architecture are indeed apt: The content model is the blueprint and infrastructural skeleton to which are then added the flesh and skin. It is relatively easy to change the decoration of a room or the clothes you are wearing—to change outward presentation—but it is much more difficult to change the infrastructure that underpins it.

If you look back to the e-consultancy example in the previous chapter, you see many of the core elements of the site's content model. There are individual content sections such as white papers and glossary and forums, each content object having its own set of data elements, and then there are higher level categories of information such as keywords, topic categories, user permission levels, and industry sectors.

NOTE   **A Site Map Is Not a Content Model**

Which comes first, the content model or the Web page? Do you build up from your content model and end up with a Web page, or do you design a Web page that will work for your users and then work out what the content model to support it is? Well, both. Ideally, you should create your site focusing on your users' needs but also have in mind commercial constraints and requirements, one of which is your ability to support a particular content model. As ever, iteration is required and a multidisciplinary team who can juggle priorities and make the best trade-off decisions.

A site map outlines what the content sections of a Web site are, as seen from a user's point of view. A site map is hierarchical: It shows what content is in what section or subsection. Thus, a site map typically also dictates the site's navigation. Site maps, as visual representations, are very bad at showing interrelationships or cross-references. If you have tried to show these, you know you end up with an organogram that has arrows drawn all over it to the point where it is useless.

A site map shows what is on a site and where it is located within a navigational structure from a user's point of view. This is not the same as a content model. For a start, a content model does not need to be hierarchical. Parent > child relationships are needed with navigation, but the information axes that make up the content model matrix are not hierarchical. In the e-consultancy example, there is no parent > child relationship between topic category and industry sector. Also, there is no hard-coded relationship between the navigation, as a content access method, and the underlying content model, whereas there is a very definite correlation between a site map and site navigation.

In the e-consultancy example, the content model structures content by 24 topics, and yet these do not appear in the navigation. They are used for filtering searches and for tracking what subject area a user is interested in across all the content sections of the site. Is it more useful to know that a user looks at particular content sections (e.g., white papers) or that she is interested in interactive advertising generally? Either way, the point is that the content model, although often closely related to a site's navigation and site map, is separate. If you have well-structured content according to a well-defined content model, it is quite easy to change your site structure and rejig your site map. If all you have is a site map, restructures are painful. ■

Think of your content model as a matrix rather than as a hierarchical tree, with different axes that allow you to view your content in different ways. You need to figure out what you need to do with your content and then design a unified framework that will serve your purposes. The following are common content axes that go together to build a content model:

▶ *Users.* Users can be grouped by numerous attributes: by behavioral characteristics, by name, by client, by permission level, by gender, by age range, by interest group, by job, or by geography.

▶ *Products.* If you are in the e-commerce field, you are no doubt quite used to product taxonomies and catalogs that structure your product information.

▶ *Topic.* If you are in publishing, you will likely need to structure content according to its subject matter.

▶ *Type.* This might be the type of content asset in terms of format (video, text, imagery) or other classification (article, news item, case study, press release, white paper, etc.).

▶ *Channel.* If you are delivering your content across multiple channels, you are going to need a way to retrieve the right content for the right channel. This does not necessarily mean creating different content for each channel, which is sometimes necessary but defeats the objectives of content reuse and repackaging offered by content management. However, in your content model, you must think through how content might need to be tagged in order to then automatically configure it for use through the particular channel.

▶ *Business area.* Particularly for business-to-business sites, you may want to structure your content according to business disciplines, by sector or industry.

▶ *Location.* This is particularly important if you are dealing with a multilingual or international site where different content, or slightly different versions of content, are required for each location. If your content model does not contain a way of retrieving content by the relevant locations, how can you effectively manage and publish that content?

The content model is at the heart of any content management system. It is the intelligence that the engine needs, not only to drive the collation, management, and publishing of content to a site, but also to provide the framework for personalization, community, analytics, and reporting. Thus, it is extremely important to get right. Yet it is very tough to define within the organization. Why? Because the content model is a distillation of everything that the company is, understands about itself, and wants to be. The architecture may be defined by customer segments, by content types, by business units, by country, or by product lines as outlined earlier. Who is to decide? Who can decide what is, effectively, the blueprint for the company now and in the future?

Imagine you are a global financial services organization that is structured internally by business units, some of which have international branches and some of which do not. Most of your financial products must be sold differently in each country because of legislation. Some of them, however, can be sold only to certain types of clients, irrespective of which country they are in. Then you have your customers, who you group not by product line but by characteristics that define the way they invest to help you cross-sell your products. You can see that there are fairly clear axes here along which to build a content model, but you can equally imagine how hard it will be to reach consensus over which elements are required and which are not to create the desired end result.

Defining a content model forces you to go to the very core of your business and draw up and prioritize fault lines that will enable you to deliver the most value. Choosing and integrating a content management system may seem a daunting task, but it is far easier, and far less important, than defining a content model, a process which must be fully integrated with overall corporate strategy. Your content model is an important strategic intellectual capital asset, representing the ultimate distillation of business and customer.

Case Study   Developing and Evolving a Content Model

Company: Magicalia, *www.magicalia.com*

Company Overview

Magicalia is a specialist Internet publisher operating six Web sites in participation sports markets as well as licensing their publishing platform to magazine publishers. The platform is a flexible and sophisticated content management system with a strong focus on community features.

Background to Case Study and Objectives

We always knew that we needed to develop an architecture that could support multiple specialist community sites. The original aim was to differentiate our offering by providing a high level of localization and personalization. To do this, we needed to build a central member profile database underpinning the whole site.

The specialized sports and leisure pursuits we deal with have strong communities and a lot of the activities are localized (e.g., around clubs or shops). So our content model had to have users and locality at its core.

We also believed, and still do, that the Web is not the same as print. To make the most of the Web medium, you must exploit its powers of interactivity and relationship building (between content and people). We knew that without an underpinning content model you cannot deliver or maintain the levels of interrelationship and interactivity required to create a compelling Web proposition.

Process and Practice

The entire process has been iterative and organic. Importantly, it has also always involved a team representing all areas of our business: commercial, marketing, creative, and technology. It is almost 4 years since we launched with the original content model and architecture. It has since evolved, morphed, and coalesced in many ways and directions in reaction to user needs and requests as well as for commercial reasons.

What has not changed over this time is the fact that our user profile database, containing site members' details, preferences, and so on, remains the engine that drives everything else. Over time, we have added further databases (articles, forums, shops, clubs, picture galleries, product reviews, classified ads, etc.) as required and "stitched" them together so that everything interrelates. The whole is genuinely an organic system—everything relates to everything else in one way or another. This includes the business-to-business applications that we run. Thus, for example, an advertising client of ours might also be a shop that sells particular brands that have associated products that have associated user reviews that have associated user profiles that have associated nearest shops and so on.

At each stage of development, it has been a matter of getting the team together to discuss the requirements, sketching out the top-level architecture ramifications before detailing the data elements and interrelations, and then finally creating the database schemas.

There is nothing on any of our sites that is not stored in a database. Every piece of content is an object with associated metadata that enables the system to manage and publish that piece of content appropriately. Those metadata include standard data elements (create dates, author, last update, etc.) as well as keywords (to improve searching), cross-referencing to other related content (including "smart" referencing), and

continued

personalization "bins"—the interest categories that users select so that we can target content accordingly.

Currently, we are concentrating on building "bridges" between our own systems and those of our retail partners, thereby extending our interrelational architecture externally. As we are starting to build these XML gateways with partners, we are defining our content and data structures more rigorously to facilitate communication and integration. We also continue to stitch together various nodes within our own architecture, allowing new ways of serving and interrelating content. This is driven primarily by user feedback and requests.

Results

It is clear to us that without our content model and information architecture we just could not deliver what we need to acquire users, keep them happy, and keep them coming back. On one of our sites alone, we often have more than 2000 forum posts a day, not to mention the articles, reviews, product updates, and so on that must appear on the site every day—and all of them are interrelated. It would be an impossible, and impossibly expensive, task to do this manually rather than exploit the power and "intelligence" of our architecture. So in many ways, a good content model delivers huge operational efficiencies while improving the quality of the user experience.

Furthermore, the more intelligently we have been able to exploit the interrelationships of our content model, the more we have seen direct revenue benefits in the form of increased user loyalty, increased viral activity (users referring other users), and increased page impressions per visit.

Finally, although the architecture itself is now complex, after many years of evolution, it is robust and very easily replicable. This means that we have a tried and tested platform that we can use to develop and deploy new sites, for us and for clients, in next to no time and at minimal cost. The content model is thus a hugely valuable intellectual property asset that embeds our learnings and experience over the years into a form of "DNA."

Lessons Learned

Our experience would lead us to make the following recommendations:

▶ Put the users at the center of your model. The one-to-one, interactive nature of the Web means that whatever the site, the user is the most important element in the equation—the unique key off which all other data, content, and information hang.

▶ Don't think you can predict the architecture at the beginning. The only way is to iterate and evolve organically over time in response to user and business requirements.

▶ Development and ownership of the model must be done by a senior, mixed-skill, cross-departmental team. It is important that the conceptual integrity and homogeneity of the architecture are cascaded from the top down to suffuse all elements of work on the site.

▶ Listen to your users. The best way to develop and evolve the model is to listen to suggestions and feedback from real users. Technical smartness and complexity are one thing, but the end experience must be user simple and user relevant.

▶ Treat all content as objects with certain qualities and attributes (defined by good metadata) that allow you to manipulate and milk the value of that content.

▶ Although we still believe that localization and personalization will be differentiators in the long term, they have not been as important and differentiating in the short term as we thought. However, having good content interrelations has proved to be incredibly important. This is another reason to make sure you spend quality time on getting your architecture and content model right.

▶ The front end (design, look and feel, user interface, etc.) and back end (databases, applications, etc.) should be developed in parallel and by teams working in close collaboration. The end experience should be driven by the user, no doubt, but the back end must also be considered and, realistically, sets certain parameters.

Finally, it is clear to us, as a relatively small company, how much harder all this is for a very large company. As stated, a lot rides on the conceptual integrity and homogeneity of the "organism" you are creating. With the attendant decisions by committee, changes in direction, and so on that are more typical of a large company with many departments, it is very hard to hold the model together.

Jeremy Tapp
CTO
Magicalia

5.3 Content Objects and Classes

Content objects are the actual pieces of content: assembled data elements that create a single sense unit. Content objects are called a variety of names: *pieces of content, content chunks, components, units,* or *record sets.* Unfortunately, there is no agreed-upon term, at least at the time of writing. None of the terms seems quite right. Chunk is almost the best in terms of its neutrality, but it is hard to take chunk seriously. Object and component have strong programming connotations, which are helpful in some ways because there are some shared attributes, but they risk being confusing if you use these terms a lot already. It is important to have a common language, but it is more important to have a common understanding.

In the earlier e-consultancy example, the white paper content capture page shows all the elements that go together to create a white paper content object. The same is true for the provider example given. Product details are also very common content objects.

One level up from content objects you have a content class that defines the properties of all the content objects within it. In the e-consultancy example, there is a white paper content class that has numerous white paper content objects within it. The data within each white paper object are different, but the elements themselves are the same. The elements of a provider object, however, are different, so a provider class is required.

Your content model provides the framework for structuring your content, but your content classes and objects provide the level of granularity that you require to easily reuse and repurpose your content with a high level of finesse. For example, it is not much good having the information related to a particular product (e.g., price, size, weight, color, features, description, or image) stored as a single data element because you have no way of breaking out the different attributes. You would have a very hard time finding and managing product information, and site users would not be able to search, browse, or compare the products as they most likely want to.

Content objects contain two types of data:

▶ *Display data.* This is content that users can see on the site. In traditional terms, this *is* the content itself, albeit broken down into more granular constituent parts.
▶ *Management data.* This is data that users do not see but that is used to manage the content object. This management data are, in fact, metadata. There will be more on metadata shortly.

Display data and management data can be created and updated either manually, semiautomatically using first a tool and then human review, or fully automatically. Figure 5.1 shows the e-consultancy white paper content object used earlier with annotations showing the different data elements.

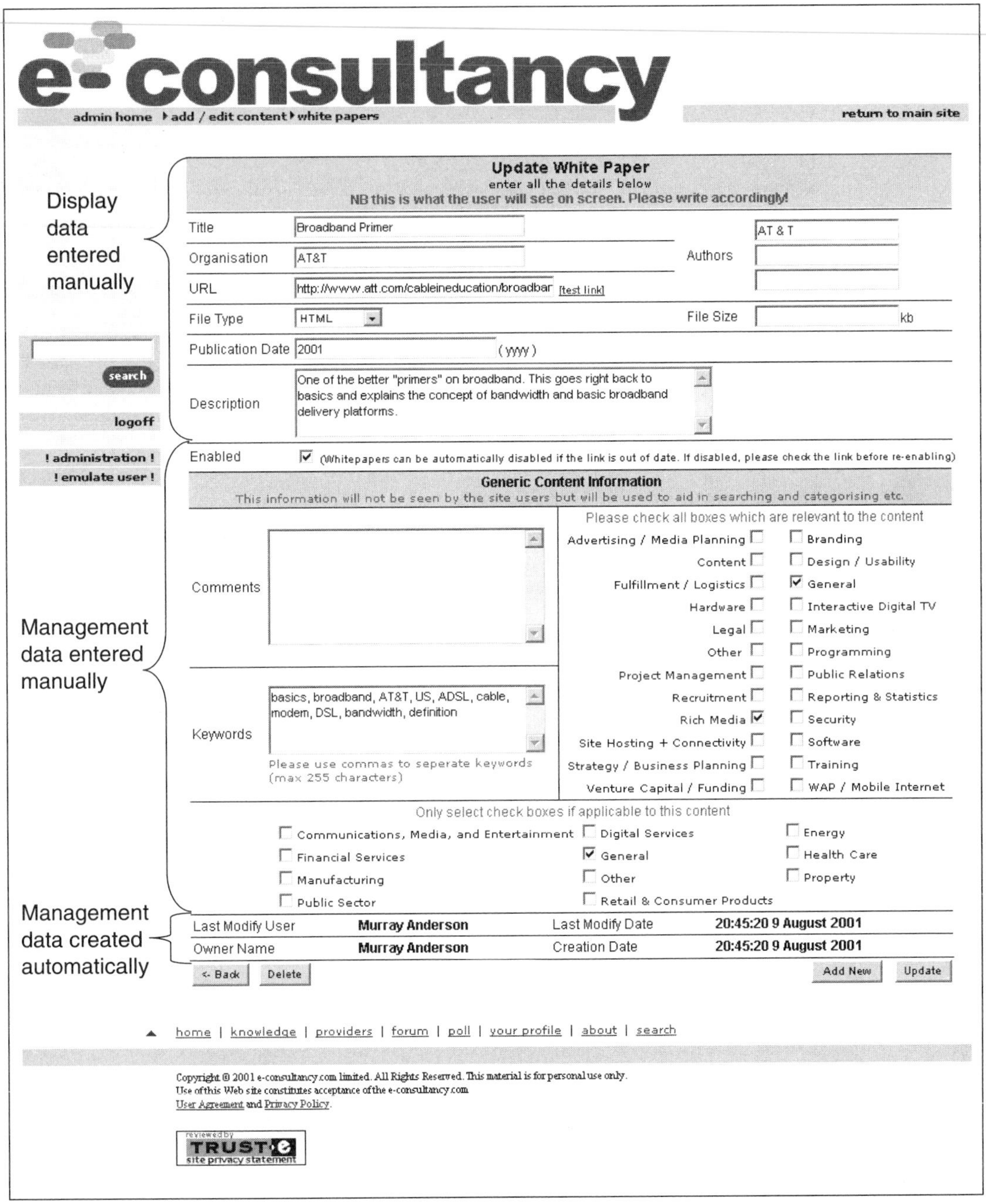

Figure 5.1 Management and display data in a content object.

5.4   Content versus Functionality

Functionality enables you to do things on Web pages. Whereas content just is, functionality allows you to perform tasks. However, from a content management point of view, you should treat functionality just as another form of content. It is not a question of content versus functionality because there is no distinction in the first place: Functionality is just a form of content.

Imagine a Web page that is trying to sell you a loan. There may be information on the page telling you about the interest rates and repayment schedule associated with the loan: the content of the page. There may also be a repayments calculator that allows you to enter loan amounts and a repayment period to find out how much you will have to pay back in total. That is a piece of functionality. However, the two can be managed in the same way. In an earlier example, we looked at how you might give structure to a video clip file by wrapping it in supplementary data to manage it better with a content management system. If you look at the piece of functionality as just another content object that happens to contain code rather than words, you can see how it is possible to wrap it up with the same sort of data to then manage and publish it.

5.5   Separation of Content and Presentation

We have seen how important it is to explicitly define a structure for your content if you are to manage it. The structure is separate from the content: It is like the way you choose to organize your filing cabinet. The content management system itself is the filing cabinet.

However, another fundamental concept of content management is the separation of content and presentation. That is, there is a difference between the raw piece of content itself and the way it is rendered to whatever medium for consumption. Splitting out content and presentation makes it infinitely easier and more cost effective to manage content. Consider the following simple piece of text content:

```
Welcome to our Products section.
```

Imagine this piece of raw content needs to appear on a Web site you have and also on an interactive TV site, on your Wireless Application Protocol (WAP) site for mobile phones, and finally in a print brochure. These are quite different media that are consumed in different ways, but let us assume for the sake of simplicity that this piece of content—that is, the words themselves— is exactly the same for each delivery channel. However, even if the content is the same, the way it is presented cannot be. In the print version, you might choose a large, graphical rendering of the text. On the Web, you would choose a font that site users could display. For the TV, you would have to think about the size of the font to ensure its legibility at a distance, and for the mobile phone, you would need to keep things very basic.

So what would you do to accommodate all these instances where the same piece of content needs to be presented differently? You could create four different versions of the content. This would work, but you can imagine how difficult and time consuming it will soon become to manage all those different versions. What happens if you make an important update to the content itself? Perhaps the word *products* needs to be changed to *services* in the wake of an important company repositioning exercise. Will you remember to change all the instances of the word *products* for all the various channels? Of course, it would be much easier just to store the content once in a raw form, as previously, and then use templates to add the presentation layer for each target publication. You then only have one piece of content to manage, and if you change the content in one place, the modifications will be automatically replicated everywhere else.

Earlier in this chapter of the book, we talked about content management as a way for organizations to reassert control over their increasingly chaotic and overwhelming Web operations. Separating content and presentation is fundamental to this ability to control because not only can you manage all content instances from a single central source, but also you can also ensure consistency of presentation. Art direction, branding and creative executions, which risk becoming inconsistent with many different teams working in different areas of the business, can be much better controlled if the presentation functions can be centrally administered. Typically, the bigger the site and organization, the more important the separation of content and presentation, as it becomes not just a content management issue but a management issue more generally.

5.6 Metadata

Metadata are data about data. Metadata are the data that we wrap around other data to make them more useful and manageable. The management data we looked at with the e-consultancy example earlier are metadata. The data we talked about adding to a piece of functionality or a video clip file are metadata. When we talk about "tagging" content, we are talking about adding metadata.

As more and more content becomes available for use and reuse, the quality of the structure of content and the quality of its metadata will become enormously more important. Success increasingly hinges on the ability to tag, index, store, search, access, retrieve, use, and reuse content. In the cases of commodity content, it is likely that the metadata—those parts that the end user does not experience directly—will become more valuable than the content itself.

Let us say that you run a leisure and entertainment portal carrying all sorts of information and listings. There is a limited WAP version of your site and you are planning an interactive TV version, too. One section of your portal is a directory of restaurants. Within that section, users can browse and search the directory in various ways: by location of the restaurant, by type of cuisine, or by price range. Each restaurant listing has address details, reservation phone numbers, a photo, a description, and a critic's review. There is a summary version of the critic's review text that users can read before clicking to see the full details. On the WAP site, there needs to be a version of the review that is shorter than 160 characters to fit on the screen. For TV, you want an even shorter version.

Imagine you have two potential suppliers of restaurant review content. One provides great reviews, but you would have to structure all the content to serve it up in the forms you want. The other provides mediocre reviews but beautifully structured content, with all the necessary metadata, that you know you can integrate, manipulate, and maintain with ease. Which one do you go with? Obviously, the choice will depend on all sorts of factors, such as price and the degree to which the quality of restaurant reviews is important to your brand or competitive proposition. However, the point is that the actual content itself is no longer the only thing of value. The structure of the content and the quality of the metadata are fast becoming extremely valuable assets.

Metadata can be used to support all sorts of content attributes. For example:

▶ *Defining relationships.* You can use metadata to define cross-references and other dependencies between content objects.

▶ *Time-related attributes.* For example, content object creation date, last up-date time, review date, expiration date, or move to archive date.

▶ *Content object attributes.* Metadata can define any number of attributes specific to a particular content object: size, file format, associated work-flows, status, keywords, and so on.

▶ *Versioning.* Controlling versioning is very important in content manage-ment (e.g., if you need to roll back to previous versions of a site), and in-formation about a content object's version is metadata.

▶ *Access.* Metadata can be used to control who has access to what by tagging content with permission levels or user groups who then have permission levels assigned.

In fact, your metadata framework is also your content model. If you look back to the previous section on the content model, you will note suggested axes for structuring your content such as user groups, products, topics, types, channels, business areas, and location. But how to do you actually understand and manage your content according to these axes? You do it through the metadata associated with the content.

5.7 Templates

Templates provide a structured way of capturing or displaying content. There are two main types of templates: content capture templates and page display templates. Content authors and editors use content capture templates to input or modify content. Programmers and designers use templates to con-trol what is presented on the Web page. Figure 5.2 uses the e-consultancy white paper example to highlight the two forms of template and how they fit into the content management process.

You need page display templates to merge back the content and presenta-tion elements that you have carefully separated: One without the other is of no use. The page display template bridges the gap between the content man-agement system and the content it manages in the repository and the final Web page or other target publication.

Templates can vary a lot in their complexity. Some are like simple place-holders or containers that then call upon other files and objects to do the work required to form the final page. This can include bringing in nested subtem-plates. Others contain functional code themselves. You can even include actual

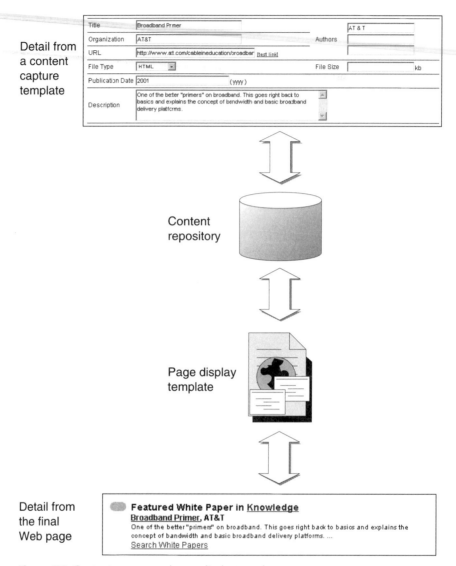

Detail from
a content
capture
template

Content
repository

Page display
template

Detail from
the final
Web page

Figure 5.2 Content capture and page display templates.

content in a template if you wish, though it would only be sensible to consider this if that content was fixed and likely to change very seldom. Figure 5.3 gives three scenarios showing how page display templates might be implemented depending on the complexity of the requirements.

Scenario 1. The template asks for data directly from the content repository to populate the page. The template does all the formatting.

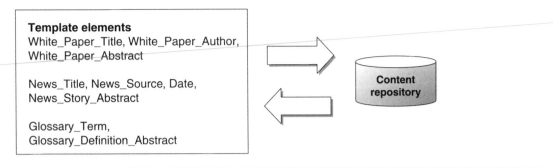

Template elements
White_Paper_Title, White_Paper_Author,
White_Paper_Abstract

News_Title, News_Source, Date,
News_Story_Abstract

Glossary_Term,
Glossary_Definition_Abstract

Content repository

Scenario 2. Templates are nested. One master template calls upon other templates to do specific tasks and then brings the results together onto the final page. The templates do the formatting work as well as retrieving the content.

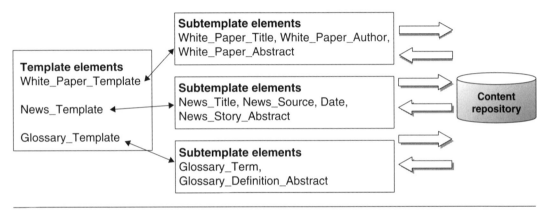

Subtemplate elements
White_Paper_Title, White_Paper_Author,
White_Paper_Abstract

Template elements
White_Paper_Template

News_Template

Glossary_Template

Subtemplate elements
News_Title, News_Source, Date,
News_Story_Abstract

Content repository

Subtemplate elements
Glossary_Term,
Glossary_Definition_Abstract

Scenario 3. There are some nested subtemplates and the templates also call on the help of other code to do tasks in the preparation of the final page for delivery. In this case, a programming object may do layout work instead of, or in combination with, the templates.

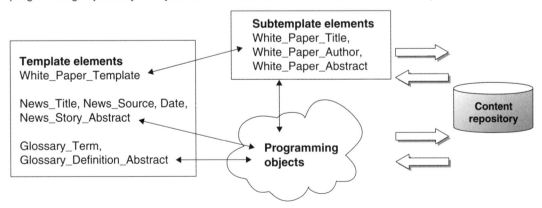

Subtemplate elements
White_Paper_Title,
White_Paper_Author,
White_Paper_Abstract

Template elements
White_Paper_Template

News_Title, News_Source, Date,
News_Story_Abstract

Glossary_Term,
Glossary_Definition_Abstract

Programming objects

Content repository

Figure 5.3 Scenarios for page display templates.

5.8 Personalization

For more on successful personalization, refer to Chapter 10, Personalization.

Personalization is about matching content to users either at a segment or individual level. It is often one of the reasons for a content management initiative. Although it is clear to most that to do personalization you need to capture information about your users and then analyze that information to understand and segment your user base, it is perhaps less evident that you also need content tagged with the right metadata to successfully make the matches dynamically and automatically. Personalizing an email message by analyzing a user base offline and then crafting targeted messages by segment is one thing, but real-time personalization requires the system to intelligently understand both users and content and have the rules available to bind the two together with templates, as shown in Figure 5.4.

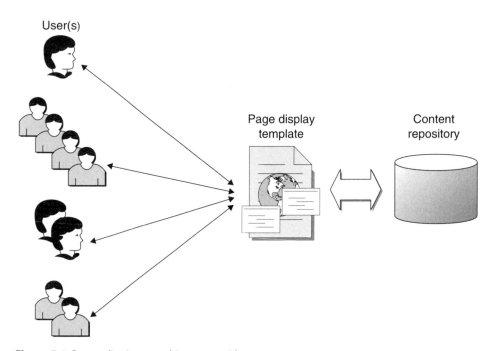

Figure 5.4 Personalization: matching users with content.

In the earlier e-consultancy example, we saw how the site navigation could be personalized based on a user's permission levels. Once the user is known to the system, either by manual or automated cookie log on, his or her permission level is then known. In the XML file that stores the site's navigation, each navigation element has a permission level access attribute, so the system knows which elements to show which users. The template matches the two and performs the necessary formatting and layout work to render the page to the screen.

5.9 **XML**

XML (eXtensible Markup Language) has become the industry standard way of adding structure and meaning to content. XML uses tags that define and describe individual pieces of content so that they can be intelligently understood and manipulated as part of an overall content structure. When we have been talking about content tagging, content models, content structure, and separating content from presentation in the abstract, XML is one of the tools to make this all possible.

NOTE   **A Brief History of XML**

When using a word processing tool like Microsoft Word, do you make extensive use of the styles function to automatically apply and update different styles to the various hierarchies of text that you are creating, such as headings, subheadings, or body text? If not, it would help if you did: You can easily make documentwide changes, automatically create tables of contents and indexes, and much more. You are separating content from presentation and using the styles as a way to link and control the two.

My point here is that you probably know the advantages of using styles in this way, but do you actually use them? It is much easier just to bold that text and make it a bit bigger than to apply a heading style, isn't it? You may get away with your lack of discipline with a small document, but imagine a larger one, like this book. I really do not want to have to individually change every figure caption from one font or size to another, so it becomes worth my while to have a single figure caption style that I can update bookwide in one place. Imagine thousands, even millions, of books worth of information and content, and you can understand that it is totally unmanageable unless there is a central and structured means of representing it.

These dilemmas represent much of the story of the road to XML. XML is a subset, or "dialect," of SGML (Standard Generalized Markup Language), the international standard for the structural and content mark-up of electronic documents from which HTML was also derived. SGML was created to meet the need for managing large catalogs and large amounts of documentation. However, SGML suffered in the same way that Word's style functions may go unused by many: It works very well, but you just cannot be bothered to do it unless you have to. HTML, born of SGML, was so much easier, and you could do the formatting then and there—just make that text bold and a bit bigger. But then Web sites began getting bigger and bigger and the fixed formatting and lack of structural intelligence embedded in HTML meant the amount of information was fast becoming unmanageable.

The aim of XML, developed in 1996 by a working group composed primarily of members from the SGML community, was to develop a language that would offer benefits over HTML in terms of extensibility and the separation of content structure and format but would be less complex than SGML.   ■

XML documents contain a number of text string elements that are held within tags. However, whereas HTML has a limited, and fixed, number of tags that can be used, XML has an unlimited set of tags. The "extensibility" comes from your ability to create as many of your own tags as you wish. You do, however, need to provide a means to interpret your custom tags as well as a central definition of what your tags mean and the rules governing how they can be used if they are to be manageable and reusable by others. Whereas HTML represents format, which is needed for presentation (and what ultimately needs to go to the browser), XML represents structure, which is needed to determine content use.

Take a look at the following simple description of a men's T-shirt as might appear on a list either in a catalog or on a Web site:

Men's T-Shirt, White, Large, $20

In HTML, this could be represented as follows:

```
<font face="Arial" size="-1" color="Black">Men's T-Shirt, White,
Large, $20</font>
```

The HTML simply specifies the font face and relative size of the text. An XML version, however, might look as follows:

```
<PRODUCTS>
        <CLOTHING>
            <MENSWEAR>
                <T-SHIRTS>
                            <T-SHIRT stock_number=12345>
                                <COLOR>White</COLOR>
                                <SIZE>Large</SIZE>
                                <PRICE>$20</PRICE>
                            </T-SHIRT>
                </T-SHIRTS>
            </MENSWEAR>
        </CLOTHING>
</PRODUCTS>
```

Even visually, it should be clear that the XML version is much more structured with nesting of information to show the hierarchy. Even with no programming knowledge, it should be pretty evident that the HTML version shows formatting information, whereas the XML version clearly shows structure. To get formatting across for the XML version, you would need to define how <T-SHIRTS> should be displayed and have a tool to interpret and translate the XML into HTML so that it could be presented as shown. This requires some work, but once it is done, it can be used to manage a lot of information (in this case, product information) efficiently.

Consider the HTML version. How, for example, would you or your site users be able to view or sort your T-shirts by size, color, or price? This structure is not explicit in the HTML, so the only way you could try and find it would be to write code to try and sift it out. For example, you might create code that looked for price information based on content that is preceded by the dollar sign and ends with a white space following a number. This may work to some degree, but it is highly inefficient and bound to break down before long as you can no doubt imagine. It is much better to have the structure of the content explicit within the content itself, working to a known and rigidly enforced content model, with you then deciding how to present that content separately.

NOTE   **Translating XML into HTML**

There are four ways to add back the formatting for content presentation purposes.

1. Let the browser translate the XML.
2. Put formatting tags into the XML.
3. Write custom code to translate the XML.
4. Use Extensible Stylesheet Language Transformations (XSLTs).

Looking at each of these in a little more detail:

1. Let the browser translate the XML.

Although some browsers can interpret and display XML directly, their capabilities are varied and limited. This should change over time, but for a while to come, this option is unrealistic except for the simplest of tasks.

2. Put formatting tags into the XML.

You could put the formatting into the XML file itself, but this seems rather to defeat the point of using XML. It is fine if you want to end up with HTML only and insert HTML formatting tags, but not much good if you want to format for mobile phones, TVs, print, and other target publications.

3. Write custom code to translate the XML.

This is a common approach and has the advantages of being flexible and powerful. However, you need the programming skills and you also need a programmer to change the code every time you want to change formatting, which is not ideal.

4. Use Extensible Stylesheet Language Transformations (XSLTs).

XSLT is a transformation language allowing XML data to be manipulated, rearranged, and processed very quickly. XSLT also has the advantage of being a standard defined by the World Wide Web Consortium. The disadvantages of using XSLT are a lack of familiarity and widespread use (though this will change, of course) and the inability to do complex processing on the XML data. It is quite restrictive in the output formats it is capable of (e.g., XSLT cannot currently transform an XML file into a Word document), and you need valuable programming resources skilled in XSLT to use it.   ■

5.10 Content Life Cycle

As Figure 5.5 shows in simple terms, content follows a life cycle. It is created or otherwise sourced and manipulated into the required form. It then needs to be stored and managed in ways that make it accessible and usable. Finally, it is published, leaving the system for a target publication and users. Workflow practices occur throughout to manage the work of moving the content through its

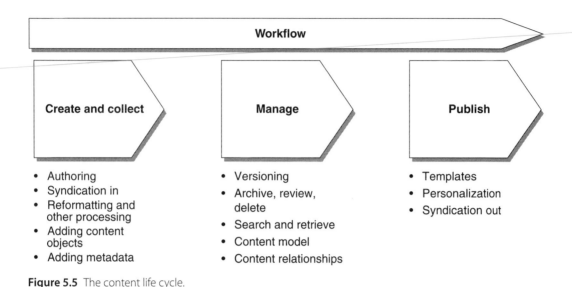

Figure 5.5 The content life cycle.

life cycle as efficiently as possible. As you will see in Chapter 6 on content management systems, a CMS is built very much to follow this basic content life cycle.

5.11 Workflow

Workflow is the series of tasks and triggers that connect the tasks in a particular cycle of work. Workflow is about formalizing and codifying work processes. In the case of content management, workflow is important at all stages of the content life cycle, helping to smooth the flow of content through the create, collect, manage, and publish stages. Workflow has two principal benefits:

▶ *Improving productivity.* Workflow can automate routing, review, and approval of tasks. The more people and the more interconnected tasks involved, the greater the potential for lower levels of productivity through higher wait time as the flow of work between staff falters. Particularly where patterns of interaction are repeated frequently, workflow can help maximize productivity by minimizing the wait time between successive steps.

▶ *Improving quality and consistency.* Workflow formalizes and codifies business processes, which improve consistency and quality. This becomes particularly important as the Web operation becomes larger. Review and approval processes are good candidates for having workflow applied to them. Multiple people, departments, and stages are often involved, and the longer the approval process takes, the more value is being lost in the content not being live on the site. Appropriate approval procedures should not be cut short (e.g., legal sign-off), but the time to get the content through the process should be minimized as much as possible. A further advantage in having workflow managed electronically is that it is easy to keep a log of what has been done, when, and by whom, giving you an excellent audit trail for management information purposes as required.

Content management workflows typically contain tasks that change the state of content. That might not be a change to the content itself but still a change to the status of the content, such as approved versus unapproved. The triggers between each task in the workflow can be based on a range of things: dates; times; content object creation, deletion, or modification events; emails; system events; or even a manual trigger following a verbal instruction based on a real-world event.

The e-consultancy provider example given earlier shows a practical example of a specific workflow in action. Figure 5.6 shows a more generic workflow that applies to a content authoring, edit, and review process. The rectangles show the tasks, with the corresponding task owners and estimated task

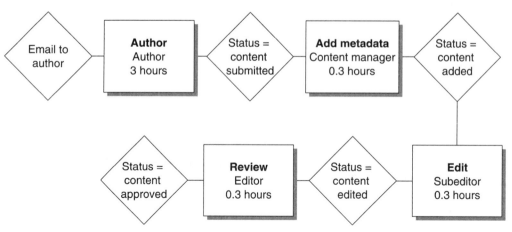

Figure 5.6 An example workflow.

durations, and the diamonds show the task triggers. In this case, most of the task triggers are based on a change of content object status. The notification of change of status, to alert the next task owner in the chain, is often done by email but might also be automatically added to a job queue for the task owner, which can then be displayed via a Web site, through project management software, or within an electronic calendar or other personal organizer. More generic workflows such as the example given can be built in a modular way and then combined like building blocks to create more complex workflows.

6

Content Management Systems (CMS)

T o manage all of the processes and content as discussed, you need a content management system (CMS). In this section, we look in more detail at what makes up a typical CMS, how it works, and how to go about choosing one.

6.1   What Is a Content Management System (CMS)?

It is easiest to understand a CMS in terms of how it maps to the content life cycle. You will note that Figure 6.1, which shows the three main parts of a CMS, is very similar to the earlier diagram of the content life cycle. The "create" wording has been dropped from the first part of the system because a CMS does not actually create content. Ideally, it integrates with authoring tools to a high degree and provides content capture interfaces such that your content creators feel part of the CMS when originating content. But the system itself is not creating the content; it is only facilitating its collection.

Collect	Manage	Publish
• Authoring • Syndication in • Reformatting and other processing • Adding content objects • Adding metadata	• Storage • Versioning and rollback • Archiving • Search and retrieve • Integration with other systems • Workflow • System configuration and administration • Link management and validation	• Deployment • Templates • Syndication out • Replication to/integration with other systems

Figure 6.1 The three parts of a CMS.

N O T E   What a Content Management System Is Not

Although different CMSs provide varying levels of functionality and features, a typical CMS is not:

▶ *An authoring tool.* It is not a text, graphics, video, or audio manipulation tool. It manages the content that these authoring tools create.

▶ *A tool for automatically organizing or structuring content for you.* Although some CMSs have modules or work with third-party software suppliers to provide tools to try and automatically categorize and structure content, this is not the core function of a CMS.

▶ *A transaction processing tool.* CMSs do not process transactions in the way an e-commerce engine does. The CMS can manage the product and pricing information as well as any other elements of content the user experiences in the online transaction process, but it does do the actual transaction processing.

▶ *An analytics platform.* Although most CMSs will give you analytical reporting both on how the system is being used and how users are requesting the content it manages and serves, a CMS will typically work with other analytics tools to meet reporting and analysis requirements. Most of what is discussed in Part IV of this book, Site Measurement, would not be provided directly by a CMS but through specialized data analysis or by using analytic software tools.

▶ *Only a publishing tool.* Of course, a CMS is a publishing tool, but it is much more than that, which is sometimes overlooked. The role of the CMS in collecting content, in particular, is often underestimated. Only by collecting content in the correct way can it later be manipulated and published as required. ■

6.1.1 Collect

The collect part is about getting content into the system in the right format and structure.

▶ *Authoring.* This is the human process of creating original content. A CMS can help provide an authoring environment as well as input templates and workflow to facilitate the authoring process. In many cases, however, authors may prefer to stick to using their own tried and trusted authoring tools, which may or may not integrate well with your CMS. You will need to decide what degree of pressure you can apply to authors to conform to your preferred means of authoring.

▶ *Syndication in.* This is where you buy in content from external sources. Increasingly, you would expect syndicated content to be well structured so that it can be imported and integrated with relative ease.

▶ *Reformatting and other processing.* In many cases, much of your planned content will be based on existing content that is in an array of formats and structures and needs converting and processing before it can be managed within the CMS. Structure needs to be added to the content or remapped to fit your content model, and unnecessary data must be discarded.

▶ *Creating content objects.* Once you have the content in a form that meets your requirements, you add it to your CMS as content objects. In some cases, content will be added directly to the system as objects, but in other cases, you may use automated batch, or even manual rekeying, processes. In the earlier e-consultancy example, life is made easier because content is authored and added to the system as objects all at the same time.

▶ *Adding metadata.* Either at the point of creating the content objects or subsequently as part of an editorial and review process, you will need to add the necessary metadata to your content objects to manage them within your system and publish them to users.

6.1.2   Manage

The manage part is about storing and managing the content once in the system as well as administering the system itself.

▶ *Storage.* Most obviously, you need a way to store all your content in a central repository. This will be a database system that itself contains or references other content databases and files.

▶ *Versioning and rollback.* Version control is very important both in ensuring that content creation and editing processes run smoothly and in providing previous versions of content in case they need to be retrieved. It is quite possible that you will have content that is created and managed collaboratively by a distributed team, making version control facilities all the more vital. Most version control works on a check-out and check-in process, where each file or content object is temporarily locked by the person working on it, but more sophisticated tools also allow parallel working on the same content with subsequent merging. By taking snapshots of the entire Web site, you are able to roll back to previously known good versions of it or back to a particular point in time, which is very important for disaster recovery purposes and often for legal reasons.

▶ *Archiving.* Although storage space is increasingly cheap these days, you still do not want to be storing more content in your CMS than you are actively using because it only increases the amount you have to manage and can slow down performance or the run time of core processes such as backup or other data transfer. Content objects should first be archived on the CMS itself. They are no longer live on the system and so do not appear in any end publications but can be recalled for rollback purposes, if necessary. Past a certain point, however, you should archive the content to another database or to offline storage.

▶ *Search and retrieve.* With all the content that the CMS manages, you need effective mechanisms for finding what you need. Access to content is provided by search, browse, and indexing facilities that work on both the content itself and any associated metadata.

▶ *Integration with other systems.* It is through the management part of the CMS that you connect with other systems. These systems might be other CMSs, internal or external systems, which take content, data, and information from the CMS or feed it in. For example, you might be integrating a customer relationship management (CRM) system, a supply chain system, a human resources (HR) or accounting application, or perhaps taking a data feed from the CMS into a separate management information system. You may simply be ensuring that your CMS is synched with replicas of itself distributed around the world.

▶ *Workflow.* As we have seen, workflow is used across all stages of the content life cycle. Within the management part of the CMS, a workflow module is available to set up, configure, and manage all your workflows, allowing you to apply different workflows to any content object or set of content.

▶ *System configuration and administration.* Clearly, the CMS itself needs configuring and administering. This is done through the management part of the system and includes the following: managing access levels to the system and security via logons and passwords; logging system activity (e.g., event logs); storing software configuration settings and registries; maintenance routines, scheduled tasks, and scripts; and performance monitoring to check that all the elements of the system are functioning as expected.

▶ *Link management and validation.* The management part of a CMS also typically contains functions for validating and managing links. These might be external links, to other Web sites for example, or internal links within the site such as "next page," page references, cross-references, table of contents, or indexes. Any of these links might be created dynamically by the CMS, in which case it is easier to ensure the links are valid, or they might be hard-coded into the content, in which case the CMS needs to validate them using a link-checking tool. Note that although a link may be valid, it is not necessarily correct or meaningful. That can only be decided by a human.

6.1.3 Publish

The publish part is about getting content out of the system to suit target user, publication, platform, and channel requirements.

▶ *Deployment.* Deployment refers to the processes and practices involved in moving content from a development environment, such as a development or staging server, to the live environment. Deployment seeks to ensure that the right content is transferred at the right time. In some cases, deployment is not a defined process step. In the case of the e-consultancy example, as soon as content goes live on the system, it also goes live on the site: The CMS is the site. In other cases, a CMS may be used to publish full versions of the site that are first reviewed and tested in a development environment before being deployed to the live servers according to a release process. If it is pages that are being published, generated through templates and content, then the live site cannot dynamically personalize content in real time. However, entire databases and applications as well as page content can also be deployed, effectively replicating the CMS to a live environment (or often just those elements that have changed are updated) so that dynamic personalization is possible.

▶ *Templates.* The publish part of the CMS contains the templates that bring together content and presentation elements to create the end publication for the user.

▶ *Syndication out.* Just as you might be buying in content you might also want to syndicate content out, either as a revenue-generating activity in selling content to other sites or, perhaps more commonly, as a means to share your content with other parts of the organization that can use it in other systems.

▶ *Replication to/integration with other systems.* This is very similar to the system integration mentioned in the management part of the CMS, only in this case, the CMS is first producing a "publication" of some sort that is then replicated to, or integrated with, another system. Integration with the management part of the CMS gives access to the "heart" of the system, the content repository and all that it contains. However, the publish part of the CMS can do a lot of useful work in shaping and preparing the elements contained within the repository so that they are in a published form that is more readily digestible by another system. For example, if you had a document management system, you might prefer to use the CMS to create publications that were a suitable versioning of the content for direct integration with the document management system rather than have to do that work elsewhere by plugging your document management system directly into the management part of the CMS.

6.1.4   Related Systems

Table 6.1 looks at other types of commonly used system and how they relate to CMSs.

Table 6.1 Systems related to CMSs

System type	Description and relation to CMS
Document management systems	Document management vendors have well-established and mature products that have historically focused on the management and delivery of predominately textual material. Document management systems are most relevant for internal and intra-organization use (intranets and extranets), but many vendors are now moving into the Web content management arena, beginning by Web-enabling their existing products. This needs to be taken a lot further before these systems can be considered proper CMSs (e.g., personalization and templating features need to be more advanced), but some vendors are rapidly evolving in this direction and benefit from a relatively long heritage in creating systems to collect, manage, and deliver content.
E-commerce platforms	Web sites are sometimes categorized into one or more of the three Cs: commerce, content, and community. Clearly, CMSs cater ideally for content and community sites, but their lack of transactional capabilities has meant that commerce sites have often opted for an e-commerce platform as the principal engine behind their site. E-commerce platforms typically offer advanced transaction processing and management facilities (e.g., dealing with multiple currencies, payment methods, shipping details, and taxes), personalization that is related to selling (principally merchandising, cross-selling, and up-selling), and advanced sales reporting and management information. They do offer limited content management with regard to products or services that are for sale, although this is more like advanced catalog management with some stock and inventory control features than full content management. E-commerce has been around longer than Web content management: There was a need to sell things online long before there was a need to manage vast sites. This means that the range of e-commerce system solutions is much more highly evolved than for content management, although CMSs are quickly catching up, particularly in the low- to middle-range solutions.
CRM systems	Customer relationship management (CRM) systems focus on areas such as community, customer service, customer segmentation, lead qualification and management, and sales-force automation and personalization. As with document management, CRM has been around for a long time, and many existing vendors are reshaping their products to cater to the online environment. There are also new vendors who have sprung up focusing on eCRM for the Web. CRM systems are designed to maximize the potential value of customers by ensuring that every point of contact with them is an opportunity to deliver exceptional customer experiences and capture more of their time and money. CRM systems typically do not offer transactional capabilities and only very limited content management features. For this reason, CRM systems are often integrated with e-commerce platforms or CMSs to enhance core capabilities.
Infrastructure systems	As Web sites grow in complexity and the demands on them increase, some vendors are concentrating on providing technology infrastructures and platforms upon which to run Web operations consisting of multiple application servers. Although these systems may provide some out of the box functionality that touches on content management, CRM, or e-commerce, their principal function is to provide a stable, reliable, scalable, and secure environment in which other systems, such as those detailed earlier, can run.

6.2   Selecting a CMS

If you want to find out more about particular CMS vendors or recommended sites, you will find a list in the Resources section at the end of the book.

The field of content management is still young but rapidly evolving. CMSs have been the preserve of the very wealthy, or well funded, for quite some time, but lower and midrange solutions are increasingly appearing to cater to all shapes, sizes, and budgets. As with the e-commerce solutions that came before, we can expect increasing commoditization of core elements required to do content management and a greater array of solutions that cater to more specific needs. There is likely to be consolidation in the marketplace around a smaller group of big players with tiers of suppliers below them. At the lower end, we can expect more vertically targeted solutions, which are also likely to be offered through an outsourced application service provider (ASP) model. The higher end solutions will offer increased capabilities for enterprise integration, hooking the CMS as seamlessly as possible into other systems such as enterprise resource planning (ERP) or supply chain systems.

Finally, the increased uptake and standardization around XML will make content reuse, data interchange, and integration between systems far easier, reducing the complexity and cost of CMSs.

6.2.1   Build versus Buy

The build versus buy dilemma has existed since packaged software solutions first appeared, and unfortunately, it applies very much to content manage-

---

TIP   **Go through a Selection Process to Help You Decide Whether to Build or Buy**

You typically go through a vendor selection process once you have decided to buy a CMS. However, it can be a good idea to go through a selection process even if you decide at the end of it all to build your own because you find there are no products out there to meet your needs or because the exercise has helped clarify in your own mind what you really want. Although choosing a CMS may be hard, it is not as difficult as thinking through exactly what you want and why. Going through a vendor selection process will force you to clarify both to yourself and others what your requirements are and how they are prioritized.

A common, and perfectly reasonable, approach is to build your own CMS to cater to short-term requirements while you go through the longer process of defining your fuller and longer-term content management requirements. By the time your own CMS is reaching the limits of its capabilities, you should be in a position to replace it with the exact long-term solution you need.

---

ment systems. The decision is made harder when the market is still young and rapidly evolving because the temptation might be to build your own system so as not to be exposed to the volatility and dramatic change as vendors appear, disappear, and reinvent themselves overnight. As things settle down, it perhaps becomes more attractive to buy a solution that someone else has sweated blood developing in an intensely competitive market. There is no single answer, but Tables 6.2 and 6.3 summarize some of the key arguments for and against building or buying your CMS solution.

Table 6.2 Buying versus building your CMS.

Reasons not to build your own CMS

You are doing complex software development	CMSs are not simple systems, so you are biting off a lot in deciding to build your own. You will need a very strong development team and good technical project management to succeed. CMSs not only require the development team to have a thorough understanding of databases and programming languages, but they must also appreciate the importance of user interfaces and editorial processes if they are to create an effective publishing system.
You are going to have to keep building it	Software companies only continue to survive if they aggressively develop their software to meet the changing needs of the market. You too will have to continue to develop the software you create as more requirements emerge. If you do not keep pace with the commercial market, your solution will quickly lag behind what is offered and you will end up buying anyway.
You are going to have to support your solution	Supporting an enterprise software system is no small task, and you will have to take on the many headaches that this will entail. Just because you develop a CMS in house does not mean that the organization will not expect high levels of ongoing support as if you were an external vendor.
Time to market	When do you need your solution by? Usually, the answer is "yesterday." It will take you some time to build your own CMS even though you can choose to prioritize those elements you most need. If you buy a CMS, you might find that you can get much of what you need out of the box, reducing the time requirement to get a useful, working system up and running.
Robustness and scalability	You would, of course, thoroughly test your own system and you would design it such that it could support existing and expected volumes of demand. However, it is unlikely, despite your best endeavors, that what you create will be as robust and scalable in the long term as a commercial solution (flaky early versions aside) that is being used in anger by a wide range of end users in all sorts of situations, a situation which forces the flushing out of most potential problems.
The market is rapdily evolving	By the time you develop your own solution, you may find that someone else has created a CMS that does everything you need and costs less than you have spent in developing your own. Furthermore, they can worry about supporting and developing the product. It can seem like the right product is always just on the horizon, or just around the corner, but perhaps you are better off buying into a solution that meets the majority of your needs and looks set to evolve to meet the rest.

Table 6.3 Building versus buying your CMS.

Reasons not to buy a CMS

They are expensive	There are midrange solutions beginning to emerge to cater to smaller budgets, but CMSs are very costly to buy, implement, and maintain. The total cost of ownership is likely to be several hundred thousand dollars, if not millions. For the same money or a lot less, you might be able to develop your own CMS that does exactly what you need.
They will not do everything you need them to do	And they will do a whole range of things you do not need, no doubt. Not only will you be paying for features that you do not want, but you will still have to incur development costs in customizing and extending what you buy, so why not just do it yourself in the first place? And despite the best assurances, guarantees, and service-level agreements to ensure the vendor provides adequate ongoing support for the system, you know you are still going to have to provide front-line support yourself and that, in emergencies, you would rather not have to wait on the vendor to resolve the issue. At least if you build your own CMS, you will know how to fix it if there is a problem.
The market is rapidly evolving	As much as this is a reason not to build your own CMS, it can also be a good reason not to buy a CMS. What happens if the company you buy from goes bust or is acquired? Would it not be better to wait a while until the market settles down and the products mature before buying? Will increasing competition mean that prices will come down if you wait and build your own CMS to get you through the short term? What happens if there are new technology developments that render your purchase quickly obsolete?

Case Study — The Transition to an Off-the-Shelf Content Management System

Company: Channel 4 Interactive, *www.channel4.co.uk*

Company Overview

Since 1982, Channel 4 has been making television that matters, offering an alternative to the mainstream on other UK channels and placing a premium on innovation, originality, and diversity. It is unique: a public service channel funded entirely by advertising. It reinvests all its profits in generating new creative opportunities for Britain's most talented producers and filmmakers.

Channel 4 remains committed to finding the new, the exciting, the innovative, and the different, to continue to give new talent an opportunity in a competitive media environment, and to build an ever closer relationship with audiences through new program ideas, new services, and new platforms.

Background to Case Study and Objectives

The prime function of our Web site is to extend the Channel 4 brand online and deliver revenue. Much more than just marketing support, it means using the medium in innovative ways to deliver new and platform-specific experiences. As different TV shows have different audiences, tone, and content, and run for different lengths of time, each show effectively has its own microsite under the Channel 4 "umbrella."

Over the last years, the number of sites required has mushroomed, the volume of traffic has increased exponentially, and the amount of content that needs to be updated and maintained has grown rapidly. At the same time, there has been an increasing focus on commercial return on investment, so we need to control costs without sacrificing quality.

We had been using a basic, bespoke content management system (using ColdFusion), but at the same time as we relooked at the entire site's design, navigation, and architecture, to meet the growing volumes of content and users, we decided we also needed to reassess our content management requirements.

We had been using FTP for content updates, but this had limitations, particularly when it came to version control. As the number of remote content contributors increased, robust version control for collaborative authoring was a must. We also saw a single, central CMS as a way to reduce costs by streamlining processes and also to reduce errors through robust templating, link checking, workflow tools, and the like. As we are clearly moving toward an increasingly cross-platform content proposition, the CMS had to be a "platform for the future" that could act as the hub of all content provision, irrespective of how the content needed to be delivered.

It was very important for us to consolidate all our various sites and systems around a single CMS, to increase efficiencies, and to ensure we had the skills in house to maintain the system. As we had been using Interwoven's TeamSite product successfully elsewhere in the organization, this was chosen as the core content management platform.

continued

Process and Practice

The transition from our existing templates to the new TeamSite templates was not simply a matter of automatically "translating" or importing. This was largely because not only were we transitioning to a new CMS, but we were also fundamentally rearchitecting the site, its navigation, interfaces, and content. We had over 200 sites under our top umbrella layer, the gateway to all the content beneath, and we had to make sure that the top-level pages, through their templates, enabled users to easily find the content they were interested in.

Once we had defined the content model and architecture, we set about loading the new system with page content. This turned out to be a very big job, involving a great deal of work, much of it manual. Even with automated scripts, search and replace functions, and so on, just the actual production efforts involved in resizing graphics or tagging content, for example, are not to be underestimated.

We also found that what we originally specified and what we ended up with were quite different. This was not because of any technical limitations but because, as we built the system and site, we realized there were better ways of doing things or new requirements emerged. Managing such shifting specifications is not easy, but you have to be prepared to iterate.

There was a fair amount of training of content editors that was required before they became comfortable with the new system. It uses its own jargon, processes, and concepts, which once understood are easy to use but which definitely require specific training to begin with. Life was made easier by the fact that we had created style guides and that our scheduling plan from the old homegrown system was just as valid for the new system. Also, our workflow requirements were not overly complex and had changed little from the old system to the new.

With the vastly increased capabilities of the new system, we were confronted with the age-old software problem that increased flexibility, features, and functions often correspond to increased complexity and decreased ease of use. What you gain in flexibility and control, you risk losing in simplicity. However, by not being overambitious on the scope of what we were trying to achieve, at least at first, we were able to spend time getting everyone used to using the new system.

The most time was actually spent on working out the new content model and architecture, working with internal teams and end users. This was refined over a 12-month period. As TeamSite was already being used within the organization, the technical deployment was relatively fast and straightforward. What took longer (several months) was the training and content processing work.

Results

We are successfully using the new CMS to manage the top layer of templated content that all users arrive at when they visit Channel 4 Web sites. Long-running microsites are being templated as required. However, many microsites below this top level are still static HTML because these sites are creatively highly stylized to go with their corresponding TV shows, because they are often only there for a matter of months, and because they are managed by small, tight teams. There is little point in developing templates for them and trying to integrate them with the CMS. We are effectively using the CMS as a file server.

The CMS is proving most useful at the top level. In particular, we have seen the following benefits:

► Rapid, controlled, and error-free deployment of content on a large scale.
► High levels of robustness. We prefer to use the CMS to publish static HTML pages rather than try and serve dynamic pages because this makes the site a lot more robust at the all-important top-level pages where (because of popular TV shows) we see huge spikes in traffic.
► Having a single unified system gives us a much better overview of what is happening where, when, and how. This is important not only for development and production teams but also for advertising sales and commercial teams.
► We now have many more content authors and site developers working remotely using the system. This allows us to contract out work in a cost-effective and yet controlled manner, avoid duplication of effort, and maintain file version controls.
► We have our platform for the future. Now that we have a single platform, we can much more easily publish across multiple channels, such as interactive TV.

In terms of areas for improvement, we are constantly trying to improve the usability of the system. Having a single system is good for maintaining an overview of everything and allowing the "update once, publish many" paradigm, but it can mean that the system is slow at times or it takes a while longer to navigate where you want to be within the system.

Lessons Learned

In our transition to a new off-the-shelf CMS, we learned the following:

► Loading a new CMS with content is a big job, not to be underestimated. Although not complicated, it is time consuming and resource intensive.

continued

▶ What you spec and what you end up with are likely to be different. That is the nature of interactive projects, and CMSs are no different. Compromises will be needed. You still need to think through your requirement and plan properly, but there comes a point where the returns on ever more detailed planning are not worth the time and money. In the case of a CMS, the content model and architecture are the most fundamental things to get right.

▶ If you are going to transition to a new CMS, you might as well take the chance to redesign and restructure the whole site. The amount of work required to do a transition is almost the same as starting from scratch, so it is a good chance to start afresh.

▶ Recognize that there is an inevitable trade-off between flexibility and control. Controls and processes can feel restrictive, but really that's the point—they are often supposed to be. They are only advisable when you have a very precise specification for the content. If not constant, changes will be expensive. You cannot edit a locked file for a reason. Getting used to new controls can be frustrating at first but is beneficial in the long term, especially as you scale up.

▶ The more flexible and powerful the CMS you have, the more complex it can be. Don't use everything for the sake of it. You are actually best off concentrating on a few key areas that are most important as these will deliver 80% of the total benefits.

▶ Clear structure and architecture have huge benefits in reducing the effort to manage the site. However, they will only be enjoyed in the longer term.

▶ Change management for the users is often neglected, especially in the case of dropping a legacy bespoke system that had been tailored over the years to very specific requirements. Users will very likely initially resent any replacement.

> **Paul Coombs**
> Production Manager
> Channel 4 Interactive

6.2.2   Selection Process

Assuming that you have decided to buy a CMS, or at least want to go through a vendor selection process, what steps should you take? Figure 6.2 shows an eight-step vendor selection process that you can use. You will note that this process is not specific to choosing a CMS but valid for any selection process

Figure 6.2 CMS selection process.

you might go through when making a large investment decision. The details at each stage will, of course, be specific to a CMS.

NOTE   **Vendor Selection Processes**

There is much debate around what the best process for vendor selection should be. The debate swings one way and then another depending on what is fashionable as much as anything else. Many organizations already have established procedures for vendor selection, and if this works, then there is little reason to change things just because it is a CMS. Ultimately, there is no one right answer. The approach will vary depending on the project requirements, the company, the state of the market, and the individuals involved. What is presented here represents a traditional and standard process for selecting an information technology (IT) systems vendor. ■

Looking at each step in some more detail:

We look at selection criteria in more detail in Section 6.2.3, Selection Criteria, and examine the important task of defining your requirements in Section 7.1.6, Requirements Gathering.

1. *Define Requirements.*   This is the hardest part of the selection process: defining what you need. Your requirements will be defined by your business strategy (where you want to go) and where you currently are. You should create both a plain English overview of your objectives, what you are trying to achieve and why, and a much more detailed list of selection criteria to meet your requirements. You should have a weighted scoring system to evaluate vendors against your selection criteria. At this stage, it is also important to build consensus on what the selection process is going to be, who is going to be part of it, what the deliverables are, and who will do scoring and make the final decision. You must treat the process as a project in itself with its own project team, milestones, tasks, and deliverables.

2. *Canvas Market.*   During this step, you cast your net quite wide to understand the CMS vendor market and the players in it. You should soon

get a feel for those that are likely to suit your needs. In doing your canvasing, you might consider the following approaches:

▶ Do research on the better Web sites dedicated to content management. For some suggestions, refer to the Resources at the end of this book. If there are discussion forums or lists, you can ask advice there and search the archives.

▶ Buy analysts' reports. If you can afford it, it is worth buying the most up-to-date and relevant report that you can find from an organization that has done much of the research and analysis work for you. It would not be sensible to base your decisions completely on what these reports say, but they do help get you up to speed quickly and collate much of the information that you will otherwise have to find yourself.

▶ Ask friends and colleagues. This is usually the first choice for most decision making. Even if they do not know anything themselves about content management, they might know someone who does.

▶ Ask the experts. If you have read features, articles, white papers, even books on content management by experts who have impressed you, or attended conferences where speakers have talked competently on the issues that concern you, try contacting them for advice. They may not have the time to help, but usually these are people who like to help and like to communicate, so give it a try. Many now have their own Web sites through which they can be contacted (and I am no exception).

Make sure you document your findings (e.g., by company) so you can refer back to them later. By the end of this step of the process, you should end up with about 10 companies. If there are much fewer than that, it is likely that you have narrowed your options too early unless you can be very clear and confident in your choices.

3. *Vendor Short List.*   You now need to reduce your 10 or so vendors to a short list of about 5. To help you do this, try the following:

▶ Use your selection criteria to weed out unsuitable vendors. You do not need to go through every detail at this stage, but by scanning through the selection criteria you created as part of the first step of the process, you should be able to eliminate a few vendors. If you involve a few people in this process, you might find that different people have valid reasons for excluding particular vendors from further consideration. For example, your technical specialist may be able to rule out particular vendors knowing that their systems will not integrate as required.

▶ Search the Web on the vendors' product names. Targeted searches, especially on technology portal sites, will yield links to further information, comment, opinions, and analysis on the particular products you are interested in. This can lead you to individuals or discussion threads that can give you excellent insider insight into the products in question, helping you further narrow your selection.

▶ Have an initial meeting with the vendors. It may not be appropriate to hold a meeting at this stage, and indeed, depending on your attractiveness as a client, the vendor may not want to meet this early on, but if possible, it is worth having a brief, informal, introductory get-together to discuss the product, the vendor, and its working practices a little more. More than anything, this is just to get a feel for the vendor organization and the way they respond to you. This can often help exclude vendors who you know you will have difficulty working with.

Make sure that you keep notes as you go against each company's profile, including reasons for dropping a particular vendor.

4. *Send out RFP.*   A request for proposal (RFP), sometimes called an invitation to tender (ITT) or other name, is a more formal and rigorous document to be completed by each vendor so that you can then assess their suitability in meeting your requirements. Creating an RFP and managing the process of sending it out and collating the results are a lot of work for you, just as filling it in completely is for the vendor, so it is important to have done the initial short listing diligently so as not to waste anyone's time.

The RFP you send out should include the overview of your objectives and a detailed list of selection questions as defined in the first step of the process. The vendor needs to respond in detail to your requirements but must also understand your wider commercial goals and business context. Their ability to understand your business and strategic issues is likely to be very important to you. Suggested selection questions are given in the following section.

5. *Vendor Meetings and Presentations.*   In this step, you should follow up your RFPs with face-to-face meetings. This gives the vendors a chance to present their thinking and their response to your RFP. It is also likely that

they will try and bring along some of their best people to the meeting to impress you, so you should get a feel for the caliber of their staff. Above all, this is a chance for you to hone in on areas of strength or weakness that you identified in the vendors' response to the RFP, giving them a fair chance to further explain and justify themselves. During this step, do the following:

▶ Score the responses to your RFP according to your weighted scoring system. Apart from helping you see any clear winners or losers in overall score, this process will help you identify particular areas of strength or weakness to further explore when meeting each individual vendor.

▶ Do a little more asking around. Now that you have a better idea of which vendors you are most interested in, you can focus your research and use your network of contacts to try and get more feedback. For example, find out who the vendors' clients are. Do you know anyone who works at those client organizations that you might be able to speak to informally?

For more on project plans, see Section 7.1.9, Initial Project Plan and Budget.

▶ Go through your project plans with each vendor. As part of the initial stages of your content management project, you should have created project plans to begin to define and scope the work, refining them as you go to get an ever clearer picture of costs, deliverables, timings, and other resource requirements. However, your choice of CMS is likely to have quite an impact on these plans. Going through them with each potential vendor helps you as follows: You get a much better feel for the quality of the vendor's delivery process and experience; you get a clearer idea of the way in which the vendor would work with you (very involved and hands on or distant?); you are able to refine and improve your plans and projections based on the valuable expertise and experience of the vendor. If nothing else, your project plans are a good concrete framework around which to base and focus a discussion.

6. *Final Short List.*   Now that you have all your research, scored responses to RFPs, and have held follow-up meetings with each vendor, you should be in a position to narrow the list of contenders to two, perhaps three, finalists. In all probability, you will have a favorite at this stage, but some important steps still remain. At this stage, it is important for members of your project team to really come to grips with the few short listed products so that you can be absolutely sure the chosen product will suit their needs and they will be able to work with it. Involving more operational members of your team at this

stage also involves them in the decision-making process, ensuring their buy in and commitment to the final decision.

It is particularly important to make sure your technical and editorial team members find out all they need at this stage. They need to "get under the hood" of the system, and if at all possible, they should see a live system in action. A simple demo is not sufficient at this stage. Most vendors are able to provide a working implementation of the system on site at their offices. Some may even have clients who are prepared to allow your team to spend some time with them. This is a chance for your team to ask all the little questions that may have been troubling them and to think through the practical implications of choosing one system over another.

7. *Commercial Negotiations and Due Diligence.* By this stage, you may already have a clear winner, or the decision may still hang in the balance. Either way, you still need to conduct the commercial negotiations and due diligence step. On the commercial side, you will be agreeing to pricing, payment schedules, and service-level and support agreements, as well as any other terms of engagement and factors affecting the ongoing business relationship. For any sizable investment, you would expect to finalize these negotiations, after a decision is made, with both parties signing a legally binding contract.

Due diligence involves following up references, talking to existing vendor customers, and double checking the business circumstances (financial status, ownership, commitments, history, future vision, etc.) of the vendor just to make absolutely sure that there are no nasty skeletons hiding in the closet.

8. *Decision.* It is time to decide. Hopefully, the decision will be clear by this stage. If not, it may be because of internal problems at your end or because you have found no suitable product. In the latter case, you will need to reconsider building your own system (now, at least, armed with a lot more knowledge) or face the fact that you will need to do a lot of customization of the CMS you choose. In the former case, if you agreed with the decision-making process and final decision owners up front, then you should not encounter a problem. However, if you do, you will need to escalate the problem higher up your organization for a decision.

Unless you are also the budget holder for the CMS investment, you will need to present and justify your decision to someone above you who will take responsibility for signing off the money. You should synopsize the mountain of information you will by now have into a report that focuses on the process you followed, the reasons you have chosen the final product, an overview of the product and vendor, and an update to your project plans, including any revised costs and schedules.

6.2.3   Selection Criteria

What exactly your selection criteria should be, and what will be the "right" answers to your selection questions, will depend on your particular requirements and resources. Of course, the temptation is to want to have every possible feature and piece of functionality in your CMS and go for the best system available on the market, but budgetary realities, among others, mean this is not always possible. You will no doubt end up making some compromises, so it is important to be clear in your mind what your priorities are so that you can compromise where it least matters and focus your attention and resources on ensuring that you do get what you really need most.

Following are a list of questions, grouped by topic, that you can use as the basis for drawing up your own selection criteria. The list tries to cover most of the areas you would typically need to cover but is not exhaustive, and you may need to go into more detail in the areas that particularly concern you. You should create a matrix, using a spreadsheet or even a database, with each question in a separate row and each product to be evaluated in a separate column. Your cells should contain formulas as required for weighting the scores that you enter. For example, the level of multilingual support of the CMS might be particularly crucial to you, and you may choose to double the scores given under this heading. By totaling the scores for each product, by topic section, and overall, you can see at a glance which products are coming out on top and where each is strong or weak.

Although there are no "correct" answers to the suggested questions, you should certainly be looking for the following:

▶ *Real experience.* Content management is a relatively new field, but you still want to see real experience in delivering solutions. Look for real examples and real clients dealing with real problems. You might prefer a company with a larger installed customer base and heritage in a related field, such as document management.

▶ *A good working relationship.* A CMS is a large and ongoing commitment, so you need to be sure that you can comfortably work in partnership with your CMS vendor. You should feel comfortable with the vendor's staff, working practices, and culture at all levels. Are they honest? Are they reliable? Have you met staff from all levels of their organization rather than just sales staff? Do they understand the human and project process factors you are facing, not just the technology issues? What do their partners seem to think of them?

▶ *Open standards.* It is increasingly rare to find a CMS solution that relies on proprietary code or standards. This may have been required in the earliest phases of commercially available CMSs to achieve what was required in the time available and protect the intellectual property of the system, but there is now no reason for a system not to be fully compliant with open standards. You want this not only to ease integration with other systems, but also so that you can readily find skilled personnel to develop and maintain the system.

▶ *Good support and training.* As the field of content management is still quite new, this is particularly important and should not be limited to technical staff but include editorial and other staff. How good is the documentation provided? Are you given a dedicated point of contact, available 24/7 in your chosen country, with solid escalation procedures? If the company is small, has it partnered with a credible and informed partner to provide support and training services?

▶ *Good version control, security, archiving, and backup.* These are basic services but extremely important for a CMS, so be rigorous in probing the quality of capabilities here.

▶ *Nonrestrictive authoring and workflow application.* One of your biggest potential headaches is changing or integrating authors' content creation practices to fit in with your new CMS. For this reason, the more flexible the CMS can be in terms of integrating with external authoring packages and providing multiple content capture options, the easier your life will be. Likewise with workflow: You do not want to be constrained to managing, say, just content objects within workflow because you may need to go to a more granular level (e.g., data elements within a content object). You should be able to apply workflow to creating and managing workflows.

▶ *Performance specifications.* Make absolutely sure that the CMS will be able to perform to accepted levels for your existing circumstances and scale easily to meet future demands.

▶ *Personalization.* Requirements here will vary but make sure that if personalization capabilities are very important to you, then you do not buy a CMS expecting it to do all you need only to find out that you must purchase and integrate a separate personalization engine to achieve your objectives.

▶ *Fit with your production environment.* Obviously, you will ensure that the CMS meets your basic technical requirements, but probe carefully to see whether there might be less obvious network, architectural, or other issues involved when integrating the CMS with your current environment: How will the CMS be split across servers? Are firewalls likely to cause a problem?

Implementation

▶ What consulting services do you provide? How involved would you be in any implementation? How much would you expect this to cost?

▶ How long would you expect an implementation of your system to take, given our circumstances, and who from your organization would be involved?

▶ Can you give an example of where your system has been successfully deployed to support global and localized multilingual sites?

▶ How would we migrate our existing site(s) into your system? Do you provide any tools, support, or processes to aid this? How long might this take in your experience, given our circumstances?

Technical and Integration

▶ What operating systems can your CMS run on?

▶ Which Web servers are supported?

▶ What database systems do you use or support?

▶ What hardware, software, and network requirements would you recommend for your system as we intend to use it? Is a proprietary, or dedicated, application server required? Which application server platforms does your CMS integrate with?

▶ Is there any particular software required for client machines accessing your system?

▶ What browsers and versions does your system support for content authoring, management, and publishing?

▶ What skills, languages, and tools are needed to customize and extend your system?

▶ What content authoring tools do you integrate with and to what extent?

► What translation tools do you integrate with and to what extent?

► Do you integrate with, or provide, tools to aid the structuring of unstructured data?

► Can you launch and use other applications from within the system?

► What connectors do you provide to common external enterprise applications, such as supply chain, ERP, HR, and accounting systems?

► How does your system share data with other systems? What protocols and formats are used?

► What syndication capabilities does the system have to take content into the system and automatically feed it out?

► What documentation do you provide with your system?

► How would your system typically be configured in terms of hardware and software, including clustering considerations, networking, firewalls, and security?

► Does your system support user session management and the use of cookies?

► What proprietary code is required, if any, and for what purpose?

► What caching capabilities does your system have?

► What administration tools and interfaces are provided for configuring and administering the system? Can the system be entirely managed via a Web interface?

► What skills are needed to administer the system?

► Can distributed servers that are part of the system be administered both locally and centrally?

Scalability and Disaster Recovery

► How does your system scale to efficiently handle increasing numbers of content objects and authors? How does the system scale to meet increasing load demands?

► What known performance limitations does the system have in terms of a maximum number of concurrent users, number of templates that can be simultaneously processed, number of content objects that can be stored in the repository, or maximum file sizes?

► How does the system support the n-tier distribution of work environments that are not in the same place?

► What is the upgrade path for more advanced or future versions of the system?

► What fault-tolerance or automated recovery features does the system have to avoid system failures?

- ▶ What archiving and disaster recovery features does your system have?
- ▶ How reliable is the system? What availability can you guarantee?

Content Authoring and Version Control

- ▶ Do you provide your own authoring tools?
- ▶ What tools does your system directly integrate with?
- ▶ What file formats can your system recognize and manage?
- ▶ How does your system deal with streaming media content?
- ▶ Do you provide, or integrate with, any tools to help automatically convert between content formats?
- ▶ Are your Web-based forms automatically generated from a database schema or manually set up? How can they be edited and customized?
- ▶ What level of form validation can your CMS provide for form-entered content? Do you provide any spell-checking or grammar-checking tools?
- ▶ Do you provide levels of undo for authors? How would an author go back to an earlier version of a piece of content?
- ▶ What preview functions do you provide allowing an author to see content in its final state?
- ▶ How do you enable formatting within your Web-based forms for content capture? And how do you link to or embed rich media files associated with the text?
- ▶ What personalization capabilities does your CMS have based on an author's permission level?
- ▶ Does a content author have to be online to use the Web forms?
- ▶ How does an author add metadata to a content object? Can metadata be automatically pulled from other sources such as a database file?
- ▶ To what degree can content authoring be enforced by setting mandatory or optional fields?
- ▶ What version control tools do you provide? Can content authors choose to view and work with previous versions of a content object? How can earlier versions be restored?
- ▶ What support do you provide for simultaneous, collaborative authoring? Can different versions of the same content be used at the same time across multiple sites? Can the same piece of content be worked on at the same time and changes merged later?
- ▶ Does the platform include audit-trail capabilities to capture relevant information on each version of a content object so that changes to the content can be easily tracked?

▶ What levels of rollback does your system provide (files, content objects, pages, complete sites)? How are "known good" versions of the site captured and stored for rollback purposes?

Storing, Managing, and Publishing Content

▶ How does your system store content in the repository (file system, object database, relational database, hybrid)?

▶ Can you store content to support international character sets as well as multiple date and currency formats?

▶ What link management features does your system provide? Can it validate both internal and external links?

▶ What indexing and searching does your system support? Do you use your own tools, or are they augmented by third-party search tools?

▶ How does the system support the replication and distribution of content to multiple locations while maintaining data integrity, system availability, and content synchronization?

▶ How does your system fit in with a two- or three-stage production environment (development, staging, and live servers)?

▶ What content deployment features does your system have? Can updates be done incrementally, or must the whole site be replicated? How can updates be automatically scheduled, manually overridden, done ad hoc?

▶ Can you set go live, archive, review, and delete attributes to content with the system?

▶ Can you use the system to publish content in file formats such as PDFs or proprietary formats such as help files or for CD-ROM?

▶ What tools can the system make available that might benefit the end user of the site, such as advanced search options?

Templates

▶ How do your templates work? What languages can be used to develop templates for your system? Do you provide standard templates, or libraries of template code, for modification?

▶ Does your system provide particular enhanced features for publishing to multiple channels, both digital and offline? How would your templates recognize and work with different end user devices?

▶ Can your system generate pages using templates both in real time and according to scheduled processes?

▶ How do your templates integrate with other systems?

Personalization

▶ What levels and forms of personalization can your system deliver and how? How do you typically integrate with third-party tools or systems (e.g., CRM or e-commerce systems)?

▶ Does your system rely on business rules defined by us or does it also have automated forms of intelligent personalization such as dynamic navigation created depending on inferred site user interests? Do you provide any predefined rules we can use?

▶ What range of rules does the system support for personalization? How are these entered and edited? What skills are required to configure the business rules?

▶ How do you store user profile data? How can user data be analyzed? How does the system report on user data? How can user data be imported into, or exported from, the system?

▶ What forms of data does your personalization engine work with (session data, user profiles, page history, metadata, rules)?

▶ What range of publications can your system personalize for? Is your personalization engine capable of running personalized, outbound, marketing campaigns?

▶ Can your system report in any way on the effectiveness of the personalization being used in order to improve it?

Universal Language Support

▶ Does your system provide user interfaces in different languages?

▶ Does your system integrate with any language translation aids?

▶ What language content cannot be entered or retrieved from your system?

▶ What are the configuration implications of deploying the system to non-English operating systems?

▶ How would multilingual servers be synched so that content is uniformly up to date globally?

Workflow

▶ What workflow tools does your system provide? What tools do you integrate with?

▶ What activities can have workflows applied to them in your system? Can external parties be included in a workflow? Can you apply workflows to all levels of content, not just files, right down to data elements within a content object?

▶ How are workflows created and managed? What is the interface for designing workflows?

▶ What triggers and alerting functions do you support in your workflow steps?

▶ How do you configure the roles of users in a workflow?

▶ Can multiple workflows be seen from the perspective of a single user's participation in them? What task queuing functions do you provide for users?

▶ How do you audit workflows? What tracking and reporting tools and analysis does the system provide?

Security and Rights Management

▶ Does your system allow for multiple layers of security rather than simple read/write/execute constraints?

▶ How are users, groups, and roles managed by the system? Do you support a hierarchical security model?

▶ Can your system work with, or import, existing user permission and security level settings?

▶ How can your system help us protect our intellectual property rights? Do you provide any digital rights management tools?

▶ Does your system come with any standard encryption or security certification features? How can the system help protect and encrypt content stored on it?

Management Information Reporting

▶ What reporting and logging features does the system have? What tools does the system integrate with?

▶ Does the reporting concentrate principally on noncustomer facing processes or on end user interaction with the content?

▶ What metrics can the system report against? Can the reporting be customer-centric, using an individual user as the starting point, rather than content-centric?

▶ How accurate and reliable is the reporting? What are the margins of inaccuracy? Does the reporting comply with standard-defined metrics?

▶ What interfaces are provided for configuring reporting and retrieving reports?

▶ What standard reports are provided? How are custom reports set up?

▶ How can reporting be configured to run regularly or ad hoc?

▶ What format can the reports be delivered in and via what channels?

▶ What technical performance measurement and monitoring tools does the system have?

▶ How can reporting and analysis be personalized to the user?

► Can the logs that the system generates be exported in standard data formats and shared with other applications?

► Can workflow be applied to the reporting?

Training and Support

► What training do you provide as standard? What additional training can you provide and at what cost?

► Where do you hold training sessions?

► Do you have certified partners who can offer additional training services?

► What levels of technical support do you provide? What hours is support available and in which countries and languages? What response times do you guarantee? What are your escalation procedures?

► What other support services can you provide through partners or self-help facilities?

► How do you cost your levels of support on an ongoing basis?

► What is the upgrade path for future releases of the system? How are patches and bug fixes communicated and distributed?

Case Study   **Building versus Buying a Content Management System**

Company: Teletext, *www.teletext.co.uk*

Company Overview

Teletext Limited was formed in 1992 to bid for the UK's public teletext license and began broadcasting on January 1, 1993. The ITV1 and C4 service is now used daily by 11.9 million people and weekly by 20.1 million. It is the largest vacation advertising medium in the UK, and the most successful commercial teletext service in the world. The first digital Teletext service was launched on the Internet in 1994, and the company now broadcasts on seven digital platforms in addition to analog television.

Background to Case Study and Objectives

In the early days of Teletext, we had only one system with a single output in a single format. It was "Teletext in and Teletext out" using our own production systems. This did the job we needed very well at the time. However, by the mid-1990s, we identified the challenges and opportunities represented by the emerging digital channels. It was clear we were heading for a multiplatform future, so we needed to reexamine our information model and how we managed content from end to end.

Our vision was not to have multiple systems, one for each channel, but to have a central database, or series of closely interconnected databases, that could manage all the content coming into it and then out to the appropriate channel in the appropriate format with the appropriate content.

As we began to look at our information model and the channels it would need to support, it was clear that there was some content that would carry almost directly across multiple channels (e.g., news headlines or sports scores) and other content that would need to be tailored specifically to the channel. It was also clear that whatever system we went for would need to be capable of integrating and processing a large number of content feeds from multiple supplier sources in a robust and scalable fashion.

Along with a centralized content management model, we were also convinced that we needed to remain platform and technology neutral to protect against future market volatility. Our strategy was to stay "agnostic" in the face of uncertain and unpredictable markets. To some degree, this meant we wanted to keep our own independence and control in terms of any CMS.

At the time, we had to make an investment with no obvious up-front return. In a sense, it was a leap of faith based on our convictions of future requirements and what would best serve them.

Process and Practice

The first system that we began sketching out was not conceived or described as a content management system per se but rather a content processing system. Our heritage in dealing with very large volumes of fairly predictable data meant we were used to processing content effectively. However, our system design soon began to take shape split down into content production and content publication: getting content into the system in the right form and then getting it out the other side in the right form.

Once we had a clearer idea of our vision and our requirements, we had to make the buy versus build decision. On the one hand, we were keen to buy a product because of the speed to market advantages, lowered development risks, and the peace of mind of working with a tried and tested product. Equally, the build arguments were appealing: retaining ownership of the core database and having the skills to develop and administer it, not

continued

becoming dependent on a third party, and being able to create the system exactly to suit us rather than having to customize extensively. These are the usual dilemmas.

We spent a fair bit of time looking at commercial CMS products with an eye to going down the buy route but in the end found nothing that could convince us. We felt that the systems were flaky or we could not be confident that they would provide the industrial strength and robustness we needed. Solid processes seemed to be lacking, and above all, most products tried to be too "all in one" for our liking. Rather than succeeding very well on a few fronts, they appeared to promise the world on every front.

At the same time, we were still not keen to be solely responsible for building a CMS product in house with all the associated risks and development costs (start up and ongoing). In the end, we partnered with a technology company to help them build a CMS product that they could then freely sell to other companies. By working closely with this partner, we managed to get exactly what we wanted, retain the in-depth understanding of the product in house, and reap the benefits of shared risk, lowered development costs, and a robustly tested system that would continue to be improved through exposure to other clients.

Results

We now have a system that publishes to seven different platforms from a single repository. More than 120 journalists successfully use the system to input content that is then served to millions of end users on many different devices—TV, PC, and phone.

Our analog TV service continues to run separately as an analog system but only because of advantageous long-term commercial contracts made many years ago. Eventually, this too will migrate to the digital system.

We are now increasingly concentrating on more seamless integration with partners and suppliers. XML data interchange, for example, is supplanting CSVs via FTP. We are also working on ways to give journalists more control of the front end to allow for editorial and creative flexibility while maintaining the efficiencies, control, and cross-platform interoperability at the back end.

Lessons Learned

▶ Things take longer than you think.
▶ It's hard getting there, but once you're there it is great. Getting the processes in place and the people and system working in harmony is hard, but once you've got your machine well-oiled, the efficiency and quality gains are significant.

▶ Finding bridges in the organization is vital to success. "Bridges" are people who can facilitate, translate, communicate, interpret—build bridges of understanding and cooperation within the company.

▶ Use open standards and be as technology neutral as possible. As you come to integrate further with external systems, this becomes all the more important.

▶ Retain ownership of the core CMS. Even if you go down the buy route, you must have in-house resources who know the guts of the system so that you can effectively develop, maintain, and customize it without being overly reliant on a third party.

▶ There is an inherent tension between control and flexibility, particularly when working across multiple platforms: More control means more efficiencies, ease of management, and "guarantees" that the end product will work (TV, for example, is much less forgiving than the Web), but flexibility is important for the front end. A balance has to be struck.

▶ Trust your templating. Once the system is underway and processing millions of content objects for millions of system and end users across numerous platforms, you simply cannot check every single page of content that goes out. So you must make sure your templates are as good as possible. You have to be able to rely on them.

Perhaps above all we have learned that you have to understand and define your compromises. No system can make content ultimately easy to manage and control and yet be ultimately flexible. Even if the system is, the people and processes that govern it won't be. The key is collaboration, cooperation, and a mutual understanding of goals and constraints.

Gordon Maynard
IT Director
Teletext

6.3   Evolving toward a CMS

Before we move on to how to tackle a medium to large-scale content management project in the next chapter, it is worth considering how a site typically evolves to this stage. Some sites launch with a full CMS in place from day one, but these are the exception. Most sites grow and evolve through phases toward requiring a full CMS.

Figure 6.3 shows three main phases in the typical evolution toward a CMS. More details on each phase follow showing what is happening in terms of content management and what you can be doing at each phase to prepare

Figure 6.3 Phases of evolution toward a CMS.

effectively for a full CMS. The distinction between the phases is rarely as clear-cut as the diagram might suggest, with much more overlap and blurring of boundaries in reality, but the phases do represent a linear progression that fits with the typical requirements of a Web site that is growing over time.

6.3.1   The Early Webmaster Phase

This phase is called the Webmaster phase because the job of managing Web site content is usually up to a Webmaster of some kind: someone charged with managing and updating the Web site whether part time, full time, in house, or outsourced.

Smaller, less complex sites or sites that do not change that often can quite happily be managed by a Webmaster. In the case of many sites, this phase is as far as they need go in terms of content management because the returns for investing in more complex content management solutions are not worth the extra investment.

Development Environment

Site changes are typically made directly to the live site by the Webmaster. He or she will have a local copy of the files of the Web site to preview changes through a browser before setting them live and also to act as a rudimentary form of backup. Testing of changes is often done once the changes have been set live with any errors fixed directly as they are found. Uptime is not business critical for this stage of site evolution, and the number of files to be managed is likely to be not much more than 100.

Content Management Tools

At this stage, HTML editors and authoring tools typically suffice. Initially these tools just helped HTML coders remember tags and syntax, but now they have evolved to include full "what you see is what you get" (WYSIWYG) authoring capabilities as well as built-in FTP clients for managing uploads to the live site.

Preparing for Full Content Management

Whether or not you plan to evolve all the way toward a full CMS, it would be prudent to undertake the following CMS-related activities:

▶ *Documentation.* At this stage, you have very informal, if nonexistent, processes and controls, and you are (over)reliant on the Webmaster. You should at least create documentation detailing style and technical guidelines. For more on this, refer to Section 2.1, Documentation, in the chapter on procedures for managing site updates. This sets in motion the drive toward standards and processes that a CMS will require.

▶ *Change processes.* There is no need for anything very formal, but you should document how changes to the site are made. This is workflow in its most nascent form.

▶ *Audit trails.* Keep a record of how content is updated and why, even if this is just storing emails and introducing consistent file naming practices for content assets. This is a basic form of version control and logging for reporting.

▶ *Backups.* Make regular backups of the entire site and store these complete site versions in an archive. As a Zip file, this should not take up much space or take long to do. Not only is this useful for disaster recovery, but it gives you a rudimentary rollback system because you can go back to an earlier version of the site if required.

▶ *Relative, not absolute, links.* Instead of using absolute HTML hyperlinks (beginning http:// . . .), use relative ones so that it is easier to move your entire site to another server setup, including offline, and the site will still work. This will help in later stages.

▶ *Centralize the storing of image files.* Organize your file directory such that image files (and other media files such as video or audio) are stored in one central directory and referenced from pages rather than in section-specific image directories. Centralized management of media assets, rather than a page-centric view, works best for content management.

▶ *Site stats.* Track usage of content on your site using a site stats software package. For more on this, read Part IV of this book, Site Measurement. This will help you understand which content is most popular.

▶ *Link management.* There are plenty of free, or nearly free, tools on the Web to check your site for broken links and alert you when any are found. Try one of these to get used to elements of link management practices. Similar tools can be found to check file sizes and monitor uptime.

6.3.2   The Mature Webmaster Phase

1. Webmaster phase

This stage is simply a more advanced form of the earlier Webmaster stage. By now, the site has grown, probably to several hundred or a thousand files; there is a little more functionality and more demands on the Webmaster coming from more people. The site has become of increased interest and importance to the business, so quality control and uptime are more of an issue.

Development Environment

The principal change in the development environment at this stage is the introduction of a staging server that allows all changes and additions to the site to be previewed and tested before going live. This is very helpful for quality control and sign-off purposes. The Web development team consists of several people by now, although we are still in the Webmaster phase because all changes are still channeled through the Webmaster, causing a bottleneck problem at times. There are enough people in the development team, and enough work going through, that it is becoming increasingly difficult for each person to understand which changes belong to whom and which are ready, or not, to go live. Without version control, there may be problems with one team member overwriting work by another. As the number of content contributors increases, inefficiencies and quality failures begin to appear.

Content Management Tools

The HTML editors of the early stage have advanced and been upgraded to include some management tools. For example, uploads to the staging and live sites can be scheduled and managed through basic deployment functions; links can be automatically checked and managed; version control capabilities are available to help manage code development; site maps can automatically be created to see an overview of the entire site structure; basic templates can be created with editable and locked areas of the page; status can be assigned to pages, with comments, giving a basic form of workflow with task lists. These tools incorporate some aspects of a content management system at a basic level, but they are file and page-centric rather than designed to manage content objects with associated metadata. These tools are less likely to be database-driven and contain little in the way of workflow or personalization capabilities. They are still a long way from being able to publish personalized content to multiple targets on different sites, devices, and platforms.

Preparing for Full Content Management

In addition to the suggestions given in the early stage of the Webmaster phase, the following steps will help take you further down the road toward full content management:

▶ *Version control.* Start using a version control tool at least to help manage collaborative code development.

▶ *Change processes.* You should start to formalize the way in which changes to the site are requested and carried out. For more on how to do this, refer back to Chapter 2, Procedures for Managing Site Updates.

▶ *Introduce cascading style sheets (CSSs).* If you are not already using CSSs to help manage the presentation of your site's content centrally, you should do so. Create a central style sheet which individual pages reference. This way you can make sitewide cosmetic changes in a single place. You should also follow the discipline of using only a fixed set of styles as defined by your style sheet rather than hard-coding a presentation using HTML. A CSS is an important step toward separating content and presentation and making site management a great deal easier through centralizing the control and configuration of styles across the site.

▶ *Introduce XHTML.* This is simply HTML that follows the rules of XML. Not only is this discipline good practice, even if you do not evolve toward XML, but it is certainly helpful training and preparation for when you do begin to grapple with XML, as you no doubt will as you evolve toward a full CMS.

▶ *Use templates.* Templates are fundamental to content management in their role bridging the gap between content and presentation, bringing the two together dynamically in multiple configurations and instances. Although templates can become quite complex programs in themselves, at this stage you should begin to use templates even though there is nothing dynamic about them. The content can be hard-coded into the template, so this is still a page-centric approach, but you should standardize how different areas of the page are used and what sorts of content appear in those areas. For example, you should begin to set rules about where and how navigation appears and think about header, footer, and column regions on the page. Think not only about the actual content itself, but also more about what sorts of content should go where. Draw templates as simple boxed areas of content on a page.

▶ *Automated link checking*. This should be offered as part of a more advanced HTML editing and site management tool.

▶ *Site cleanup*. At regular intervals, perhaps once a month, the Webmaster should go through the site and get rid of any orphaned or unused files that are on the site cluttering it up. A basic site management tool will help identify these unwanted files. Obviously, back them up somewhere rather than deleting them for good in case they turn out to be important. Doing this regularly keeps the site tidy and clean so that when it needs to be moved or migrated, time is not lost working on redundant content.

6.3.3   The Early Database Phase

This phase is called the database phase because it signals the change from a site that consists of many individual files that are brought together via HTML into static pages to a site where content is stored in a database and pages are created dynamically using languages such as ASP or JSP. The reasons for moving into the database phase are principally to solve the Webmaster bottleneck by partly automating site updates and partly allowing content contributors to make their own site updates; to more effectively manage the volume of content that was getting out of control as thousands of files; to allow for more advanced functionality and increasingly dynamic content, including personalization and more advanced search features; and to be in a better position to share content with other databases.

Development Environment

The technical skills required to manage and develop a database-driven Web site are far greater than for a simple file-based HTML site. Not only do the databases themselves need configuring, managing, and administering but optimal schemas and architectures need to be designed, and code needs to be written to read and write content to the database as required. Hardware, software, and networking considerations greatly increase as the database application demands its own resources and maintenance. The points of potential failure, especially for highly dynamic sites, greatly increase with the complexity.

At this stage, the development team probably consists of more than five people, managing many thousands of content assets within the database. As well as the staging and live server environments, there may be additional server farms or clusters on which the site is replicated to enhance performance or provide fallback and recovery options. Load balancing may be required to manage the demands on the live site. The development team is likely by this stage to have a development environment as well as the staging and live areas, which allows them to independently test and preview changes.

Content Management Tools

With the wider range of skills required, the range of tools will also be much greater. As well as the more advanced HTML editors and site management tools, there will be many more development environment tools and database management applications. However, most of these tools are for empowering individuals to do their jobs more effectively. There is still nothing like an overall system for managing content from creation through to publication.

However, for the first time, content contributors are empowered to manage their own content more directly. The "tools" provided are custom coded and typically consist of Web-based forms giving content authors a visual interface through which they can add and edit the content stored in the database. Another common option is to upload specially formatted text, Comma Separated Values (CSVs), or other files that are then automatically read into the database by a script. Once the content is in the database, it can be incorporated in an HTML page that is either displayed dynamically, as requested by the user, or generated automatically by the system (e.g., once a night) and then served as a static page. Dynamic pages are required where you do not know beforehand what will appear on the page, such as anything user specific or requiring interaction with other live data systems.

These content management tools are often not out of the box software but custom coded for the purpose. Although they function in the same way as parts of a content management system, these tools do not constitute a full CMS. Typically, these tools do not work with a content model or cater to metadata, there is little or no integration with content authoring tools, only basic workflow capabilities, and multiplatform personalized publishing would take a lot of specialized coding. The tools provide support at specific points in the content life cycle, particularly in the management stage, but do not provide the entire system to underpin the full content life cycle as does a CMS.

Preparing for Full Content Management

At this stage, your preparation is directly relevant to the planning and implementation of a full CMS.

- ▶ *Change processes.* As with earlier stages, you should continue to refine and evolve your change management processes. By now, they should be in a form that could easily be translated into a workflow to automate them.
- ▶ *Single content repository.* It is now time to begin the large task of migrating and reformatting all your content and storing it in a single content repository, which should be a relational or object database or an XML structure. Unifying your content into a single source like this will help you enormously in managing all your content (with all the advantages of "create and update once, publish many"), and it will make the transition to a full CMS much quicker and easier when it happens.
- ▶ *Web-based content capture.* Now that you have a database underpinning the content of the site, you should provide form interfaces to the content allowing content authors and contributors to submit and edit content online. Use client and server side form validation and content parsing techniques to help enforce consistency and standards in how content is created. Introduce basic editorial processes to ensure that all submitted content is properly checked before going live, even if this is just a check box that needs to be ticked by an editor before a piece of content can go live. You are on your way toward devising a content collection and management system with attached workflow.
- ▶ *Mix static and dynamic.* Generate both static files, using a batch process, and simple dynamic pages based on unique user history or preferences. You do not need to know who the user is, only that he or she is the same user, which can be adequately accomplished using cookies. This is not yet advanced personalization, which requires richer user profile information, but it is the beginning of matching content to users according to rules. Mixing dynamic and static pages through various page generation techniques will also be helpful preparation for the full CMS.

▶ *Define user segments.* You should have done this already, even for a less advanced site, but now is certainly the time to be defining your user segments, giving them appropriate names and understanding their attributes and how you want to interact and do business with each segment. This thinking must be done before you can really do the more advanced personalization a full CMS is capable of.

▶ *Define your content model.* We discussed what this is and how to do it earlier. Although the deliverable is quite simple in itself, the thought process is less easy, and building consensus and acceptance of a single content model takes time, so you should start now.

▶ *Refine templates.* You should be using templates by now, even if all they are doing is pulling a few elements directly out of the database onto the page. As you move toward increasingly dynamic pages and personalization, however, you will need to refine your templates and build increasing intelligence and rules into them to cope with the growing number of combinations and configurations of content and user. Start the thinking now, again using simple wire frames (black-and-white boxes and line drawings) to outline how content objects will be used in a template.

▶ *Capture metadata.* Once you have defined your content model, you should know what metadata you are going to need. Even if you do not yet use the metadata, you should begin to capture it at the content creation and collection stage. Not only will this give you something practical and real to test your new CMS with, but it will also help get content contributors used to the concepts and practices of metadata. You will learn a lot that will help inform your design of workflow and editorial processes in the coming CMS. Perhaps start by introducing the automatically generated management metadata associated with content objects, such as status, creation date, last edit date, or author, to get content contributors comfortable with this before asking them to manually add further metadata.

6.3.4   The Mature Database Phase

By this stage, you are all but using a CMS, which means that if you have not bought a commercial CMS, you have pretty much built your own. However, even if you come this far just by developing your own content management tools and processes, giving you the features you need, it may still be necessary to migrate to a commercial CMS to give you the robustness, scalability, and out of the box advanced features that you increasingly require. Equally, you may no longer wish to support and develop your own in-house CMS, even if this is possible, preferring rather to outsource these efforts to someone else.

By this stage, the site itself is clearly a core business channel, no doubt with transactional capabilities and other systems integrated with it. Content is published not just to a Web site but also through other interactive channels such as mobile phones or even TV. In the most advanced cases, the system will be supplying content to offline publication channels as well. Producing and managing multilingual and international versions of the content often become a key focus at this stage. Whereas earlier stages have seen a shift from no system and no control to a central system with all the control, it is now desirable to have a centralized platform but localized control and content ownership.

Development Environment

The development team has grown to more than 10 people, and the number of content assets is likely to exceed 10,000. The most noticeable difference, however, is that the development environment is becoming increasingly distributed. There may be a core team, but this is supplemented by freelance specialists from time to time, who may be working from home, and satellite development teams, who may be distributed around the world to cater to local versions of the site. It becomes increasingly important to have tools and processes to manage communications and work in this distributed, and yet still collaborative, development environment. Different time zones add to the challenges. Virtual project management tools and extranets with work management features such as task queuing, approvals management, discussion threads, and file sharing can help.

The technical infrastructure will have become more complex as well. The demands for system availability will have risen sharply as the site has become increasingly important as a business channel, meaning redundancy needs to be built into the system. If localized versions of the site are being created and maintained in foreign countries by development teams based there, then further development environments need to be set up, and they may even require their own dedicated servers to serve their version of the site to acceptable performance levels in that region of the world. Keeping all systems in synch and maintaining a centralized management control, and yet localized content ownership, become a considerable challenge.

Content Management Tools

The tools in use at this mature stage of the database phase are the same in concept, and often in practice, as employed with a full CMS. It is merely a question of degree and sophistication. It is also possible that as your in-house tools have grown organically and haphazardly to meet needs as they arose, you have a disparate collection of nonconsistent tools that could benefit from the uniformity brought by a CMS developed as a single product.

It is likely that your content management tools will be quite advanced in terms of content capture and maintenance. You will probably also have well-developed workflow, templating, versioning, and rollback. The areas that are likely to benefit most from a full commercial CMS are features for helping automate the structured acquisition and syndication of content; features for automating the conversion and reformatting of content; more advanced analytics and reporting capabilities; improved multiplatform publishing; more advanced forms of personalization and business rule management; and easier integration with other systems. Although these are all things that you could do yourself if you have managed to come this far, you have to ask yourself whether it is worth doing and having to support the system.

By this point, the tools will be of less interest than the processes and the actual content itself. Of course, the actual content should always be of primary importance because this is what attracts users to a site and keeps them coming back, but until this point, you have needed to focus on building tools to manage the content adequately. Now that you have most of what you need in place, you should have more time to focus on improving the processes throughout the content life cycle and ensuring you are deriving the greatest possible value out of your content. This will include looking at ways that you can exchange data more efficiently with other systems and ways to reuse, repackage, and even resell your content to milk its value.

Preparing for Full Content Management

Although you might be almost there in terms of a full CMS, the following are some areas you might want to refine:

▶ *Workflow.* You should now be able to implement workflow, even if not to a fine level of granularity or complexity. What have been change processes to date can now mostly be automated and made more efficient using workflow. If there are things you would like to be able to do in terms of workflow that you have not had the time or resources to develop yet (e.g., more advanced trigger and alerting functions between tasks or more advanced reporting features), keep a wish list. It will be useful when defining your detailed CMS requirements.

▶ *Templates.* You will have been using templates for quite some time by this stage, but there may be more you can helpfully do in preparation for migrating to a full CMS. The more that you can separate content and presentation, the easier the migration will be. For example, if your navigation is not yet automatically generated (whether via a batch process or on demand), you should make it so. If you are currently maintaining different content and systems for different target platforms, you should be looking instead to develop templates for each platform that can work from a single content source.

▶ *Content structure.* Although you may have your content management tools at quite an advanced stage by now, there is no doubt more that you can be doing to improve the value, quality, and consistency of your content. For example, you might want to standardize your content around XML and define an enterprise-wide document type definition (DTD) that sets rules to help enforce a standard content structure. You might want to work with customers, suppliers, and partners to standardize content structures to make data interchange more efficient. If you have not already gone multichannel and multiplatform, you can begin to define the metadata you will require to publish your content in these new forms.

▶ *Personalization.* There are endless opportunities here. You can experiment with different forms of personalization and evaluate which are most effective both for the customer and your organization. Again, keep a wish list of the personalization you would like to be able to do, or the ways in which you would prefer to do it, to help inform your CMS selection process.

▶ *Reporting and analysis.* Now is a good time to focus on really understanding how both site users and system users are interacting with the content and the system. This intelligence is invaluable in informing the definition of your requirements of a CMS. If you are planning a site overhaul as part of the migration to the new platform, a thorough understanding of current usage will also be extremely useful.

▶ *Systems integration.* The larger your site gets and the more core it becomes to the business, the more it will become integrated into the fabric of everything that goes on within the business. And that means there will always be more systems integration work to be done. Bearing in mind a possible migration to a new CMS platform, you should ensure all integrations are properly documented and use open standards in any connector code.

▶ *Content migration plan.* Do an audit of all the content you are currently managing in your system and the structures that it adheres to. Assuming you are going to migrate all this content into a new, single platform, what needs to be done? What work will need to be done on the existing content to give it a unified structure and access methods? You may not yet have defined your final content model, but you should be able to start planning basic content migration tasks. Failing that, it will still be useful to audit and document what you have.

▶ *CMS project.* If you are planning to buy a full CMS, or to significantly enhance your existing system to give it full CMS capabilities, it is time to start a CMS project. The steps involved in this are detailed in the next chapter, Tackling a Content Management Project.

6.3.5 Full CMS

3. Full CMS

By this stage, your content creation, collection, management, and publishing processes should be unified under one CMS platform. However, the CMS is quite possibly only one piece of a much larger jigsaw that includes all sorts of other enterprise systems networked together, exchanging data, content, and functionality.

Development Environment

There are likely to be several distributed development teams in multiple geographical locations with tens, if not hundreds, of developers in total. Likewise, the number of content assets being managed is likely to be in the tens, if not hundreds, of thousands. The trend toward centralized system configuration, maintenance, and management but localized content creation and control continues.

Content Management Tools

The entire suite of tools available as part of a CMS is now available. Depending on how advanced your site was in the database phase before migrating to a full CMS, this may mean you have a whole load of new tools at your disposition or it may just mean the same tools but, ideally, within a more unified and consistent environment. Many commercial CMSs include more advanced features, functions, and tools that are bundled with the fundamental content collection, management, and publishing tools. These might include digital rights management (DRM) tools to help manage and protect the intellectual property value of your content; more advanced syndication tools to help manage the way content is shared between your site and others; analytics tools to gain further insight and intelligence into your site's users and the way they are interacting with the site's content; community functions such as discussion forums, polls, or email lists; marketplace features for the exchange of goods, services, or information; customer service tools to help manage and improve the way your organization interacts with customers and deals with their inquiries; advanced personalization tools, such as collaborative filtering; and merchandising tools to help promote, cross sell, and up sell products.

As you can tell, at this stage the lines between a CMS, an e-commerce platform, a personalization engine, an electronic customer relationship management (CRM) platform, and many other sorts of systems become increasingly blurred. Each offers elements of what the other can do, and ongoing consolidation in the vendor marketplace—with e-commerce platforms buying CMS vendors, and vice versa—means the lines will continue to blur. It is unlikely that there will ever be a single solution that does everything you need, or it will be prohibitively expensive, so some systems integration work is inevitable.

Content Management in Action

Now that you have a CMS, what are you likely to be concentrating on? Following are some ideas for evolving the CMS (more details are in the next chapter):

▶ *Training and education.* Clearly, a big part of the ongoing success of a content management system is to ensure that everyone knows what it is, how it works, and how to use it. Different users are going to require different types and levels of training. Senior management and commercial and business teams can benefit from more educational workshops, even if they are not operationally involved with the CMS.

▶ *Documentation.* Not least to aid with training, you need to keep your documentation up to date. This includes not only system documentation and project documentation but also the guides that are required on a day-to-day basis: editorial and content submission guidelines, details of workflow processes, template guidelines, and explanations of what metadata to add and how.

▶ *Maintenance.* Once your CMS is up and running, you clearly need to maintain it, so you should have a plan in place to cover maintenance issues such as disaster recovery, backups, security, technical support, issue resolution processes, logs and reporting, monitoring and alert functions, archiving or deleting old data, and service-level agreements.

▶ *Migration.* Although you now have a CMS, it is quite possible that you also have other systems running concurrently whose content or functionality needs to be migrated and subsumed by the new CMS. For example, you may have a print publishing system that you would like to replace with the CMS, although this may take some time to do. Rather than migrating an existing system "into" the CMS all at once, think about using the CMS to gradually take over the tasks of the existing system until one day the CMS can do it all. For example, you might use just the content repository of the CMS at first and continue to collect and publish content using an existing system.

▶ *Localization.* You may have your CMS working fine for publishing content in one language or for one country, but if you work for a large international organization, it is likely that localized versions of the site, or completely separate sites, will be required, each with their own development groups, workflows, and content creation processes.

▶ *Content authors.* Content authors can be your biggest ongoing challenge. Depending on the nature of the content and the individual author, you may find content authors to be the least technically savvy and most opposed to changing their content creation process and working tools. It is likely that you will spend quite some time refining the way that content authoring and collection happens, working with an increasing number of authors, each with his or her own way of working.

▶ *Content conversion.* Just as content authoring is a time-consuming and very human process, content conversion can also be very time-consuming, but should be as nonhuman as possible. Now is the time to optimize the ways in which you acquire and convert content for efficiency.

▶ *Integration and multiplatform publishing.* The work of integrating other systems with the CMS is unlikely to stop. Equally it is likely that the CMS will be called upon to publish to increasing numbers of platforms and through multiple channels. Expect this to form a large part of your work in evolving the CMS.

▶ *Customer relationship management.* Not forgetting the actual end users of your published content, you should expect there to be an increasing focus on using the CMS as a tool to build and strengthen relationships with customers. Building increasingly refined user segments, improving personalization and customer service, building communities, and offering user-to-user services are likely to feature strongly.

▶ *Plug-in enhancements.* Although your CMS may be feature-rich, there may be some areas where specialist tools that plug-in to the CMS can deliver benefits. Examples include the digital rights management software mentioned earlier or tools to help structure unstructured data.

Tackling a Content Management Project

Previous chapters have looked at the need for content management, the key concepts and building blocks as well as details of content management systems, and how a site might typically evolve toward a CMS. But how do you actually tackle a whole content management project? What are the key stages and deliverables? This chapter looks at how you might tackle a full project to plan, implement, and integrate a CMS solution, concentrating on what you need to do at each stage and what the deliverables are.

Although there are different levels and complexity of content management systems available, we are assuming for the purposes of this chapter that a fairly large-scale, fully featured solution is being sought. Not everyone will be looking for a solution on this scale, but at least most of the considerations will be covered and can always be scaled down or cut for smaller projects.

Figure 7.1 presents a method for tackling entire Web projects. These four phases and eight work stages constitute the framework for Web project management that I explain in much more detail in my first book, *Web Project Management: Delivering Successful Commercial Web Sites.* I use this same

Phase 1			Phase 2			Phase 3	Phase 4
Preproduction			Production			Maintenance	Evaluation
Project clarification	Solution definition	Project specification	Content	Design and construction	Testing, launch, and handover	Maintenance	Review and evaluation

Figure 7.1 The four phases and eight work stages of a typical Web project.

framework to shape how you would tackle a content management project. This is not in order to force you to buy my first book (although it will be helpful for anyone who is familiar with my proposed method to integrate content management into their project planning) but rather to show how content management could be tackled as part of an overall Web project life cycle. If your content management project is a stand-alone one, which is not part of a wider initiative, you can still use this approach, albeit in an accelerated manner. You will notice that I use this same project framework for Chapter 18, Tackling a Web Site Measurement Project.

NOTE   **Web Project Management Fundamentals**

My first book, *Web Project Management: Delivering Successful Commercial Web Sites*, goes into more detail on Web project management covering topics such as budgeting, scheduling, resourcing, critical paths, milestones, team management, testing, documentation, change control, and risk management. These are not addressed in detail in this chapter; instead, the focus is on the process, what work needs to occur at each stage, and what the deliverables are. Some elements you will recognize as being generic to most projects; others are specific to the needs of a content management project. ∎

7.1 Project Clarification

During this work stage, you focus most on really understanding what it is you want to achieve and why. We are assuming that there is an overall business strategy in place and, indeed, a content management strategy. This would contain the business justification for starting on the project in the first place, and you should be able to draw on much of the work and thinking done there. This work stage is also often referred to as the *discovery phase,* and it includes the "requirements gathering" work typical of other large software integration projects.

NOTE **Content Management Is a Strategic Issue**

Hopefully, having read this part of the book, you will realize that content management is powerful and valuable as well as complex and challenging. It is not something to be undertaken lightly and is worthy of serious strategic consideration involving the most senior figures in a business. Content management is important enough for such high-level involvement for the following reasons:

► It is expensive and will take up a lot of management time and company resources. For this reason alone, it must be done properly and with the blessing of those at the top.

► It touches all parts of the organization. Content management and a CMS are not just the concerns of the technology department or the marketing team. They require input and ongoing commitment from all areas of the business to succeed, and this will only happen if driven by senior management.

► It affects how your customers see you. Customers are any company's most valuable asset and therefore are of extreme importance. The quality of your Web site in terms of what content management can do for it (more up-to-date content, fewer errors, more relevant content, improved functionality, and content retrieval) has a direct bearing on your customers' impression of your company.

► It is a tool for increasing competitive advantage. Content management can help increase efficiencies, allowing resources to focus on improving quality to stay ahead of the competition.

► It affects working practices. Content management involves a lot of processes that affect working practices. Workflow, for example, is a means of managing work through automated processes. There is likely to be some degree of change to the way people work. This can only be achieved if supported from the top.

► The content model is the strategic blueprint for the company. The content model, with its structure of information axes, categorization, indexing, and metadata, is at the heart of any CMS. It is the engine that not only drives the collation, management, and publishing of content to a site, but also provides the framework for personalization, analytics, and reporting, which become of increasing importance in the war for competitive advantage. Thus, it is extremely important to get right. Yet it is very tough to define within the organization. Why? Because it is a distillation of everything that the company is, understands about itself, and wants to be. The architecture may be defined by customer segments, by content types, by business units, by country, or by product lines. Who is to decide? Who can decide what is effectively the blueprint for the company now and in the future? Only the most senior figures in a business can make or ratify the content model.

7.1.1 Project Sponsors

Decide who are going to be the sponsors of your project. Ideally, these should be a combination of people with relevant experience and senior decision-making authority. The more areas of the business that the sponsors represent, the better. This will help build that all-important consensus and commitment across the organization.

7.1.2 Project Team

Identify who will form part of the project team, their level of commitment, their role, and their responsibilities. Identify also broader project stakeholders who may not be directly involved in the project. Again, try to ensure there are representatives from across the business. All your initial project planning work and certainly this project clarification work stage should be done by the core project team. Whereas the sponsor's role is to provide the senior support and organizational commitment to the project, the project team is there to ensure the project itself is properly planned, managed, and implemented.

7.1.3 Project Mission

Briefly articulate the goals and success criteria for the project. This is your mandate to get project buy in and commitment. Make sure that your success criteria are clearly defined and can be properly measured.

7.1.4 Organization Interaction Plan

It is important that your project gets off to a good start. It is also important that you do not waste the time of members in the organization. Create a plan for how you want to interact with the organization: Who do you need to talk to and why? What are you going to ask them? How much of their time do you need and when? Get your project sponsors to ratify this plan. They will know better which boats not to rock.

7.1.5 Audits

To plan how best to move forward with your content management project, you need to clearly and fully understand what has been achieved so far and the state of readiness within the organization for content management. The following are the principal areas to concentrate on:

▶ *Readiness.* This is a more cultural gauge of to what degree the organization is ready to embrace content management. By talking to stakeholders across the business, you should get a feel for the levels of support and interest that exist, the issues and problems there currently are that might be addressed through improved content management, and the willingness to change working practices. You should gather together and document any previous work conducted in an effort to improve the way content is created, collected, managed, and published throughout the organization. You might even come across pilot projects or prototypes that have already been created.

▶ *Content and functionality.* You should audit what content and functionality of value exist within the business and how they are currently managed and used. Document both the details of this content, as exemplified by Figure 7.2, and any content structures, information flows, or maps that chart the way in which content moves through the organization and is categorized. You should also document existing editorial or workflow processes governing the way in which the content production and publishing are controlled.

▶ *Users.* If there is an existing system of some sort in place, document who the current users of the system are and their roles and responsibilities. Perhaps more important, you should audit the business' current understanding of who the target users are, broken down into segments, including each user segment's attributes and needs. This knowledge may not exist at a very granular level of segmentation but find out at least what has been done and what customer intelligence already exists.

Content ID	Content name	Priority	What is the purpose of the content?	Where is it?	What format?	What volume?	What file size?	Who is the content owner?	What is the process for creating the content?	Who are the end users of the content?
1	Press releases	High	Communicate company activities to the press, investors, and other interested parties	Stored as files on E: network drive in "PR" directory	Word documents and RTF files	There are about 200 press releases dating back over 10 years	Around 40KB per press release as a Word document	PR manager (name)	Press releases created either by PR agency or in house then reviewed, edited, and approved by PR manager and relevant buiness unit manager. All done by email with attachments.	Journalists, analysts, investors, customers, other interested parties

Figure 7.2 Example content audit details.

▶ *Localization.* Find out how much work has been done to create localized sites for different regions or target users. Document how this localization is currently managed in terms of systems, people, and processes. This will become useful later if you are planning to create and manage localized sites using your CMS.

▶ *Management information.* In your travels, you will no doubt find out what tools and processes exist for providing management with information on business and systems performance to aid decision making. Keep track of what management information (MI) capabilities already exist and what they deliver so that when you come to choosing your CMS, you can make sure its capabilities complement and enhance those already in place.

▶ *Systems.* What systems are currently used? What technology is used? What architecture, networking, security, platforms, and browsers are already in place?

7.1.6   Requirements Gathering

The most important thing about requirements gathering is to get as many people involved as possible, particularly any eventual end users of the system you will be developing or anyone else directly affected by what you will be doing. It matters less that you end up with a whole host of varied requirements because they can always be prioritized and trimmed. It is more important that people feel you are taking their particular requirements into account instead of guessing what they might need or, worse, ignoring them. In some ways, the actual process of gathering the requirements is more important than your final requirements. The requirements will change and evolve quite a bit over time, but if you do not get off to a good start with the wider organization, the project will falter and possibly fail.

Even though the requirements may change, it is important both to prioritize them and to have them formally signed off. Both the prioritization and approval should be done by those giving the requirements (most likely business units) so that you can understand what they feel most strongly about. Once you have all the requirements, you can then begin to prune and shape them with the inevitable compromises that occur. The main areas for requirements gathering are described next.

▶ *Business requirements.* These are the commercial requirements that you are likely to get from people such as senior managers, marketing and sales

teams, strategists and business analysts, and financial and legal representatives. The business requirements define what the project and system
must be able to do, or not do, to meet the needs of the business in line with
the strategy. For example, if you are a newspaper publisher, your business
requirements would likely include the ability to handle very high volumes
of content publishing with advanced workflow capabilities to suit the editorial process and a well-featured content creation and authoring environment to allow for large numbers of widely distributed content contributors
with very different ways of working. However, if your business focus was
more about selling products online, then your requirements for the project
might center more around enabling advanced online merchandising and
integration with stock control and inventory systems. Other business requirements might include legal constraints, multilingual capabilities for future expansion, management information reporting features, training, and
levels of postsale service and support.

▶ *User requirements.* In this case, *user* refers to a system user as opposed to
an end site user. These users will include members of the content contribution and editorial team, system administrators, developers, and management information specialists. It is extremely important to make sure
that you fully understand user requirements if the system is to have any
chance of actually being used. You should find out who the actual users of
the system will be and talk to them. What is their level of technical expertise? How many of them are there? How do they work? What skills do they
have? Where are they based? What technologies does their working environment support? Once you have understood the current environment,
find out from the users how they would prefer to work. What would make
their lives easier and their work more efficient and productive? What levels
of technology might they be comfortable with? What tools would they prefer to work with? How do they prefer to communicate with each other?
Would it help to be able to work more remotely? Clearly, there will be discrepancies between what one user wants in contrast to another as you collect individuals' requirements, but these can be ironed out or catered to
once you have the overview of all user requirements.

▶ *Content requirements.* This is less an inventory of what content currently
exists (this should already have been done as part of the content and functionality audit) and more what content is required to meet the goals set
out. This is the domain of the editorial team, although they should be
working closely with the marketing and commercial people. Requirements

for the process by which content is created and published should also be included. Questions to ask include: What content must you deliver to meet your users' needs? Who is needed to create this content or how will you otherwise acquire it? What different formats of content (text, video, audio, streaming, PDFs) will you need to manage? Do you have any particular requirements to archive content or have it auditable in any way? What publishing procedures do you want to follow? Who authorizes the content to go live? What current or future multilingual capabilities are required?

► *System requirements.* These requirements will define hardware, software, and other technical infrastructure and environment choices. The IT department will be responsible for maintaining the system so they should input most into the requirements. Questions to ask include: What existing systems will you need to integrate with? What technical, hardware, and software standards do you adhere to? What development environment do you require? What performance levels do you expect? How scalable does the system need to be? Are there any special security considerations or requirements? What measurement tools and reporting do you expect? What levels of caching and cache management do you require? What system administration and maintenance tools are required? What deployment architecture must the system work within?

► *Localization requirements.* You should conduct the same requirements analysis and gathering for each locality that you intend to support, working with the local teams or local users. The complexity of localization can vary from straightforward translation or alternate currency displays to a site that has its own structure, content model, and templates. Depending on the number of localities and the degree of variance from the main site, you may wish to run each locality as a separate subproject with its own team that is nonetheless integrated with the overall efforts.

7.1.7   Change Management

Having spoken to members of the organization about their requirements and your project, you will have a much clearer appreciation of how far content management is actually understood within the organization. Being a relatively new discipline, there are probably large gaps in knowledge and some resistance to the change it will bring. Ignorance risks damaging the project, whereas if people feel they are learning and being involved in the process, you have a greater chance of their commitment.

To manage the changes that will occur, you should draw up a change management plan, a large part of which will involve educational initiatives such as introductory training in content management concepts and then more specific training related to the system later in the project. Make sure in particular that this change management work stream embraces senior management who are not directly involved in the content management project because it will help heighten organizational awareness of what you are trying to achieve and engender more interest and commitment.

7.1.8   Risks and Issues

As you go, keep a list of risks that you fear might impact the project, with suggested ways to avoid the risks, and issues that are already impacting the project and need resolution. You may find this list is very long near the beginning of the project because all sorts of organizational pain bursts to the surface as you talk to more people. Do not bear all this pain yourself. Document it and discuss it with the project sponsors at review meetings.

7.1.9   Initial Project Plan and Budget

Create a Gantt chart with tasks, milestones, timings, dependencies, and resources as far as you can. Also draw up cost estimates. Neither will be comprehensive or fully accurate, especially for later stages of the project, but you will refine the plan as you go. Try to ensure that at least your short-term plan is as accurate as possible, which should be feasible. This will allow senior management to commit to budgetary decisions at least for the initial stages. It will also make people take you, and the project, more seriously.

7.1.10   Deliverables

The deliverables for the project clarification work stage, based on the work described, are as follows:

▶ Project brief (including details of project sponsors, the project team, and project mission)
▶ Organization interaction plan
▶ Content management status report (including audits and readiness assessments)
▶ Requirements document

▶ Change management plan
▶ Risks and issues document
▶ Initial project plan and budget

7.2   Solution Definition

This work stage involves thinking through and defining the best solution to your needs and requirements that, by the end of the project clarification work stage, you should be clear on. Although the solution definition work stage may not take as long as the actual implementation or involve as many people full time on the project, it is nonetheless perhaps the most important work stage and the one that requires the most intensive thinking, planning, collaboration, and iteration. It is both conceptual and practical in nature and requires a real blend of skills to get right: commercial, technical, marketing, and editorial across the business.

If you get this part right, the rest may still be a lot of work, but then you are just carrying out what you have planned at this stage. The temptation is to curtail the solution definition work stage, or gloss over thorny problems, to move on to the later work stages that seem to produce more tangible results: actual specifications, prototypes, interfaces, working models, hardware, and software. Hard as it is, you should try to resist this temptation to rush on. If you have not thought things through properly at this early stage, they will come back to haunt you in a bad way later on, and the cost and time implications could be nasty.

7.2.1   Content Model

We discussed the concept and importance of the content model at the beginning of Chapter 5, Key Concepts and Building Blocks. It is not easy to reach consensus on what this overarching content model should be, and unfortunately, there is little alternative other than to openly discuss and constructively debate until agreement is reached. Earlier, we described the content model as resembling a matrix, rather than just a hierarchical tree—so what are the axes of this matrix that you need to define to build your content model?

▶ *Content classes.* This axis is more hierarchical within itself because you need to define a name and description for each content class, then drill down to define permitted data elements of each class and, finally, at the lowest level, the element types (management or display) and allowed element values.

▶ *Metadata axes.* These are overarching metadata structures, and there can be any number of them, each representing and enabling a different view or slice of your content. As discussed earlier, these axes might be based around structuring attributes such as user groups, product groups, topic, type, distribution channel, or location.

NOTE   **Deciding on Your Content Classes and Metadata Axes**

Although it is not necessarily the case that your content classes will exactly match your site map (i.e., content sections in a navigational hierarchy as experienced from an end user's point of view), they often do, and your site map is as good a place to start as any when deciding what your content classes should be.

If you do not have a site map yet, or are unclear of the process behind creating one, I would suggest a two-pronged approach to classifying and organizing your content: one business-driven and the other user-driven. Start with the business-driven approach by canvasing opinions within the organization as to how they see the content should be organized into "buckets" of content that make sense to them. Settle on names for the content sections as well as their hierarchy. Then ask end users what they would expect to find on the site in terms of content and how it would be best organized and named to suit them. *Card sorting* is a great technique at this stage. Put the names of all your individual content sections on cards and lay them out in no particular order or structure and ask users to group them and assign headings to the groupings as makes sense to them.

The results of this two-pronged approach should help clarify the best way to group your content into classes. You may find that the classes the business needs to sensibly and effectively manage the content are not the same as the navigational hierarchy users require. Or the classes are the same as the navigational content sections, but they need to be named differently to make sense to the business on one hand and users on the other. As you can imagine, the closer the two are in both structure and naming, the easier your life will be.

The metadata axes are easier to define inasmuch as they are for management purposes. The axes are defined by what is needed to manage the content in the way you require to do the things you want to do. So if you want to personalize by content topic, then you need to know what content topic each content object belongs to; if you want to be able to apply workflows to content objects based on their status, you need to have content object status metadata. ■

You should capture information on your content classes and metadata axes using a spreadsheet or database tables, but it is helpful to use wire frames to show the details. Wire frames are simple black-and-white diagrams, easily done in tools like PowerPoint, that allow you to mock up pages and show data elements, and how they relate, more diagrammatically. These can then be discussed and modified on paper, iterated electronically, and then used to help define content capture screens, templates, and database schemas. The advantages of wire frames are that they are easy and cheap to create, require no special tools to update, and are easy for everyone to understand and collaborate on. Furthermore, they are useful prototypes for the Web forms that will need to be created further into the project.

Let us take the earlier e-consultancy example. There are various content classes: white papers, e-business solution providers, quiz questions, glossary terms, forum posts, and events. These content classes are given a unique name, ID, and description. We then need to define the permitted data elements of each class and the element types (management or display) and allowed element values. Using the wire frame technique, and taking the e-business solution providers content class as an example, we might come up with the wire frame shown in Figure 7.3. You can see how this then translates to the final Web form shown in Figure 7.4, which allows the content to be input into the CMS and then managed and updated.

What the wire frame does not show adequately are the data elements names and their allowed values. Consistent naming and consistent validation are important, so this information needs to be defined as part of your content model and should be captured within your spreadsheet or database as exemplified in Figure 7.5.

7.2.2   User Segments and Personalization Rules

For more details on how to understand and segment your users, and create personalization rules, refer to Part III, Customer Relationship Management, particularly Chapter 9, Understanding Your Users, and Chapter 10, Personalization.

Understanding and segmenting your user base are very valuable exercises even if you do not plan to use the segments within your CMS. But if you plan to do any kind of personalization, more advanced user-centric reporting, or targeting marketing, then understanding your users by segment is a prerequisite. Personalization is a process of matching content to users via rules. Once you have your content model defined, it is clear what chunks or slices of content you will have at your disposal to serve up. Understanding and segmenting your user base to create a user model are the same idea, and very similar processes, as creating a content model, only you are dealing with people, not content. Once you can "slice and dice" your user base and content base, you have all the ingredients to be able to dynamically mix and match the

E-business Solution Provider Content Class

Display Data

Company name	(Text field)	**URL**	(Text field)
Address	(Text field)	**Email**	(Text field)
	(Text field)	**Postcode**	(Text field)
Region	(Drop down) ▼	**Telephone**	(Text field)
Clients	(Text area with clients comma separated or on separate line)	**Expertise**	(Text area with areas of expertise comma separated or on separate line)

Description

(Text area)

Office locations	(Text area with office locations comma separated or on separate line)	**Number of staff**	(Drop down) ▼
		Comments	(Text area)
Turnover	(Drop down) ▼	**Project budget**	(Drop down) ▼
Comments	(Text area)	**Comments**	(Text area)

Management Data

Comments	(Text area)
Keywords	(Text area with keywords comma separated or on separate line)

Industry sectors

Communications	☐ ☐	Energy
Property	☐ ☐	Health Care
Public Sector	☐ ☐	Financial Services
Manufacturing	☐ ☐	Digital Services
General	☐ ☐	Retail Consumer Products
Other	☐	

Functional disciplines

Advertising	☐ ☐	Branding
Content	☐ ☐	Design/Usability
Fulfillment/Logistics	☐ ☐	General
Hardware	☐ ☐	Interactive Digital TV
Legal	☐ ☐	Marketing
Other	☐ ☐	Programming
Project Management	☐ ☐	Public Relations
Recruitment	☐ ☐	Reporting & Statistics
Rich Media	☐ ☐	Security
Site Hosting	☐ ☐	Software
Strategy	☐ ☐	Training
Funding	☐ ☐	WAP/Mobile Internet
Venture Capital		

Set review date	(Text field)
Set auto-archive date	(Text field)
Status	● Live on site ○ Pending approval ○ Archived

Record last modified by	[Name]	**Last modified date**	[Date]
Record created by	[Name]	**Creation date**	[Date]

Figure 7.3 Wire frame showing data elements and types within a content class.

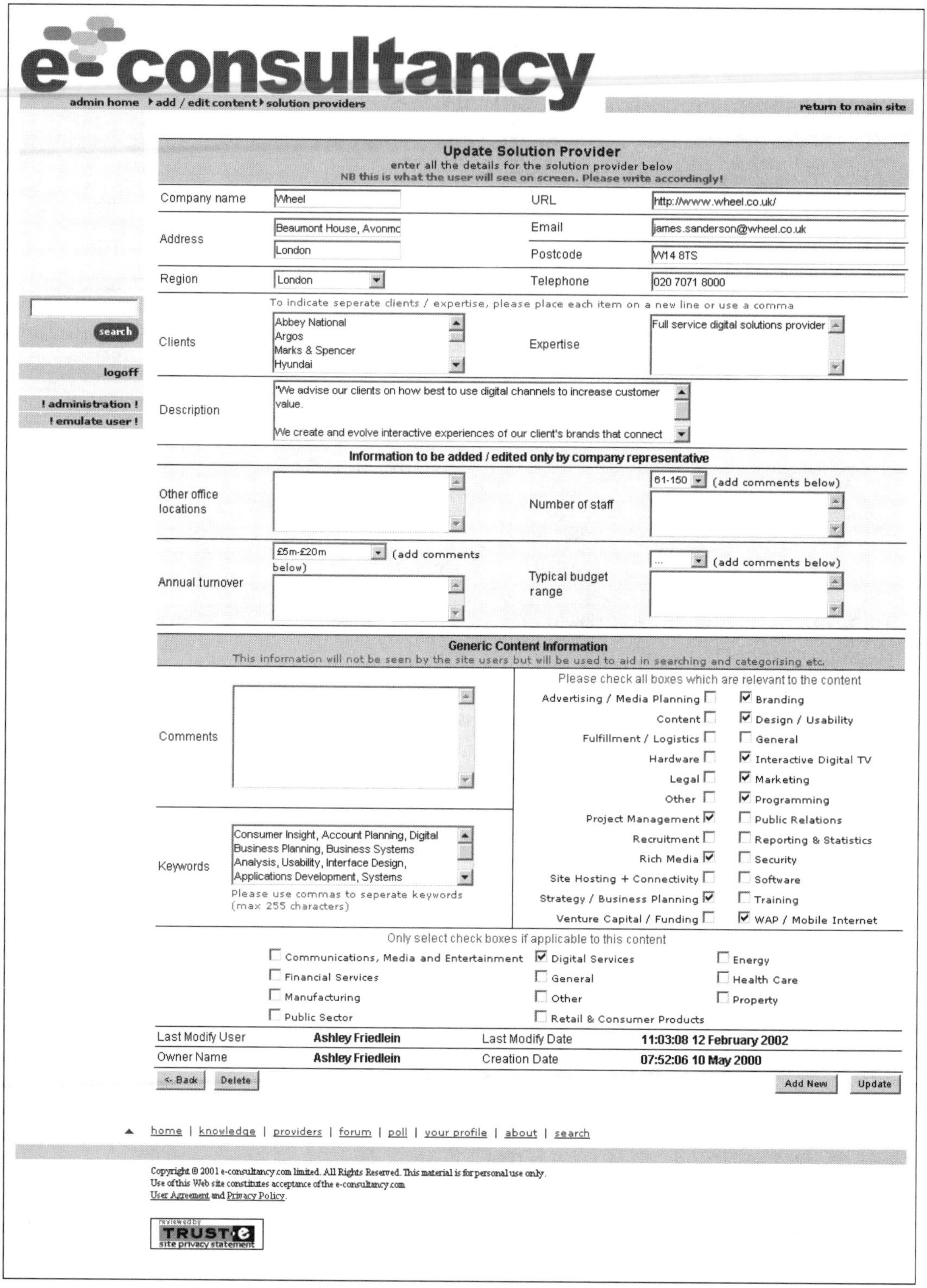

Figure 7.4 Web form for collecting and managing a content object.

Content Class ID	Content class name	Data element name	Data element type	Permitted values	Validation
CC3	Providers	email	Display	Free text limited to X characters long	Check for well formed e-mail address (something@something.something)
CC3	Providers	region	Display	Drop-down box choices defined by database table: London, Northeast, Midlands, Southeast, Northwest, Southwest, West, South	If default selection "London" is selected, check that the telephone field begins "020". If not show alert: "Are you sure that this company is based in London?"
CC3	Providers	review_date	Management	Date format DD/MM/YYYY	Check for well-formed date format

Figure 7.5 Content model data elements, values, and validation.

two together. Once you have your content and user model, you should then define the personalization rules that you intend to use in the CMS to bring the two together.

The user audit you conducted during the project clarification work stage will be your starting point for creating a user model and then personalization rules.

7.2.3 Templates and Page Designs

As we discussed earlier in Section 5.7, Templates, there are two types of templates: content capture and page display templates. At this stage, you need to define both. The content capture templates should be straightforward once your content model is defined because they are there to capture the content objects, with all their accompanying elements with correct values. If you have created wire frames as I described earlier to define the elements of each content class, the content capture templates should correspond very closely.

How to define the page display templates is usually a more controversial matter as it involves end users and is interwoven with the page design. This means that graphic designers, brand strategists, and any others who feel a responsibility for getting the look and feel of the site right, which usually means everyone, get involved. Whereas most are happy to leave content capture templates to business analysts, developers, and usability engineers, the content display templates attract everyone's comments, usually not directly but indirectly. People love to comment on page design (the look and feel, images, colors, and fonts), but this has an impact on the content display template design, and vice versa.

TIP	The Balancing Act between Page Design and Template Design

Which should come first? Should you create your content model and then extract pages from it or should you design pages that look good and then work out how to support them via the templates and content model? The latter approach used to be the norm when sites were smaller, less functional, brochureware initiatives. The former approach is increasingly required as solutions become more complex and need to remain manageable. Ideally, you should use a mixture of both approaches and come to a consensus via iterations and constructive debate.

In the past, I have successfully run two parallel work streams at this stage, one of which was very "blue sky creative," focusing very much on tone, feel, and brand, while the other focused on information architecture, templates, logic, and content object analysis. Managing the two and bringing them together into a harmonious union, however, are not always easy and require a multidisciplinary team that works well together with individual members who respect the knowledge and experience of the others.

If you have less time, resources, or a team that you feel will not be able to work together collaboratively, then (assuming you have a site that is moving toward a CMS) I would favor doing the content model first, then the content display template analysis and design, and only then the look and feel design. I would certainly do usability tests on the final page design, which is all that end users see. Does this relegate graphic designers to mere page decorators who just put an "on brand" skin over page content that is dictated to them? Does this rob them of their chance to have a creative vision of what the page should be like? Well, yes and no. Yes, their job is then largely to render defined content elements into a page design that works for the brand, but no, this is not a matter of relegation or robbing them of their creativity. It is an extremely challenging and skilled task where there is still ample opportunity for creativity and finesse within the detail. I do not think designers are best placed to decide what should go on a page, but they are well placed to define how it should go on a page and where and what it should look like.

With your content model in mind, start by using wire frames to create initial content display templates. These should define what content objects will be used within the template and according to what logic. Differentiate between static and dynamic content and make clear what is navigation and what is page content. Do not worry too much about where on the page each of your content elements goes because this is more a question of interface design, which is better addressed by the page designers.

Taking the e-consultancy example we looked at earlier, Figure 7.6 represents what an initial wire frame for the home page content display template

Header
(Logo)

"Breadcrumb" navigation	Site tools (contact, search, site map)

Local section navigation

Standard "quick link" navigation
(Your profile, email services, About)

Search

Admin section navigation

Best of the Forums
Message_Subject, Author, Date, Star_Rating
Message_Content (first 250 characters)
Logic: select a forum post at random but the post must be rated at least three stars or higher on average and must have been made within the last three months. If author has a photo, then display it.

Featured White Paper
White_Paper_Title, Organization
White_Paper_Review (first 130 characters)
Logic: Select any white paper at random

Spotlight on a Provider
Provider_Name, Region
Expertise (first 80 characters)
Clients (first 80 characters)
Logic: Select any provider at random

Today's Quiz Question
Quiz_Question
Logic: Select any quiz question at random

Glossary term of the day
Glossary_Term, Definition (first 130 characters)
Logic: Select any glossary term at random

News feed1
News_Category
News_Headline
News_Source, Date
News_Headline
News_Source, Date
News_Headline
News_Source, Date

Logic: display three most recently updated news headlines

News feed2
News_Category
News_Headline
News_Source, Date
News_Headline
News_Source, Date
News_Headline
News_Source, Date

Logic: display three most recently updated news headlines

Promotional Area

Personalization
(Since last visit: forum rating change, number of new forum posts, number of times your posts have been read, position in the quiz)

Footer
(Links to key site sections, conditions of use, privacy policy link and TRUSTe logo, copyright)

Key to types of content

Static content	Dynamically generated (not on the fly)	Dynamically generated (on the fly)

Figure 7.6 Home page template wire frame.

might look like. Notice how the page elements and logic clearly show an understanding of what the content model is: How else could you know what content elements were there to use on the page? Figure 7.7 then shows the eventual page design version of this template. Note that although the page el-

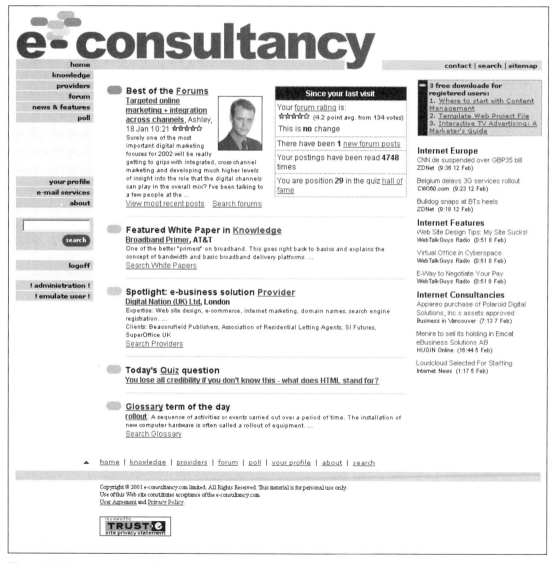

Figure 7.7 Home page page design.

ements, logic, and content elements have not changed, the layout has, and of course, there are design elements such as graphics, fonts, and colors.

Once you have a set of templates such as these, you should create some example content for each that adheres to the rules of the template (e.g., the content should be of the correct length) and brief the page designers who can then see not only how the page works, but now also have some real content to use in their mock-ups. The page designers should have the freedom to move, perhaps even resize, the content elements you have suggested in your template wire frames. They will add the look and feel skin to your bare bones template wire frames, and with some iteration, you will end up with something that fits the brand, is easy to use, looks appealing, and most important, you know your CMS will be able to deliver because the page is based on a template, which is based on your content model. Keep going through this process until you have defined all the templates and page designs you need.

Case Study   **The Development Process from Content Model to Web Page Design**

Company: Wheel, *www.wheel.co.uk*

Company Overview

Wheel Group uses imagination to combine strategy, marketing, and technology to help a broad range of clients use digital channels to communicate with their customers and service them better. Wheel Group's areas of specialist expertise are retail, financial services, entertainment, and luxury goods.

Process and Practice

Obviously, different sites have different objectives based on business and customer needs. However, you might broadly categorize sites into two groups. One group includes sites that have a much more tactical brand and marketing purpose. These might include competitions, games, special promotions, microsites, and similar sites. Simple, static brochureware sites can also be included in this broad group. These types of sites often have

continued

a limited shelf life and are designed to meet a particular purpose for a finite timespan. For these reasons, the maintenance and evolution of such sites are less important. Equally, there is a lower requirement for well-defined processes to support such sites.

The second, much larger group of sites serves longer term strategic objectives. These sites are more complex, perhaps in multiple languages, with a higher volume of content turnover and more contributors. These types of sites are likely to grow in importance. They require processes to optimize efficiency and quality. The larger or more complex these sites get, the greater the requirement for a robust content model, information architecture, and page templating. Without these elements, it quickly becomes uneconomic to maintain and evolve such sites.

Clearly, sites cannot be rigidly classified according to just these groups. Each site will fall somewhere on a continuum between these two poles. However, it is important to realize the difference in approach required as sites gravitate toward one pole or the other.

Two quite different forms of creativity are required when designing pages for these two groups of sites. For the first group, the creativity required is perhaps what is more commonly thought of as creative and focuses most on look and feel, branding, layout, colors, fonts, and so on. The second group of sites requires this too, but there is a further requirement to think creatively about functionality and understand how the front end (the page that the user ultimately experiences) ties in to the back end.

In this latter case, creativity needs to occur with the parameters set by the underlying content model in mind. In this case, there is much creativity required in exploiting the way the presentation layer interacts with the content layer via business logic, templates, and rules. This is not a form of creativity that is solely the domain of an interactive designer but is the joint responsibility of a multidisciplinary Web development team. This kind of creativity requires a fusion of business acumen, customer insight, and an in-depth understanding of the medium and its technology. Unlike the actual design of the point of interface with the end user, most of this creativity is invisible, like the majority of the iceberg that is not seen below the surface.

Assuming we are talking about the second group of sites and assuming you have the right mix of skills in your development team, what is the process to follow in moving from a set of requirements to a designed Web page? We would typically follow these steps:

1. *Business and customer requirements.* We draw up a list of business requirements and customer requirements—that is, things that we know from our customer research work that the customer really wants. We use these to drive our initial conceptualiza-

tion of what the customer offering might be and how this might best be supported on-line.

2. *Audits.* If the first step looks at the requirements in abstraction, at this stage we look through what is actually available and possible given the resources of the project. We do content and functional audits both on any existing client sites and on competitor sites to benchmark best practice. We also audit existing customer behavior through both qualitative and quantitative analysis.

3. *Recommendations.* By mapping the requirements against the audit results, and given project resources, we come up with a set of recommendations for the customer experience, including content and functionality.

4. *Content model and site map.* At this stage, we do not define the final content model, including details of every content object, attributes, metadata, and so on. However, we do start to build a working "skeleton" and a framework that works at a content class level. Closely aligned to this, we also develop the first site map, showing the content sections of the site. This is likely to iterate through the project in its details but not so much in its top-level categories.

5. *Customer journeys.* We then begin to model examples of customer journeys. We use Unified Modeling Language (UML) practices to construct use case scenarios. This is sometimes supported by other techniques such as action/response tables for more precise definitions of the expectations of the system and wire framing of pages in PowerPoint. We begin with the ideal customer journeys (i.e., what we would like the customers to be doing) and then look at the likely most common customer journeys before addressing exceptions, deviations, and less likely routes. At this stage, page content is not defined in detail. What we are ensuring is that the primary routes that will create customer value and serve our clients' business needs are properly thought through and outlined at this stage.

6. *Navigation.* Having mapped out key customer journeys and iterated the content model and site map accordingly, we are now able to define the navigation that will best support the user in achieving his or her goals. At this stage, we define generic navigation and navigation rules, as opposed to specific in-page navigation.

7. *Page content.* Now we really begin to look at every page in detail and define what content, navigation, and functionality will be on each. We typically do this by starting with simple flip charts and a group brainstorm to capture ideas for each page. We then create paper prototypes in PowerPoint and use these as a tool for iteration.

continued

8. *Page templates.* As we become clearer on what content and functionality will be required across a range of pages, we are able to begin defining templates as we can see common content and functions emerging. We then create a set of templates to deliver all pages in the site. We seek to minimize the number of templates without compromising what we are trying to achieve at a specific page level. By the end of this process, we have a set of templates and are also in a position to drill down to the detailed data elements of the content model.

9. *Page design.* Only now is a look and feel applied to the templates and specific pages. Effectively, the skeleton we have developed is now being "skinned" with the brand in question.

Although it may be only at the last step that *graphic* design begins, we see this whole process as being about *interactive* design. Interactive design is needed if you are to successfully deliver the kinds of sites I talked about earlier.

> **Jonathan Hilton**
> Head of Solutions
> Wheel

7.2.4   Content Creation, Migration, and Collection

Once you have defined your content model with all the corresponding classes, objects, and elements, you know what content you will require to fuel the system. The content and functionality audit that you did as part of the project clarification work stage gives you a good idea of what content you currently have at your disposal, who creates it, and how. However, you should take your content classes as the starting point for defining your content creation, migration, and collection solutions. That is, you should begin with what you want to end up with rather than what you currently have. Look at each content class in turn and define how you are going to create, migrate, and collect that content: Create from scratch? Repurpose and migrate what you already have? Syndicate in? For each content class, you will need to drill down to the element level within the content objects as it is likely that different authors will contribute to the same object: Metadata, for example, may be added by someone other than the original content author.

Start your analysis and design going out from the content, but once you have done this, pivot your analysis so that it can be viewed from the content originator's viewpoint. In the e-consultancy example, you would analyze how to create or acquire the content starting with the classes, but you would then pivot this analysis to see which content originators contribute to multiple content objects across the site. It is likely that those adding metadata will do so across all the content classes of a content model for consistency.

There is no particular trick or shortcut to this analysis. You must systematically go through every piece of content and define where it will come from and how it will get into the system in the right format and structure. If you have defined the tone and quantities of each content element, then this will at least help you decide where best to source the content and who would be best suited to create it. Details to consider for content authors or syndication sources include:

▶ *Authors.* Who are the authors and how will they interface with the CMS? What authoring tools will they use? What access levels, permissions, and edit rights will each author have? How will you track system usage and contributions by author?

▶ *Acquired content.* What are the acquisition sources and how will they integrate with the CMS? What data transfer routines are required? How often and when will content be taken into the system? How will you know if the content collection process fails? How will you track what content you have taken from whom? What formats and structures does the content need to comply with?

To complete your content collection solution, you should also define the following:

▶ *Conversion processes.* Based on your knowledge of how content will arrive or exist in its raw form and your knowledge of how you need the content to end up to get it into the system smoothly and efficiently, you should be clear on the gap between the two and the resulting content conversion that needs to occur. Define how this conversion is going to work, both one-off bulk conversion efforts and ongoing processing requirements in terms of reformatting, stripping out unnecessary elements, and adding structure.

▶ *Editorial guidelines.* If you have not already developed editorial guidelines, you should do so now. These guidelines should cover the usual things you might expect to brief an author with (tone, style, target readers, length, format, delivery schedule), but you will also need to develop guidelines for those who are interfacing directly with the system that explain how to do it, how to submit and revise content, how to add metadata, how to structure content, and how to set review dates. These guidelines may not seem editorial at first, more like system help notes, but what is done here does have a direct impact on what content the end user will see and in what context, so I would argue that this is indeed an editorial function. Deciding what content category to assign a content object and when to auto-archive it, for example, requires an editorial style insight into the value, nature, and target user of the content.

Once you have these processes and sources defined, you can then organize them into jobs and tasks that can be governed by your CMS's workflow capabilities.

7.2.5   Workflows

In the content and functionality audit of the project clarification work stage, you should have reviewed and documented existing content management processes. The main purpose of this is less to define the solution to come and more to understand the way the organization works and to get to talk to those who will become actively involved in the end solution. There is nothing worse than enabling a bad process just because that is what is there and because your new system has the ability to do so. As one client once said, that is like "putting lipstick on a bulldog." It is a very poor attempt to make an ugly process look good. Instead you should design your workflows to support your requirements. This may involve using existing processes as a starting point for discussion and refinement, or it may involve starting from scratch.

The focus of workflow is often on the content creation and publishing processes as this is where editorial processes and sequenced tasks are most evident and map most easily into a workflow. However, workflow can equally be applied to any set of tasks related to content management: archiving or deletion processes, producing reports and analyses, testing cycles, system maintenance routines, or data transfer cycles with other systems.

The process for analyzing and designing workflows is as follows:

▶ *Identify candidates for workflow.* During your interaction with the organization, you should easily be able to identify interaction sequences that would benefit from automation. Look for often repeated jobs where a group of people have to work through multistep tasks. Each of these jobs is a candidate for becoming a workflow. Assign each workflow candidate a unique ID and name that you use consistently thereafter.

TIP	Keep Workflows Simple at First

If you are just beginning to implement workflow, keep things simple at first. Focus on automating just a few simple processes. Choose commonly repeated interaction sequences that involve the same few people each time to minimize the complexity of the workflow and maximize the benefits gained. Even if you only save a small amount of time through process efficiencies, this will soon mount up if the process is often repeated. You will learn a lot from these first few workflow implementations, particularly about the people and process side of workflow within the organization, which will be of enormous value as you roll out workflow to other areas of work.

You should also aim not to have workflows with an overly long task chain. The longer the task chain, the more likely a workflow will break down at some point. Workflows with shorter task chains are simpler to understand, implement, test, maintain, and train people on. If necessary, break down an overly long task sequence into several modular workflows that are linked together. These workflow modules can then also be used elsewhere.

▶ *Create an ordered task list for each workflow.* For each workflow candidate identified, create a list of all the tasks that occur to get the job done and then sequence them from beginning to end as a series of linear steps. Give each step a unique ID and name that you use consistently thereafter.

▶ *Assign task details.* Describe each of the tasks in each step. Detail the task owner, task duration, and frequency. Each step may contain multiple or single tasks. If you wish, you can also create a master list of individual tasks, each with its own ID and name, so that you have a hierarchy of workflow > step > task, each fully and individually identifiable.

▶ *Define triggers and transitions.* For each step within the workflow, you should define what needs to happen for a particular step to commence and then what needs to happen for its completion to be signaled for the next step to begin.

▶ *Define notification mechanism for transitions.* Describe how each trigger or transition will be communicated to the next step in the workflow: Email? Verbal? Fax? Phone? Short Messaging Service (SMS)?

▶ *Check integrity of workflows.* At this stage, go back through each of your workflows to ensure there is no way that your process can break down. Have you covered all eventualities and outcomes? In particular, you should look at how your workflow deals with exceptions, rejections, and refused approvals. What happens in these circumstances?

▶ *Iterate workflow with end users.* Once you have your workflow in a state that you think works, you should present it to those who will actually use it to have them test it, question it, and enhance it until, after a few iterations, everyone is happy that the workflow will indeed work.

Figure 7.8 shows how you might use a spreadsheet to capture workflow analysis as has been described. In this example, the step has only one task, as is often the case, but one step could include multiple tasks. Spreadsheets are handy for managing consistent information during the analysis stage, but they are not nearly as powerful as databases when it comes to ordering, filtering, grouping, retrieving, and embedding relationships within information. A spreadsheet will do a reasonable job for a smaller amount of information, but a database is required if you have a lot of workflows, steps, and tasks. Both require the consistent use of IDs and naming to make the most of their capabilities.

Having the details of your workflows, steps, and tasks stored in a spreadsheet or database is great for managing, organizing, editing, and manipulating large amounts of information in one place. However, it can be difficult to understand a single workflow in this form. Once your workflows have been iterated and agreed upon, you should create diagrammatic versions of each to show all the elements in a much more digestible form. As an example, Figure 7.9 is what we looked at earlier when discussing workflow concepts. It shows a workflow with steps, triggers, transitions, task owners, and task durations (the notification means is not shown).

7.2.6 Localization Plan

Localization is the process of creating sites that are specifically targeted at a particular region to reflect the language, business, and cultural requirements of

Workflow ID	Workflow name	Step ID	Step name	Task(s)	Task owner(s)	Task duration	Task frequency	Step trigger	Step notification	Transition trigger to next step	Transition notification
PR001	press release	R001_1	Press release —first draft	Write first draft of press release	Press officer (name)	3 hours	Ad hoc	Request from press manager (name)	Non-automated: verbal or email	New press release content object created	Email sent to editorial team for the addition of metadata to new press release content object

Figure 7.8 Workflow analysis.

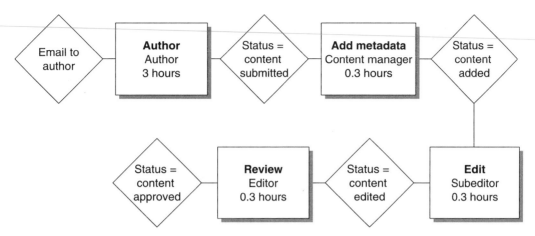

Figure 7.9 An example workflow.

site users from the region. In the vast majority of cases, localization is about creating versions of a Web site to suit users in other countries where the principal requirement is to provide sites in the native language. However, although strictly speaking *locality* must refer to a physical and geographic difference, the process of *localization* is also used to embrace instances where a site needs to be created that caters to particular subsets of users or requirements. For example, a French language version of a site might be considered a localization process, whereas in fact, it is really only translation until it is localized for France, Canada, Madagascar, and any other French-speaking countries.

Ultimately, localization is not about places but about target users. It is just that target users and their needs are often thought of and most easily understood in terms of a country or locality. With the world becoming a global village, with more and more international travel, it will become increasingly important to understand localization as user specific rather than location specific. You can more broadly understand localization as the creation and management of versions of the main site or sites that have some form of interdependence and relationship with the main site.

You may not be planning to deliver Web sites other than for one locality, so a localization plan may not be required, but increasingly, it is localization requirements that are driving the move toward content management systems. Localization very quickly increases the complexity and volume of processes, content, and functionality that need to be managed, and CMSs are seen as a way to ease the pain that often results as organizations confront the alarming growth and complexity of their Web operations. It is certainly the case that a CMS can help, but as stated often already, it is only a tool, and success depends on the quality of the team and the planning behind it. Localization is difficult, painful, and often fails not because of content management problems or an inadequate CMS, but most usually because of internal political problems and organizational structures that throw up walls and barriers against cooperation and progress. This is not the book to tell you how to resolve these people management challenges; rather, we are looking at localization from a content management point of view.

Although translation is the first thing that comes to mind when people think of localization, it is clearly much more than that if you think of how many languages are spoken in lots of very different countries. Over and above language differences, you need to consider the following: cultural and religious differences; the tax regulations and currency of the locality; the way addresses are constructed in the locality (for delivery purposes, your Web forms will need to have different fields accordingly); and the format of dates and times. Furthermore, you need to think about how you are going to provide customer service in the locality (taking into account different time zones among other things), and you must recognize that local business teams are going to want to do promotions, merchandising, and other business activities that are specific to their locale and their customers.

For all these reasons, you might think that only completely separate sites for each locality will work. However, from a business point of view, consistency and shared resources between sites make them easier and more cost effective to deliver and maintain. Even from a user point of view, consistency of look and feel and navigation can be a good thing as the user may like to feel that she is interacting with her one trusted brand wherever she is in the world. This tension between how far to keep things the same versus make them different is at the heart of the localization challenge. To make things easier for yourself, recognize the challenge and begin planning to address it at this early stage even if you do not envision localization being required for initial launch.

During the project clarification work stage, you have gathered your localization requirements. In terms of defining a solution, you now need to look at all these requirements—see how they differ from or are similar to each other and the primary locality—to work out how best to structure and deliver the local versions. Your requirements should give you a good enough indication to help you decide whether your localized versions are significant enough to require dedicated teams, each of which would run its own full project, including a full solution definition work stage as described here. In this case, you must run parallel projects but ensure collaboration, communication, and integration with the primary team, which governs the main site and the CMS itself. If your localization requirements are not significant, you can handle them as part of your main project.

Your localization requirements will tell you what degree of overlap there is between the primary site and localized sites both in terms of content and functionality and also in terms of processes such as workflow. Table 7.1 looks at varying degrees of overlap and the content management implications for each.

TIP   **"Think Global, Act Local"**

Getting the globalization versus localization balance right is hard. On the whole, the more globalized the content, the more generally applicable it is, and the easier it is to create, manage, and publish. At the same time, this means that the content cannot be very specific or targeted to the particular needs of a locality. In trying to be all things to all people, it risks becoming of no genuine interest to anyone. With the multitude of dedicated, specialist sites out there, your content will have no compelling competitive value. There is no perfect answer to this challenge, but what might be the optimal compromise?

In my view, the "think global, act local" approach works well:

▶ All your technology should be standardized and centralized, although there may be server farms that are replicated local versions of the central master system.

▶ Standards for all sites should be defined centrally. This does not mean ignoring local needs; it means working with all localities to come up with a solution that will adequately cover all their various needs. Note adequately, not ideally. Standards should not just include technical standards but also editorial guidelines, brand guidelines, customer service levels, and response times.

▶ As far as possible, all the sites should use the same content model, templates, and navigation mechanic. Think primarily of the user here. If the same user came to the various local site versions, he or she wants to be able to feel at home and part of the same overall organization. Simple things like the links to search, contact us, help, and site map should be in the same place, the navigation should work in the same way, and the content sections should be as consistent as possible even if how they are named varies for the locality.

▶ Give control of the content to local teams. On all aspects, it makes great sense for teams across localized sites to share expertise, knowledge, infrastructure, and

Table 7.1 Content management implications of localization.

Degree of overlap	Content management implications
Very Low Different content, functionality, site structure, navigation, content model, and design.	In this case, it makes sense to share infrastructure, hardware, and software for cost efficiencies, but that is about all. The sites are independent and separate to the degree that it is questionable whether this is a localization at all or just different sites. If the localized site attracts high volumes of traffic or there are very high processing demands, then you may require a local deployment of the infrastructure because a single central system may not be able to cope adequately or serve content and functionality fast enough to end users. Also, if the local team needs a high degree of control and access to the physical infrastructure, a local deployment is required.
Low-Medium The content and site structure vary from the primary site as required, but many of the same templates are used and design, navigation, and other site elements are shared.	The same infrastructure should be used and common resources should be shared to maintain the "publish once, update many" approach that minimizes management work and ensures consistency. The different sites need to be managed through different branches of the system such that there are "Chinese walls" between each, allowing them to be managed as separate projects and entities and yet be part of the same overall system. For example, each will have different workflows as suited to the working practices of the locality, but all will use the same workflow subsystem of the CMS. At this level of overlap, the sites are still distinct enough that you would gain little by tagging content with locality attributes because each piece of content is destined for one locality only.
Medium-High The site structure, navigation, content model, templates, and design are fundamentally the same, but the page content and functionality are all different as required for the locality.	The infrastructure is shared but, most important, so is the content model, which means that the content collection, management, and publishing elements for all sites can be shared. You need to ensure that content and functionality can be tagged with a locality attribute (metadata) at the point of collection so that they can then be managed and published according to processes and rules that suit the locality. For example, you can then define different workflows by locality. The CMS can use the locality attributes of the content to serve the right content to the right local users. Equally, the locality attribute allows content authors and editors to manage content at a local level, working only with the content that is relevant to them.
High Everything is the same except for certain content sections or elements (e.g., pricing), which need tweaking for the relevant locality.	An example of this might be a U.S. site that needs small tweaks for a Canadian localization. The same language is used and most of the content is the same, but some elements (such as pricing and currency) are different. This situation is not dissimilar to the previous one inasmuch as locality attributes in each content object's metadata are the means to manage the localized content, but it is more likely that the content authors and editors will not themselves be local but part of the central team. The level of shared, common content is much higher, and the localizations are small adjustments to this core content, which can probably be done by a single team. Workflows are more likely to be consistent across all content and will be important in reminding the content team to create or update the localized version of a particular content object. If the content object is shared exactly across all localities, then the create or edit work needs to be done only once. If there are local variations, then use workflow to ensure that changes are made to them as well as the master or that versions are created to match the new master.

other resources for efficiency, speed, and quality. I think the content for localized sites, however, must come from a local team. Not only do they best understand the users and the local ways of doing things, but they must take responsibility for the ongoing growth, maintenance, and support of the localized site.

▶ Naming and actual page content should be localized and, ideally, created by a local team that knows the users and their needs. Design elements (not the template itself) such as colors, imagery, and fonts should be localized. So too should workflow, personalization rules, merchandising, marketing, and promotions.

▶ Country level domain extensions such as *.com.au, .co.uk, .fr,* or *.de* should direct users straight to the relevant localized home page, but all site home pages should provide links to the other localized versions. This is particularly true of the *.com* site, which is often used as a doorway or portal to localized sites.

Your localization plan should detail your approach to localization based on your analysis. Will each locality be treated as a separate subproject, each with its own team and each to create its own project specification in collaboration with a core team? Or will you integrate localization requirements within the main project and detail them along with other requirements in a single central specification? You will probably find that there are some elements of localization that are best handled centrally, such as infrastructure, and others that need to be defined locally, such as content creation and workflow.

7.2.7 Reporting and Analysis

Taking your management information audit and business requirements from the project clarification work stage, you now need to define what reporting and analysis your solution will provide. What will your standard reports contain? How often will you deliver them? Who will have access? What format will the reports be delivered in? How will you support reporting? Depending on your desired metrics and reporting, you will require different forms of analysis and corresponding resources and support.

7.2.8 Technology

Based on your systems audit and systems requirements, you are in a position to define more of the desired technology solution without specifying a particular system. Your systems requirements define the environment in which your chosen content management tool must operate: platforms, operating systems, languages, protocols, and network environments. Based on this, you should define an initial systems architecture and proposed integration and configuration solution but not actually choose your software solution at this stage. Once everything is buttoned down in the project specification, you then have the criteria and requirements you need to go through a vendor selection process.

7.2.9   Testing

Define how you are going to test your content management solution once it has been built. You should create a plan that details what process you are going to go through. This should include the usual forms of testing for any software integration or application deployment project (user acceptance testing, scenario and load testing, usability testing, and security and penetration attack testing as appropriate), and you should create sample test routines and scripts.

In particular, you should focus on stress testing and checking that all the points of integration with other systems are working as expected. Real-time personalization, complex templates, and simultaneous authoring and usage greatly increase the pressures on the Web server and demand much more processing power, so you must test the system under increasing loads with all these things going on to check it copes as expected. You may find that the system does not crash, but it might become unacceptably slow to use and functions may begin to time out.

If the system is to tie into other data sources, you will have to pay particular attention to ensuring these function correctly. Again, you may find that there are no obvious errors reported but that in fact the update is not happening at all or the data elements are being mismapped and incorrectly displayed. In your test plan, you must allow enough human testing time (for meaning and sense can only really be tested by humans) and enough time to go through all the dependencies under various load scenarios.

Usability testing is very important for the interfaces that a site's end user navigates, but it is also important that the system itself is easy to use. Allow time in your testing plan to test the interfaces and Web forms that content contributors, editors, and other system users will be using on a daily basis. Indeed, you should include usability testing of this sort throughout your project plan, testing a little as you go, so that the final testing is only small tweaks and not big changes that could derail the project schedule at the last minute.

7.2.10 Deployment and Rollout Plan

A CMS is typically an enterprise application that involves a large number of users and ties into other enterprise systems. This means its deployment and rollout are likely to be complex and take some time, requiring a dedicated plan to manage all the activities that must occur. You need to define when and how the system is going to become operational and how it will be integrated into the organization both from a systems viewpoint and from a working practices viewpoint.

Depending on the size of the project, it is unlikely that everyone who will use the system will immediately be able to do so or that all systems that will eventually integrate with it will simply slot into place. A step at a time, you will need to fully integrate with organizational systems and ensure that all relevant staff can comfortably work with it. This is not just a technical or process challenge but an emotional one. Change must be carefully managed: You should update the change management plan you created as part of the project clarification work stage to specify more of the details around the actual system rollout and what this will mean for each individual. Training will obviously be a large part of this change management to bring systems users up to speed on how to work with the new system.

TIP   **Rollout**

There are a number of ways that you might choose to power up and roll out your CMS, but it should be done in carefully managed stages, little by little. Both from a system and user point of view, I would start at the most basic level and gradually increase system complexity and the number of users. Begin with getting the system up and running in a simple stand-alone environment with the basic configuration. If this works smoothly, you can gradually migrate to the real environment but without any external systems integration. Keep the number of users who have access to the system to a few core members of your team at this stage. Then begin your systems integration work so that you get to a point where you have a complete beta version of the system running. Only once you are confident you have a fully working system should you begin to roll it out to a broader set of real end users.

You can choose to stage your rollout to users a number of ways: by individuals, department, business unit, country, language, even by digital channel (e.g., mobile or PDA). Again, it is advisable to begin where things will be easiest. Not only will this build your confidence, but it will also give you a more forgiving environment to fine-tune your process, training, support, and documentation. Generally, increasing the number of system users creates more work than increasing the complexity of the system because you have a lot of training and change management work to do as well as any bug fixing. It is easier to deliver an all singing, all dancing system to a few people than a more basic system to many. For this reason, even though you have a fully functioning system now running, you should release its capabilities in stages: Roll out basic features to a select group. Next roll out the full system to the same select group, then basic features to a wider group, and finally the full system to the wider group.

7.2.11   Maintenance and Staffing Plan

Even at this relatively early stage, you need to be planning for what will happen once the system is up and running, thinking through how it will be maintained and who will be needed to staff it. In particular, you should analyze and define solutions for the following areas:

▶ *Training.* Training features as part of your change management planning and also as a large part of your deployment and rollout planning. However, you should also consider what forms of ongoing training and support you intend to provide once this initial push is over.

▶ *Maintenance.* Define the ongoing maintenance requirements for your content management system including backups, data archiving and deletion, technical support, service-level agreements with third parties, periodic testing practices, system reporting, log management, and scheduled system reviews. Make sure you have processes in place to deal with issues and problems: designated contacts, problem escalation procedures, response times, system monitoring, and alert services.

▶ *Documentation.* You will have produced a lot of documentation by the end of the project. However, some of this documentation will need to be updated and supplemented on an ongoing basis. Define what documents you will need, who is responsible for creating and maintaining them, when they will be released, how they can be accessed, who will have access to them, what format they will be in, and how they will be distributed.

▶ *Staffing requirements.* At this stage, you should have a reasonable idea of the likely staffing requirements for each of the areas that you have analyzed and defined a solution for. Furthermore, you need to break this down into staffing requirements for the initial development and launch phase versus the requirements in the run phase of the system. Typically, you will need a larger number of short-term staff to define, develop, and deploy the system and then a smaller number of full-time staff to maintain and run it. For this reason, the initial phase is often outsourced with in-house staff then taking over the ongoing work. For each staff member, define a job description, roles and responsibilities, skills required, tasks to be undertaken, and reporting structures. Depending on how far advanced you are with defining workflows, you might even include the relevant ones for each job.

Table 7.2 describes the main job functions you are likely to require to staff a CMS.

7.2.12 Project Documentation

Based on your recommended solutions, you should be able to refine and update your project plan and budget as well as your risks and issues documentation and any other project management documentation you are maintaining. Change control could begin at this stage but is perhaps best commenced after the project specification stage.

7.2.13 Deliverables

The deliverables for the solution definition work stage, based on the work described, are as follows:

► Content and user models
► Content collection solution (including creation, migration, workflow)
► Content management solution (including systems architecture, technical environment, and system administration)
► Content publishing solution (including templates, page design, personalization rules, and workflow)
► Localization plan
► Reporting and analysis recommendations
► Testing plan
► Rollout and deployment plan (including training and change management)
► Maintenance and staffing plan
► Updated project documentation

Table 7.2 Job functions for a CMS.

Job function	Roles and responsibilities
Project management	The project management function will be heavily involved during the planning, development, and launch of the CMS and then to a much lesser degree once it is up and running.
	You are likely to need a project director to be in overall charge of the project, supported by project managers and more specialized technical project managers as required.
Editorial	The editorial function will be heavily involved throughout. In particular, once the system is running, the editorial team will be those most involved on a day-to-day operational basis.
	The editorial function will consist of content creators, authors, editors, and reviewers as well as those in charge of adding value to content through metadata.
Production	The production function may be involved in the start-up phase helping to mass convert and format content for the launch of the system, and it is then certainly required on a regular and ongoing basis to help maintain the flow of content into the system.
	Production roles consist of those responsible for content conversion and processing and system administration and maintenance, among others.
Designers	The design function will be heavily involved in page, template, and interface design at first and then to a lesser degree once the system is operational day to day.
	Designers' skill sets vary and range from system interface design to more graphically focused page design, animation, line art, and 3D graphics. For a CMS, you will mostly need those who can work with templates and design pages for them.
Developers	Like the designers, the developers will also initially be very busy in the development, construction, delivery, and integration of the system. Once running, developers will still be required to maintain and evolve code, templates, functionality, and integration with other systems.
	The developer function covers a whole range of skills: server and client side coding, template programming, database development, business logic, and integration coding.
Analysts	The analyst functions are quite varied but tend to be more specialized and so are called upon as required, with the bulk of their commitment likely to come in the start-up rather than run phase of the CMS.
	Analyst roles include systems architecture, information architecture, personalization rules, workflow analysis, business process analysis, systems analysis, technical evaluations, infrastructure design, and management information reporting and analysis.
Specialists	Specialist job functions, like the analysts, will be called upon as required. Depending on the specialist, the skills may be in demand either before, during, or after system deployment.
	Specialist is a catchall term that includes roles such as change management consultant, educationalist, training specialist, documentation specialist, and testing and quality control specialist.

7.3 **Project Specification**

During this work stage, you will be choosing a content management system and documenting in detail the specifics of the project. Whereas the previous work stage was about thinking through and defining the optimum solutions, this work stage is really about nailing down the details in specifications that then become your team's marching orders for the production phase of the project.

7.3.1 **CMS Selection Process**

To find out more about how to run a CMS selection process, refer to Section 6.2, Selecting a CMS. To learn more about specific CMS vendors, refer to the Product Vendors section of the Resources part of the book.

When exactly to do the selection of your CMS is a bit of a chicken and egg conundrum. Which comes first, the planning or the CMS? Without doing the planning, you are not in a position to know what you want, but without knowing what CMS you are going to have, how can you plan accurately? Often companies will go into a selection process almost as soon as they have begun a content management project, probably because it feels very tangible. The result will be the purchase of an actual system, and everyone can see that this is a step forward. However, hard as it may be, I think it is better to put off the selection process until as much of the planning and solution definition has been done as possible. The thinking and planning work are ultimately more valuable and more important than the system itself. The thinking is unique to the needs and requirements of your organization, whereas a CMS is just an enabling tool that anyone can buy. Any tool is only as good as the person using it, so the quality of your thinking, planning, and analysis will be a much bigger determinant of ultimate success than the CMS you choose.

Leaving the selection process until the beginning of the project specification work stage means that, based on all the solution definition work you have done in the previous work stage, you should be clear on what you need, and creating the request for proposal (RFP) and corresponding selection criteria will be easy. Without knowing precisely what system you are going to end up with means that some of your planning will be based on assumptions, and some of the specifics and details cannot be known. However, once you have gone through the selection process and know the system you will be using, you are able to turn the solutions you defined in the solution definition work stage into detailed specifications in this work stage.

7.3.2   Create the Project Specification

Now you should formally document the solutions that you have defined in the previous work stage and bring them together into a single, authoritative specification. Where there are finer levels of detail missing from the solutions so far defined, now is the time to specify those details. As you bring all the elements together, now is also the chance to see the bigger picture and make final iterations of the various elements such that the whole hangs together.

The project specification document you create is the single document that all relevant parties must sign off and agree to. For this reason, it is often the basis for contractual relationships. If you take the time to do the work on the project specification, the subsequent implementation and maintenance work stages will be much easier. You may have taken some time getting to this point, but you are unlikely to have committed large sums of money to the project. Larger capital expenditure and resource costs will, however, be incurred from here on, so it is doubly important that key project stakeholders and sponsors have signed off the project specification.

7.3.3   Final Project Plan and Budget

By now you should have all the information you need to confidently plan and budget the remainder of the project, including resourcing, time scales, tasks with dependencies, key milestones, and sign-off points.

It is quite possible that in putting this together you find that the project is much more expensive and will take much longer than was originally imagined. You will need to confer with the project sponsors and key stakeholders to decide the best path to take: ask for more time and money, reduce the scope of the project, try and negotiate down quoted times and costs, or break the project up into phases. It is rarely a good idea simply to try and force down quoted times and costs as this usually results in poor end quality and results. Asking for more time and money is not always the best way to make friends either. I would favor delivering less but doing it really well, either by reducing scope or, perhaps best of all, breaking the project into phases. This ensures people are not disgruntled if they can see their full requirements will eventually be met in later phases, and it gives you a much better chance of actually delivering the first phase on time, to budget, and to a high level of quality. If you can do this, you are much more likely to get the time and money to do the remaining phases, which by that point are likely to have been refined in any case. If you cannot get agreement on scope reduction or phasing, then try at least to build consensus around prioritization of requirements.

7.3.4   Risks and Issues

Now that you know which CMS you will be using and have specified as much as you possibly can, you should update the risks and issues document that you created in the first work stage. Ideally, as you have been going, you should note down anything that you feel could pose a risk or that is already an issue. Document the risk or issue, including details of owner, impact, severity, type, probability, and steps planned to avoid it. The kinds of areas in which you are likely to come across risks or issues might include system integration, third-party content syndication, resource levels, changes to the specification (in particular, the content model), delayed decision making, cost overruns, late delivery, or the bankruptcy, merger, or acquisition of your CMS vendor or other major supplier.

7.3.5   Sign-Off and Change Control

Of course, you will be building consensus throughout the project and getting sign-off where appropriate, but the project specification with accompanying final project plan, budget, risks, and issues are the most important documents to be signed off. You do not want to be the one held responsible for hitting the expensive "go" button as you enter the production phase of the project.

Once the project specification has been signed off, you should begin change control.

7.3.6   Deliverables

The deliverables for the project specification work stage, based on the work described, are as follows:

▶ CMS vendor selection process
▶ Project specification (including final project plan and budget as well as updated risks and issues)

7.4 Content

We are now entering the production phase of the project, otherwise termed *delivery, implementation,* or *build.* This is where the planning, thinking, and specifying end and the doing really begins. If you have done the first three work stages diligently, there should be little to say other than go ahead and do what you have planned to do. You will be implementing what you specified for the content collection solution.

Content is not a work stage that you usually see as part of most software delivery methods or project management approaches. However, I think it is very important to Web projects and, of course, particularly important to content management projects. A CMS with little or inadequate content is of little use. You can run this work stage in parallel with the next work stage, design and construction, but the important point to note is that you should begin the content work stage as soon as possible. This should certainly be as soon as you have finished the project specification, and in some cases, such as mundane content conversion tasks that you know all along will need to be done, you can begin even earlier. Creating, acquiring, converting, and otherwise manipulating content often take much longer than you imagine, and there are rarely many shortcuts, so the sooner you can get started, the better. Depending on how large your overall project is, you might want to turn this work stage into a subproject or multiple subprojects as some of the work is stand-alone, requiring adherence to specifications but having a low degree of interdependence with the rest of project. For example, if you have a large amount of existing content that needs to be migrated into a new form according to clear guidelines, then this can happily be run as a small stand-alone project.

7.4.1 Content Authoring and Capture

Begin working with your content authors, contributors, and editors such that their working environments, tools, and practices integrate with your content management requirements. Even before the CMS itself is fully up and running, you should be introducing your content authors and editors to the concepts and practices of content structuring, metadata, and templates. Whatever means of content authoring and capture your end solution will use, you should introduce it early on even if the content is not yet being submitted directly to the actual CMS's repository. For example, you can ensure that all content created in Word is done using the correct template, or you could create Excel or Access input forms that mirror what the eventual Web forms will look like. You could even create the Web forms and have content submitted to an existing database you have available and then simply migrate to the CMS once ready. At least if you are capturing the content in the required manner and form, it will then be much easier to transfer to the full CMS because the authors and editors will be used to working in the new way and importing the content will not be a problem as you know that it is in the correct form.

7.4.2 Content Conversion and Processing

You should have defined what content you need to convert and how it must be formatted and processed to become usable. Now is the time to write the scripts, routines and batch processes to actually do this conversion as well as take on any human resources you need. Begin doing the content conversion and processing. You will soon learn which areas need fine-tuning and whether your project plans need adjusting because the work is taking longer than, or indeed not as long as, you imagined.

7.4.3 Content Acquisition and Syndication

Whether it is content that you are taking into your CMS or content that you are delivering from your CMS to an external system, you should begin your talks with content partners as soon as you can. This is because the process of getting content acquisition and syndication feeds up and running and working smoothly invariably take longer than you think. This is in part for technical reasons, in part for customization work that is usually required, but largely for commercial reasons in coming to an agreement on what exactly will be supplied, at what cost, and on what terms. On the positive side, once these feeds are up and running, they tend to stay working reliably and efficiently.

Whatever else you do, you must be sure to work with sample content before signing up for anything. One test of samples is insufficient. An ongoing feed is required so that you can test it for quality, consistency, and reliability. Do tests to make sure there are no unexpected problems with importing or exporting the content from your system as required.

7.4.4   Testing and Quality Control

As you assemble content from various sources, you should, of course, be checking it for quality. You should be checking not only the quality of the actual content itself but also the quality of the structure of the content, its metadata, the reliability and consistency with which the content is produced, and how closely the content meets your editorial guidelines. The earlier you spot quality problems, the more time and money you will save in the long term. As your processes and production volumes gear up, a small unnoticed problem can become quite a painful issue. For example, you might find that there is a problem with the way content is being mapped during a conversion process, or a metadata field on one of the content capture templates is incorrectly named, or your validation is not picking up the fact that dates or times are being stored in multiple formats.

7.4.5   Training

Your change management plans should include training for your content authors and editors to help them learn to integrate their working practices with the new system. The editorial guidelines that you have created will further support them.

7.4.6   Update Project Documentation

Once you have actually begun work on content authoring, conversion, and acquisition during this work stage, you will quickly appreciate how accurate your planning for it was. Is it taking longer than expected? Is it going to cost more than expected? Do you need more people to make it happen? Is the quality of what is being produced not high enough? Depending on how things are looking, you may need to adjust your plans (e.g., by cutting scope) and update the relevant project documentation accordingly.

7.4.7   Deliverables

The deliverables for the content work stage, based on the work described, are as follows:

▶ Content collection tools, processes, scripts, and routines (including content authoring, conversion and capture tools and environments, content capture templates, and sample content)

▶ Updated project documentation (in particular, any revisions to project plan, budget, risks, and issues)

7.5 Design and Construction

During this work stage, you implement the project specification using your chosen tool. This work stage runs in parallel with the previous work stage, content, which is split out largely to emphasize its importance and because it often makes sense to run content as its own work stream or subproject.

Within the design and construction work stage, you may wish to structure the work according to the three main areas of your CMS (collection, management, and publishing) or by work streams and subprojects that focus on particular areas such as templates, integration coding, technical infrastructure, change management, documentation, testing, editorial, or project management. Although it makes most conceptual sense to define the solution in terms of the three main elements of content management, reflecting the content life cycle, the reality is that most people operationally involved in the project will be doing things in more than one element and, most likely, all three. For this reason, it is easiest to create separate work streams, each with its own team and project plan, to tackle particular areas across content collection, management, and publishing. Each work stream should have a project management function that reports in to a central project management team that coordinates all activities across all teams and subprojects.

7.5.1 Project Management

Although this work stage may take the longest and involve more resources than any other work stage, there is little to say about it other than you do what the project specification says. Once you begin the design and construction work stage, there is no difference between a CMS project and any other systems integration project. The hard work is in managing all the people involved, ensuring that good communication continues, and that problems are prevented or resolved. Just keeping up to date with progress and project status with regard to the project plan is a large task.

7.5.2 CMS Installation and Configuration

Once you have chosen and purchased your CMS, you should begin the process of installing and configuring it as soon as possible. Do not wait on other elements of the project, such as the full content, to begin installation because the longer your technical team has to play with the CMS, the better they will know how to run and fix it and the more time they will have to ask questions of the vendor. The aim at this stage is not to fully deploy and roll out the CMS but to get a full beta version of the system running, with real content, so that it can be tested in the next work stage.

7.5.3 Content Collection and Migration

With your content collection specification and the outputs of the previous content work stage, you should have plenty of content for your beta version CMS to begin managing and publishing. There is likely to be some content that you have batch prepared and can import into the system en masse and other content that is entered directly to the system using Web forms and workflows. Now is your chance to really find out how well your content collection solution is working.

7.5.4 Training and Consulting Services

If you have bought a CMS, then there will be training required, at this stage particularly for the development and technical teams that may need support from the vendor or systems integration partner.

7.5.5 Change Control and Risk Management

Change control and risk management are likely to feature much more strongly during this work stage as you juggle potential changes to requirements and fend off challenges that might derail the project's progress.

7.5.6 Deliverables

The deliverables for the design and construction work stage, based on the work described, are as follows:

▶ A beta version of the full CMS (including real content)
▶ Project milestones as defined by the project specification
▶ Updated project documentation (including change control, risks and issues, and the project plan)

7.6 Testing, Launch, and Handover

You ensure that the system is working as expected before deploying and rolling it out to the organization. *Launch* refers to the deployment of a public-facing Web site with all the attendant fanfare and marketing efforts. It is often the case that the deployment of a CMS is also the occasion for the launch of a complete site redesign and overhaul. *Deployment* is a more standard term for the go live and integration of an enterprise software application. *Handover* is the changeover from the start-up phase of the project to the ongoing run and maintenance phase, which typically involves a handover from one team of people to another requiring a transfer of knowledge.

7.6.1 Testing

Follow the testing plan that you created in the solution definition work stage and which should also be part of your project specification. Do not underestimate the time that testing will take, in particular the testing of all the points of integration with other systems, and do not forget to include final usability testing of the system interfaces. Finally, make absolutely sure that you are confident your system will more than be able to cope with the levels of load and demand put on it once live. Start by testing your CMS beta version, test the system again in its final version, and then finally, once it has gone live, test again. These rounds of testing should flush out as many potential problems as possible.

7.6.2 Deployment and Rollout

Once you have a version of the system that you have fully tested and are confident works, you can set it live by following your deployment and rollout plan, also created in the solution definition work stage and included in the project specification.

7.6.3 Localization

Depending on the complexity of your localization requirements and how you have structured the approach to localization, you may be carrying out simultaneous multilocality deployments and rollout or staggering them. The latter is perhaps a more realistic and manageable approach. Particularly if each of your localities has its own team, you will need to be going through all of the elements of this work stage for each locality.

7.6.4 Documentation

Perhaps now more than at any other work stage, you need to bring your documentation up to date and ensure it is complete and accurately reflects what you have actually delivered, which is often not quite the same as what was originally planned despite the best intentions. Documentation should certainly include full systems documentation but also editorial guidelines, brand guidelines, training documents, and all project documentation. This documentation will be relied upon as the basis of future training and system development.

7.6.5 Training

Many system users will already be aware of the system and have used it during development and testing and so should be comfortable with it. Certainly, you should make sure that there is a core team that is already fully up to speed and can work with the system once it goes live. However, there will be plenty of other more occasional users who now require introductory training and subsequent support. Your documentation, including standards, guidelines, glossaries, support information, problem resolution procedures, and training contacts, will form an important training resource.

7.6.6 Handover

As you move from the initial development phase of the CMS into the ongoing maintenance phase, there will be changes to the project team. Indeed, the project itself comes to an end around the same time that maintenance takes over. The team involved with the CMS postlaunch may be a reduced version of the team that developed it or a completely different set of people. Either way, you need to plan a series of handover sessions to facilitate the smooth transition from the initial project team to the maintenance team. There needs to be a final cutoff point where the maintenance team accepts full responsibility for the CMS, thereby "releasing" the initial project team. Often this is the point at which consulting partners, systems integrators, and other third parties' involvement comes to an end.

7.6.7 Internal Communications

Be wary of overtrumpeting the arrival of your new system as this may then set you up for a fall. At the same time, you should not let your team's efforts go unnoticed, and you will have failed if the system goes unused. You must be the judge of what internal communications and marketing are most appropriate. Do not forget to celebrate your achievements. If you have made it this far, you and your team deserve it.

7.6.8 Deliverables

The deliverables for the testing, launch, and handover work stage, based on the work described, are as follows:

- ▶ Testing documentation and results
- ▶ Handover briefings and process
- ▶ Training
- ▶ Internal communications initiatives
- ▶ Updated documentation

7.7 Maintenance

Once the system is up and running, it needs to be maintained and refined. Note that this work stage is likely to run in parallel with the following work stage and extends beyond the lifetime of the initial CMS project. Follow the maintenance and staffing plan that you created earlier, which covers ongoing training, maintenance, documentation, and staffing needs. Make sure that backup, archiving, and content expiration functions are running smoothly.

As demands on the system increase, through increased numbers of users and increased usage per user, check that the performance of the CMS is not suffering; work with the vendor to ensure software upgrades occur as necessary; improve support and service levels; update and refine documentation and guidelines; provide ongoing training; conduct ongoing testing; and continue to improve the usability of both the system and the site.

7.7.1 Managing Changes and Updates

For more on change management practices, refer to Part I, Change Management.

During the maintenance work stage, you will receive requests to change and modify the way the system works. For example, users may request alterations to the content capture Web forms, and workflows are bound to need refining. Depending on the nature of the change request, you might wish to save it up and tackle it as part of a new project, or it may need addressing as part of a regular change process. Effective change management during the maintenance work stage helps you keep an audit trail of who requested what and what changes have been made. This is important for effective future planning and ensures that knowledge of what has changed does not reside solely in the head of a single person or scattered around the organization. The system status should reflect system documentation plus subsequent documented changes. For this, you need to define a change request process and provide associated documentation. Among others things, this will help protect you from the tidal wave of changes and ideas that are likely to come your way once the system is live.

As you get used to maintaining and running the system on a day-to-day basis, you should also be in a position to improve development and release processes and cycles. You will have a better understanding of how to manage different types of change: scheduled (regular or one off), on demand (typically urgent changes), and event driven (e.g., on content submission) being the main three. A fourth kind of change is rollback where you return the site to a previous known good state. Your CMS should have rollback functionality to help you do this, but it is very important that as part of your maintenance you ensure you can roll back. Check that the system is archiving snapshots of the site that you can roll back to and test that the rollback function does actually work. As your working practices settle down and evolve, you can develop more efficient scripts, rules, automation, and workflow to help manage changes and updates. The editorial team should be able to provide a publishing schedule that will further help you plan for and manage change.

7.7.2   Service-Level Agreements

Service-level agreements are particularly important where third parties are involved, but even internally, it is important to define and document the levels of service that the maintenance team is committed to. This ensures a certain level of quality, it clarifies the expectations of the maintenance team, and it gives measurable objectives to which the maintenance team can be held and by which their performance can be monitored and appraised.

Pay particular attention to the processes by which problems and issues will be addressed: Who are the contacts? What is the escalation process? How are problems classified? What audit trail is there to show how problems have been addressed? Are there any additional costs involved in resolving issues? What response times are guaranteed? Who has what decision-making and authorization powers?

7.7.3   Phase 2 Project Planning

If you have phased the implementation of your project, you will by now already be planning the next phase. You should not miss the review and evaluation work stage that follows, but you should be able to accelerate the project planning work stages that you go back into. As you begin to maintain the phase 1 system, you will learn a lot that is likely to affect your phase 2 planning. Note improvement and enhancements that could be made. Users are likely to give feedback and suggestions. Unless they have spotted critical bugs, which should have been ironed out during testing, resist pressure to make significant changes ad hoc. Little things can be changed in the course of maintaining the system or compiled into a list that is treated as a miniproject and implemented all at once.

Larger changes will require a full project to implement and should go through the full project cycle and work stages as described here. If your CMS is a success, then you will quickly find requests for content to be published to new platforms and devices, for the CMS to be integrated with other systems, and for increasingly advanced personalization. What is large and what is small are a matter for some debate, but on the whole, changes to existing content and system functionality can be handled as part of ongoing maintenance and change management procedures, whereas new content and new functions require a phase 2 project treatment. Do not dismiss requests because they cannot be done in the foreseeable future. Keep a wish list that can be revisited when the time and resources are available.

7.7.4 Deliverables

The deliverables for the maintenance work stage, based on the work described, are as follows:

▶ Change request process and documentation
▶ Service-level agreements (including troubleshooting and issue resolution procedures)
▶ Updated maintenance documentation
▶ Phase 2 project proposals and planning

7.8 Review and Evaluation

You conduct a review of the content management project and evaluate the results it has achieved against the goals defined at the beginning.

7.8.1 Project Review

Conduct a project review that focuses on assessing how well the project itself was run and how things might be improved in subsequent phases. Elements to address include quality of planning, communication, expectation management, efficiency, team morale, milestone management, budgetary control, key project processes (e.g., reporting, review, and sign-off), and documentation. Refer back to the success criteria defined in the project brief right at the beginning of the project to evaluate to what degree the project has underdelivered or exceeded expectations.

7.8.2 Content Return on Investment

Much as a CMS may deliver efficiencies, there is no getting away from the fact that good content costs money. Thus, you need to be sure you are spending your money only on content that is delivering a return on its investment. You must be ruthless when deciding which content is worth publishing. If it is not

Part IV goes into a lot more detail on the ways and means to measure the performance of a Web site, both qualitatively and quantitatively.

serving a user need that in turn delivers value to the business, money is being wasted. As we have said before, although a CMS helps you manage large quantities of well-structured content efficiently, it cannot help you identify which content is the most valuable. It may provide some reporting and analysis tools that will help you reach this decision (e.g., showing the number of views per content object), but ultimately, only you can know the strategy and objectives and therefore what is valuable and what is not.

For the majority of Web sites, the 80/20 rule holds good when it comes to content: 80% of value is delivered by just 20% of content. So it is all the more important to identify that 20% and focus your resources on that. There are numerous approaches to finding out which content is most valuable from data analysis through path analysis to focus groups.

Everyone thinks that their own piece of contributed content is useful and interesting, but you must find out the objective truth. In particular, you should analyze the value you are deriving from syndicated content or other external content that you are paying for. Are you getting value for money? Do not forget to consider the value of the content over the entire length of its usefulness ("lifetime value"): Some content is great for a day but then worthless the next day, whereas other content has a much longer shelf life, extending its lifetime value. Because of the speed and volume of content updates online, the value of content typically depreciates very quickly, so you should look at ways of extending the content's usefulness, by repackaging it for another audience perhaps.

TIP   **Don't Forget the Authors**

Authors write for an audience. They want to communicate with their audience, and they thrive on getting feedback in a way similar to an actor or actress on the stage. Unfortunately, a CMS tends to take away this direct connection with the audience, depersonalizing the author-reader relationship, because authors cannot know how and when or who exactly will see their content or in what context. Creating content and entering it into a CMS can feel like sending your carefully crafted content into a black hole.

If you are to win the commitment of your authors and keep them interested in communicating the best they can with users, I believe you must try and keep alive as many feedback mechanisms to authors as possible. That may be user comments or it may be custom reports for authors showing utilization of content that they have created (which, if you have stored "author" in your content object's metadata, is not hard).

7.8.3   Recommendations

Based on your experiences so far and your analysis, you should make recommendations for what can be done next. If you are going into phase 2 of a large project, then it is highly probable that phase 1 will have taught you some lessons and uncovered requirements that will necessitate some refinement of plans for the coming phases. Your analysis of content value should give rise to recommendations for site content and functionality enhancements.

7.8.4   Deliverables

The deliverables for the review and evaluation work stage, based on the work described, are as follows:

▶ Project and content review (including performance against objectives and recommendations)

Summary

tructure and process are at the heart of content management. Structure and process enable efficiencies and increased quality control even as a site's scales and volumes and complexity of content turnover increase. Content management helps meets the challenge set for e-business managers: improve quality but streamline costs.

But content management is more than just this, as I hope you have realized. It is not only the preserve of the well funded or the megasites, nor is it only about streamlining maintenance costs. It is also about thinking intelligently about how to get the maximum value out of your content—how it can be repackaged and presented to suit the needs of different users via different channels. In the case of Web content management, it is about maximizing the business value of what you have by exploiting the unique interactive capabilities of digital channels and digital media. This should be the goal for Web sites and organizations of all sizes.

The next part of the book examines how best to manage your most important assets: your customer relationships. Customer profiles can be managed as content objects like any other by a content management system, but of course, there are real people behind these profiles, and they need to be treated as real individuals.

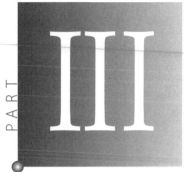

CUSTOMER
RELATIONSHIP
MANAGEMENT

To maintain and evolve a successful commercial Web site, you need to be able to effectively manage change, manage content, and measure your performance as the other parts of this book discuss. However, all these activities are more or less behind the scenes. They do not directly touch the customer. They can affect the customer experience, but mostly they are about improving business processes in the quest to reduce costs and improve efficiency. Yet we have all learned that customer-centricity is fundamental to Web success. If you do not provide customers with a Web experience with which they are satisfied, they will go elsewhere. So if you are serious about evolving your Web site and improving that customer experience, you must continue to improve the way in which your organization interacts with its customers via digital channels.

Customer relationship management (CRM) has become quite a hot buzzword. It has also caused a lot of confusion because everyone claims to "do" CRM. I considered naming this part of the book something else to try and avoid being sucked into this confusion, but no other description worked as well. This is not a book about the wider world of CRM. It is about how to improve your

Web site, and a large part of that is about how to evolve to create better relationships with your customers, which is good news for them and for you. We begin with a broader discussion of CRM to give some context to the CRM phenomenon and introduce some key concepts, but we then move on to the specifics of how CRM manifests itself through Web sites and can be used to evolve them.

NOTE   **The Human Touch**

For all that CRM has—process, technology, and management theory elements—it is essentially all about interacting with real people. As we know from our experiences in the real world, people are very different, and the way they choose to conduct their relationships with others varies enormously. So, although this book strives to stick to the practical and to give concrete advice, this part on CRM necessarily contains some more subjective opinions about how people do, or do not, like to be treated and how they prefer to interact with one another. My observations are based on experience, observation, and research, but they cannot be seen as answers; rather, they are merely guidelines for framing your CRM activities. So much depends on who you are dealing with that there can be no substitute for that hard-to-define, yet all important, human touch. ■

Key Areas We Will Cover in Part III

▶ What is customer relationship management? Why is everyone talking about it? And what is eCRM—what are the opportunities afforded by digital channels? We cover the key concepts, such as the single customer view and lifetime customer value, that make up CRM.

▶ Understanding your users. You cannot do CRM without understanding your users, so here we address customer segmentation, customer data, and how to capture and manage it, along with permission and privacy issues.

▶ Personalization, online communities, and customer service. We examine each of these three topics, which are central to eCRM, to understand what each is, what each promises, and what we have learned so far about managing them online.

8

A CRM Primer

I f you are not familiar with CRM, the following section will introduce you to as much as you need to know in terms of background and context to then apply CRM to your Web site. If you want to find out more about CRM, refer to Resources at the end of the book for some recommendations.

8.1 What Is Customer Relationship Management (CRM)?

Almost everywhere you look these days, you run into CRM in one form or another. The number of articles discussing CRM has skyrocketed over the last years. Try a search on CRM on any search engine and expect to get several hundred thousand results. And yet there is no one standardized definition for either CRM or its electronic sibling eCRM. This does not matter very much as long as you at least have a clear idea of what you mean when using the term. Any two parties discussing the subject should also clarify up front what their frames of reference are to avoid confusion. To get you started, following are two alternate definitions from reputable sources:

1. Official *CRMGuru.com* definition:

"Customer Relationship Management (CRM) is a business strategy to select and manage customers to optimize long-term value. CRM requires a customer-centric business philosophy and culture to support effective marketing, sales, and service processes. CRM applications can enable effective Customer Relationship Management, provided that an enterprise has the right leadership, strategy, and culture."

2. Paul Greenberg, from his book *CRM at the Speed of Light:*

"CRM is a complete system that:

   1. Provides a means and method to enhance the experience of the individual customers so that they will remain customers for life
   2. Provides both technological and functional means of identifying, capturing, and retaining customers
   3. Provides a unified view of the customer across the enterprise"

Despite the various definitions that you are likely to come across, there are a couple of key concepts that most people seem to agree on:

▶ Customer-centricity is the strategic imperative.
▶ CRM helps companies to better understand and serve their customers to help acquire and retain them. You cannot do CRM without knowing who your customers are and having data about them.
▶ An understanding of customer value by segments is vital in ensuring that CRM delivers a measurable return on investment: CRM is about measurable return on customers.
▶ Customers can be internal, external, business partners, or consumers. CRM is not limited to business-to-business (B2B) or business-to-consumer (B2C).
▶ CRM is not a technology thing, although technology is fundamental to making it work successfully. It is about people and processes.

8.2   eCRM: The Digital Opportunity

There has been much debate surrounding the differences, or lack of differences, between what is called CRM and what is called eCRM. Is eCRM just Web-enabled CRM? Is it merely symptomatic of companies hoping to strengthen their proposition or valuation? Or is eCRM fundamentally different?

Clearly, the Internet and e-business are responsible for the *e* in eCRM. It is basically about delivering increased value to the customer and to the business using digital channels. The differences between CRM and eCRM are mirrored in the differences between business and e-business. Increasingly, all businesses are becoming, in part if not in whole, e-businesses. Once we are all used to everything being digital as well as material, the *e* will appear increasingly redundant, and so we come back to just business again. Currently, e-business makes new things possible, which require new skills and technologies, but this will become business as usual. CRM will never go away; it will just become e-enabled.

NOTE   **The eCRM Umbrella**

As you can tell from the chapters within this part of the book, the term *eCRM* encompasses a range of topics related to managing customer relationships via the Web: customization, personalization, online customer service, targeted marketing, and community building. Anything that affects the point of interface and interaction between a customer and a company online can be called eCRM.   ■

Although the fundamental principles of CRM and eCRM are the same, there are significant opportunities offered by the new and evolving interactive digital channels.

8.2.1   Build Closer Relationships with Customers

The greatest strength of CRM is when you can really create a relationship with your customers. The digital channels offer great opportunities for building relationships because they are interactive, because they can be personalized, and because they can be available anywhere in the world at any time of day, creating an open channel for dialogue with customers.

8.2.2   Understand Your Customers Better

Digital channels are particularly effective at delivering insight into customers and their needs. For example:

▶ Analyzing how users interact with sites gives a good indication of what people like and dislike, what works and what does not, and what attracts them and what does not. For more on this, see Part IV, Site Measurement, in particular Chapter 15, Measurement Approaches and Techniques.

▶ Analyzing users' search terms on your site will help you understand what people are most interested in, what they may be having problems finding on the site, and what their unmet needs might be.

▶ Users are more likely to fire off an email giving their feedback and opinions than they are a letter, partly because of the potential for anonymity and partly because of the time and cost involved with writing and sending a letter, so email feedback can give useful qualitative user feedback.

▶ A survey, questionnaire, competition, or similar mechanism for soliciting user feedback can quickly and cost effectively deliver customer insight.

▶ By allowing customers to manage their own data and details via the Web, you have a much better chance of maintaining valuable, up-to-date customer information and knowing when their needs and circumstances change. Indeed, these points of change are often crucial "moments of value." For example, a customer who buys a house, gets married, or has children will have new and pressing needs.

8.2.3 Increase Competitive Differentiation

Consumers are increasingly demanding to be able to interact with a company through multiple channels. They expect to receive a consistent experience across all channels. This experience will inform their perception of the quality of the company and its brand, and this in turn will inform that customer's propensity to spend some of their value with the company, be it money, referrals, or time. As consumers continue to migrate to emerging digital channels, it is here that the greatest opportunities exist for companies to differentiate themselves and their offerings.

8.2.4 Higher Levels of Accountability

CRM, in the form in which it has existed for decades, has a bad name when it comes to justifying returns on its investment and for delivering accountable solutions. There are many reasons for this, and none of them, I would argue, are due to the fact that CRM as an approach is fundamentally flawed. However, eCRM does at last offer the opportunity for CRM to be much more accountable. This is because it is generally much easier, and more realistic, to measure and track customer activity online than offline. It would be difficult and expensive to accurately track the number of repeat visits that all customers made to a shop to gauge levels of loyalty and interest, but this is straightforward on the Web. eCRM initiatives have ample opportunity to work to quantifiable and measurable objectives ensuring increased levels of accountability.

8.2.5 Tactical Strengths

Digital channels typically allow for many more tactical initiatives than is possible offline. To make the most of these tactical opportunities often requires rethinking business processes and demands new skills to cope with more iterative, fast turnaround and dynamic tactical projects. However, if this can be achieved, the results can be dramatic. Companies that have successfully embraced email marketing, for example, have seen the number of campaigns that they run per year grow at least tenfold, with the same number of staff and at almost the same cost, relative to what was possible with, say, direct mail. Equally, a retailer or manufacturer who wants to clear excess inventory can very quickly use promotions through digital channels to reach a large number of customers at relatively little cost.

8.2.6 Cost Efficiencies

Here are some of the ways that CRM through digital channels can further help decrease costs:

▶ Customer servicing is the obvious one. If customers transact via a digital channel, companies can save costs and improve their margins because there is a decreased need for expensive physical presence or staff. As customers take greater control and manage their own profiles and relationships with companies (online banking is a good example), it is possible to hand back much of the costly administration overhead to the customer.

▶ Proposition and product development. Using digital channels' enhanced capabilities for data tracking and analysis, combined with the ability to capture qualitative user feedback through tactically deployed and targeted campaigns, it is possible to "test drive" products, services, and propositions online. The online customer can help inform and shape future developments, which can lead to faster development times, avoid costly mistakes, ensure that developments are in line with customer needs, and uncover previously unimagined ideas.

▶ Online questionnaires and surveys can be a cost-effective alternative to focus groups. It should be noted, however, that this does not invalidate the need for face-to-face customer insight. But for certain forms of surveys (e.g., regular panel studies involving users who are geographically distant), digital is ideal, giving richer data at a reduced cost and in shorter time frames.

8.2.7   Improved Testing and Proposition Development

Use the digital channels to test and refine new customer propositions. The speed and relative low cost with which propositions can be delivered digitally to customers make the digital channels an ideal route to test, learn from, and refine customer interaction processes. For example:

▶ You might trial, preview, or request feedback from select customer groups on a new product or service you are developing to gauge interest.

▶ You can test the potential for viral marketing by leveraging your existing customer base to acquire new customers at low cost.

▶ You can provide multiple channels and alternatives for customer (self-)service to understand what combination of services most appeals to which customer segments and at what cost to you.

▶ You can experiment with targeting a new customer segment (e.g., in another country) to monitor interest and refine your proposition.

▶ If your organization is undertaking other CRM initiatives, the digital channels are a great place to test run propositions and validate business cases.

These kinds of activities help you understand how best to deal with different customer segments: what to present them with, when, and how to create the most value for both the customers and the business.

To exploit the potential of eCRM, however, it must be noted that new skills and knowledge are required. Unfortunately, just as digital channels offer companies an excellent opportunity to positively differentiate themselves from their competition, it is also possible to get things wrong and damage the brand. With the competition only one click away, the consequences are grave. Digital customers have shown themselves to be merciless in the exercise of this free will. While the industry matures and new skills are acquired, it is important to recognize and understand the skill set required to devise and implement outstanding digital offerings. More than any other discipline, eCRM represents the ultimate fusion of marketing and IT skills and knowledge. You need to understand customer insight processes, have a good grasp on the technology options, appreciate new working methods and practices, and understand human-digital device interaction. These skills all exist but are often spread across technology vendors, direct marketers, management consultants, advertising agencies, customer service experts, and the like. To really evolve your Web site, you need to have a team that brings together all the components.

8.3 The Business Case

The severe market downturn of 2000, fueled by a multitude of dotcom failures, has, if anything, heightened interest in CRM as an approach that promises to increase value and profitability by both lowering costs and increasing sales:

▶ *Higher sales.* Conversion rates improve through better targeting, better merchandising, better understanding of customer needs, and better feedback from customers leading to better product configuration and proposition development. There is better retention of loyal and profitable customers through improved, personalized services, raised switching costs, cross- and up-selling, better customer service, increased dialogue with customers, and more effective customer life cycle management.

▶ *Lower costs.* Marketing is more targeted, customer acquisition costs are lowered through higher conversion rates and customer referrals, customer self-service efficiencies, and savings through using lower cost channels such as email.

Perhaps the single biggest aim of CRM is to improve customer retention: to focus on keeping your current customers happy and loyal rather than chasing after new customers. This has become particularly beloved of the dotcoms who found out just how much it cost to acquire each customer in the first place. Whereas their offline counterparts had an established brand to help draw customers to their Web sites, the dotcoms spent fortunes on advertising in an attempt to build a brand. The bottom line was customers that cost more to acquire and retain than they generated in profit, which was not a viable long-term business proposition.

NOTE   **The Power of Customer Loyalty**

Here are a few statistical and research snippets, as well as other well-worn business truisms, that testify to the enormous importance of customer loyalty. Some of the statistics may be out of date but not the core message.

▶ The Web customer is only one click away from the competition.
▶ It typically costs at least five times as much to acquire a new customer as it does to retain an existing one.
▶ A McKinsey study showed that the average new customer spends $24.50 at a given Web site in the first 3 months as a shopper. The average repeat customer spends $52.50 every 3 months.
▶ "Some companies can boost profits by almost 100% by retaining just 5% more of their customers." *Harvard Business Review* (Reicheld and Sasser)
▶ In traditional markets, a dissatisfied customer will tell 8–10 people. In an electronic market, this is more likely to be 85 people. (British Telecom)
▶ Most companies lose half their customers in 5 years. (Harvard University study)
▶ On average only 15% of a site's customers consider themselves loyal to it. The loyalty rating among people who had experienced a problem was only 6%. Customers who had not experienced problems indicated a customer loyalty rating of 19%. The loyalty rating among customers who had experienced problems but were satisfied with the way they were handled: 21%. (Digital Idea)
▶ "20% of our customers generate 150% of our profit." Chase Manhattan Bank
▶ 70% of repeat purchases are made out of indifference, NOT loyalty. (eLoyalty)
▶ Half of the Fortune 500 companies have "grievance sites" allowing customers to air their grievance with the company in order that they can be addressed. (Lazard Freres)
▶ The average online marketer needs three purchases to break even after acquiring a new customer. (Boston Consulting Group/shop.org retailing study)
▶ 40% of customers expect a response to an email within 6 hours but only 12% of online retailing sites deliver on this. (Jupiter Media Metrix)   ∎

Whichever way you look at it, and whether a household name or a dotcom, you must conclude that customer retention and loyalty, which are largely driven by the quality of ongoing customer experience a company delivers, are fundamental drivers of long-term profitability and success.

In reality, CRM must be seen not primarily as a way to grow a customer base but as a means to defend and retain it. The battleground as markets and channels mature is increasingly in the retention and loyalty sphere, as well as winning over existing market share, rather than the acquisition of brand-new customers. The Internet still offers the opportunity to reach out to completely new markets, but it has turned out not to be such a limitless pool of willing global customers as many thought.

NOTE   **Customer Lifetime Value (LTV)**

Customer *lifetime value* is a phrase you will often hear in a CRM commercial context. It refers to the revenue a customer generates over the period of their entire relationship with a company, less the costs of acquiring, converting, and retaining the customer. So, when everything has been taken into account, how much profit does each customer generate over the time that he of she is a customer? You will note the focus that this gives to the value of ongoing relationships: By extending the length of the relationship with the customer by just a little, you can increase his or her LTV significantly. CRM business cases often focus their return on investment (ROI) arguments on improving customer LTVs. Just finding out which of your customers actually have the highest LTVs is a CRM project in itself. In theory, if you can work out what sorts of customers generate a high LTV and what keeps them loyal, then you have the intelligence you need to get and keep more of these most welcome customers. Or in business speak, you can "leverage customer intelligence to maximize the value of your customer assets." ∎

8.4 Customer Value

In the real world, you might aim to treat everyone you meet fairly and courteously, but this does not mean you want a relationship. There has to be some value exchange for a relationship to occur, some incentive to enter into anything deeper than a cursory interaction. Digital channels allow interactions to occur in new ways such that different forms of relationships can grow over time. However, the notion that a fruitful relationship is based on a mutually appreciated value exchange is no different. As in real life, there are likely to be those who you are happy to treat politely but are certainly not interested in developing a relationship with.

Clearly, a company needs to make value propositions to its customers. The more differentiated, the more targeted, the higher the perceived value of the proposition, the more likely it is to succeed in attracting and retaining customers. However, what about the other side of the value exchange: How does a company understand the value of its customers?

Understanding customer value is key to being able to develop a CRM strategy. To understand and measure customer value, it is necessary to define the

If the customer value metrics given mean nothing to you, or you are wondering how to measure and track them on your Web site, refer to Part IV, Site Measurement, in particular Chapter 15, Measurement Approaches and Techniques.

appropriate metrics for your business and put the systems and processes in place to ensure that customer value is tracked over time. You cannot manage what you cannot measure after all. The metrics you define can be used to create valuation formulas and to rank, segment, and prioritize your customer, or prospect, base. Customer lifetime value is a core metric to help a company understand how much a single customer is worth to them over the likely lifetime of that customer's relationship with the company. To calculate the lifetime value of a customer, you will need to establish relevant customer value criteria such as:

▶ RFM (recency, frequency, monetary) transaction values
▶ The length of a customer's relationship with the company
▶ Churn rates by customer segment
▶ A customer's propensity to create value in the future
▶ Relationship maintenance costs by customer or customer segment
▶ Marketing expenditure by customer or customer segment
▶ Cross-sell ratios (the number of different products owned by a customer)
▶ Sphere of influence (ability to generate positive word of mouth or referrals)

Once you have an understanding of your customer segments and their value, including future and potential value, you can begin to devise strategies for migrating or retaining customers relative to value areas as shown in Figure 8.1. These strategies should be mapped to the customer life cycle and, at a more granular level, to the customer touch points where the customer actually experiences the effects of your strategy. Clearly, your Web site represents one very important such touch point.

A question that is often asked is which customer segments should you focus on first? There is no definitive answer to this, as it will depend on the type of business, the stage that business is at, and the nature of the value proposition. However, the following order of priority, by customer profitability segments, is a solid approach:

1. *Your most profitable current customers.* Here the focus of your value propositions must be to increase loyalty to the company, increase the amount of disposable income that they spend with you ("share of wallet"), and lengthen the amount of time spent with the company.

2. *New customers with a propensity to become very profitable.* Here the focus must be on excellent service levels so that these customers stay with the company long enough to become profitable.

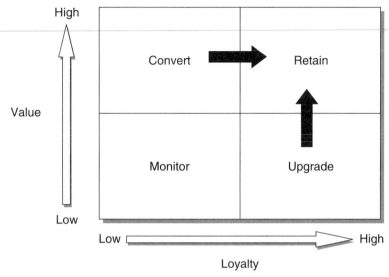

Figure 8.1 Customer value migration map.

3. *Past customers who were profitable.* For varying reasons, these customers are no longer profitable, but they have spent a lot of time and money with the company in the past. Thus, they are likely to be the company's best advocates and a rich source of valuable referrals. The focus must be on keeping service levels as high as possible while minimizing cost.

4. *Customers who are not profitable.* It may be that the greatest return on investment you will get from your CRM program is cost savings through working out how to handle the large number of customers that are not profitable more efficiently. For example, if you identified your bottom 20% of customers by profit margin, you might then increase service-related charges, influence these customers to use less expensive interaction channels, remove them from telesales lists and direct mail campaigns, and curtail the number of costly outbound communications to them. Here the focus is on reducing the costs of doing business with certain customers.

Case Study   Increasing Customer Loyalty and Value

Company: Channel 5, *www.channel5.co.uk*

Company Overview

In comparison to other broadcasters, Channel 5 is small, very young, and very ambitious. Since launch in March 1997, we have pushed our way to the forefront of UK commercial television and forced viewers and industry pundits alike to sit up and take notice of us.

Five facts on our 2001 performance:

1. Channel 5 was the only commercial terrestrial channel to experience an increase in share year on year in 2001.
2. We claimed a 5.8% share of viewing among all individuals and a 5.9% share of adults viewing.
3. Our profile has become younger and more up-market than it was in 2000.
4. We now reach 86.6% of the population, and 38.3 million people now tune in to Channel 5 in a typical month.
5. Airtime sales were $320 million in 2001.

Background to Case Study and Objectives

As a broadcaster, our primary objective is to drive ratings of our TV programs to sell advertising. Our viewers become increasingly valuable if they watch Channel 5 more often, so anything we can do to encourage and demonstrate increased interaction with the channel is of direct benefit.

Furthermore, all commercial broadcasters are under pressure to grow, or even just maintain, revenue in the face of a tough advertising market. For this reason, we and other broadcasters are looking at other ways that we might derive more value from our viewers.

In the last year, we have run two Movie Bonanza competitions. This competition was a piece of marketing activity that had secondary revenue opportunities. It had four core objectives:

▶ Build closer relationships with Channel 5 viewers
▶ Increase ratings to the 9 PM movie
▶ Add people to our customer database
▶ Deliver revenue

Process and Practice

The first time the competition was run, viewers needed to watch one particular Channel 5 film per week (all Tuesday 9 PM with one exception) and correctly answer a question relevant to the film. They would then be entered in the weekly $1600 drawing. There were eight competitions you could enter across the 8-week period of January 23 through March 13, 2001. The competition was also promoted on-air one week before it began, and it was possible to preregister to play via *channel5.co.uk* or via SMS.

To enter the competition, you could phone, short message service (SMS), or enter at *channel5.co.uk*. Those that entered via SMS were sent weekly reminders about the competition and the competition question after the relevant film. Email reminders were also sent on the day of the competition to those who had registered online.

There was also a cash bonanza of $32,000 that could be won if five out of the eight competitions had been entered correctly.

The second competition ran over 6 weeks from October 9 to November 13, 2001. There were six competitions, all following Tuesday 9 PM movies, and each offered the chance of winning $1,600. There was no large prize fund at the end of the competition this time. As before, a question was asked after each movie, and viewers could enter via phone, SMS, or the Web. The 44,000 participants (SMS and Web) from the previous competition were all recontacted. Those who subscribed by SMS were sent a reminder and the competition question after the film each week, and those who subscribed online were sent a reminder on the day of the competition.

Results

The first Movie Bonanza competition led to more than 121,000 interactions between Channel 5 and its viewers over an 8-week period and increased our database by almost 50,000 new people. Average viewing across all eight films was 2.7 million and a 13.7% share. The interactions broke down as follows:

Volumes of entries

Telephone calls	62,300	
SMS entries	38,000	(29,000 opt-ins)
Web entries	21,544	(14,921 opt-ins)

Revenue was made through premium rate telephone calls, but overall, the competition ran at a loss largely due to the $32,000 cash bonanza.

continued

The second time the competition was run, more than 188,000 contacts were made by viewers with the channel due to the competition, and more than 36,000 new names were added to our customer database. Although the contacts were up on the previous competition, the entrants were down. This suggests that those who were likely to play this type of competition based around our peak time movies had already done so. There was a good response from those that were recontacted from the SMS database to play the second game—between recontacting the initial people and the end of the second competition only 5000 people unsubscribed, showing the continued interest in the game. Average viewing across all six films was 2.6 million and a 13.7% share, almost identical to the first competition.

Volume of entries

Telephone calls	65,798	
SMS entries	108,318	(28,000 opt-ins + 29,000 previous)
Web entries	14,202	(7748 opt-ins)

An increase in the cost of premium rate calls the second time around did not seem to deter people from calling. The second Movie Bonanza ran at far less of a loss than the first due to the reduced prize fund (£28,000 vs. £6,000) and excluded any potential value in the opt-in database we had built.

Lessons Learned

The Movie Bonanza competition was clearly a successful marketing activity in terms of getting viewers to interact with the channel, with both competitions attracting well over 100,000 responses. There was a very high response rate from the original SMS subscribers, which shows that this marketing has the potential to conduct very powerful one-to-one communications with viewers. However, a lack of new opt-ins suggests that this interactive competition initiative should be taken to other programs and times of the day if it is going to add value over time.

It is difficult to assess whether the competition drove viewing to the films because they were all big movies. However, viewing was almost identical across both competitions and more contacts were made with the channel via the second competition, suggesting that more people became aware of the competition rather than the competition driving ratings. Therefore, it was unlikely that the initiative drove ratings.

Using SMS and our Web site meant that players or users did not actually need to watch the film because questions could be answered if they had any prior knowledge of the film, or of course, they could guess.

One noticeable difference was the choice of channel of interaction. Whereas the number of phone entries was similar for each competition, the number of SMS entries shot up for the second run and the number of Web entries dropped. This suggests not only that the phone is a good response medium for TV but that the technology savvy (predominantly younger) viewers were choosing to use SMS rather than the Web the second time around.

Movie Bonanza ran at a loss on both occasions, although significantly less the second time around. If the aim of the competition is to provide revenue, then offering only Web and telephone options would dramatically cut down the costs as the SMS method was most costly. A reverse billing method, where the user ends up paying part of the cost, would help the figures a lot.

In terms of creating a viewer database with value, then SMS and the Web are an efficient way of collecting the data with around a 50% opt-in rate each. Alongside this, using text messaging to communicate with our viewers is an innovative and relatively new method of marketing that has shown its potential to drive increased customer interactions and also deliver revenue rather than just being a straight marketing cost.

Tamsin Denbigh
Marketing Manager
Channel 5

8.5   The Single Customer View

In this book, we are discussing CRM through the digital channels (eCRM), but of course, the digital channels are just that: channels, which happen to be digital, to reach *the same* customers. For most organizations, the digital channels are growing in importance but still represent a small part of their business. The ultimate goal is for companies to understand their customers across all the points of interaction that the customer has with the company, online and offline. To do this, you need to have a *single customer view*.

In many ways the single customer view (sometimes also called the *enterprise customer view* or the *360° customer view*) is the Holy Grail of CRM. With this in place, a company can interact with its customers in an integrated and consistent manner across all channels, with vastly improved opportunities for superior product and services offerings, improved customer service, and improved customer life cycle management.

Figure 8.2 is a much-simplified data map of how this single customer view pieces together. The left side of this customer data map shows the offline world. A lot of work continues to go into harmonizing all the customer data sources across multiple systems. To the right of the map we see the digital channels and touch points. These are creating further customer data, including behavioral data such as the way users interact with a Web site. This area also offers real-time personalization opportunities. The center shows how data can be unified to provide the single customer view. This data can then be analyzed and supplemented by external data sources to provide a deep level of customer insight to inform decision making.

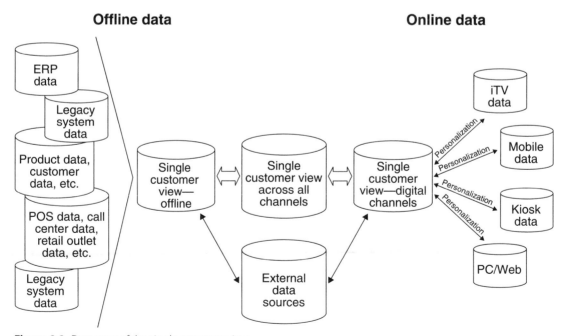

Figure 8.2 Data map of the single customer view.

Typically, the evolution path toward the single customer view goes in the following stages:

1. Tactical customer-centric initiatives. For example, online customer self-service that features order tracking, account status, and problem resolution tracking.
2. Pools of consolidated customer data. For example, customer data are consolidated by department, by channel, or by product line.
3. A single customer view. A customer profile database that unifies all customer data is finally created, but it is still stand-alone and is most probably just used as a data warehouse for analysis purposes.
4. The customer database is linked in with enterprise systems and business processes. Now the single customer view becomes more proactive and dynamic, feeding off and into other business systems.
5. The customer database drives core business processes. The single customer view has by now become the heart and engine of the business. At this stage, the business can truly consider itself to be a customer-centric enterprise.

9

Understanding
Your Users

For ideas on how to understand your *online* customers, refer to Section 15.2, User-centric Measurement, in Chapter 15, Measurement Approaches and Techniques.

AOL was able to swallow up Time Warner as it had twice the stock market valuation at the time. And why did it have such a high valuation? It was due to the huge customer base it had and, more important, because of how much it knew about those customers and the direct relationship it had with them. In hindsight, AOL's valuation at the time seems hugely overblown, but in the ever-intensifying battle for customers, there is still a great premium placed on the value of understanding, and knowing, your customers. This is vital for CRM and it is increasingly at the root of any Web project: Usability, personalization, and community building all absolutely depend on understanding your users.

Your marketing department is likely to have the most information and insight on your customers. You need to understand who your customers are, what their needs are, what influences the decisions they make, and what the longer term trends are. This customer insight is the basis for then working out the all important customer segmentation and data models.

9.1 Segmentation

Customers are typically grouped into segments to make it easier to understand and serve them. There is an increasing drive toward achieving the segment of one vision of one-to-one marketing, where customers are addressed and treated as individuals, but this is still more of a vision and a conceptual approach than a reality. Digital channels help you get nearer to this vision and perhaps create a larger number of more refined segments and subsegments, but you still need to define what those segments and their attributes are and have a notion of how you are actually going to use these groupings.

Segmentation is principally used for three reasons:

1. Reporting and analysis

   A large part of CRM is data analysis. By sifting through customer data, and other relevant data, using a range of techniques from simple rules-based processing to the more complex algorithms of data mining, valuable business intelligence can be derived. Segmentation models can be used here to provide the framework for analysis. In many cases, the goal of the data analysis is to discover the segments in the first place. Segments are built or analyzed according to the following sorts of attributes:

   ▶ *Profitability.* How profitable is the customer?
   ▶ *Monetary.* How much does the customer spend?
   ▶ *Frequency.* How often does the customer buy?
   ▶ *Recency.* How recently has the customer bought?
   ▶ *Payment profile.* Does the customer have a positive payment profile?
   ▶ *Product choice.* Does the customer tend to buy high-margin products?
   ▶ *Product range.* Does the customer buy across a wide range of products?
   ▶ *Responsiveness.* How much does the customer respond to marketing?
   ▶ *Channel usage.* Which purchase channels does the customer use (how cost efficient are they to service)?
   ▶ *Geography.* Where is the customer based?
   ▶ *Life stage.* What life stage is the customer at?
   ▶ *Income.* How much does the customer earn?
   ▶ *Profession.* What does the customer do?
   ▶ *Risk.* What is the customer's risk profile?
   ▶ *Duration.* How long has the customer been a customer?

Once the segments have been defined, they can be reported against and analyzed. The segments can be analyzed for change over time, customer migration between segments can be analyzed, and intersegment dependencies can be examined.

This form of segmentation and data analysis is not something that we are going to address in detail in this book. This is because it has only an indirect impact on maintaining and evolving Web sites. This form of data analysis has existed for a long time, it is not usually done in an online environment (rather than in stand-alone data warehouses), and it does not directly touch or change the interaction with online customers.

2. Marketing campaigns

Clearly, you need to understand your customer segments to market to them effectively. Segments are used to create and target marketing campaigns. As with reporting and analysis, there are any number of attributes that you may wish to use to create a particular segment and a corresponding campaign.

Although creating custom segments for marketing campaigns is very important for the success of a Web site (e.g., in creating targeted email marketing campaigns), this is also an area that we will not be focusing on. This is because we are concentrating on how to maintain and evolve the Web site itself rather than the marketing of it. Also, I believe the skills required to do such segmentation and marketing have long been known to direct marketers and database marketers, so there is much less new to learn here.

3. Personalization

To personalize online, you need to match content to users. To do this, you need to have intelligence about the content itself and about the users and you need to have rules that then match the two in an appropriate manner. If you want to do real-time personalization (on the fly), then you need to have live access to these data.

With the two forms of segmentation application given earlier, you may choose to use existing segmentation models, you may choose to create new ones for a specialized campaign, or you may even be looking for new segments. With personalization, however, the segments must be fixed and known to the system so that rules can be applied. We look at personalization as an approach in more detail in Chapter 10, Personalization, but how do you define the segments that you should use to drive online personalization?

Understanding your customers in general is one thing, but defining and agreeing on a segmentation model that you can use for the Web site are a very important, and often surprisingly challenging, next step. Along with your content schema, which defines the structure and metadata of your content, your customer segmentation model is the most important asset you can create to successfully maintain and evolve a Web site. These two structures of users and content will underpin and affect everything that you do on the site. Any form of personalization is only possible if you have clearly defined user segments to which you can serve the relevant content.

In the offline world, we can be somewhat flexible with our categorizations and use our emotional intelligence, or subjective interpretation of a situation, to make judgments and decisions. Online, it is a computer that has to try and be as human and customer intelligent as it can. For the moment, computers can only follow rules and process instructions and data, so the quality of treatment your customers get depends largely on your ability to properly understand and segment your user base and then devise rules that really do give customers what they want. Computers are dumb: They need logical chunks of data, names, rules, and logic to have any semblance of emotional intelligence.

NOTE   **Using Existing Segmentation Models**

It is likely that your company already understands its customers by segments for marketing purposes. If there is an accepted segmentation model, then there are some strong reasons to use it for the Web site:

- ▶ It is already agreed. No doubt a lot of work and consensus building went into creating segmentation, so why fight against this?
- ▶ It is a common "language." Usually, segmentation models have some kind of naming system associated with them that is commonly understood within the organization. If you use the same system, integration will be easier.
- ▶ Integration of analysis and reporting will be more straightforward. Again, if you can conform to existing structures and processes, integration should be smoother.
- ▶ The single customer view. We looked at this in Chapter 8, A CRM Primer. If the organization is striving to understand its customers consistently across all channels, then it will help to use the same segmentation model regardless of channel.

However, you must ensure that the segmentation model(s) that exist do sensibly transfer online. Models based on geographic location, for example, may not be of any relevance online. Equally, there may be important behavioral traits upon which you want to base your online segmentation that can be done only online. A good place to start is the user analysis work done when the Web site was created. If this was done, it probably contains some very valuable thinking about who the site is addressing, by segment, and what needs the site is meeting. If you can map existing offline segmentation models to an online version that is supplemented by online-specific details, you get the best of both worlds.   ■

In creating a segmentation model that is to form the basis of personalization, you must remember that the primary reason you create a segment is to deliver different Web content or services to that segment which better reflect that segment's needs and interests. If you do not have the content stored in such a way that it can be filtered and delivered to the correct segment, you cannot do personalization. There is somewhat of a chicken and egg situation that needs to be resolved: Do you create your user segments and then try to source content that will serve them, or do you work out from the content that you have to define the segments you can serve? If we are being truly customer-centric, we should start with our user segments and then source or create content to serve them. Of course, budgetary and other realities will impact what is actually feasible, but if at all possible, start with your users rather than your content.

What user attributes might be used to build your segmentation model? Here are a few examples of attributes that are inherent to the user:

▶ *Site user type.* Different site users might have different site access privileges defined by their log on. An administrative user would see different content from a content contributor who would see different content from a regular user.

▶ *Relationship to the company.* Is the user a customer, an employee, a shareholder, a partner, or an investor? In each case, the site might appear differently to suit the user.

▶ *Status of relationship.* An example is the status of a user's account or order. You may want to build a segment of all bad debtors or all customers whose accounts have been dormant for longer than 6 months. The Web site can then be personalized with messages and content relevant to the status of the customer's current relationship with your company.

▶ *Profession.* The user's profession might define what they see on the site. In the case of a portal for medical professionals, for example, doctors are likely to want to see and have access to different content than, say, dentists.

▶ *Nationality.* This typically defines language and geography characteristics that are likely to have a significant impact on what site content the user will be interested in and what language the content should appear in.

- *Gender.* If you sell to both men and women but have very different products or services for each, you may want to personalize the site by gender.
- *Age.* Your customer offerings may be split into age bands, in which case you may have different sites, or site sections, for different age groups.
- *Location.* This is not always relevant but could be. A large chain of stores that likes to give customers a friendly, local feel might want to show only details of the user's local store on the Web site or at least set the local store as a default.

TIP   **Customer Profile Standards**

At the time of writing, the first customer profile standards are beginning to emerge. These are data models for user data that if adhered to make the exchanging and sharing of customer information between different parties much easier and more uniform. These models are tending to come from particular industry sectors and address the typical customer data needs for that sector. However, standardized customer profile information is likely to become more the norm, particularly as browsers store more user information and broker it according to the user's preferences with Web sites. You should check whether any such standardized profiles or initiatives exist for your industry because much of the thinking about what data to include will have been done. Compliance with the model is also likely to help you in the long run with integration.

The attributes given are the same sorts of attributes that are used to build traditional segments, so you may find that your company already has segments based on a combination of these attribute variables that you migrate for online use. These segments can then be used as the basis of site personalization. Simple rules such as "if the user belongs to segment X, then show them Y content" can be created and delivered, assuming you can ascertain that the user does indeed belong to segment X.

However, the real advantages of the Web come when you overlay online behavioral attributes to the underlying user segments so that your personalization rules can be based on who is doing what. Behavioral attributes include the following:

- *Looked at.* If you know what content a user has looked at, you can use this information for personalization advantage. For example, when the user comes back to the site, you could let them know if there had been changes to what they last looked at or you could highlight areas they had not looked at.

▶ *Downloaded.* For example, if a user had downloaded an application form for a particular product or service, you might want to highlight further information on that or sell its benefits.

▶ *Last visit date.* If you log when a user has last visited the site, then this too can be used for personalization that benefits the user. For example, you could let the user know what was new to the site since their last visit.

▶ *Create date.* This might be the create date of a user's registration record, a first transaction, a customer service inquiry, or other user-specific record. Personalization could then be based on the amount of time between the create date and the current date. For example, if an online customer service inquiry has gone unresolved beyond a certain length of time, you may wish to say something specific about this to all affected users.

▶ *Last update.* Perhaps this is the last time the user updated her personal details, the last time she renewed her membership, or the last time she logged a customer service inquiry. These behavioral attributes can trigger further personalization rules.

By combining segments based on inherent user attributes with behavioral attributes, you will note that your personalization possibilities become much more powerful. You can now say, "If someone from segment X does Y, then show them Z."

Table 9.1 gives you a template to use as you begin to detail your user segments. It has been filled out with some example data for just two user segments of a fictional medicolegal insurance membership organization. You can imagine that they have a large but static site that has different sections of content for each of its members' segments. They are now evolving the site to make maintaining the large amounts of medicolegal content they have more manageable and more accessible to their members. They also want to use personalization to improve the Web site experience and better promote their services. To do this, they will need to classify and tag their content and manage it through some form of content management system, and they need to classify and identify their member segments. The template headings are useful as follows:

▶ *ID.* This is a useful short-form reference code and could be useful later for sorting and filtering by segment. Whereas a name may change, the ID should not and is likely to be used for programming purposes.

Table 9.1 User segmentation template.

ID	Name	Identifying value	Description	Importance to the business
1	Doctors	Choice of profession type in membership details.	70:30 Male:Female. High proportion based in the southeast and concentrated in major cities. Increasing number of especially general practitioners and part time. 20,000 current members of 37,000 total market size.	HIGH. Doctors are our core customers: Their membership fees represent 50% of current revenues.
1.1	Junior Doctors	Choice of profession type/career stage in membership details.	Shift toward female and ethnic minorities, but still low here. Intake of 4000 each year.	VERY HIGH. It is at this level that the choice of medicolegal insurer is made, so this is a critical conversion point, especially as churn thereafter is very low. This segment represents the future of our company!

▶ *Name.* This performs a similar function to the ID but is more user-friendly. Whereas your programmers might prefer a segment ID, your marketing people will probably prefer a segment name.

▶ *Identifying value.* How are you actually going to know whether an online user belongs to the segment? In the example given, it is relatively straightforward: The segments are based on profession, and these details reside in the user's membership records. Once they log on to the site, the system will reference the member's records and know which segment he or she belongs to. However, you might have segments based purely on behavioral attributes, such as a segment called Regular_Visitors whose identifying value is a certain number of repeat visits per month tracked by a cookie.

▶ *Description.* You might want to include demographic information, the size or traffic volume of the segment, levels of technology savvy, other sites this segment uses, interdependencies with other segments, or even a "pen portrait" describing a typical member of the segment.

Key reasons to use site	Behavioral attributes of interest	Personalization ideas
1. Online membership applications and renewal 2. Update their clinical practice information 3. Get revalidation support	1. Have they logged on to the site? 2. Have they looked at and updated their membership details online?	1. Membership summary details on the home page. 2. Show "Number of days until your revalidation is due" on home page and send reminder emails. 3. If doctor has logged on to site but not looked at membership details, then promote benefits via home page and email.
1. To receive educational support for further exams 2. To access medicolegal knowledge base	1. Have they logged on to the site? 2. Have they come back to the site regularly? 3. Have they downloaded any of our tutorial guides? 4. Have they posted to our forum?	1. Promote "Free exam support in our forums" on home page. 2. Email our "Guide to getting through medical school" when they register on site. 3. Create user-to-user auction for used medical books only visible to Junior Doctors.

Refer to Part IV, Site Measurement, for more details on measuring and tracking how a site is being used.

▶ *Importance to the business.* This can help you prioritize your development efforts as well as focus your personalization ideas to ensure they are delivering value to the business.

▶ *Key reasons to use site.* While this attribute reminds you of the value of the segment to the business, this field refocuses you on what the segment is interested in on your site. There are all sorts of ways you can find this out if you have an existing site. Taking the user's viewpoint helps ensure that your personalization ideas meet their needs.

▶ *Behavioral attributes of interest.* Given what the business is interested in and what the user is trying to get out of the site, what behavior do you need to look for to know that the site is succeeding? Focusing on this will help you define what you actually need to measure on the site as well as help shape your ideas on how personalization might encourage, or be triggered by, certain kinds of behavior.

▶ *Personalization ideas.* At this stage, you do not need to be defining rules in the form of "if X, then Y" or "where this equals X, then show Y + 1," but you do have the material to begin articulating personalization ideas, by segment, that will deliver value to the business and the user.

You should initially use the template given in Table 9.1 to capture all the possible segments that you feel might be relevant. You can then begin to combine and refine those segments, iterating your segment definitions with members of your company to build consensus. Personalization is inextricably tied up with content management (you are matching content to users after all), which is why Table 9.1 contains information and thinking about what content on the site is of most interest to the segment. This intelligence helps when defining page templates and the template logic to deliver the most appropriate content to the relevant users.

TIP   **Subsegmentation**

In the example given in Table 9.1, you may have noted that the IDs of 1 and 1.1 suggest that Junior Doctors is a subset of the Doctors segment. If you have subsegments such as this, you should define them as separate segments, with their own names and IDs, rather than lump them together, even if you know that for the moment you have no way of splitting out your content to serve the subsegments. First, your users are unlikely to notice that the same content is being served to two or more different segments because each individual usual will typically belong to only one segment. Second, and much more important, it is easy to use programming logic to combine and then unbundle segments for the purposes of personalization, but it is not as easy to recategorize all your users.

Imagine Doctors had four subsegments. You have segment 1 and subsegments 1.1–1.4. At the moment, you can only really categorize your content by Doctors in general. This is not ideal, but you plan to create more content that will be specifically for the subsegments. In the short term, your programming logic can just say, "Anyone that's 1 or 1.something will get Doctors' content." However, as your new content becomes available, you can immediately start to say, "Show subsegments 1.1 to 1.3 the Doctors' content as before but show anyone who belongs to the 1.4 subsegment this new content." This is easy only if you actually have your users already segmented. If you lumped all the subsegments into just Doctors, you would have to go through your entire user base and recategorize them all.

Case Study **Understanding and Segmenting a Customer Base to Deliver Business Benefit**

Company: Netpoll, *www.netpoll.net*

Company Overview

At Netpoll, we provide our clients with consultative research that delivers insights into user attitudes across interactive platforms. These insights are based on expert opinion, market analysis, customer interviews, consultancy, surveys, and statistics, all aimed at better understanding the interactive user. Backed by a team of experienced researchers and analysts from a variety of backgrounds, our strategic services encompass planning, research, and analysis.

Background to Case Study and Objectives

In mid-2001, France's leading online newspaper *Le Monde Interactif* (MIA) was looking into methods by which they could monetize their content. To do this successfully, MIA had a number of key questions about their customer base that needed answers, including:

▶ Who are our online customers?
▶ For what services are they most likely to pay?
▶ At what price?
▶ How do we reach them?
▶ What impact will this have on our existing free subscribers and users?

Netpoll was contracted as the research partner to help answer these questions and provide a robust consumer-led business case for any decisions taken in regard to the final paid-for content product.

Process and Practice

The project took place over the course of 4 months and involved two key phases as represented in Figure 9.1. The most important input to the process was to establish the characteristics, behavior, and preferences of the customer base. The online survey, which received more than 10,000 responses, helped us establish four unique customer segments. These could be broadly defined as brand loyalists, news browsers, surfers, and

continued

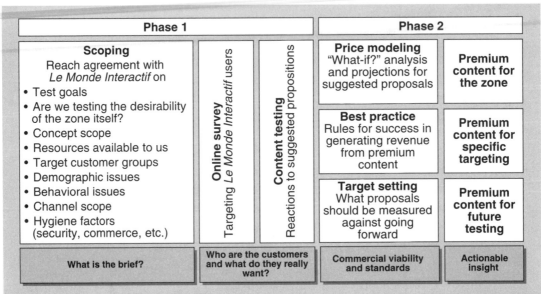

Figure 9.1 Process for user segmentation project.

payment rejecters, as shown in Figure 9.2. The brand loyalists were three times as willing to pay for online content as the next two categories, and the rejecters had an interest level so low it barely registered. Generally, the browsers were more willing than the surfers; however, we had to treat the willingness to pay of the surfers with some degree of skepticism given their youthful profile and the claim that the news was of limited interest.

In addition to the survey, we ran concept groups in both Paris and New York to probe the different motivations for both national and international users. The most interesting finding was that for international respondents, even expatriates, *Le Monde* was very much a secondary news source. This had dramatic implications for their willingness to pay. The combination of these findings formed the basis of our price elasticity calculations.

Rejecters	Browsers	Loyalists	Surfers
• Young • More students • Time rich, cash poor • Low Internet experience • Deep readers of the news	• Older • More private sector managers • Cash rich, time poor • Good Internet experience • Hungry for frequent updates	• Oldest • More public sector workers • Cash rich, time poor • Most Internet experience • Use many *lemonde.fr* services	• Youngest • Time rich, cash poorest • Least Internet experience • Least hungry for news

Figure 9.2 Example user segments.

Concept testing of different functionality and modes of payment also helped resolve an internal debate on the way to charge. A range of options had been proposed from the simple subscription model to bespoke payment and tiered access. Among other concepts, one of *Le Monde's* more brilliant ideas was a morning newsletter that gives subscribers an exclusive preview of the afternoon edition (*Le Monde* is an afternoon paper). This proved universally popular with our test subjects. Indeed, levels of interest were fairly consistent (good or bad) between segments for many proposed services leading us to conclude that tiered pricing was not either desirable or necessary. This would not necessarily be true for other online content brands. Much in the *Le Monde* work related to the unique power of their brand with a very influential audience.

Results

By understanding and segmenting *Le Monde's* online customer base, we were able to produce a set of recommendations on pricing, charging mechanism, content, and services that we were confident would work. Our recommended revenue-maximizing price of $5 per month was adopted as were many of the prioritizations on design and content. We were also able to provide a flexible price and planning tool, built upon the insight we gained, that would adjust predictions according to new information and recommendations on best practice informed by case studies from across the industry.

Le Monde's early returns for the premium zone proved to be extremely positive, coming close to and then exceeding our first quarter predictions. We believe this effect was in some part stimulated by the intense interest in the surprise victory of Jean-Marie Le Pen during the first round of the 2002 French presidential election.

Client feedback was exceptionally positive, and the future of the *Le Monde's* subscribers' edition looks extremely healthy.

Lessons Learned

One of the most important lessons from the project was that of retaining an open mind during the research. Many of the preconceptions of both the research and client teams changed during the course of the study in response to the new facts emerging. You may think that you know your online customer base and their needs well, but it pays to find out for sure.

It was of great to surprise to me, for example, that there was so little delineation in desired services between the different customer segments. One of the more universally popular online news services, SMS alerts for newsflashes, failed to register much support,

continued

and the customers who tended to read *Le Monde* in the most depth were also those who had most resistance to the notion of paying for online services.

It is a common assumption of interactive service providers that primary research is a luxury that you can ill afford in the rush to market. People who really know what they're doing don't need it, and "if you build it, they will come." No serious company would take this attitude in the offline space, and those that do tend to fail after their initial run of luck wears off. Risking putting out the wrong service at the wrong price to the wrong people is never the right decision. Understanding and segmenting your customer base through consumer research pay for themselves many times over.

Andy Mayer
Lead Strategist
Netpoll

9.2   Customer Data

Segmentation and personalization are all very well, but of course, you cannot do any of it online if you do not have two prerequisites: the actual customer data and a means to uniquely identify individuals when they come to the site. How to identify and track individual users is addressed in Section 15.2, User-Centric Measurement, in Part IV, Site Measurement. Here we look at the customer data themselves and how to acquire them.

9.2.1   Capturing Customer Data

Before you can manage your customer data, you need to get some. Actually capturing those data in the first place, considering most people are very distrustful of simply handing over their personal data to some Web site, is an art form in itself. Doing it well, or poorly, makes a huge impact on your ability to acquire and retain customers. Arguably, along with site usability, examining and fine-tuning your customer data capture processes are the quickest of "quick wins" in the arsenal of weapons at your disposal to improve the overall performance of your Web site.

The two apparently simple stages to customer data capture are first to work out what data you actually need and second how you are going to acquire them. Tables 9.2 and 9.3 suggest a structure for addressing the first stage, breaking the analysis into data required from users and data required from the system with further subdivisions according to priority and necessity.

Table 9.2 Analyzing your customer data requirements.

Customer data required from the customers

Priority	Description
Must-have	This is the bare minimum of customer data that you require to do your business with them. Examples include contact and address details to deliver your customer's products or transaction details to process the order. For a membership organization, further personal details or areas of interest may be must-have data. For some businesses, such as financial services organizations, there is a lot of must-have customer data, often for regulatory reasons.
	These data are relatively easy to collect from users as they understand why they are necessary.
Important to have	These data are not absolutely necessary but would be of great benefit either to you or to the customer. This might include alternate, or more detailed, contact information or gender or age details. It should certainly include the data you need to do all those great things you have in mind to make your site stand out. For example, you may offer some very useful personalization features on your site for which you need some additional customer data (birth dates for automated gifting reminders perhaps?); maybe you offer your customers customized SMS alerts for which you need their mobile phone number. It should be clear from your ideas for enhanced content and functionality what data will be required to make them possible.
	The key to acquiring important customer data is to make it clear to the users why it is important and how they will benefit. Of course, some data are important to you as a business but very much less so to users, in which case acquiring the data will be trickier.
Nice to have	There are no doubt many things that you would love to know from your customers but which either are not strictly necessary to operate your site or you are very unlikely to get from your customers. Most of this information revolves around marketing intelligence: What are our customers' interests? Where did they hear about us? Do they have friends who might also want to know about us? Which of our competitors do they do business with? What other sites like ours do they use? This kind of information is nice to have, but you cannot force users to provide it.
	To acquire this kind of customer data, you should ensure that it is not required information, there are as few questions as possible, and you are open and honest about why you would like to know. Customers these days are savvy to the ways of marketing and often cynical, but if you ask politely, you may just get some help.

Table 9.3 Analyzing your customer data requirements.

Customer-related data required from the system

Priority	Description
Must-have	The must-have data that are system generated and customer related are often the management elements of the customer profile record. For example, for a membership organization the create date of a new member's record is probably not entered by the customer but is recorded by the system once the membership begins. This date is a must-have for managing membership renewals. Transaction dates or customer status information might also be must-haves for operational or legal reasons.
	Customer-related data generated by the system are easy to collect because they do not require the cooperation or, in most cases, consent of the customer. However, you still have to think through what you need and then actively collect and use it.
Important to have	These are system data required in enabling enhanced content and functionality on your site. This might be user facing, as with personalization, or it might be business facing, as with more advanced reporting and analysis features. For example, by having a last visit data element stored for each customer profile, you can then show that user what has changed on the site the next time they visit. Or from a business viewpoint, you may log what content types users have been looking at on the site so that you can report on content popularity and usage by individual or by segment.
Nice to have	Perhaps there are some things that you feel are worth the system logging about users that you cannot use now but have a feeling might come in handy later. Or perhaps there is some user analysis that you would like to do out of interest but is not strictly necessary. If there are customer-related data that can be logged by the system without adversely impacting the user experience (e.g., by slowing the site down), there is an argument for capturing everything you can in case you need it later. This is fine but you do need to be sure it is not going to cause problems or impact performance: Extra data take up extra space, which costs extra time and money.

The analysis in the tables looks at all the customer data requirements from a business point of view. You now need to look at these data requirements from a customer perspective. You might begin by mapping the data elements you have come up with in your business analysis into four quadrants as shown in Figure 9.3. This gives you the additional perspective on how easy it is likely to be to get the data you want. Often you will find that some of your must-have data are also likely to be hard to acquire, whereas other elements are likely to be surprisingly easy. Looking at your data requirements in this way can help you further prioritize.

This now needs to be translated into what the customer will experience. Inasmuch as we are talking about Web sites, the way customers give data is

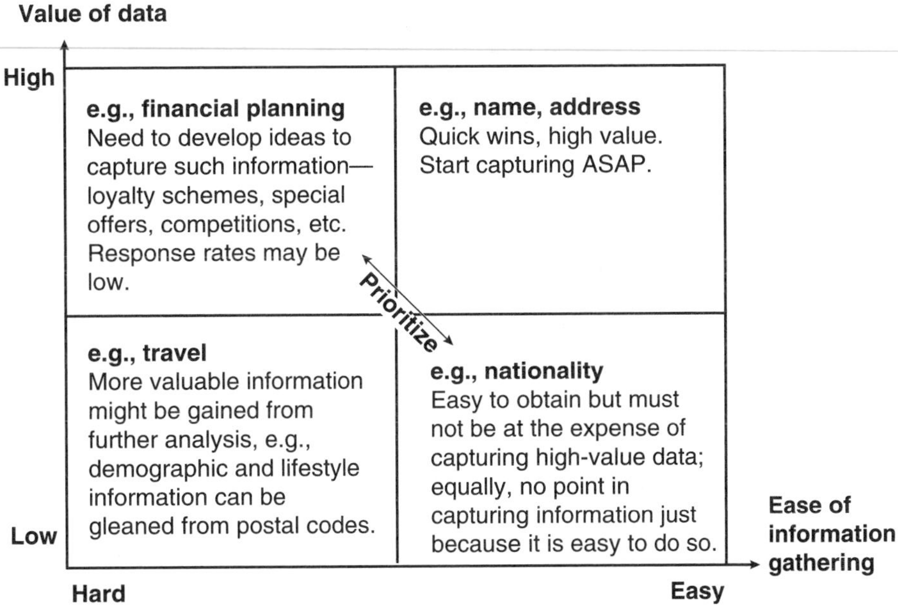

Value of data

e.g., financial planning Need to develop ideas to capture such information— loyalty schemes, special offers, competitions, etc. Response rates may be low.	**e.g., name, address** Quick wins, high value. Start capturing ASAP.
e.g., travel More valuable information might be gained from further analysis, e.g., demographic and lifestyle information can be gleaned from postal codes.	**e.g., nationality** Easy to obtain but must not be at the expense of capturing high-value data; equally, no point in capturing information just because it is easy to do so.

High

Low

Hard   Easy

Prioritize

Ease of information gathering

Figure 9.3 Mapping data capture requirements.

almost always via a Web form that they fill in and submit. Email is an alternative, or perhaps filling in a document that is downloaded and sending this as an attachment, but forms make for the easiest processing. Whichever route you are using, you should split the information into required and optional. The required information should appear on your form with an asterisk or highlighted in some other way (e.g., a different text color), so it is abundantly clear to users which information they have to give and what information you would like them to give.

As you will note, what were three categories in our original analysis (must-have, important to have, and nice to have) have now been reduced to just two categories: required and optional. Whereas the original analysis should catalog all the possible customer-related data you wish to capture, it is now time to decide what you are actually going to ask for. You should be particularly tough on yourself when it comes to what is required data. The must-have data are easy because those will be required. However, the debates will come when discussing the grayer areas of the important to have and nice to have data. Experience has shown that as a rule the more information a customer has to give on the Web, the less likely he or she is to complete the form at all. A customer can choose to skip the optional information, so you can afford to make this a little longer without risking losing customer data, but you must assume as a working basis that for every extra piece of information you make required, you are losing more customers. It is a negative way to look at things, perhaps, but a good way to focus on capturing only what you really, really need.

The absolute minimum required is no more than a single means of contacting the customer. You do not necessarily even need a name: Signing up for a newsletter is often the easy way into a relationship with a Web site, and this requires only an email address. Often companies collect gender and age information as required because they think these must be useful. They can be, but only if you know what you are going to do with them, and often gender and age appear to be really of no relevance at all, so why ask?

TIP   **"Drip" Data Capture**

Users do not like handing over all their personal data right away, particularly if they are not absolutely sure that they can trust the Web site in question. Bigger brands have an advantage in this sense as users are more willing to trust the site with their details. However, one way to build up a rich user profile and build a strong relationship is to do it slowly, little by little, over time. Just as in the real world where most relationships are developed over time, the approach online is similar: Start by asking for very little, and over time, slowly ask for more data as the user feels comfortable to give them. For example, users might be happy to start by signing up for a newsletter and giving their email address. Further down the line, they might be happy to give their home address to be sent a catalog, then their transaction details to purchase, and finally more detailed personal preferences in a survey for a competition or to personalize their special offers email.

Once you have decided what data you require of the customer and what is to be optional, you need to decide how you are going to get the data you want. There are three ways to get these data: You can ask the user for it, you can infer it based on the user's on-site behavior, or you can buy it from a third party. The second two options may have some merit for enriching existing intelligence you have about user segments, and they are easier to implement as they are less customer intrusive, but they are not nearly as reliable as simply asking the user for the data. Furthermore, only by asking the user for his or her data can you actually directly and openly begin a dialogue and a relationship. As the other two options are done without the customer's knowledge, they take you no closer to one of the core aims of CRM: building stronger customer relationships.

So how do you successfully ask your customers for their data? Following are some pointers:

▶ *Be open and honest.* Above all, you should not try and hide anything from users. The moment they become the tiniest bit suspicious about what you may be up to, you have lost their trust and hence their data.

▶ *Clear articulation of benefits.* Customers may be suspicious of why you want their data and wise to the marketing uses to which it will be put. They need to be convinced with a clear articulation of the benefits they will receive for giving their data in the first place. You must recognize that there is a value exchange taking place: The user knows that his or her data are valuable to you, so you must sacrifice something of value in return. Even splitting your form information into required and optional is a good start in showing a form of value recognition of the user. You are tacitly saying, "We recognize you are busy and don't like giving your data, so we've thought hard about requiring of you only those data that we really feel we need. The rest is up to you." This kind of approach will win you many more conversions.

▶ *Take privacy and security very seriously.* Clearly state your privacy policies, security measures, and data protection guidelines. Third-party accreditation from independent bodies (e.g., TRUSTe) helps you show your customers that you take their security and privacy seriously.

▶ *Capture data over time.* Rather than trying to capture the data you want all at once, maybe you can do it little by little over time. Think of a reason users might be happy to give you their email address to start with and plan how to build out their data profiles over time from there.

▶ *Use form validation.* To improve the quality of captured data, you can perform client-side checks on what has been entered to ensure quality before submission. For example, you might want to check for the @ sign in an email address or, very commonly, alert users to any required information fields that they have not filled in.

▶ *Form usability.* It is extremely important to make the form clear and easy to understand. Test it on real users first. Include any instructions or example data where necessary. Make it clear to users where they are in the form-filling process (e.g., "step 1 of 2").

▶ *Customer data integration.* You should centralize your customer data with a common format for ease and accuracy of subsequent analysis and, particularly if you are going to be integrating or exchanging the data with other applications, use "open" data standards to store the customer data (e.g., XML) so that it can easily be shared or exported to other systems. Increasingly, there are customer data profile standards beginning to emerge, particularly by industry sector, which could help you define the data model and standard to adhere to.

TIP   **What to Do Immediately after Data Capture**

Once users have filled in a form giving their data, typically for registration or purchase, they are typically in a slightly more relaxed and open state of mind than before. They have accomplished what they wanted and therefore are more open to following other avenues of interest. They have more of a browse mentality than a focused "just get it done" attitude. This moment after data capture presents several opportunities:

▶ *The thank you page.* After the purchase or registration, you should show a thank you screen to confirm to the user that the form has been successfully sent. This screen can also have interactive hooks, preferably relevant to the purchase just made or the registration data just given, that lead the customer on to other areas of your site and your offering. Make the most of the customer's mind being open, with guard down for a moment, to gently present cross-sells or perhaps offer email newsletters so you have an ongoing reason to contact the customer.

▶ *Email confirmation.* As well as the thank you screen, you should send an email to the user confirming the registration or purchase. Not only is this good practice and fills users with confidence that their data did get through, but it serves several other important functions: You can verify whether the email address given actually works, you are establishing a more personal and direct contact with customers by popping up in their email inboxes, and again, you have an opportunity to helpfully suggest other links, content, products, or services that the customers might be interested in based on the purchase or registration they have just completed.

▶ *User tracking and identification.* Just after the point of user data capture is the time to set a cookie on that user's machine so the next time the user comes back to the site you know who he or she is. Once you can track individual users, you can start to measure customer loyalty, which is the fundamental barometer of CRM success.

▶ *Personalization.* Whatever other personalization you have planned, there are some basic things you can do once you have a user's personal data to improve his or her experience on your site. Prefilled forms are a good example or various alerts and reminders, what has changed on the site since her last visit, and so on.

9.2.2 Permission and Privacy

The R in CRM is for relationship, and you cannot have a relationship that is one way. Direct mail that you receive and throw straight in the bin or spam email that you receive and angrily delete is not about relationships. It is what Seth Godin, in his book *Permission Marketing*, refers to as "interruption marketing." Godin preaches the growing importance of permission marketing where the customer gives his or her consent to be marketed to. Whatever, you want to call it, and whether or not you buy into all of what Godin says, there is no doubt that if you are trying to leverage the interactive powers of the Web to build stronger customer relationships, you can only do so effectively with users' permission and subsequent commitment to the relationship.

The depth and levels of permission you have to interact with your customers are very valuable intangible assets that you build over time. You have to invest a lot of time, effort, and money to get this permission, but it is a very powerful commercial advantage as it is very hard to copy or steal. Like strong brands, deep levels of permission take a long time to build, but if nurtured, they endure and grow well too.

For all the marketing revolution speak, permission and privacy are about common sense and courtesy. Just ask yourself honestly how you would like to be treated, and as often as not, your customers will be little different. If you abuse your customers' permission or privacy, then it is possible you might gain in the short term, but it is highly improbable you will do so in the long term. Nothing can be quite so scary as the power of online customers whose personal data have been abused. In the examples that I know of where a company has stepped over the lines of acceptable use of customer data, the downsides have always outweighed any upsides. By themselves, the measurable customer service costs in dealing with resulting complaints are enough to learn the lesson the hard way, not to mention the harder to measure but even more damaging lost customer count.

The data protection and privacy laws vary from country to country, so it is difficult to give any hard and fast guidelines on how to do permission and privacy online. However, the basic premise must be: Ask users for their permission to do what you want to do; tell them clearly what it is that you want to do; and allow them to opt out of whatever it is you are doing at any later stage. The specifics of what this means in practice are being hammered out by governments and various industry bodies around the world, but it is Internet users themselves who are the strongest enforcers of personal privacy and permission.

If you are not sure where to begin with implementing permission or privacy best practice on your site, then there are several places to begin. First, look at what other leading Web sites are doing. Use their policies as a template for your own. They have put a lot of thought and money into getting these right and have kindly posted them on the Web to help you out. Second, look to industry bodies for guidance. For example, to comply with the certification requirements of TRUSTe, you have to satisfy them with details on the following seven key questions:

1. What personally identifiable information is collected by you through the Web site?
2. Who is the organization collecting the information?
3. How is the information used?
4. With whom may the information be shared?
5. What choices are available to the user regarding collection, use, and distribution of the information?
6. What kind of security procedures do you have in place to protect the loss, misuse, or alteration of information under your control?
7. How can users correct any inaccuracies in the information held on them?

NOTE   **The Complexities of Interactive TV and Mobile Internet**

This book is primarily about Web sites, but you should note that customer data issues become markedly more complex once you start to introduce other digital channels such as interactive TV and mobile Internet. This is partly because someone actually owns the platform or infrastructure that delivers the data (whereas nobody owns the Internet), meaning they have greater levels of access and control over customer data, and also because there are existing regulators (e.g., telecoms and broadcast regulators) who are still in the early days of grappling with trying to define standards for the new interactive channels. Every regulator in every country can be different. Mobile Internet is made even harder because with prepay phones, which in most countries account for a large part of the market, you have no idea who the user is, rendering applications of customer data of little value. Existing subscriber contracts, between mobile phone subscriber and operator, may also complicate your ability to collect and use customer data. ∎

Third, you must ensure that you comply with any legal requirements depending on the applicable jurisdiction. For example, in the United Kingdom, the UK Data Protection Act of 1998 requires every data controller who is processing personal data to notify the UK Data Protection Registrar. If you are processing customer data and are not registered, you are breaking the law. In the UK, anyone processing personal data must comply with the eight enforceable principles of good practice. They state that data must be:

1. Fairly and lawfully processed
2. Processed for limited purposes
3. Adequate, relevant, and not excessive
4. Accurate
5. Not kept longer than necessary
6. Processed in accordance with the data subject's rights
7. Secure
8. Not transferred to countries without adequate protection

9.2.3   Managing Customer Data

The focus of CRM, and this part of the book, is to think of users as the individual people they are, not as inanimate blobs of information. Although CRM involves processes and technology, if it does not work at the more human relationship level, then it will fail. However, from a data and content management point of view, customer data profiles can be treated and understood in the same way as any other content object that needs to be acquired, managed, and published. Just as a content object has management and display elements to it, so too does a customer profile object. (If you are not sure what is meant by content objects and management and display elements, refer to Part II, Content Management.) Consider, for example, the content object for a restaurant review, which might contain the following management and display elements:

Management elements: CreateDate, ReviewDate, ExpireDate, ReviewAuthor, Language, ChannelType, PublicationName

Display elements: RestaurantName, Address1, Address2, Address3, PostalCode, Tel, Web, Email, StarRating, OurOverallRating, ReservationsYesNo, PhotoDetail, PhotoLarge, Chef, ReviewAbstract, ReviewFull

A customer data object would be structured and managed in a very similar way, with relevant management and display elements. For example:

Management elements: UserID, CreateDate, LastVisitDate, NoVisits, SegmentID, CustomerServiceInquiries, ContentTypesLookedAt

Display elements: FirstName, LastName, Address1, Address2, Address3, Zip Code, Tel, Web, Email, Password, UserName, Photo, NewsletterSubscribedYesNo, EmailFormat

In this example, there are elements within the display category that you might think were for managing the object rather than information for display. However, if you imagine that in this case users have access to their personal profile and can choose what of their personal profile they wish to make public to other site users, then you can see that this is indeed information used for display purposes. Management and display elements for customer profiles are not hard boundaries, just as they are not for content objects; rather, they are a useful way to ensure you consider what information you need about your customers not just to make the site work from a display point of view but also to efficiently manage your customer data. Although we are dealing with real people here, a customer data profile can be considered a content object for management and maintenance purposes.

For more details on content objects and how to manage them, refer to Part II, Content Management.

10

Personalization

Personalization is perhaps the most often-cited advantage afforded by digital channels. However, companies have found the practice of delivering personalized digital propositions much more challenging than the theory. It is undeniable that customers want increasingly relevant offerings that meet their needs and save them time. As it is so easy to switch providers online, personalization is increasingly becoming one of the key differentiators and barriers to switching in the competition for acquiring and retaining customers. Real-time personalization clearly is not possible through offline channels (human interactions aside) such as retail presences, direct mail, or advertising. Multiple digital platforms, however, do hold out the promise of delivering a consistent personalized experience to the customer at any time of day and in any location. Doing this successfully is one of the largest CRM challenges that many companies are currently tackling.

In the following sections, we briefly look at the theory of personalization, what it means, and what it promises, followed by the reality of personalization in terms of what we have learned about it over the last few years, and finally the practice of personalization.

10.1   What Personalization Is and What It Promises

The Personalization Consortium defines personalization as "the use of technology and customer information to tailor electronic commerce interactions between a business and each individual customer." The purpose of personalization, they say, is to:

▶ Better serve the customer by anticipating needs
▶ Make the interaction efficient and satisfying for both parties
▶ Build a relationship that encourages the customer to return for subsequent purchases

You might also add other business objectives such as improved customer retention, more effective marketing, greater customer insight, higher conversion rates, increased switching costs, higher order values, and share of wallet. Personalization promises to deliver on the core CRM objective of improved value to both customer and business.

On a more macro level, personalization, enabled by technology, is about trying to recover the highly personalized levels of customer service apparent in the era of the village economy and yet retain the cost advantages delivered by the Industrial Revolution and the mass-market economy. Today, customers prize service and their own time above all else, yet they also expect highly competitive pricing. In theory, technology-enabled personalization can make this possible.

NOTE   **The Different Forms of Personalization**

You come across many different variants of personalization, with customization and collaborative filtering being two common examples. Are these all personalization or something different? If you are being strict, you might argue that they are different. Customization is where users proactively configure, or customize, their online experiences using tools at their disposal, such as choosing a preferred layout or selecting content display options. Customization requires little customer intelligence or the creation of rules, only some functionality and the ability to recognize a unique user. Collaborative filtering requires no intelligence on the browsing customer; rather, it performs an analysis of past transactions or customer preferences to display relevant content and options to anyone: "[We don't necessarily know who you are, but you might be interested to know that . . .] customers who chose X were also interested in Y." Personalization, however, is about matching content, functionality, and services to known and recognized users according to rules that you have devised. Personalization is not actively configured by users; like customization, it happens transparently for them. All this said, the lines between all the different variants of personalization can quickly become blurred, and it does not matter too much what you call things as long as you and your team understand what you are trying to achieve, why, and how.   ◼

Whatever your understanding of the term personalization, the following process is required to personalize:

▶ *Identification.* Obviously, you cannot personalize an experience if you do not know who the user is, so unique user identification must be the first step.

▶ *Customer data capture.* Once you have identified a unique user, you require further information about them to form the intelligence you need to personalize. You can collect data about the user through implicit and explicit techniques. Explicit data capture is when users are aware that data are being captured, typically because they are being asked to fill in a form, whereas implicit data are captured without the user's knowledge. Inferred preferences based on online behavior or supplementary third-party data are examples.

▶ *Recognition.* As well as initially identifying the user, you must be able to recognize the user when he or she comes back to the site. Once recognized, the system can tap into the customer's data profile to use it for personalization purposes.

▶ *Match.* Once you have recognized a user, you match content, functionality, and services to their profile based on rules that you have set. These rules define how the personalization works.

▶ *Merge and deliver.* Based on the rules and the relevant match, the system determines the interface and content for the user and merges the two dynamically at the point of delivering the page to the user.

10.2 What We've Learned So Far

During the dotcom heyday, personalization was a hot buzzword. Since the bursting of the bubble, personalization's image has also been tarnished, and many see it as overhyped and underdelivered. The practice of personalization online has so far come up against the following realities:

▶ *Privacy, security, and regulatory challenges.* If you have ever had to deal with the complexities of data protection across multiple international jurisdictions, you will appreciate just how complex (and expensive) this can be to get right.

▶ *Cost.* Achieving real-time personalization is very expensive, often prohibitively so. Systems integration and maintaining accurate data alone are expensive mountains to climb.

▶ *Skills gap.* There are not that many people who really understand how to implement personalization. Many implementations of enterprise personalization platforms are actually being used for content management and not personalization (yet).

▶ *Return on investment.* There has not yet been enough published proof that personalization actually delivers a clearly demonstrable return on investment (ROI). In fact, in some cases, there is evidence that personalization actually destroys value—for example, through losing customers whose preferences have been incorrectly inferred by a personalization engine.

▶ *It takes time for users to use personalization features.* Very few site users leap into personalization or hand over all their precious personal data right away. They first have to establish a relationship of trust and comfort with the site. It takes time to configure personalization features and time is precious, so uptake is by no means swift or guaranteed. Many users can quite happily do without personalization.

▶ *Multichannel challenges.* Achieving cross-channel, integrated personalization (which requires the single customer view) is a very large systems, data, and process integration job. Furthermore, different digital devices have specific technology considerations: Some mobile phones do not support cookies, and most interactive TV users do not have keyboards, making text entry, and therefore, logon, an issue.

▶ *The technology is the easy part.* Although personalization technology may be quite complex and advanced, it is not as hard to get right as ~~are~~ the people, proposition, and process elements of a personalization project. Doing personalization is a lot easier than working out the whats, whys, and hows.

Perhaps the single biggest lesson learned from personalization work so far is not to attempt or expect too much too soon. Personalization is rightly a part of the CRM family as it is about improving the relationship and point of interface between customer and company. As we have pointed out, however, relationships are not implemented out of the box, nor do they grow overnight.

They must be nurtured and grow over time. Be wary of any "turnkey" personalization solution. Personalization, like a relationship, grows from small beginnings. It is better to start small with your personalization initiative, develop what works best, iterate, and grow over time than to throw every personalization feature you can buy out of the box at your customers. Typically, you might start by giving customers access to their profile, account details, or order status and then allow them to edit and update that and other information before moving on to more sophisticated content, product, and service personalization features. Before you can successfully devise personalization rules, you need to spend time observing and learning about your customers and their preferences, so give them the opportunity to show you what they like.

TIP   **Sorting Out the Basics**

I am a great believer in the power of personalization and have seen it deliver measurable benefits on many occasions. However, in your quest to maintain and evolve your Web site, there is no point even thinking about personalization until you are sure you have other more important basics sorted out. No amount of personalization is going to make up for poor navigation, poor content, or poor customer service, for example. Focus first on what customers care most about. And that is not personalization. In many cases, they can live quite happily without it.

10.3 How to Personalize

We briefly looked at customization and collaborative filtering as forms of personalization. By far the most common form of personalization, however, is rules-based matching. The rules create matches between users and content typically based on one or more of the following three user characteristics:

▶ *Profile.* Assuming you have segmented your customer base and have collected the necessary information to be able to identify which segment a user belongs to, you can personalize according to a rule for that user's segment. For example, "if a user has a profile that means she belongs to our Doctors' segment, then show her the Doctors' navigation."

▶ *Behavior.* Here you personalize according to rules based on what the user is doing, or has done in the past, rather than on who he is. Past behavior could be anything from when the user last visited the site, when he last bought something, or when he last checked his account. Obviously, you need to be able to identify individual returning users (usually via logon) to do this form of behavioral personalization. You can also create rules for behavior that is in progress and does not necessarily require unique user identification. For example, "if the user has visited page X, then show him product X promotion when he returns to the home page."

▶ *Characteristic.* This third category is somewhat of a catchall, typically used when you are creating rules to identify and target a group of customers for a particular campaign or other "push" marketing initiative. You might have your regular personalization in place, which is based on behavioral or profile-based rules, but then you want to send out a promotional email to a range of customers who cut across your existing groupings. In this case, you need to identify a characteristic that can be used to create a rule that will filter your users accordingly. For example, you may not normally use age or gender as the basis for your personalization rules, but one day it becomes relevant for a particular campaign, and seeing as you have these user data stored, it is a characteristic that can be applied.

The process for creating rules is quite simple if you have the right data and information on hand. Creating rules that work really well, however, is certainly not self-evident and requires a very good understanding of your customers' needs and interests. The following five-step process describes how to define and implement your rules.

1. You need to understand your users by segments. These segments may be based on any of the three personalization criteria (e.g., profile, behavior, characteristic).

2. In segmenting your users, you may have come up with some initial personalization ideas. If these are not already in the form of a "plain language" rule, then try to rephrase them such that they are. Plain language rules are not phrased in the logic that a programmer might eventually use; they are simply descriptions of what you would like to happen in a particular case. For example, "whenever doctors come to the site, they should get a link to our Doctors' research material that other site users don't see."

If you look back to Section 9.1, Segmentation, in Chapter 9, Understanding Your Users, you can see how you might segment your user base.

3. The plain language rules should now be further refined into a set of "If . . . then" statements that constitute your rules. Again, these do not need to be programmatically correct syntax, but they should be clear enough for a programmer to translate into code logic. The if part of your rule will be based on one of the three user characteristics given earlier: something to do with who the user is or what he or she does. The then part of your rule defines what should happen on the site. At this stage, you should also try to be more specific about what pages, or even better, templates, your rule applies to. For example, "if a user from the Doctors' segment is using the site, then the Main_Navigation template should show a link to the Doctors_Research_Home template."

TIP   **Don't Target Too Tightly**

It is true that the more refined your targeting and matching of content to users, the better results you will get. If you could ideally match everything that you had to every single user's needs, then you should be laughing all the way to the bank. Of course, it is not quite that easy. Indeed, if you target too tightly and your aim is even slightly off, you risk alienating a section of your customers. Also, the more rules you have to refine your targeting, the greater the demands for well-tagged data, which in itself is a lot of work to create and maintain. You need to try and ensure that whatever personalization you do repays the cost and effort to do it. Despite the power of targeting, it is better to have an all-inclusive easy-to-use static site than a dynamic personalized site with poor rules, which means users do not get to see the content they are actually interested in. I would personalize based on one simple rule first. Learn from this. Do not be overambitious and risk making incorrect assumptions in your rules. Design your rules so that they prioritize, rather than exclude, content for matching users.

---

4. You need to ensure that you have the required supporting data to actually enable your rule. This means the necessary user data and the necessary content data to match the two. In our Doctors' example, how do you know that a user is indeed a Doctor? Once you do know that she is a Doctor, how does the main navigation template, or the Doctors' Research template, know what is Doctor content that it should be linking to and displaying?

The obvious way to match a user from the Doctors' segment is to have corresponding content that is tagged "Doctors." There is then a direct match, making it
easy to correlate one with the other. However, if your rules assume that there will
be a direct match like this, then clearly you need to make sure that all your content
is dutifully and correctly tagged if it is not to get lost as a result of not being associated with any user segment. If you have created a large number of user segments
with associated rules, then you have a lot of work on your hands ensuring that all
those user segments are applied as tags to the relevant content. In the case of an
indirect match, you might decide that all your content that is already tagged as
type Research matches the user segment Doctor. If you are only managing a few
content types and have the content already tagged, you might save yourself a lot of
work by using indirect matching. However, the quality of the matching is likely
to be less precise. There is no definitive answer as to which approach is best. It
will depend on your time and resources, your customers, and the nature of your
site and its content. In some cases, you may be lucky and find that your content is
already stored and tagged by the same user segments that you have based your
rules on.   ■

5. Your rules are implemented. The logic and code that drive your rules can
   be within the page template itself. The code executes within the template as the user requests it and connects with the various data sources
   it needs to build the appropriate page to return to the user. Equally, you
   might have a personalization application server that is integrated with
   your Web site and whose sole purpose is to do your personalization. In
   this case, the template would call up your personalization engine, which
   would do the necessary matching and return the appropriate content to
   the template for display to the user. Indeed, there is no reason that your
   personalization should be conducted on the fly, in real time as the user
   requests a page. For some forms of personalization, you may wish to run
   your rule via a script overnight, or every hour, to create a set of "preper-
   sonalized" static pages that are referenced on the site and appear to be
   dynamically generated. This may not always work if users come back to
   the site more than once a day and your script is only running once a
   night as discrepancies may become obvious. However, there are definite
   speed and other performance advantages in avoiding personalizing on
   the fly.

Case Study   **Increasing Customer Value by More Personal and More Frequent Online Contact**

Company: First Direct, *www.firstdirect.com*

Company Overview

First Direct was launched in 1989 to take advantage of a gap in the market by catering in particular to busy people who could not deal with their bank outside office hours when they wanted to. At launch, First Direct created a revolution in banking by organizing the bank around the customer and using the telephone to deliver the service.

Since then First Direct has taken on an average of 100,000 customers every year totaling more than 1 million. First Direct makes 500,000 product sales per year and has fully integrated delivery channels: telephone, Internet, and mobile phone. First Direct is the most recommended bank in the UK and has the most satisfied customers.

Background to Case Study and Objectives

As a direct banking organization (we have no branches or physical presence), we have always differentiated ourselves through outstanding customer service. This is in part made possible by our single customer database, which allows the same customer to interact with us through any channel (mail, phone, Web, mobile) and have a seamless experience. It also allows us to be very sophisticated in measuring and managing customer value across all channels.

When we first started evaluating the potential for e-channels to support our direct banking model, we looked at our existing customer base to identify trends and attitudes toward new technologies. We found that our customers were much more technically savvy than the average member of the public. Mobile phone ownership, for example, was twice as high as the average. On the back of this, we launched a PC banking service in 1997, which required a special software download, and then full Internet banking in 1999.

The business case for a large e-channels investment in 1999 was based on what we had learned from the previous 2 years about our customers who were using online channels. We had identified that e-customers were in fact our most valuable customers. This was true even before they became e-customers, but they became even

continued

more valuable afterward: Not only did they buy a wider range of products at higher values, but they became more cost effective to service as the number of their inquiries to our call centers dropped.

Our key insight was that e-channels gave us a way to increase the frequency of contact with our customers, which allowed for a greater dialog and a closer relationship while reducing costs. Increased frequency of contact not only helps our brand awareness (very important for an organization with no high street presence) but also gives us more opportunities to communicate our products and services to our customers. Furthermore, we found that the more personal and relevant we made our online contact, the greater the customer response and value created. One of our key objectives therefore became to use e-channels to increase customer value by more personal and more frequent contact.

Process and Practice

To make our e-channels more personal and relevant to our customers, we concentrated on content, services, and functionality, which related specifically to customers' accounts and dealings with us. All our research indicated that this is what people were most interested in and most valued. It also had to be as fast and easy to use as possible. We have also always been scrupulous about ensuring any contact with our customers is permission based.

We reviewed every page of our site, looking at each very much from a direct marketing perspective to optimize the value that each could deliver: What response were we trying to get from this page? What call to (inter)action did it have for the customer? How would it help increase customer value? Would it encourage increased contact with the customer?

Perhaps most interesting, however, has been our success with the use of mobile phones as an e-channel. In our pursuit of more frequent and personal contact with our customers to increase their value to us, it was clear that mobile phones presented an exciting opportunity. If we could establish an e-relationship via mobile with a customer, then we were that much closer to them, mobile being an even more personal and direct medium than the Web. We started to offer SMS alert functions. For example, customers can request to be sent an SMS as soon as their account reaches a certain level. This has proved immensely popular, and we have since extended the range of services available to customer via their mobiles.

Results

It has become clear that the more personal the message and the medium, the better the response rate and the greater the value. We carry promotional messages both on external sites and within our own site. Although response and conversion rates from external sites can be low (less than 0.5%), they quickly climb as the promotions become more personal and relevant. For example, promotions to customer segments within their own account areas of the site get efficiency rates in excess of 4%.

Our SMS alerts service for mobile phones has surprised us with its success. We now have nearly 200,000 mobile banking customers. Over 30% of all our new customers are gained via referral, and we have taken on over 100,000 SMS customers with no marketing to them at all. The response rates we have been getting to SMS have been very encouraging and, so far, much higher and much more immediate than any other medium. Perhaps even more encouraging is that these alerts have given customers a confidence to spend closer to their limits than previously because they know they will be alerted before they go too far. This means they are using more of their credit facility, which is good news for us.

We have also noted that by using e-channels for more frequent and personal contact, we see much less of a degradation of marketing efficiency (in terms of cost/response) over time than offline equivalents such as direct mail. Response levels do not dip nearly as quickly, and the efficiency of sales is higher.

Lessons Learned

Here are the key lessons we have taken from our experience so far:

▶ The power of more personal e-contact. For all the talk of personalization and the power of online channels, we have actually proven to ourselves that it works. E-channels really can facilitate increased personal contact with customers, leading to increased customer value, at a reduced customer servicing cost.

▶ The importance of the human touch. For all that technology can deliver, we have also learned that you cannot replace humans when it comes to dealing with customers. The contact may be SMS or email, but it still needs to be dealt with by a real human. Automation can help basic processes and there is a lot to be gained in efficiency and quality of customer service by unifying customer data, but you cannot afford to cut out the human touch.

continued

▶ Permission is paramount. It is not an option; it is a starting point. The more personal you get, the higher the rewards but the greater the risks. As you get more personal, the level of permission and trust must be correspondingly higher. Whatever you do must be permission based, well executed, and supported by excellent customer service if it is to succeed.

▶ Beware of underestimating response rates and overestimating deliverables. We have been surprised by the speed and level of customer response to our new e-channel initiatives. In order that the quality of your customer service does not suffer, you should have contingency plans for unexpectedly high response rates. Equally, we have found that we have sometimes overestimated our ability to deliver new IT systems and functions within time and resource constraints. It does work, but it takes time to do well.

Andrew Davies
Head of e-Marketing
First Direct

11

Community

In many ways, online communities represent the Holy Grail of what the Internet is supposed to make uniquely possible, opening up new ways for companies to interact with their customers and for their customers to interact with each other. As with personalization, however, the early theories have transpired to be a lot more difficult to do in practice. The following sections look at the promises of online community building for creating stronger customer relationships and what we have learned so far. Community building, perhaps more than any other aspect of CRM, is ultimately a people skill even if it is facilitated by processes and technology. For this reason, there are few hard and fast answers on "how to do community." What follows are observations and conclusions based largely on personal experience and talking to the people behind some of the best community sites on the Web.

11.1 What Community Is and What It Promises

Community is about user-to-user interaction. Customers get a sense of other customers through community. This might be through direct interactions, like forums or chat rooms, or indirectly through user-generated content such as product reviews. In some cases, the actual interaction may be between customer and company, but if it is shared and open for all to see, then there is still a sense of community. For example, a billboard allowing customers to post complaints or grievances online that the company then responds to fosters a sense of community even without customer-to-customer interaction.

Loyalty and customer retention are arguably the key drivers behind CRM as a business approach. Certainly, the most likely reason any business would invest in building online communities is customer retention. In all cases, customer retention leads directly or indirectly to increased revenues.

For a business driven by advertising revenue, community must deliver more users, more visits, and longer visits. Equally, research has shown that members of an online community are more responsive to advertising, and their trust transfers into greater propensity to transact with advertised brands. E-commerce operations also hope to use online communities to build trust and awareness within their customer base, which benefits their brand and translates into a higher frequency of purchase, across a broader product range, with a larger average basket size. Communities are also seen as the platform for creating user-generated content such as articles, views, reviews, and ratings. User-generated content not only costs next to nothing, but it can also be a good sales driver, a brand tool, and a point of competitive difference. For example, Amazon's user-generated book reviews and ratings are clearly a very important part of the sales process.

11.2   What We've Learned So Far

Much has been said about the merits of online community building: its ability to increase customer loyalty, build site "stickiness," increase switching costs, and encourage customer advocacy and referrals. Experience has taught us that community can indeed be a very powerful tool for achieving these things, but it only works if done correctly. Talking community is one thing; walking it is much harder. There is now an increasing realization of what a big and costly task it is to set up and, most important, manage an online community. However, it is an undeniable attribute of digital channels that they can greatly facilitate intrauser dialog and communication. After all, the Internet has grown so successfully chiefly as a result of its communication and information sharing powers.

NOTE   **Implementing Community**

There is little to be said about how to implement community in terms of process, tools, and practices that has not already been covered. You are managing users and content and matching the two. The hard part is getting the spirit of the community going. Communities do, however, offer a good chance for personalization because you can segment community members by their community status: Top-ranking members might be able to see and do things that others cannot. As individuals contribute content to the community, you should add this to, or at least associate it with, their customer data so that when you are looking through individual profiles you know the value and nature of what each user has contributed to the site. Although the user may not be creating much direct value for you, if she is an active member of the community, she is still contributing a lot of indirect value that will benefit your CRM initiative.   ■

So what makes a successful online community, both for the customer and for the business? Here are some of the lessons we have learned so far:

▶ *Don't do community for community's sake.* Community always used to be one of those things that appeared on the shopping list of what every company wanted on their Web site. It was usually a subcategory of "sticky content." However, creating a community without real purpose and value is futile. Token discussion boards to promote a sense of community comments or ratings, which help people decide if and what to buy, are very powerful. Amazon has long shown the power of this use of community. The discussion boards of personal investment site Motley Fool are thriving because they are extremely valuable in helping you make an investment decision. iVillage has built a successful community of women because their forums help women share knowledge and expertise to make better decisions. In some rare cases, community features have successfully been used purely for brand purposes. Shell, for example, allowed members of the public to discuss environmental issues on its site which, though risky, proved successful in showing a positive commitment to discussing hot topics that Shell might otherwise have been accused of avoiding for reasons of self-interest.

▶ *Don't overestimate your ability to create an online community.* As a general rule, the number of people a company thinks will want to take part in a community is smaller than is actually the case. Depending on the site proposition and target market, you might expect 1 in 10 site visitors to be interested in community. Within any discussion or chat area, a read-to-post ratio of 200:1 is average. That means you will need 2000 site visitors to generate just one contribution. Furthermore, building a good online community takes time, typically several years.

▶ *Be explicit in how you are generating money from people.* People are smart. They know that you have to make money to continue to provide the services they value. Do not be afraid to point out to them how you are making money. Do not try and covertly generate revenue from your community (e.g., by selling customer data without proper permission or disguising advertising), or it will quickly turn against you.

▶ *Employ expert community staff.* If you look behind some of the best-known community sites on the Web, you will find community producers with years of proven expertise in managing communities online. They are passionate about the issues the community is centered around, they are able to mediate between community members effectively, and they are intuitive and sensitive to the emotional dynamics of the community.

▶ *Have a strong community philosophy.* Communities will only succeed if there is a reason to be there, a reason to care, and a kernel of passion about the issues that matter to members of the community. If you try to create and manipulate an online community with purely commercial goals in mind, you will fail.

▶ *Focus on meeting users' information needs.* You must assume that the majority of people are not coming to the community out of a sense of great benevolence but because they have an immediate and specific need that they want the community to help them with. This might be advice to support a purchasing decision or help in finding relevant information or services.

▶ *Only the community can effectively police the community.* You can, and should, create guide rules for people to refer to and mechanisms to allow intrauser policing (e.g., ratings and reporting offensive posts), but ultimately, you must create an environment that people will not abuse because they can see that nobody else is behaving is such a way.

▶ *Growth has to be managed carefully.* Empty discussion forums may be one problem, but successful communities can also become victims of their own success. If the community grows out of control, its value can quickly dissipate, alienating previously committed members.

▶ *Create a physical sense of place.* Despite being virtual, online communities like to feel a sense of place, a "grounding" that helps give the community a stronger sense of identity than just anonymous interactions over the Web.

Commercial partners can help in this regard, as can real-world events, press coverage, or simply giving contact phone numbers for people to call.

▶ *Reward community members who contribute value.* If people are contributing value, they need to be rewarded to show others the benefits of contributing and to further win the commitment of your most valuable community members. Reward may be in the form of heightened status (e.g., a "top reviewer" rating), access to premium content or services, or more direct access to your staff.

▶ *Let the group take its own course.* Rather than trying to force the evolution of a community down a particular path, it is much better to see what is popular and what works, and capitalize on it. This allows you to spot opportunities and grow business value in areas that were not perhaps initially apparent. It allows you to mold your value proposition to the needs of the community. Their pull is a much easier sell than trying to push your products and services. Equally, advertising will be much more effective if it fits with the evolving needs and interests of the community.

Make no mistake. Doing community on the Web is a big undertaking. Information sharing and networked communications between people with a common interest may have been the reasons that the Internet took off in the first place, but trying to use the community power of the Web for business benefit is a very challenging task. To mix business with online communities is to walk a fine line between genuine, selfless, almost idealized, dedication to the group's cause on the one hand and yet a much more deliberate and calculated evaluation of commercial returns on the other. If done properly, it can pay dividends. But if done poorly, it can be very damaging to both your brand and your bottom line.

12

Customer Service

In our service-driven economy, it has long been recognized that the intangible qualities of a company are becoming increasingly important as points of competitive advantage and differentiation. In many sectors (e.g., financial services), there is often little difference between the products, so the battle for customers is fought more on brand and other intangibles, and customer service is a key component. Furthermore, there is an underlying social change whereby customers are becoming increasingly self-empowered. Customers want to take control of their interests and control their personal affairs more closely than before.

This climate would seem ideal for the Web to capitalize on. If you think about it, every Web site is a self-service operation inasmuch as it is interactive and driven by the customer. Unfortunately, as we all know, the quality and levels of customer service experienced by so many on the Web have undermined users' confidence in the medium as a channel for resolving their customer service needs. As a result of this disappointment and frustration, however, Web-based customer (self-)service has become a key area of competitive advantage: If you can do it well, you will surprise and delight your customers. Improving the quality of customer service you deliver via your Web site is thus an important part of maintaining and evolving a successful commercial site.

The topic and practice of customer service in general go way beyond the scope of this book. However, it is undoubtedly a key component of CRM (many people think that customer service is CRM), and it has an important online face. It is this Web "front end" of customer service that the customer experiences that we are addressing here. For Web-based customer service to really work, the site must be just that: a front end to a much larger, and integrated, customer service back-end system.

In Chapter 8, we looked at the concept of the single customer view. When it comes to offering really top-class customer service across all customer contact points, this single customer view is vital. If every customer service representative or Web-based self-service system is to be fully up to date on who a customer is; what the status of their account, inquiry, or order is; and what their interaction history has been, you need a fully integrated customer service operation that can feed off a single customer view. The Web site will be just one channel that inputs to the system and takes feeds from it at the same time as call centers, Internet-enabled mobile phones, kiosks, interactive TVs, and paper-based inquiries. Getting all the back-end systems integrated and the processes in place to make all this possible is no small task, but it has to happen if companies are going to meet the rising expectations of their customers.

12.1   What Online Customer Service Is and What It Promises

Web-based customer servicing is considered less about growing revenues and market share and more about reducing costs and improving the quality of the customer experience. As customer servicing requires valuable time spent interacting with the customer, even if the interaction is nonhuman, there are opportunities to introduce customers to other products or services that they might be interested in. If you have a rich customer profile to work from, ideally drawn from a single customer view, then your suggestions to the customer can be much more intelligent and relevant. Despite the apparent attractions of seizing such opportunities, you have to be very wary of frustrating the customer further. Imagine she is contacting you with a problem, which is often the case, and all you do is try and sell to her further. You will not hear her scream at her computer, but neither will you hear from her ever again. The most common reasons for pursuing Web-based customer servicing solutions are as follows:

▶ Reducing customer servicing costs by using more cost-effective channels. Depending on whose analysis you read, it is claimed to be $10 to $110 more expensive to handle a customer inquiry by phone than via the Web.
▶ Faster and more effective customer service means increased customer satisfaction, which means fewer lost customers.
▶ Global 24 × 7 support is a fraction of the cost of face-to-face and local support.
▶ Closer customer relationships and giving customers control lead to a stronger bond between company and customer.
▶ It can free staff resources busy dealing with routine inquiries to work on more complex customer inquiries and more valuable strategic initiatives.

12.2   What We've Learned So Far

The realities of implementing Web-based customer servicing have suggested the following challenges:

▶ Customer expectations are rising faster than companies' ability to meet them, leading to disappointed customers.
▶ Companies are typically behind on the skills, technology, and processes to manage the Internet channel in an efficient and integrated way.
▶ Companies are avoiding e-service because they fear it will overload their call center, swamping already stretched customer services staff.
▶ Automation may work 90% of the time, but the 10% where it does not work can create frustrated and angered customers who spread the bad word. The most expensive form of service is self-service that doesn't work: You simply train the customer to pick up the phone, assuming that you don't lose the customer altogether.
▶ Customer data are still not integrated; thus, delivering a seamless cross-channel service experience is extremely hard.
▶ Customer inquiries are often not stored and analyzed, leading to a lot of unnecessary rework as staff respond to the same questions.
▶ They are large organizational and process challenges. For example, should you have different agents for voice and data inquiries because of

the different skills required? How long can an agent spend on emails and text messages? Which should be prioritized?

Faced with these challenges, how should you approach Web-based customer servicing to ensure both the customer and the business benefit? Here are some pointers for evolving your Web site's customer service offering.

▶ *Open the organization up to customers.* Not only do customers want access to their own information, but you want them to have access to save yourself administration costs and to help ensure the data you do have are as up to date as possible. Certainly, you should try to achieve the following: Let your customers have access to their customer profiles and be able to update them; give customers access to their accounts, transaction histories, and order statuses; and let customers manage their incentive awards programs online.

▶ *The 80/20 rule.* It is important to look at ways that the Internet can help improve the quality of customer service you offer, but perhaps more important, you should be seeing the Web as a way to reduce the need for a customer inquiry in the first place. Customer service demands typically follow the 80/20 rule: Most service demands are for the same reasons. Use the Web to try and address these most recurrent questions. Do not delay and try to cover everything. You can add and iterate later.

TIP   **Improving Your FAQs**

A common way to address the most common inquiries is to create a list of frequently asked questions (FAQs). You need to properly maintain these, and you should also promote them to get maximum value. A customer in need of help may overlook a link saying FAQs or something similar and instead head straight for the Contact section. It is here that you should promote your FAQs and do so with needs-driven calls to action: Want to know your order status? Can't remember your password? Worried about security? Delivery and returns questions? Doing this can divert dramatic amounts of inquiries away from the phone and back to the Web.

▶ *Focus on site usability.* If you are asking customers to proactively service themselves online, you must be proactive in ensuring that their experience is as positive as possible. Before you think about buying expensive software, you should ensure that the Web site itself is doing its job properly. In

For more on site improvement techniques, refer to Chapter 17, How to Improve a Web Site, in Part IV, Site Measurement.

many cases, the fastest returns will come from improving site usability and content: update your FAQs, analyze customer click paths through key areas of the site to identify bottlenecks, improve your product information, improve your search function, cross-link between sections more effectively, give clear and ubiquitous contact options, and make sure your Contact Us page has clear links to your online support content. These measures may not help reduce the number of offline customers' inquiries, but they will certainly reduce your Web site visit-to-inquiry ratio.

▶ *Capture customer needs and build a knowledge base.* Customer emails are often routed to separate members of staff without being centrally stored for tracking and analysis purposes. These explicit customer needs must be captured to begin the building of a knowledge base that can then be made available to customers online. Further enhance the knowledge base by analyzing implicit customer needs such as terms used in site searches. This knowledge base does not need to be big, complicated, and expensive to start with, but it is a very valuable asset that you should start building and updating as soon as you can.

▶ *Automation.* Automation, where the system handles customer servicing without human intervention, is clearly desirable in reducing unnecessary repetitive work for staff. However, if handled poorly, it can be one of the most annoying things for a customer to be confronted with. Clearly, you should automate processes such as a forgotten password, sending registration details, or confirming orders, but where a customer has made a specific inquiry, the only decent way of handling it is through a human. For email inquiries, agent review of autosuggested answers provides a better level of service than pure autorespond and retains many of the benefits of automation. If you are going to interact with customers using an automated tool, you must tell them up front that it is automated and let them know how to contact a human if they wish. By all means automate, but manage expectations very clearly and offer alternatives.

▶ *Recognize and reward best customers.* Retaining high-value customers is a key CRM concept, and customer service has a large part to play. As a first step, you need to define, identify, and then recognize your best customers online. In terms of rewarding them, you might offer them guaranteed response times, special hotline contact numbers, access to premium support content, more personalized responses, or even a dedicated service representative.

▶ *Offer multichannel contact options.* You might say, "Why put our call center number so prominently on our site if we're trying to divert customer servicing to the Web to reduce costs and relieve call center backlogs?" Offering clear, multiple (in particular, phone) contact options to customers online reassures them. This sense of reassurance—that if they need help from a real human being, it is always at hand—actually emboldens customers to try and succeed in getting what they want using the Web site first (often they are online at home and may need to disconnect to phone, which is undesirable). The sense of trust this approach engenders also improves browse-to-buy conversion rates. Some may still want to use the phone route (which is fine because you do want their business, don't you?), but increasingly, many site users will not resort to calling unless they become frustrated with your site. In that case, you need to know about it and quickly improve things.

TIP   **Error Handling**

It may be the case that customers expect the world and become frustrated when even the slightest thing goes wrong. But it is also strangely the case that if you resolve customers' problems particularly well, even if they are your fault, they tend not only to be extremely pleased (and often surprised) but will see you in a better light than if the problem had not occurred in the first place. They may also tell their friends about how impressed they were with your handling of a problem.

One thing that you can do online is customize your error pages. Instead of serving the standard 404 or 500 error pages, which look highly unprofessional, you should replace them with customized error pages that your Web server will display instead. Take this a step further and give the user an error log number or code, which they can use to follow up with you and which you can use for tracking and resolution purposes. If you know who the user is, send an email to say you are sorry for the error and that you have now fixed it.

▶ *Cross-channel customer data integration is vital.* One of the most frustrating aspects of customer service is the need for customers to repeat their account details and the nature of their inquiry more than once during an inquiry. As mentioned earlier, it is increasingly important to integrate customer data across all channels and departments. A system architecture based on open standards is key to successful cross-channel integration.

The easier you make it for the various components of your organization to relate to each other, the easier it will be to create a truly seamless customer service operation.

The bottom line is that you cannot afford to do customer service badly. Web-based customer servicing indeed offers great opportunities in evolving your overall proposition. It is incorrect to make excuses that introducing on-line customer servicing would overburden you as this would only be true if your site was poorly implemented. It should in fact reduce the burden on all fronts as customers begin to help themselves.

Summary

With CRM, the biggest longer term challenges are not technological but centered around bringing your people and processes up to speed and turning your organization into a truly customer-centric one. This is not always easy but your customer relationships are your most valuable, and yet potentially most fragile, assets. Thus, CRM in some form is increasingly becoming a strategic imperative, not an option. With customers' expectations continuing to rise, you cannot afford to risk these relationships (e.g., by giving poor online customer service), as this undermines customers' trust in you and your brand, both of which are increasingly vital for business survival and success.

Digital channels offer an extremely powerful medium for delivering on the promises of CRM. Their interactive nature means that it is possible to build a true dialogue, and stronger relationship, with customers. Furthermore, you cannot do CRM without customer data, and online offers excellent opportunities for capturing these data and using them to the benefit of both the customer and your business.

If you are managing your customer relationships and your content well, then it is likely you are already successful in maintaining and evolving your Web site. But how can you be sure? The truth is that you cannot manage what you cannot measure. So the next part of the book is about measuring, analyzing, and reporting on the success of your Web site, and taking steps to improve its performance based on the intelligence you gather.

SITE
MEASUREMENT

Competitive advantage is now less about being fast; it is more about being smart. This means it is no longer acceptable for Web sites not to answer to business success criteria and performance evaluations in the same way as other projects and initiatives, although the metrics and measurement techniques themselves need to be specific to the Web.

The Internet provides opportunities for unparalleled levels of customer and management information intelligence, but only more recently have companies really begun to address these opportunities. In many cases, e-business managers lack some of the usual core tools and techniques required for successful management. They need to be able to answer questions such as: What types of customers are driving profitability? What do our most profitable customers do on our Web site? Which of our marketing activities are proving most valuable? How can we best respond to new and potential competitive threats? What returns are we getting on our Web investments?

In more traditional channels, senior managers have a significant arsenal of fundamental metrics, often sector or industry specific, that help reveal major trends, key opportunities, and hidden hazards. These metrics facilitate more confident strategy decisions and help businesses navigate through unfamiliar and volatile business conditions. As Web sites become an increasingly integral part of business, decision making regarding site development becomes a larger responsibility and one that managers will feel uncomfortable taking on if they have no support and no information upon which to base their decisions. As they will be held accountable, they rightly expect the Web site to be accountable.

A lack of understanding and standardization of metrics and measurement processes has damaged credibility in the online channels to date. Online media buying, for example, has been adversely affected by the lack of clarity around standards and a mistrust of the figures that sites quote as they have proved to be misleading in some cases. However, with the help of various industry bodies, and the will of the industry itself, the fog is gradually clearing, and standards and accepted accreditation processes are emerging.

This part of the book charts the typical evolution path a Web site will take on the road to advanced site measurement and optimization and looks at the different metrics, measurement approaches, tools, and techniques at your disposal. By the end of this part, you will have a clear idea of how to go about managing a project to measure and optimize your site.

Key Areas We Will Cover in Part IV

▶ What are the promises and challenges of Web measurement? What is different about it?

▶ The evolution of e-intelligence. How have Web metrics evolved over time and why?

▶ Measurement approaches and techniques. What are the pros and cons of the various measurement approaches? Which should you use for what purpose? What data sources are required?

▶ Reporting and analysis. How do you avoid information overload? What should you measure? How do you design your site to make it easier to analyze? How do you schedule and distribute reports? What do real example reports look like?

▶ Choosing a measurement tool. What different types of solutions are offered? What selection criteria should you use?

▶ Improving your site. How do you use Web measurement, and the intelligence you gather, to take action to optimize site performance? What areas should you concentrate on? How can you use approaches such as usability testing and viral marketing to improve the success of your site?

▶ Tackling measurement projects both small and large. What process should you follow? What are the tasks and deliverables at each stage?

13

The Promises and Challenges of Web Site Measurement

The Internet is often heralded as the ultimately accountable medium with huge sales and marketing opportunities arising from greater levels of customer intimacy made possible by analyzing customer interaction and site usage data. In theory, Web analytics and measurement enable the following.

13.1 Promises

13.1.1 More Effective Marketing

By observing and capturing customers' behavioral data, you understand individual customer preferences and needs. This affords much more valuable marketing insight than traditional demographics, which crudely lump people together.

Equally, by tracking performance in real time, marketing messages can be quickly and cost effectively optimized. For example, by tracking the response to an email campaign, marketers can test alternate versions of the message and gravitate toward the version that gets the best results.

Finally, richer customer profiling gives the intelligence required for improved targeting and more refined communications, which means costs can be reduced and revenues increased.

13.1.2   Improved Customer Retention

Using customer-centric metrics to deliver customer intelligence, the necessary knowledge and information are in place to provide the platform for more advanced Web personalization and customer relationship building. This binds customer and company together, improves the customer experience, and reduces the likelihood that he or she will switch to a competitor.

Further, by tracking the types of customers who churn and the behavioral attributes they display before they are lost, it is easier to predict and avoid future customer churn. Greater intelligence on what customers are finding hard to do on the site, or what they most often inquire about, also leads to improved customer service and an improved customer experience.

13.1.3   Increased Sales

Richer customer profiles improve customer service agents' interaction with customers and lead to additional sales opportunities. Analysis of these customer profiles leads to an improved capability to predict the profitability and revenue potential of customers and a clearer insight into how best to acquire and convert them. Cross- and up-selling of products can become increasingly sophisticated and effective as it becomes clear from measuring previous results what works best for which customers.

13.1.4   Automated Site Performance Management

Software tools can monitor and maintain site performance quality, automatically alerting you to problems and, in many cases, resolving the problem before it becomes apparent to site users, guaranteeing an optimal customer experience.

Yet despite all these great promises, many have found that the practice of Web site measurement and analysis is not quite as easy as the theory. In particular, the following challenges need to be surmounted.

13.2 Challenges

13.2.1 Information Overload

To avoid information overload, define your measurement framework. This is covered in Section 16.1, Defining a Measurement Framework.

Online interactions may give you enhanced capabilities for data capture, measurement, tracking, and analysis, but this can lead to data paralysis if you are not sure exactly what you want to be measuring and why. The temptation is to try and analyze everything because you are capable and because the default reflex when you are not sure of your metrics and measurement strategy is to capture as much as possible for future benefit.

13.2.2 Data Quality

Your measurement, reporting, and analysis are only as good as the source data you base them on. Poor data equal poor results. The preparation and cleansing of data for analysis are time consuming and costly. If data are really poor, it is not worth the expense trying to clean them at all. Much criticism has been aimed at Web data in particular for their lack of reliability and accuracy. The benefits of going to the effort of using the much vaunted behavioral data for personalization and customer insight have also been called into question.

13.2.3 Few Common Standards or Metrics

The Internet is still a relatively new channel, and although great efforts are being made to standardize around particular protocols, metrics, practices, and processes, most companies are finding it hard to build a robust measurement framework without further clarity and agreement. Misunderstandings and loose interpretations of existing terminology have confused the issue and undermined the credibility of Web site measurement.

13.2.4 Privacy and Security

Personal privacy and security of personal information are clearly big issues that must also be confronted. Best practices continue to evolve and customers' expectations continue to be molded by what is reported in the press. Capturing, storing, and analyzing customer data, particularly customers from many countries and jurisdictions, present considerable challenges in meeting legal and customer expectations for privacy and security.

13.2.5   No Single Customer View

We looked at the single customer view in Section 8.5 on electronic Customer Relationship Management (eCRM). It is clear that without customers' data being consolidated from all touch points into a single view such that a true picture of all of the customers' interactions and dealings with the company arises, it is not possible to understand and measure that customer in a true and holistic manner.

The reality is that few companies are that close to achieving the single customer view even though they may know it is ultimately required: The systems, data, and process engineering work are typically complex and costly. For the moment, measurement and analysis still tend to be around silos of data with Internet channel data typically being one of those silos. However, in isolation of other channels, this only goes so far and does not accurately show how customer value is created through channels complementing each other. Just because a customer never buys through the Web site does not necessarily make that person a low-value customer, as they may be researching online and purchasing offline.

13.2.6   Slow, Error-Prone, or Unavailable Sites

Despite much evidence that slow sites frustrate users and adversely affect usage and sales, there are still too many sites that force bloated graphics or rich media on their visitors in the name of innovative design, pushing the boundaries, or exploiting the opportunities of broadband. Equally, sites are often down or contain dead links and errors. There are numerous possible reasons for these problems, but they must be addressed if the customer experience is not to suffer and customers are not consequently to take their business elsewhere. Proper site monitoring, quality control, service-level agreements, and testing may not be the most exciting things in the world, but they absolutely must be done properly and form part of any Web performance management and site improvement process.

14

The Evolution
of E-intelligence

It is very rare, and very difficult, for a company to jump from almost no Web site measurement to having advanced analysis and reporting capabilities. Be wary of any turnkey solutions that promise they can make this jump happen in very little time.

It is much more normal, indeed preferable, to work incrementally and iteratively toward full e-intelligence, ensuring that what you do along the way is delivering real insight and value as you go. This chapter looks at the typical evolution path that most companies take as they journey from basic traffic reporting to advanced site measurement.

14.1 The Arrival and Development of E-metrics

Metrics are the fundamental units of measurement that can be used to gauge and calibrate success against given objectives and benchmarks. Solid metrics are the required foundation of robust measurement frameworks.

NOTE   **Who Sets E-metrics Standards?**

The following industry bodies are among those leading the way in defining Web standards, protocols, and e-metrics:

▶ Internet Advertising Bureau (*www.iab.net*): "The industry's leading interactive advertising association. Its activities include evaluating and recommending guidelines and best practices, fielding research to document the effectiveness of interactive media, and educating the advertising industry about the use of interactive advertising and marketing."

▶ Audit Bureau of Circulation Electronic (ABCe) (*www.abce.org.uk*): "The source of independently audited data in Internet traffic measurement in the UK and Ireland using internationally agreed standards."

▶ International Organization for Standardization (*www.iso.org*): "The mission of ISO is to promote the development of standardization and related activities in the world with a view to facilitating the international exchange of goods and services, and to developing cooperation in the spheres of intellectual, scientific, technological and economic activity."

▶ Institute of Electrical and Electronics Engineers (*www.ieee.org*): "The IEEE ('eye-triple-E') helps advance global prosperity by promoting the engineering process of creating, developing, integrating, sharing, and applying knowledge about electrical and information technologies and sciences for the benefit of humanity and the profession."

▶ The World Wide Web Consortium (*www.w3c.org*): "The World Wide Web Consortium (W3C) develops interoperable technologies (specifications, guidelines, software, and tools) to lead the Web to its full potential as a forum for information, commerce, communication, and collective understanding."   ■

As the Internet burst upon the scene, generating new business models and ideas, and threatening a "revolution" that would overturn traditional ways of doing business, we were forced to look for new metrics to try to understand and measure e-business. E-metrics such as hits, stickiness, page views, and unique users came into existence and were liberally used with little clarity over their precise meaning and relevance: Hits were used synonymously with page views, and sessions were confused with unique users. Even where the metric was clear, the accuracy of the reported figures was quickly called into question: How are page view figures affected by the use of frames or caching? How are unique user figures distorted by proxy servers and dynamic IP addressing?

E-metrics quickly moved on as the market turned away from a volume-based, market-share approach to more of a focus on revenues and profitabil-

If you are not sure what any of these terms mean or how to answer these questions, see Chapter 15, Measurement Approaches and Techniques, for more details.

ity: Along came conversion ratios, average basket size, browse-to-buy rates, customer acquisition costs, and the like. E-metrics continue to evolve in the quest to use business intelligence to make better tactical and strategic decisions, to outinnovate and outmanage the competition. The strongest influence on the future development of e-metrics is coming from the following quarters:

▶ *Standardization.* There is increasing momentum and industry desire to define and agree to e-metrics standards. Most common terms have standard definitions championed by industry bodies.

▶ *Custom metrics.* The relevant metrics for a business to use will vary depending on the type of business. Particular industries and sectors focus on different metrics or have metrics unique to what they do.

▶ *Integration with the rest of the business.* As the Internet is increasingly integrated into the core business, new hybrid metrics are emerging that are a blend of new and old.

▶ *Customer focus.* As the next section explains, the fundamental shift to a more customer-centric economy is affecting the sorts of metrics that are emerging and being used to gauge success.

14.2 Increasing Sophistication and Customer-Centricity

Most companies report at least basic site traffic statistics using a low-cost data analysis tool. However, generally the results and reports generated are of little value to business managers faced with forecasting revenues and optimizing profitability. There is often more value there than is perceived, but it is lost through poor analysis and reporting. Even at its best, traffic analysis does not deliver the most valuable commercial and customer information.

As we have seen in Part III, Customer Relationship Management, there is a fundamental shift toward a customer-centric economy. This means that metrics and key performance indicators (KPIs) are evolving to have more direct relevance to customers: They are increasingly perceived to be a company's most important asset. So the metrics that many Web sites are working toward focus on who a customer is, what that customer's attributes and preferences are, what segment that customer belongs to, how valuable that customer is to the company, and how that customer feels about the company. These metrics become the determinants of customer and business value.

NOTE   **New Metrics for Old**

First Generation e-Metrics
Hits, Sessions, Page impressions, Users, Accessed pages, Referring sites

Second Generation e-Metrics
Average basket size, Average revenue/customer, Click through rates, Conversion rates, Repeat visits, Customer acquisition costs, Recency, Frequency, Monetary

Next Generation e-Metrics
Loyalty/churn by segment, Propensity by segment, Customer (lifetime) value   ■

Focusing on customer-centric metrics and measurement methods is nowhere more relevant than on the Web. It is customers who are in the driver's seat as they interact with a company through its Web site. Furthermore, it has been shown that the 80:20 rule of thumb for traditional channels (80% of revenue from just 20% of customers) is even more acute online: Approximately 10% of a Web site's customers typically account for 90% of revenue. This is likely to even out over time, but it emphasizes just how important it is to hold onto those few good customers. Figure 14.1 outlines the typical evolution path toward more sophisticated and customer-centric e-business intelligence.

Evolution toward e-customer intelligence →

Site stats
- Page views
- Hits
- Unique users
- Visits
- Sessions
- etc.

E-business intelligence
- Recency, frequency, monetary
- Customer acquisition costs
- Conversion rates
- Sales trends
- Average basket size
- etc.

E-customer intelligence
- Segmentation
- Custom metrics
- Click stream
- Loyalty/churn
- Propensity
- Customer value modeling
- One-to-one relationship
- Maximize ROI/customer
- etc.

Figure 14.1 The evolution of e-intelligence.

As e-business becomes just part of business, the next big challenge, as we have seen previously in discussing customer relationship management, is to ensure that customers are not understood only by particular channel interaction data but according to the totality of their relationship with the company. E-customer intelligence will become part of the customer intelligence that is so necessary to build stronger, more personalized relationships with customers that in return protect and grow the company's share of that customer's time and money.

Case Study

Applying Traditional Management Performance Measurement Techniques to e-Business

Company: Netpoll, *www.netpoll.net*

Company Overview

At Netpoll, we provide our clients with consultative research that delivers insights into user attitudes across interactive platforms. These insights are based on expert opinion, market analysis, customer interviews, consultancy, surveys, and statistics, all aimed at better understanding the interactive user. Backed by a team of experienced researchers and analysts from a variety of backgrounds, our strategic services encompass planning, research, and analysis.

Background to Case Study and Objectives

One of the key problems emblematic of the dotcom hysteria was a desire by businesses in all kinds of industry to believe that interactive technology meant you could reinvent *everything*.

Proving just how incorrect this assumption was is unnecessary given the bonfire of businesses that followed this route. However, although there is now agreement that the new can learn from the old, the where and how are still matters for discussion.

In Netpoll's industry, market research and consultancy, the classic error made by clients and suppliers is to believe that accumulating log files and databases is a substitute rather than complement to traditional research techniques. This is wrong for a number of reasons:

▶ Knowing what is going on is of limited impact if you don't know why.
▶ There are still few clear industry agreements on standards for interactive metrics.

continued

▶ Measurement of cross-channel effects is almost redundant if your benchmark is various channel-based data files rather than the customer journey.

▶ CRM systems are frequently installed by and run by the IT department. What information architects understand about customer insight is roughly similar to what market researchers understand about IP networking.

A large number of companies have a lot of data sitting around doing very little that is useful.

Process and Practice

One area in which Netpoll uses an established methodology to inform interactive business is the balanced scorecard. The objective of a balanced scorecard is to weave strategic accountability into the target setting and development of a business. Implemented successfully, a balanced scorecard is a dashboard of KPI (key performance indicator) targets that has consistency and relevance both to the overall plan for a business and component parts.

The original scorecard was developed by Kaplan and Norton in the United States and was largely designed to help companies manage change by identifying the strengths of a business according to four perspectives:

▶ The shareholders' perspective: Financial
▶ The customers' perspective: Customer
▶ The internal perspective: Internal
▶ The future perspective: Growth and learning

It has since been adopted by a number of corporations in a wide range of industries from big oil to hospitals. What is interesting about the scorecard from a corporate point of view is also extremely relevant to interactive business.

In the dotcom boom, we might say there was an overemphasis on customer metrics. Firms were going to make supernormal profits because they had a one-to-one relationship with their customers and could intuitively tag them at the very moment they were thinking about buying exactly what the store had available. Advertisers would flock to this medium and pay vast sums for the privilege of accessing the forbidden knowledge. This was clearly wrong.

In the bust, too many companies started hyping financial metrics as king. Perfectly good businesses that were generating significant sales for their offline sponsors went bust as accountants poured over cash-flow projections, debt restructuring deals, and business-unit level profitability targets. This was clearly wrong as well.

Every interactive service, particularly those that are part of a wider channel strategy for a traditional business, has a sales and marketing function. Measuring the effectiveness of these functions requires attention to all four areas of the scorecard. Figure 14.2 is an example of a scorecard that Netpoll produced for an interactive travel client. With this scorecard, the client was better able to assess future research requirements and ensure their effectiveness criteria were in line with the business strategy.

Lessons Learned

One of the key benefits of a scorecarding process is the facility to get buy-in to any measurement project from every stakeholder in the business. The scorecard can clearly communicate the value of any interactive service at the board level and retain realistic targets for departmental heads to achieve in line with their strategic plan.

The weaknesses are generally related to the up-front time investment required for setup and resource allocation for ongoing development. A business that implements the scorecard should have the flexibility and accountability to adapt effectiveness measurement to

Financial	Customer	Internal	Future
Profitability • Average gross margin per sale **Customer value** • Customer acquisition cost • Customer retention cost • Lifetime value • Share of wallet	**Brand equity** • Brand awareness • Brand meaning **Customer satisfaction** • Migration • Usability • Perception of service **Market share growth** • Customer segmentation • Reach • Share of wallet • Competitor activity	**Quality and reliability** • On-time delivery • Service error rate **Efficiency** • Revenue per spend on channel development • Time to buy • Calls per booking • Effective public relations	**Leadership** • Market position • Customer champion **Diversification** • Effective partnerships • Expansion • Personalization **Intelligence** • Industry intelligence • Product intelligence • Competitor intelligence

Figure 14.2 An example interactive scorecard.

changing market conditions. Practically, this is often not the case when tight budgets and resourcing make monitoring a low priority. An underfunded or ad hoc scorecarding process is a worse decision than no process at all. If the data aggregation and buy-in are not continuous, you are simply left with an occasionally applied bandage rather than a true support for the business.

Our experience has proved to us that the same techniques and management tools that have traditionally been used to measure and guide business performance can apply equally well to online initiatives. This is particularly valuable where a multichannel strategy is being adopted because a single measurement approach can be used to gauge performance across all channels. There are areas, and particular metrics, that require a more specialist e-business approach. However, there are great benefits in aligning the way digital channel projects are appraised to the way the rest of the business is measured as it means e-business becomes accountable and is given the same level of senior management attention as other areas of the business. Ultimately, this level of senior sponsorship is what Web sites require to progress.

Andy Mayer
Lead Strategist
Netpoll

15

Measurement Approaches and Techniques

We have looked at the theoretical benefits of Web site measurement and the real challenges you are likely to come up against, and we have outlined in broad strokes a typical evolution path. We will move on to the processes involved in managing the implementation of Web site measurement, including looking at how to define and deliver appropriate reporting and analysis, but first we should review the measurement approaches and techniques available to us. These are the nuts, bolts, and tools at our disposal to build the component parts of our measurement system.

15.1 Site-Centric Measurement

Site-centric measurement is a category of measurement approaches and metrics in which users are often referred to, but it is not actually known who the individual users are. Users only exist as unidentifiable people who have interacted with a Web site. This category also includes measurement of the technical performance of the site (reliability, speed, error checking, etc.) as well as the analysis of transactional data. The next section, User-Centric Measurement, focuses on forms of measurement where the identity of the user is actually known.

15.1.1 Metrics

The most basic metrics for site-centric measurement are those that give a measure of Web site activity, or traffic. These are well-known to most and are summarized by Figure 15.1.

Site-centric measurement answers four key questions about a Web site and how it is being used:

1. What are people doing on the site?
2. What technology are they using to view the site?
3. Where have they come from to get to the site?
4. How well is the site performing technically?

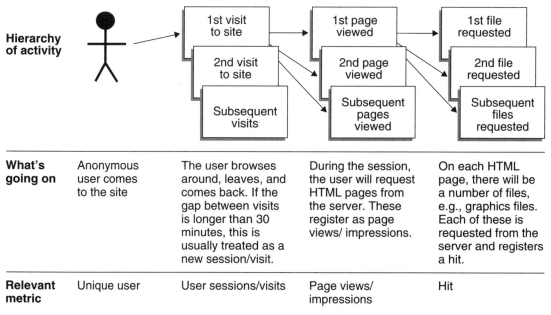

Hierarchy of activity	1st visit to site / 2nd visit to site / Subsequent visits	1st page viewed / 2nd page viewed / Subsequent pages viewed	1st file requested / 2nd file requested / Subsequent files requested
What's going on	Anonymous user comes to the site	The user browses around, leaves, and comes back. If the gap between visits is longer than 30 minutes, this is usually treated as a new session/visit.	During the session, the user will request HTML pages from the server. These register as page views/ impressions.	On each HTML page, there will be a number of files, e.g., graphics files. Each of these is requested from the server and registers a hit.
Relevant metric	Unique user	User sessions/visits	Page views/ impressions	Hit

Figure 15.1 Basic Web site activity metrics.

It should be clear how answers to these questions will aid site development and marketing efforts, but what metrics are required to give answers to each of these questions? Now we look at each of the questions and the most common corresponding metrics used to help answer the question. The next section explains what data sources and measurement techniques can be used to provide these metrics.

What are people doing on the site? (Table 15.1)

What technology are they using to view the site? (Table 15.2)

Where have they come from to get to the site? (Table 15.3)

How well is the site performing technically? (Table 15.4)

15.1.2   Measurement Techniques

Now that we understand the metrics that we can use to help answer our site-centric performance questions, it is necessary to understand the data sources and methods that are used to arrive at the measurements. This is important because the method that you choose will affect the type of tool you opt for and can have large implications in terms of how you would set up and manage a project to implement them. Later sections deal with how to choose a measurement tool and how to run the project.

To report against the metrics we have been looking at, two things must be done: Site activity must be recorded, and there needs to be a way of identifying unique users. Most often, log files record site activity, and either IP addresses or cookies identify unique users.

NOTE   **"Packet Sniffing"**

It is also possible to log site activity by monitoring the flow of HTTP packets as they are passed between the user's browser and your Web server. Activity is being measured at a network level in this case. This technique has been much less common in the past than log file analysis for Web site measurement. It has, however, been much more common for network administration functions or security applications monitoring the integrity, authenticity, validity, and origins of network activity. It is finding increased popularity as a Web measurement approach primarily because you are able to measure Internet protocols other than HTTP, so it can offer a solution for tracking not just Web site activity but file transfers, email, chat, and messaging activity. ■

Table 15.1 Metrics for measuring what people are doing on a site.

Relevant metrics	Description
Hits	A request to the server for a file. Now not considered valid currency because one page can contain as many hits as you desire. If you cut one graphic into 100 files, you get 100 hits instead of 1. Not worth tracking and analyzing to find out what people are doing on the site.
Page impressions/page views + most accessed pages/directories	A request to the server for an HTML page. Be aware that frames, proxy servers, and caching can distort the validity of page impression figures. Nonhuman traffic such as search engine spiders also needs to be filtered out for an accurate reading. Useful to gauge levels of site activity by time of day and by section of the site. This gives an indication of relative popularity of each page or area of the site. If tracked over time, this becomes particularly useful following a redesign because you can work out the impact on normal levels of activity for particular sections.
Top entry and exit pages	The pages most users enter the site at or leave from. Can be distorted by nonhuman traffic. Useful to see if lots of people are following a particular link out of the site or whether visitors appear to have a bookmarked page other than the home page.
Unique users/ unique visitors	Users distinguished by IP address or by cookie. Dynamic IP addressing used by ISPs can give you a falsely high number of users. Proxy servers, on the other hand, cause the number of unique users to appear lower than the real value. Nonhuman traffic will also account for some unique users. Despite the inaccuracies, this is the best indication (other than users actually logging on to the site) of how many different people you have using your site.
Repeat users/ return visitors	The number of unique users who come back to the site. This is usually tracked using a cookie on the user's computer to tag them. Again there are some inaccuracies because two different users could be using the same machine, but this metric, which is easy to track, is the first step in beginning to understand your users' loyalty and the effectiveness of your site in drawing users back to it. Tracked over periods of time, you can gauge the number of users gained, returning, or lost since the previous period. For example, you might decide to call users lost if they do not revisit within 6 months.
Sessions/visits + average user session/ visit length	A session spent on the site with no breaks in activity of longer than 30 minutes (usually). This will be defined by the session timeout that you set on the Web server. This is usually set to a default of 30 minutes, but you could positively skew results by shortening this period. Where machines are shared, or due to a proxy server, it can be hard to tell where one user leaves and another takes over. Different sites would expect different average session lengths.
Average number of page impressions per session/visit	This is a composite metric based on dividing the total number of page impressions by the total number of sessions in a given period. Other such composite metrics can be created. An example is average session length per repeat user to gauge whether repeat users spend longer or less time on average in successive visits. Page impressions per visit gives an idea of how much content each user looks at on average. This is clearly important to sites trying to maximize advertising revenue per user.

continued on next page

Table 15.1 Metrics for measuring what people are doing on a site. (continued)

Relevant metrics	Description
Conversion/browse-to-buy/browse-to-apply/browse-to-register/click through	These metrics are typically expressed as percentages, rates, or ratios and give a measure of the number of people who are doing something that you want to track: Buying, clicking on an ad, registering, inquiring, or applying are typical examples. These ratios, when tracked over time, become useful benchmarks against which targets can be set such as to increase the browse-to-apply ratio from 2% to 4%.
Abandonment	The opposite of conversion, this is a measure of how many people do not complete what you (usually) wanted them to do: Shopping cart abandonment is the most common example.
File downloads	The number of times particular files have been downloaded. You can set the types of file that you wish to monitor and see which downloads are most popular. By cross-referencing the number of visits to the download page with the number of actual downloads, you can see how interested users are in the download.

Table 15.2 Metrics for measuring what technology people are using to view a site.

Relevant metrics	Description
Browser	Details what version of which browser users have. This is useful for future site developments as you will have a good idea of what levels of technology your users will be able to support and what you will need to test for.
Operating system	Details what version of which operating system users have.
Screen resolution	Details what screen resolution users have their monitor set to. This information is not contained in standard log files (unlike browser and OS information) but can be logged using JavaScript inserted into a page retrieved by the user.
Java/CGI/cookie support	Details of what technologies users are supporting on their machines.
Plug-ins	Details of what browser plug-ins users have installed on their computers (e.g., Flash or RealPlayer). This is often one of the most useful technology metrics to look at because, although plug-ins typically give much enhanced multimedia capabilities (allowing for richer experiences), they must be downloaded and installed before content can be displayed—clearly a potential source of user frustration. If you can be confident about levels of plug-in support in your user base, you can be much more confident in deciding the pros and cons of using plug-ins.
Connection speed	The speed at which the user is surfing the Internet. Unfortunately, this is not a metric that can be automatically or easily captured. You will have to rely on market research to get a feel for how fast your users' connections are. This is clearly an important metric, however.

Table 15.3 Metrics for measuring where people have come from to get to a site.

Relevant metrics	Description
Referring IPs/ URLs/top referring domains	Details of the IP address, URL, or domain that users came from to arrive at your site. The referring site's IP address is passed in the HTTP header as a user arrives at your site. This IP address can then be looked up to find out the domain associated with it. This is useful to see where the majority of your traffic is coming from. If you are controlling the link that the users click (e.g., a banner or text ad), you can track even more precisely where users have come from by sending them to a special tracking URL on your site that logs details of inbound traffic and then immediately redirects to the page the user is expecting.
Country of access/ city of access/ geographic usage	Where site visitors have come from geographically. This is not a very reliable measure as it is based on country domains. For example, many users will have a dotcom domain rather than their country of origin. However, it might be useful to highlight unexpected traffic from a country where you thought you had no interested customers. Equally, it might help you weight or adjust traffic figures to exclude traffic from countries that are of no business value to you.
Search engines/ keyword searches	Details of the search engines that users have come through to get to your site and the search keywords that they used before clicking on the link to your site. These are useful in determining how important search engines are in referring you visitors, which search engines are delivering the most traffic, and the terms that users search under to find your site. This insight helps you decide how much search engine optimization work you need to do (promoting your site to the search engines to get better results rankings) and on what search engines. It also helps you in deciding what metatag keywords you should insert in your code to be picked up as users search for them.
Organization	Details of the types of organizations using the site. This, like the geographic information, is not always that helpful because it is based on domain extensions such as *.com* (commercial company) and *.org* (nonprofit organization) where the categorizations are not strictly adhered to. However, there are extensions such as *.edu* (educational body), *.gov* (government bodies), or *.mil* (military) that could give you valuable insight into what types of organizations users are coming from.

IP Addresses versus Cookies

Using an IP address (see the section on Log File Analysis that follows to understand where the IP address comes from) to identify unique users is not especially reliable. Three factors in particular will distort the accuracy of the data:

1. *Several users sharing the same machine.* If the machine has a fixed IP address, then it will appear to be the same unique user each time that machine comes to your site.

2. *Firewalls and proxy servers.* Used principally for security, network management, and to minimize the use of bandwidth, firewalls and proxy

Table 15.4 Metrics for measuring the technical performance of a site.

Relevant metrics	Description
Client and server errors	Details of client side errors and server side errors such as 500 Internal Server Error or 404 Not Found. Useful for spotting missing pages and broken links, debugging Web servers, or other application errors. Beware, as some errors are not actual errors: Some 404 file not found errors are not broken links; they are caused when users have incorrectly guessed a URL.
Site response times/speed/ download times	How fast pages load and data are retrieved. A useful benchmark to see how the site performs over time with changing traffic levels, fluctuating processor demand, and following site updates and redesigns. You should compare the performance of your site with that of competitors or other benchmark sites to ensure the experience you are delivering your users matches their expectations.
Server uptime/ server availability	Percentage of time that the site is available. This must be as close to 100% as possible. Any downtime equals lost revenue and disappointed customers. Uptimes should be guaranteed in a service-level agreement with your Internet service provider—typically 98% or higher.
Bandwidth usage/ busiest periods	The number of bytes of information delivered by your site across the Internet and the times of greatest bandwidth usage. These figures typically correspond to traffic levels but could also be skewed by backup routines you may run across the Web, FTP to and from the site for updates, as well as email traffic. Useful for load management, capacity planning, and planning downtime for upgrades. Can also be useful in spotting illicit traffic such as someone else taking up your bandwidth by using your mail server without permission.

servers have the effect of underrepresenting the number of actual unique visitors because all users going through them will have the same IP address.

3. *Dynamic IP addressing.* ISPs have a certain number of IP addresses allocated to them, and they share these among their users. As a user comes online, he or she will be allocated an IP address from the pool for the duration of that session. The next time that same user comes online, he or she is unlikely to be allocated the same IP address. This has the effect of overstating the number of unique users your site has, especially if you have a lot of return visitors.

NOTE   **Broadband and Fixed IP Addresses**

With broadband "always on" connections, users' machines are assigned a fixed IP address, which in theory means that unique user identification by IP address will become more reliable as the penetration of broadband users increases. However, there will remain a large percentage of users who do not have broadband, so IP address user identification will never be 100% reliable. ■

Cookies (small text files that are on the user's machine and store information that can be passed back to the server that first set them there) act like flags to tag a particular user so he or she can be recognized when returning to a site. This overcomes many of the problems encountered with IP addresses, but cookies are machine specific, so if a machine has more than one user, your data will still be distorted. Furthermore, cookies can be refused or deleted by the user or by corporate firewalls as they are perceived by some to infringe on personal privacy or to be a security threat. Studies have shown that the number of people rejecting cookies in this way is unlikely to be higher than 5% and typically closer to 1%. In lieu of user registration and logon, cookies are good enough for unique user identification and preferable to using IP addresses because the margins of error are that much less.

Log File Analysis

Although compulsory user logon is a much more powerful user tracking technique, log files remain a powerful tool in helping you understand user activity on a site and, indeed, are the only tool if logons are not desirable and cookies are disabled by corporate firewalls or users' browser settings.

The real value in log file analysis comes over time. It is the ability to see trends and therefore anomalies that is most useful. Log file analysis is certainly not 100% accurate, but at least the levels of inaccuracy are consistent so that observations over time are valid relative to each other.

One week's worth of log file data will give you a snapshot understanding of the volume of activity on a site, but you need more like 3 months' worth to get a real insight into the trends. Once you understand the trends, then spikes and anomalies become evident, and usually, their cause can be traced and evaluated.

NOTE   **Dealing with Nonhuman Traffic**

You need to be aware that some of your page impressions and users are not in fact generated by humans but by search engine spiders and other automated bots. It is not uncommon for nonhuman traffic to account for 10–20% of site accesses.

As well as spiders sent by search engines to index sites, there are many other kinds of bots: They copy sites for offline browsing, follow pages to harvest email addresses in mailto links, or check links to see if they have been updated.

Unfortunately, all these have different behaviors in terms of paths and the number of pages visited. Some bots are sent by known search engines and can be recognized from the hostname/IP and agent string and thus filtered, but many are programs run by individuals or are designed not to be spotted by changing their agent string for each hit in a visit.

If you are keen to try and gauge, filter out, or control as much bot activity as possible, there are several lists of bots online that you can reference. Most bots will attempt to access a file called robots.txt at the root directory of your Web server, and you can include specific instructions here like requesting search engine spiders to index only the home page.   ■

To understand *why* things happen, you need to talk to users. This is covered in Section 15.2, User-Centric Measurement.

Although log files do not tell you *why* things are happening, they do tell you *what* is happening, and if you analyze them pre- and postsite updates, you can get a very good idea of how successful your changes have been.

As well as being valuable for trend analysis and assessing the impact of site changes, the trail that log files leave can be used to glean information about frustrations in the customer experience as they try to navigate through sections of the site. This is looked at in more detail in the later section on path analysis.

The log file most commonly analyzed is that created by the Web server. However, there are other ways to log activity that can prove superior. The different forms of log files and their merits and drawbacks are outlined in the following pages. It is important to be aware of these differences to help you choose a measurement tool and to help you properly interpret your metrics and measurement results.

Web Server Logs

Browsers and Web servers communicate using the HTTP protocol. When the browser sends a request to the Web server, it includes a header that contains information that is logged by the Web server. Our ability to analyze site activity is confined to the information that is thus logged. Figure 15.2 shows a typical log file and the information we get from it.

TIP   **Managing Web Server Log Files**

▶ *ECLF or CLF?* You can configure most Web servers to create common log files or extended common log files. You get a lot more information with the ECLF format,

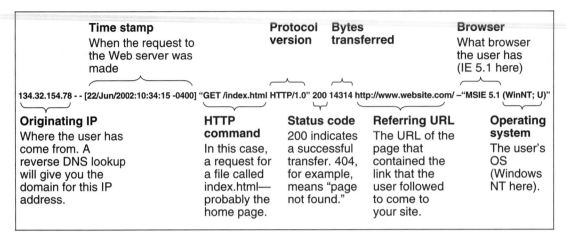

Figure 15.2 Anatomy of a typical log file.

so in general, go for this. However, bear in mind that ECLF are much larger than their CLF equivalent and more CPU power is taken up creating them.

▶ *Large log files.* Although log files are only plain text, they can get very large—over 100MB a day on busy sites. Be careful about filling up your disk space, which can cause problems with the proper functioning of the applications. Consider writing log files to a larger nonsystem drive. Back them up and zip them up to conserve space. Storing log files by month is a common practice for month-by-month analysis and reports.

▶ *CPU demands.* Remember that running a log analysis tool on the server uses up a fair amount of CPU power. This could adversely affect the performance of the site, and it might take several hours to run the report. Set the analysis tool to run automatically when the site is least busy. Many software tools allow for real-time log analysis. Although exciting to look at, remember the performance overheads this incurs.

▶ *Corrupt log files.* If the log file is there but the analysis software cannot read it, the log file might be corrupt. Try deleting the last and first 10 lines of the log file and rerunning the software. Often this cures the problem.

▶ *Missing log files.* Are you sure they have not written elsewhere on the system? Have they written to their default location on the system drive? If they are really missing, there is not much you can do other than estimate site activity, based upon an equivalent day's log file.

Log files were originally designed to let server administrators gauge server performance and not for purposes of tracking how users are interacting with the Web site. There is much information that could be considered redundant (do we really need to log every file request?), and as we have seen, there are dangers in relying too heavily on the accuracy of the information.

It is possible to clean up log files and filter out much of the inaccuracy and redundant information. This is a process that is typically carried out before importing the log file information into a data warehouse or other database for analysis. Analyzing raw log files can be done, but it is slow. This works fine if you only require standard reports that can be automatically run overnight but becomes very restrictive when you need to do more ad hoc and real-time analysis or mine the information to answer specific questions. Ideally, one would like clean, accurate data stored in a relational database, into which one can integrate other data sources, with an analytics and reporting tool to help extract and display the answers and intelligence you are after.

Do-It-Yourself Logs

One way to try and eliminate some of the inaccuracies and redundant information contained in Web server log files, thus reducing the time and effort required to clean them up for analysis, is to create your own source of log files. There are two key approaches to this:

1. Create logs on a remote machine by tagging pages
2. Log activity to a file or database on your own servers

Create Logs on a Remote Machine by Tagging Pages

You insert a piece of code in your HTML pages that makes a call to a remote server, which is then logged for analysis. This piece of code may be in the form of a file request (e.g., for a transparent 1 pixel × 1 pixel GIF image), or it may be a piece of code (e.g., JavaScript, CGI, Java). Typically, you can include variables, such as page or product name, in this inserted code that are passed to the remote server, logged, and can then be more easily interpreted during analysis. This technique is variously called *page tagging, page dotting,* or *browser-based measurement.*

For more details on measurement tools, including a summary of the advantages and considerations in opting for an ASP solution, refer to Section 16.4, Choosing a Measurement Tool.

There is no reason you cannot log activity to a remote server like this yourself, but usually this is provided as an outsourced ASP (application service provider) service. Table 15.5 summarizes some of the differences between using Web server logs and using the page tagging approach for data collection.

Table 15.5 Comparison between using Web server logs and page tagging for data collection.

	Web server logs	Page tagging
Accuracy and data management	Issues with identifying users by IP address and inaccuracies in activity reporting through caching and proxy servers. Nonhuman traffic and redundant data also logged. Web server logs need to be cleansed and processed before they can be accurately reported against.	Page view data are more accurate without the need for filtering as you specify which pages log what. There is also less data generated as only a single request needs to be logged per page viewed as opposed to log files where all file requests are stored making the size of the raw data much larger. Page tag data are thus easier to import into a database for analysis than Web server logs, which need more cleansing.
Ease of implementation	To analyze your log files, you will need to purchase log file analysis software that you then configure to run either on the site's server itself or locally, in which case you need to download the log files before you can analyze them. You will also need to ensure that your Web server is writing the log files correctly, and you will have to analyze the structure of your site to work out what data you will need to filter out of reporting: requests from navigation frames, for example.	Web server logs can be written automatically by the Web server, but someone has to do the page tagging. The results will only be as good as the tagging work. Imagine you have a site with half a million pages and no well-structured content management system with a limited number of templates. Do you want to be the one who goes through every page adding a piece of code to each? How much would that interfere with other ongoing developments? Who defines all the tags for reporting purposes? It is quite a logistically frightening task. If you have a relatively small site or one that is template and database (CMS) driven with well-indexed and labeled content, it should be relatively straightforward to add the tags. You need only add the tags to the templates, and the necessary variables will be created and passed on as the page is dynamically served. If you fall somewhere in between, as many sites do, you need to carefully consider the amount of work involved in doing the tagging. On the plus side, if you are using an ASP, the data are logged to a remote server, so there is no systems integration work, and the analysis and reporting infrastructure is already all set up.
Quality of reporting	You will need to resolve the file path data that resides in the log file to something more meaningful.	The clarity of the reporting will depend on the clarity of the tagging schema you have used and whether the tags have been inserted in the correct places. As tags rather than file names are used, the information and reporting can be much more marketing friendly. A very popular page such as *Products_Kettle_Steel_Large* is somewhat easier to understand than *http://www.Website.com/products/kitchenware/product_id=23.html*.

continued on next page

Table 15.5 **Comparison between using Web server logs and page tagging for data collection.**
(continued)

	Web server logs	Page tagging
Cost	Varies from $5,000 to $10,000 for entry-level software up to $200,000+ for enterprise-level, though if all you wanted was Web server log file analysis, this would be substantial overkill. Usually, you purchase the software license up front and then pay a regular fee for free support and upgrades or simply pay for upgrades as and when you wish.	Assuming you are using an ASP, price ranges vary greatly depending on the complexity and levels of the service you require. Entry-level site activity analysis costs around $5,000 to $10,000 (the same as the Web server log file analysis software licence fee), but this is a service fee that is payable each year. You are buying a service not software. Increased costs are for increased levels of service.

Log Activity to a File or Database on Your Own Servers

Of course, you can write your own scripts and applications to log user activity. This is particularly valuable if you want to track quite specific actions to answer specific questions. It can also be more cost effective than implementing an all-singing, all-dancing, out-of-the-box measurement system.

For example, say you have a site that has registered users and a newsletter that is regularly sent to subscribers. For starters, you can set a cookie on each registered user's machine so that they do not need to log on each time they visit the site. The cookie ID that is communicated to the server allows the system to know who the user is and automatically log them on. There is some margin for error, of course, where machines are shared, but a "Not Ashley Friedlein? Click here" prominently displayed (plus required reentry of password to access sensitive information) gets around the worst of that.

With users thus cookied, you know who they are when they come back to the site and can chalk up another visit to their user profile information. By inserting a tracking URL in your email newsletter (e.g., *www.Website.com/redirect. asp?FV951*), you can also log what links are followed from the newsletter to what content. Using codes that might indicate content, version, or time, for example, you can log information that provides the data you need for your analysis. Whether you log information to a file or directly to a database will depend on levels of activity and resulting demands on the CPU and database. If you are logging directly to the database, you must be careful that the extra CPU demands do not adversely affect the customers' experience of the site.

ISP Logs

Internet service providers monitor and log the activity that occurs on sites that they host. In most countries, they are required to monitor this activity and keep records of it for legal reasons. Many ISPs use the information they have to provide traffic measurement and analysis services to sites that they host. There are also third-party service providers (see Resources for examples) that purchase the log file information from numerous ISPs to aggregate it and provide traffic information across multiple companies, types of site, or industry sector. This is using the same techniques and information as per Web server logs, but because there is information from other sites included, it is possible to compare the performance of your site with that of peers, a useful benchmarking exercise.

Using Metadata and CMS Application Data for Analysis

Log file analysis, in its different guises as outlined, is the most common form of site-centric measurement. However, it does have its limitations, as we have seen. Log file analysis could not tell you (at least not without a lot of cumbersome analysis effort) whether a particular person, or users in general, is tending to look at products marked with a reduced price, or products that are blue, or content from a particular source provider, or content updated by a particular author, or content with similar associated search keywords. This sort of information is often not particular to identifiable sections of the site (file directories from a log file point of view), so is not embedded in the actual file path, particularly if you have a dynamic site powered by a content management system. The information exists in the metadata: the information that describes content, or data about data. As we have seen in Part II, Content Management, metadata are increasingly important in storing, indexing, retrieving, managing, and generally optimizing the use of Web assets.

The information architecture of the site and the metadata are very powerful sources of data for advanced site-centric measurement. As this information is usually embedded in a content management system, you have a lot to gain from integrating your analytics and reporting platform with the CMS. Not only does this provide you with the power to perform much more complex analysis using the additional contextual information about site content usage that the CMS provides, but it can also make maintenance much easier: As the CMS is updated, the reporting automatically adjusts to include the new changes.

Imagine you ran an e-business events listings site. You charge event organizers a commission on any bookings made for their events through your site.

The site is navigationally organized by topic: marketing, advertising, design, content, production, strategy, venture capital, and so on. You have a home page that displays personalized content, and you send out emails to registered users. The site is powered by a CMS using templates, and you have an analysis and reporting tool that is integrated with the CMS.

Through log file analysis, you could tell which areas of the site received the most interest, and through actual bookings, you could look at conversion ratios and try and glean what it is about those conferences that persuaded people to go. However, if you wanted to understand interest levels by event organizer (assuming the same organizer had events across several topic categories), by cost of the event, by venue, or by speakers, then log file analysis would not be very effective because this information is contained in the "event" content object and its location within the file structure of the site is immaterial. Using your analysis tool in conjunction with the CMS, however, you can understand your users' preferences and interests over and beyond just a topic. Imagine how much more effective your personalization, email offers, and other marketing could be. Imagine how valuable that information could be to a potential advertiser. Did you know Joe only looks at Forrester events? And Dave won't look at anything for more than $500.

Path Analysis

Analyzing the paths that users have taken to and from certain pages within a site can be one of the most useful and powerful forms of site-centric analysis. It is particularly good for answering the "What are people doing on the site?" question, especially where you want to focus on a particular area of the site.

NOTE   **Click Stream Analysis**

Path analysis is also referred to as *click stream* analysis. A user's click stream is simply the stream of clicks that he or she has made navigating through a site. This stream of clicks represents a navigation path, so click stream analysis and path analysis are synonymous. ∎

Whereas more general log file analysis works well for the reporting of volumes and nature of traffic, path analysis is preferable for examining in detail how traffic is flowing around particular areas of the site. General log file analysis will help you monitor site usage trends, whereas path analysis will give you specific before and after analysis, especially where you are focusing on a particular process within the site that you would like users to complete such as purchase, registration, and application steps.

Path analysis still uses log files, whether from the Web server or generated another way, as its data source, but the reporting is page-centric, allowing you to look at the traffic flows from a particular page and then drill in any direction continuing to follow the flows of traffic from page to page. This gives you answers to common questions such as: Where do most people go from the home page? Where do people drop out of the buying process? Which step in the registration process are users taking longest to complete?

Figure 15.3 gives a simplified example of path analysis. We are looking at the final three stages of a checkout process on an e-commerce site. The path that you would like users to follow is to go from step 1 to step 3, thereby purchasing something. For simplicity's sake, we assume 100 users have come to step 1 in the purchase process, and we can see that only 30 customers get as far as the final order confirmation page, meaning 70% of potential buyers have somehow been lost along this particular path. If this could be reduced by 20%, it would make a big difference to the bottom line. So before you try spending more money on marketing or complete site redesigns, how might you improve conversion rates just by concentrating on the flow of traffic through these crucial last three pages of the checkout?

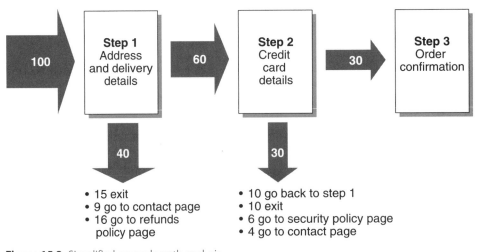

Figure 15.3 Simplified example path analysis.

You would enter the page tag name of the first page in this checkout process (e.g., "step1_checkout") or the file path (e.g., *www.Website.com/checkout/step1.jsp*) depending on how your analysis tool is set up, and you could see how traffic was flowing from that page. Looking at Figure 15.3, we can see that although 60% of users are continuing on to step 2 toward purchase, you are still losing 15% completely, 9% are for some reason going to the site's contact section, and 16% are looking at the refunds and returns policy.

As we follow the traffic to step 2, we notice that only half of your users actually purchase, with a significant number dropping out or going back a step in the path for some reason. This path analysis tells you clearly what is happening, but does not tell you why it is happening or who the users are. The following section on user-centric measurement gives more details on this, but for now let us suppose that based on this path analysis intelligence, you came up with the following hypotheses and actions:

The address and delivery details page:

▶ Perhaps people are put off when they see all the details they have to fill in. You implement a system to remember customers' address details for repeat purchases.

▶ Perhaps people have privacy concerns about putting in their personal details. You get a third party to accredit your privacy policy.

▶ Perhaps people are concerned that if goods are delivered to their home, they may not be in. You make your delivery options more prominent and add a guarantee that if the goods are stolen from outside the customer's house, you will replace the goods at no charge.

▶ Perhaps people need more up-front assurance about your returns and refunds policy. You make your returns guarantee more prominent on the page.

The credit card details page:

▶ Perhaps customers are not convinced of the security measures on the site. You emphasize that you are using the strongest encryption available and put a link to a special page detailing your extensive security measures.

▶ Perhaps there is a problem with form validation on the page. You conduct a usability test which shows that, indeed, there is a problem: The form is rejected if users enter their credit card number with any spaces. You fix this.

▶ Perhaps customers need a little enticement to persuade them to buy. You give away a free promotional gift with every first purchase.

As you implement each of these changes, you would revisit your path analysis to see the effect of each change. Figure 15.4 shows an improved checkout process where half of the users entering this purchase path follow it through to purchase, representing a 20% increase thanks just to concentrating on these few pages.

Transactional Data Analysis

The analysis of transactional data is usually done without reference to actual customers, although it can also be viewed from the point of view of actual customers (What has Joe Bloggs bought? What does that say about him? Who else has bought similar things to Joe? Where do they live?). In this sense, transactional data analysis bridges both site-centric and user-centric measurement, depending on the focus of the reporting.

Clearly, there are several inherent advantages with transaction data:

▶ *It is rich.* Typically, the customer will need to give quite a lot of information for the order to be processed: name, address, and payment details at least.

▶ *It is easy to capture.* Assuming that you can persuade people to want to buy your products in the first place, customers know that they will need to give extensive personal information to actually purchase, so data capture is quite straightforward.

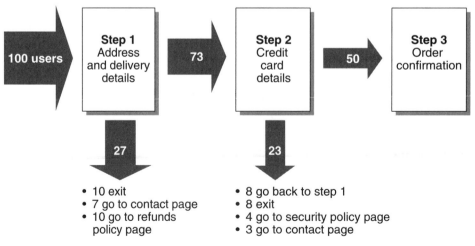

Figure 15.4 Improved example path analysis.

For more details on how personal data can be used, see Section 15.2, User-centric Measurement.

▶ *It is explicit.* Rather than trying to infer information from data sources that contain inherent inaccuracies (e.g., path analysis), transactional data are submitted directly by the user.

▶ *It is clean.* The data are typically submitted via a Web form that allows you to capture the data directly to a database or in a form that is clearly structured. This means there is much less need for cleaning and filtering the data.

For these reasons, there is nothing particularly difficult or at least nothing that makes transactional data from a Web site any different from other transactional data analysis. It is a point of sale like any other. Not surprisingly, transactional data analysis that is not user-centric tends to focus on metrics and calculations that have a direct correlation to financial performance:

▶ Sales (by volume, value, product, or customer)
▶ Profitability (by value, product, or customer)
▶ Average basket size
▶ Cross-sells/product mix purchased
▶ Customer value calculations
▶ Return on investment analyses

These metrics are clearly very important both in historical analysis of what value a site has generated over a given period and in projecting future returns. As the Web becomes integrated with the core business and there is an increasing focus on ensuring online investments meet the same return on investment criteria as other projects, these fundamental commercial metrics will remain benchmarks against which targets will be set and performance evaluated.

Case Study   Moving toward Performance Measurement across Multiple Web Sites

Company: AUTOGLASS,® *www.autoglass.co.uk*

Company Overview

AUTOGLASS® (*www.autoglass.co.uk*) is the UK's leading vehicle glass repair and replacement expert, serving over 1 million drivers each year via 1100 mobile service units.

continued

The mobile network delivers the widest UK and Ireland service, which uniquely extends to the rest of Europe through the Carglass (*www.carglass.com*) brand. AUTOGLASS® and CARGLASS® are owned by Belron International (*www.belron.com*), the global market leader in automotive glass repair and replacement.

Background to Case Study and Objectives

We implemented our first Web measurement solution in 1898, the second in early 2000, and the current one in 2001. Our evolution has probably mirrored that of many other similar sites. We started out using Webtrends' log analysis tool offline. Each month, we downloaded our Web server logs and analyzed them using Webtrends to produce reports that focused on traffic analysis: hits, page views, user sessions, and so on. We encountered some challenges with this approach. For example, at one point, the date format of our logs changed, which confused our reporting. Equally, our site's use of frames and a lack of rigorous log filtering meant there were inaccuracies in our analysis.

We then installed, and ran, Webtrends live on our server, which allowed us to do more frequent reporting, saved us time, and gave more people online access to the reporting. However, we soon realized that not only was this very resource intensive and impacted on the performance of the site but also that hits and our traffic-centric reporting were confusing, and ultimately meaningless, to senior management who could not make the connection between this and the business value that the site was delivering. So we transitioned from a page and traffic-centric approach to concentrate more on customers (e.g., analyzing customer service feedback) and measuring business value as defined by the number of leads the site generated and how many of those converted to actual glass jobs.

However, even as we refined our analysis and reporting in the UK, we recognized that site development and performance measurement across the 14 other countries within our group were progressing at different speeds and in different directions. The decision was taken to centralize systems, design, and site measurement—keeping content and marketing local—to improve consistency and quality and to streamline costs.

Process and Practice

Centralizing on a common technical infrastructure across all countries and for all sites, and developing common design templates, was a major step toward making multiple-site measurement possible and effective. Without this, it was not possible to compare like with like, so comparative benchmarking was not feasible. As we outsourced the provision of the technical infrastructure, the choice of site analysis tool was made easier because our ISP recommended LiveStats in our configuration as the best performer for our requirements.

It was very important at this transitional stage that the opportunity for change was supported by senior management, without which we would never have gotten the buy-in from the individual business units, and the project would have been much harder and might have even failed. We combined a top-down and bottom-up approach. This big change also gave us the opportunity to review and standardize our site measurement tools, reporting, and analysis across the group. So the decision-making process was perhaps largely autocratic rather than democratic, but we were very keen to end up with a common platform and base level of measurement and reporting across the group as quickly and efficiently as possible.

In deciding what this base level of measurement should be, we learned from our collective experience across the various sites what metrics were most important and most valuable. For example, earlier I described some of the experiences and learnings from the UK. Above all, we wanted to ensure that the base levels we defined were simple and effective. Simplicity was crucial to ensure successful multinational rollout, including subsequent training and take up. We believed we would be much more successful doing a few things well and consistently than attempting too much and losing quality and control. For most countries, our newly defined base levels of site measurement were in any case a big leap forward; for others who were more advanced, we could provide a base level that they could then build on. At least we could be sure of a certain standard throughout.

As we had a common technical infrastructure for all sites, we were able to set up a dedicated log file server on which LiveStats, the reporting and analysis tool we now use, runs. This means that all reporting for all sites can be managed in one place and through one interface. At an administrator level, we are able to set up logons for different users giving them access to the relevant reports for their country and function. Improving multilingual support means that single-system reporting can work in countries all over the world, which is important as we expand and integrate further businesses around the globe.

Results

Initially, we were reluctant to change from Webtrends because we already understood how it worked and what we could get out of it. We felt the learning curve of a new software package was one we did not want to make, especially as a few of the countries were using this package and it was another obstacle to overcome. Furthermore, at the time the tool did not provide click stream analysis, which was something that Webtrends, which

continued

we had been using, did. However, we felt that LiveStats would do a good enough job and would at least meet all the base-level requirements we had defined. Click stream analysis was something we decided we could live without.

Subsequently, we have discovered that in fact there is a lot more that we can do applying basic measurement techniques using LiveStats than we at first recognized. Apart from two valuable features that LiveStats provides (a real-time "who's on" the site now function and a site usage map facility), we have found the "watches" function, which is essentially little more than a counter, surprisingly powerful. For example, we use it to:

▶ Track inbound traffic to particular pages or URLs to measure response rates to marketing activities (e.g., press releases, advertising, etc.)

▶ Monitor activity from particular IP addresses (e.g., big partner organizations, potential security threats, etc.)

▶ Set up click through URLs to track referrals from online advertising to accurately measure returns on investment

However, the biggest advantage is the fact that we now have one system that works across all our sites globally. We have been able to create a standard training manual; share expertise, tips, and knowledge around the organization; and quickly roll out measurement for new sites. Senior management at a group level are able to cross-compare performance internationally on a like-for-like basis, enabling much better decision making as well as highlighting areas of over- or underperformance that might need attention.

Lessons Learned

Based on our experiences, I would advise the following:

▶ Keep it simple. Particularly when you have to manage measurement across multiple sites, you should have a simple base level of analysis and reporting. Each individual site can evolve and iterate its own more customized reporting, but there needs to be a common underlying base standard that everyone can understand and deliver. This is especially important where there are differing levels of Web expertise across the business.

▶ The tool is less important than how you use it. Most analysis tools now share core basic features and differ only in the details. These details are not where most of the value lies. You can actually achieve a lot with quite basic tools and techniques. With experience, you realize that there is more value present than you at first thought, and yet you also learn to recognize what to ignore: a log file analysis package can produce lots of information that, although interesting, may not add a great deal of value to your site understanding.

▶ Ongoing education is very important. Measurement only has any value if it is accountable and delivers actionable insight that leads to increased business value. Insight requires understanding, so it is vital that staff continue to be educated about site measurement and that knowledge is shared. Equally, you must beware that all your site measurement expertise does not reside in just one person because without that person all the value is gone.

▶ You need qualitative and quantitative measurement. I have emphasized log file (data) analysis, but we have received tremendous value from more direct customer feedback through usability sessions, focus groups, surveys, and the like. To really understand what is happening on your sites and why, you must combine qualitative and quantitative measurement techniques.

▶ Use existing standards where possible. Be very aware of getting bogged down in the details of log file analysis. It is important to apply standard principles of market research to Web analysis so that the Web channel's value can be judged in the same context as the rest of the business.

David Robertson
Program Manager
AUTOGLASS®

15.2 User-Centric Measurement

As should be clear from the last section, site-centric measurement is very good for telling *what* is happening on your site, but it does not tell you *why* it is happening nor does it tell you anything much about *who* the actual users are. As the balance of power shifts increasingly toward the customer and building strong, profitable customer relationships becomes vital for commercial success, it is rarely sufficient to rely on site-centric measurement alone because it tells you so little about actual customers and their likes, dislikes, motivations, and needs.

The metrics of user-centric Web site measurement are more fluid than for site-centric measurement. This is because on the whole they are softer, less tangible, more subjective metrics such as customer satisfaction or loyalty. There is nothing new about user-centric metrics as applied to the Web. It is the detail of the way each is measured and the actual implementation for the Web that are relatively new. For example, how do you define a loyal site user?

These intangible elements are becoming ever more important in the quest for competitive advantage. The collective experience of the Internet industry has taught us, for example, how important brand is online. Dotcoms burned through enormous amounts of money trying to build brands overnight. They may have created awareness, interest, and even site visits, but they did not create brands with real meaning and longevity in customers' minds. The more established brands have capitalized on their brand heritage, and the mass market of Web users has gravitated toward sites of those brands that users know and trust, where they understand and believe in the promise that the brand makes them. Brands exist in the minds of the user—perception is reality—so an important part of Web site measurement is understanding what effect the Web site is having on users' perception of the brand.

Customer service is also extremely important. We live in a service economy where basic product quality is usually taken for granted, and it is the brand and service elements that add value. On the Web, there is no physical product; it is all about the brand and service, so there are great opportunities to create or destroy that intangible value. The remote, interactive nature of the Web makes it all the more important to try and gain insight into your customers' mind-sets because you cannot see them, you cannot easily talk to them directly, and you cannot stop them quickly expressing their feelings to thousands of other potential customers. Once lost, you are unlikely to get them back.

User-centric measurement is thus a vital element of any Web site measurement strategy and helps evaluate whether you are reaching the right customers, whether you are successfully creating value both for your customers and for the business, and whether you are keeping the brand promise to your customers.

15.2.1   Metrics

In the same way that site-centric measurement helps answer several fundamental questions about how the site is being used, user-centric measurement focuses on answering the following three questions:

1. Who are our online customers?
2. How valuable are they to us?
3. What do they think about us?

Next we look at each of the questions and some of the most common corresponding metrics and measurement approaches used to help answer the question. Section 15.2.2 explains the measurement techniques employed.

1. Who are our online customers?

2. How valuable are they to us?

3. What do they think about us?

15.2.2   Measurement Techniques

As you can see, although the nuances of what they mean for the Web might be different, the actual metrics used in user-centric Web site measurement are the same as those in traditional marketing. Likewise, the techniques for arriving at these user-centric metrics are generally little different from traditional methods. Following is a brief review of some of those techniques with a particular focus on how they are, or can be, applied online.

Identifying and Tracking Users

It is worth remembering that despite all the Big Brother fears that the Web conjures up, the only way you *know* who users are for sure is because they tell you or because you buy users' data from someone else they have revealed their identity to, a practice that is usually frowned upon if not illegal. The section on site-centric measurement explains how you can determine some crude user attributes, but you still do not know the identity of a user until he or she gives you the information.

Once you have been given users' personal information, so that you know who they are, or at least who *they* say they are, you still need to be able to identify them on repeat visits. Only in this way can you tie activity to a particular profile. The only two ways to adequately identify unique individuals when they come to the site are:

1. *A persistent user cookie.* Cookies are small text files that are on users' machines and store information on them that can be passed back to the server that first set them there. Cookies act like flags to tag particular users so they can be recognized when they come back to a site. However, cookies are machine specific, so if a machine has more than one user, your data will be distorted. Cookies can also be refused or deleted by the user. Some cookies are only used for certain periods of time. Session cookies, for example, only store information while you are actually using a site: Keeping track of what you have in your shopping basket is a good example. A persistent user cookie, however, remains

Table 15.6 Metrics for measuring who your online customers are.

Relevant metrics	Description
Name, gender, age, and other personal details	Basic personal information that has long been used for categorizing and segmenting target markets. Gender and age can clearly be of great importance for some products or services, but reliance on these characteristics alone as determinants of likely behavior is increasingly unreliable in a modern society. However, there might be particular details about your customers that group them or make them particular relevant to your proposition.
Demographics	The factual characteristics of customers, including their personal details as well as marital status, family size, education, geographic location, income, and occupation. Demographics are widely used in the advertising industry as a means to classify people according to socioeconomic/demographic groups (A, B, C1, C2, D, E), each with particular characteristics such as level of education, types of employment, and levels of affluence. The A-E scale of demographic groups is what people are usually referring to when they say "upmarket" (A, B, C1), "mass market" (all grades though more C1, C2, D, E), or "downmarket" (D, E).
Psychographics	Used to build customer segments based on attitudes, values, beliefs, and opinions as opposed to the factual characteristics of demographics. Political views, learning patterns, or musical tastes would qualify for psychographic segmentation. Marketing research usually combines demographic and psychographic information to build a fuller understanding of customers.
	Because the Internet is still a relatively new and evolving medium, one which the mass market is still getting used to and whose usage patterns are determined both by levels of Web experience and type of person, psychographics are of great interest for the Web. The ability of an online broker to convert browsers to online traders, for example, will depend to a large degree on the type of person using the site: Are they confident people who like to give things a go or are they risk-averse followers of the masses? Psychographic segments built on attitudinal and behavioral characteristics will often be good indicators of how customers will use and react to a Web site.
Lifestyle	The way that people choose to live their lives. Lifestyle data, indicating habits, preferences, and dislikes by customer groups, have become increasingly popular as their relevance in modern society—relative, say, to demographics, age, or gender—has increased. Everyone can be considered part of the lifestyle universe, but groups of us approach life in similar ways and share interests, which means we will respond to particular propositions in a similar way. Lifestyle data might include media consumption habits or pastimes.
Interests/preferences	Customer interests and preferences can be stated by the customer, or they can be inferred from their behavior. Understanding customer interests and needs is fundamental to giving them what they want to win, retain, and maximize them as customers. The fact that the Web is interactive and dynamic makes it an ideal medium for capturing customer interests, both stated and inferred.

Table 15.6 Metrics for measuring who your online customers are. (continued)

Relevant metrics	Description
Customer segments	Many companies will have developed specialized customer segments that are often an amalgam of the various other ways of understanding customers as outlined. Customer segments will usually be given names (e.g., fruits, types of animal, types of car, etc.), and marketing and communications will be tailored by segment. This form of segmentation shows a more mature and advanced form of customer insight that is characteristic of companies like financial services organizations that have a lot of customer information and for which these customer data are a vital strategic asset. There is no reason these sorts of segments should not be extended to include Web site behavioral attributes or why new segments should not be created to cater for customers who show particularly strong online usage characteristics.

indefinitely (or at least for a long period) and is preferable for user identification as you do not know when they will next come back to the site.

2. *User logon.* Access to the user's profile information is protected by a logon, typically requesting a username or email address plus password combination.

Best practice user identification employs a hybrid of the two foregoing approaches that gives a good enough level of user identification accuracy, security, and ease of use. The hybrid approach automates logon using a persistent user cookie while catering for the possibility that the machine-specific cookie might have assumed the incorrect user identity by having a link prominently displayed on the site for the user to correct any such mistake: "Welcome **Ashley Friedlein**. Not Ashley? Click here." Although logon is automated, it does not give access to areas of the site that contain sensitive data related to the user: account information, profile data, credit card details, and the like. Access to these areas still requires logon to avoid the risk of unauthorized access.

If you want to know how to go about this, refer back to Section 9.2.1, Capturing Customer Data.

User profile data should be written to a central user profile database. The user profiles are enriched over time as the relationship grows. The deeper the user profile information, the more valuable the customer base becomes and the more potential there is for improved customer retention and acquisition. The real challenge is persuading customers to give you their precious personal data in the first place.

Qualitative and Quantitative

Quantitative data analysis or customer research projects will give you more statistically relevant results because the number of participants is higher.

Table 15.7   Metrics for measuring customer value.

Relevant metrics	Description
Acquisition and servicing costs	If a customer is particularly expensive to acquire or is very costly to service, then they will need to either spend a lot with you or have other important intangible benefits to be of value
Loyalty	Loyalty, and its corollaries churn or attrition, are very important in affecting profitability. It costs much more to win a new customer than it does to win repeat business from an existing customer. You cannot afford to lose valuable, loyal customers because they are the cash cows that keep a business going. But what is loyal? How do you measure loyalty?
	Loyalty needs to be defined to become a meaningful metric, and it is likely to vary from business to business. For a content Web site that is supported by advertising revenues, a loyal user might be defined as one who has visited the site at least 10 times in total and at least once in the last 4 weeks. For an e-commerce site, a loyal customer might be defined as one who has bought online at least three times, spent more than $100, and bought from more than two product lines. Loyalty is usually measured as a composite of the various metrics that follow.
Fit with target audience	Assuming you have a clear idea of who you want to be targeting (your "ideal" customer), you should also be quite clear how close a fit a particular customer is to your ideal.
Share of wallet	A measure of how much of a customer's overall spending power you are capturing or their spending power within the category of expenditure that your business fits. This is a measure of how successful you are in extracting money from your customers relative to the average amount they would normally spend.
Recency, frequency, monetary (RFM)	This is a metric often used by retailers to measure customer value. Monetary measures how much a customer spends. Frequency measures how often a customer buys. Recency measures how recently the customer has purchased.
Payment profile	Does the customer have a positive payment profile and credit history?
Product choice and range	Does the customer tend to buy high-margin products and buy across a wide range of products? If so, their value is likely to be higher.
Responsiveness	How well does the customer respond to marketing? This could be an important determinant in ascribing value.
Opinion former/ status/profile	This is hard to measure without some subjective input, but it is clear that some customers are of great value for their ability to sway the opinion of others. Journalists are a good example. Other high-profile, well-connected, or influential people also make very valuable customers: Celebrity endorsement is very important in the fashion industry, and good political contacts through customers might be very important for lobbying.
Channel usage	Which purchase channels does the customer use? For example, if the customer shows a high propensity to use the Web as their purchase channel of choice, then this should mean that they are more cost efficient to service, improving their lifetime value.

Table 15.8 Metrics for measuring what customers think of you.

Relevant metrics	Description
Customer satisfaction	Customer satisfaction has been measured and rated offline as standard practice for a long time, but it is just beginning to be measured more formally for Web sites. Some of the more successful and best known Web sites, however, do run ongoing customer satisfaction measurement programs to benchmark whether they are successfully improving the customer's Web experience over time.
Loyalty	Loyalty, as discussed earlier, is a measure of value to the company, but it is usually founded on the fact that the customer thinks highly of the company. This is not always the case, however. For example, there might be only one store stocking particular items for hundreds of miles. Unless a competitor comes along, this store is likely to have loyal local customers for those items. This is much less true on the Web, of course, where loyalty is more likely to be based on genuine preference, as otherwise it would be easy to go elsewhere. Brand is a very powerful contributor to loyalty online as well as offline.
Mindshare/ awareness	This is perhaps less a measure of *what* a customer thinks of you as *how much* they think of you or whether they know of you at all. How much of a customer's thinking and aware time do you take up? How well do they recall your products or services? A strong brand, again, will drive high levels of awareness. With so much choice on the Web, it is all the more important that customers know who you are, what you can offer them, and where they can find you. Higher levels of mindshare and awareness are also likely to build confidence and trust with potential or existing customers, positively affecting the likelihood of online purchasing.
Referrals	Online you can encourage customers to "Refer a Friend" or even just "Email a Friend" a Web page. These "viral" tools are excellent ways of acquiring the right kinds of customer cost effectively. It is also easy to track whether such referrals are being made and taken up and who is making them. Monitoring the use and success of these referral mechanisms will give you a benchmark for assessing whether customers feel what you are offering is worth passing on.

However, qualitative techniques often prove more useful at getting deeper levels of insight, understanding subtler shades of customer behavior, and getting more of a feel about customers' reactions to new concepts. The smaller, usually less structured nature of qualitative customer insight projects also means that they are more likely to suggest entirely new ideas that you may not have thought about. Each approach is most powerful when complemented by the other. If you make a change to your site based on qualitative insight, how do you then measure whether it has worked? This is where you need the data-driven quantitative analysis. With the two working in tandem, you ensure that you are continually refining your proposition in the right direction.

Tables 15.9 and 15.10 summarize common qualitative and quantitative techniques for user-centric measurement and where each is most effective.

Table 15.9 Qualitative techniques for user-centric measurement.

Techniques	Application	Description
Focus groups	Idea/concept development and testing; understanding customer opinions, attitudes, context; brand evaluation	Focus groups will be recruited according to set criteria depending on your objectives. Typically, a small number of customers representing a cross-section of your target market will be selected and then talked to individually and/or in groups to solicit their feedback and to try and understand their mind-set. Although the small number of people involved in focus groups may not make the results statistically relevant, it is as close as you can get to really understanding what makes your customers tick.
		Conducting focus groups for Web sites is no different than for other projects, although the facilitators and moderators should have experience with conducting Web site focus groups. This is important because they must understand enough about the Web and the site to ask the right questions, and they must also be able to empathize with a group that is likely to feel somewhat apprehensive, even embarrassed, about their lack of expertise in the Web, which means they may not be totally honest about what they think and feel.
Customer feedback	Customer satisfaction, product/service enhancement, innovation	The most obvious way to understand how customers feel about you is to listen to what they tell you: both the positive and the negative. Too often companies have no formalized process for routing, capturing, and analyzing the invaluable customer feedback they receive. On the Web, customers are usually more forthcoming and forthright when it comes to giving feedback as they do not have the embarrassment of having to talk to someone face to face. Although this means you are likely to receive some very harsh words from customers, it is better to know what you are doing wrong than to lose customers without knowing why. Impromptu customer feedback not only helps iron out flaws in the existing site, but often customers will tell you what they would really like to have, giving you ideas for site development.
Usability	Testing and validation of navigation, interface, prototype ideas, and site structure	Usability is covered in more detail in Chapter 17, How to Improve a Web Site. Usability testing is qualitative and user-centric inasmuch as it involves working with a small group of real users, but its purpose is less to find out who the users are and more to try and understand *how* customers use the site and *why* they use it as they do. Usability is thus an excellent complement to site-centric measurement that tells you *what* is happening.

Table 15.10 Quantitative techniques for user-centric measurement.

Techniques	Application	Description
Online and offline surveys	Customer profiling, customer satisfaction, product evaluation, customer loyalty	Surveys can be both qualitative and quantitative depending on the number of customers surveyed and the nature of the survey. For example, a Web site pop-up survey canvassing feedback from tens of thousands of site users would be quantitative, whereas a number of in store customer interviews would be qualitative.
		Surveys tend to be used more often for canvassing feedback on existing products and services rather than new ones, where focus groups might be more appropriate. Quantitative surveys are usually a series of numerous questions with simple yes/no or rating type answers. These are effective for capturing statistically relevant amounts of data in a structured format for subsequent analysis. These data can be used for user-centric metrics, for customer profiling, and for building customer segments.
		Online surveys are particularly powerful as they can be relatively quick and cost effective to deploy, they can reach a wide audience quickly, and the data can be captured directly to a database in the required format for analysis. Using form validation, it is also possible to ensure a high level of data integrity and "cleanliness." For example, you can check that email addresses are well-formed.
Data analysis/ mining	Customer profiling, segmentation, personalization, reporting	Analyzing collected user data for customer insight and intelligence. Typically, a database of customer information will be queried using an analysis tool by a specialist data analyst. Data mining techniques look for hidden patterns in the data to unearth unexpected insights into behavioral characteristics. Data analysis is most commonly used to report against particular metrics, evaluation frameworks, or segmentation models or to derive the necessary intelligence to build segments in the first place. Segments may be modeled on customer value, propensity, psychographics, and/or other criteria. For more on segmentation, refer to Chapter 9, Understanding Your Users.

16

Reporting
and Analysis

The previous sections should give you a background to Web site measurement and how it is evolving as well as some of the key measurement approaches and techniques. But how do you apply these tools to ensure that reporting and analysis work for you? Different businesses have different objectives, requirements, and resources, so their needs will vary in terms of both what processes and reporting structures they should adopt and what software tools will best support them. This chapter addresses how to approach defining a solution that will work for you.

16.1 Defining a Measurement Framework

Online interactions give you enhanced capabilities for data capture and analysis, but they can lead to data paralysis. The key challenge here is to avoid information overload and make sure that you focus your efforts on analyzing only those things that are of real value to the organization. You first need to define a measurement framework: the basic structure and metrics against which you wish to report. This framework should be derived from the key business drivers. These key drivers will vary from business to business; a retailer's business drivers and metrics are not usually the same as a publisher's, for example.

Map out your business drivers, creating a tree of "levers" that contribute toward your end goal. This provides a framework for measurement that has corresponding metrics that allow you to gauge what commercial effect your lever-pulling efforts are having. Figure 16.1 gives a simplified example of such a map showing some of the elements that drive total online sales for a typical e-tailer. At each point on this map, it becomes clearer what metrics are required to measure each element's contribution toward the end goal and what measurement approach, qualitative and/or quantitative, is best employed for effective reporting and analysis.

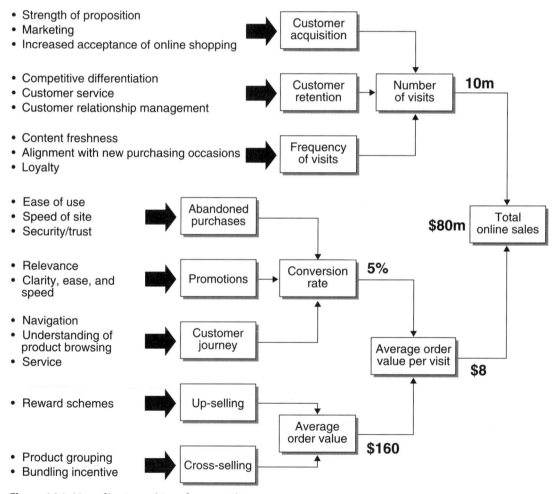

Figure 16.1 Map of business drivers for an e-tailer.

Equally, you might choose to look at your customers' life cycle and decision drivers and use them as the basis for creating a measurement framework. If you can measure and understand at what point your customers are along a purchase cycle, then you can take more effective action to optimize the likelihood of a sale or a sale of higher value. Figure 16.2 shows a very customer-centric view of key decision points when buying a car. A Web site will play a greater or lesser role at each of these stages: A customer is likely to use the Web site for researching and short listing potential cars and perhaps also for booking a test drive. Understanding these channel dynamics and being able to measure what is happening at critical points in the creation of business value give you the intelligence you need to optimize the performance of your Web site for the overall business.

The initial measurement framework should not be overly complex. It should show what the business is trying to achieve and the various contributing elements that influence success. Each of those component elements can then be further broken down and refined. Each element should have a corresponding metric or set of metrics, and each metric should have a method of measurement. The more detailed and specific measurements are likely to be of interest for particular business units or operational staff, whereas the higher level metrics will act as benchmarks for management to gauge performance and results.

Figure 16.2 The customer life cycle and decision factors in buying a car.

For example, in the car buying example, senior management are most likely to be interested in optimizing the effectiveness of the Web in contributing to the sale of cars. Among other things, they will want to know the cost of the Web site in comparison to the number of sales it helps generate to work out the return they are getting on their Web investment. If it is known that, on average, it is much more likely that a customer will buy a car if they have test driven it, it will be valuable to measure the number of test drives booked via the Web and how many subsequently convert to sales. It may be found, for example, that customers referred via the Web are more likely to purchase than others. The following set of metrics could be used by operational teams to report on this scenario:

- ▶ Metric1: percentage of visitors who visit the test drive section of the Web site
- ▶ Metric2: percentage who then actually book a test drive
- ▶ Metric3: percentage of those who booked that turn up
- ▶ Metric4: percentage who take a test drive booked online and then purchase

As with most Web development work, do not try to do everything at once. Concentrate first on developing the overall measurement framework to get cross-team and management consensus on what the goals are and what therefore needs to be measured. Put in place the measurement systems and processes to deliver on a few key metrics first and ensure that you are happy that this reporting is accurate and reliable before beginning to deliver more complex and specialized analysis and reporting at finer levels of detail. Above all, this iterative and incremental approach will help you ensure that the internal business processes to support reporting and analysis are put in place and running smoothly before you scale up the volume and complexity of measurement.

Case Study | Defining a Measurement Framework to Help Improve the Bottom Line

Company: WHSmith Online, *www.whsmith.co.uk*

Company Overview

One of the UK's leading High Street brands, WHSmith launched online in 1999 and sells a complete range of books, music, DVDs, games, magazines, and stationery. In addition to the WHSmith Web site, the company retails on digital TV and through telesales and offers a branded Internet access service. The online business is promoted through stores and aims to provide a consistent WHSmith offer in all relevant direct channels.

Background to Case Study and Objectives

Being a retail e-commerce business, sales levels are ultimately what affect the bottom line most. For a long time, we had been tracking e-commerce sales activity and so had a very good understanding of sales-centric metrics such as revenues per product type, by channel, average basket sizes, the effects of pricing, promotions, merchandising, and so on.

However, we did not feel we had a good enough understanding of why sales levels varied. Obviously, we could see peaks and troughs related to promotional, seasonal, and sales activities, but what we really wanted was to raise the base level of sales by understanding what affected them. If we could raise our base level of sales by even a few percentage points, this would have a big impact on the bottom line.

We saw customer satisfaction as the key "umbrella" metric that we needed to understand. From a strategic point of view, the business had never spent vast fortunes on marketing (in order to keep customer acquisition costs sensible) nor were we ever going to compete solely on price, although pricing is an important part of our proposition. This meant that we had to optimize our spending by converting and retaining as many customers as possible and growing their spending levels over time. How could we do this? By meeting and exceeding our measurable customer satisfaction targets.

An important objective was that whatever measurement framework we came up with for customer satisfaction, it would have to be specific, measurable, and accountable. We wanted hard numbers that could be charted, benchmarked, and efficiently managed over time. Indeed, we decided that the end composite performance metric would be tied in part to staff bonuses to ensure commitment and accountability.

Process and Practice

We first needed to define what we actually meant by customer satisfaction: How does this break down into more specific and measurable metrics to come up with an overall, weighted, composite score? Customer satisfaction is measured offline in stores through techniques such as exit polls or "mystery shoppers," and we could apply some of this thinking online, but we wanted to go deeper into the root causes of how to increase conversions and repeat buys online.

continued

To build a list of metrics that would produce a composite score that equated to customer satisfaction, we did the following:

▶ *Online customer surveys.* We conducted surveys to get customers' feedback on what elements most enhanced or damaged their online buying experience.

▶ *Feedback from our customer contact center.* We talked extensively to our own customer service staff to try and understand where the problem areas were and what customers most liked or disliked.

▶ *All staff brainstorm.* We facilitated several brainstorming sessions with our staff to get their ideas and input. (This has a positive side effect of winning their commitment to the project further down the line.)

▶ *Research and expertise.* As you would expect, we also looked at available research in this area and called upon the expertise of others who had been there and done it before.

We then took all our findings and modeled them according to the customer experience when arriving at and using our site. This made sense because customer satisfaction ultimately equates to the totality of the experience a customer has when dealing with us. This clearly includes things such as delivery on time that are not directly related to the site itself but extremely important to the customer experience. For each stage of the customer journey, we identified areas of possible measurement, possible problems, improvements, and related metrics.

We arrived at a customer satisfaction matrix that included metrics in the following categories: site availability and resilience, price competitiveness, navigating and browsing, product information, purchase process, order fulfillment, customer service, and customer relationship. Some of the metrics within each of these categories could be measured through data analysis, but others needed qualitative customer feedback. For each metric, we assigned unit values, a target, and a weighting corresponding to its relative importance in influencing customer satisfaction as indicated by our customer surveys. We then had an overall composite score.

We implemented this measurement framework with reports generated weekly and benchmarked over time. We use color coding to highlight areas of underperformance or overperformance relative to targets. We have a special team that can immediately address highlighted problem areas, so each weekly report generates specific actions.

Results

Having this "experience-centric" measurement framework to run in parallel with our sales-centric reporting has proved very valuable because it measures whether customer expectations are being met, and this ultimately leads to customer satisfaction, which leads to higher conversions, more repeat sales, and higher basket values. Customers' expectations risk being too soft and vague a metric, but it is vital to understand it for brand reasons and to differentiate your proposition. It helps us measure whether we are meeting not just our stated promises (e.g., delivery times) but also our implied promises based on customers' expectations of a Web site and WHSmith as a brand.

Now that we can accurately measure such apparent intangibles, we also have a benchmark to use in assessing the actual value delivered by new ideas and services. Once we've got the basics right, we increasingly want to wow our customers, but we have finite resources and they must deliver a return on investment, so we need to know what constitutes wow and whether doing it delivers a return. For example, our stated promise might be that there is someone you can call at our customer contact center to help you with a problem during particular hours. Our implied WHSmith promise is that the phone will be answered quickly and politely and a helpful customer service representative will deal with your problem efficiently. Our wow factor might be to proactively resolve a problem for a customer before they are even aware of it. We can track the impact of these differing experiences through our customer services measurement category.

Our measurement framework is also proving very useful as a benchmark to assess new site services, content, and functionality. For example, we can try out personalization features and see what impact they have: Do they improve overall customer satisfaction by winning us higher scores in the navigation and browsing, customer service, or customer relationship categories? Or do we find that personalization slows the site down and has a disastrous effect on metrics within our site availability and resilience category?

Lessons Learned

These are the top five tips that we have taken from our experience so far:

1. Use number values for your metrics. You must have clearly defined metrics that have a numerical value so that targets can be set and performance managed and benchmarked. Clear scoring and targets help motivate teams, make you more accountable to senior management (who will also take you more seriously), and provide a framework for performance reviews.
2. Don't just measure financial performance. You need to understand the subtler contributing factors to really optimize performance. That said, you must ultimately be able to tie back any form of measurement to financial performance—the bottom line rules.

continued

3. Include everyone in the process. Not only will you get good ideas from unexpected sources, but it is vital to the long-term, ongoing success of performance measurement to have companywide understanding and buy-in. We publish our customer satisfaction results to the whole company, and bonuses are in part tied to performance, so everyone has a vested interest in seeing that line climb ever higher.

4. Maximize ROI through a "good enough" approach. There are always a million and one things that you can measure, and some would like to measure them all. But when you come down to it, you have to be practical about what is realistic and sensible given your resources (time, money, skills, etc.). Know what you really need to measure and prioritize to make sure you've got metrics in place to give good enough results.

5. Get your metrics in place before you make changes. It is no good making improvements to a site before you know where you stand. Your improvements might in fact make things worse. You have to be able to measure the impact of any changes.

Nick Andrews
Development Director
WHSmith Online

16.2 The Importance of Analysis

For a number of reasons, the analysis of Web performance is too often given little attention: Resources are fully tied up with development efforts, management believe that software can automatically do all the analysis required, there is not enough budget allocated for proper analysis, there is no faith in the quality of the data available, the volume of data is not worth spending much analysis time on, the Web channel is yet to be integrated with other channel data analysis operations, or simply the Web is still not taken seriously enough.

Although software is a powerful tool to aid data analysis, reporting it cannot do the whole job for you. It only works as well as it is configured and the data it has to work on. As we have seen, the same is true for content management systems: They are a great tool for helping you manage your content, but they do not know how your content should be managed to your best advantage because they are not intelligent. Only human beings supply the intelligence that is required to do a proper job of Web performance analysis. This intelligence is needed to define the measurement framework, choose the best tools, configure them correctly, and then analyze results in the context of ongoing business operations and real-world events.

Managers often complain about the large, detailed, but incomprehensible reports they receive that have been churned out of a log file analysis tool. Quite correctly, they complain that this sort of reporting gives no actionable insight and little indication of trends, and is hard to correlate the morass of figures and charts with what has been happening in the business. The fault here is not with log files or the analysis tool but with a lack of time and effort spent on analysis. There is no shortcut here: An analyst is required who understands the medium, the measurement tool, and the business context. It is better to report on very little but analyze it thoroughly to derive useful, actionable intelligence than to produce huge and meaningless reports just because the software allows it.

16.3 Design for Analysis

In many cases, you will be required to try to analyze and report on the performance of an existing Web site that might be a hodgepodge of systems, files, and applications that have grown organically to meet demand and ad hoc requirements often coming from different parts of the business. In this case, it may be possible to report on specific things, but it will be difficult to give a good picture of how the entire site is contributing business value. It will take some time to introduce order and consistency, and you will need to start by defining the measurement framework as described earlier to galvanize the disparate elements and migrate them toward a more robust and holistic measurement, analysis, and reporting process. Tactically, you can introduce design and navigation guidelines, along with other standardization measures, which facilitate analysis.

If you want to ease the implementation of reporting and analysis, ensure quality, maximize speed of rollout, and minimize costs, then it is much more preferable to "design for analysis": to build your Web site and online systems with future analysis needs already in mind. As you develop a site, you should try to ensure that you are building in the necessary structure and data as the platform for future reporting. Just as human DNA contains all the instructions necessary to create an entire human being, you should build new site sections or new sites so that every element contains information that relates it to the core purpose of the site. In this way, you can measure each individual element in a way that truly reflects how it is contributing value to the whole.

So how can you ensure that you design for analysis? Following are some of the most important areas to concentrate on.

16.3.1   Information Architecture

For more on the importance of content structure and information architecture, refer to Section 5.1, Structuring Content.

The axes of information, content classifications and categories, database schemas, tables, and metadata that all form part of the information architecture provide an excellent platform for data collection and measurement. Why? Because an information architecture has both structure and business logic embedded in it: It is the Web site's DNA. The architecture may be defined by customer segments, by content types, by business units, by country, or by product lines. The same business drivers that help define an information architecture will also define the analysis and reporting requirements.

16.3.2   Templating

For more details on page tagging, refer back to Section 15.1, Site-Centric Measurement. Templates are covered in detail in Section 5.7, Templates.

To avoid having to create and update every single page on a site manually, templates help manage the deployment and automatic update of content to the presentation layer. There will be far fewer templates than there are pages on a site, and embedded in the templates will be business logic allowing the template to know what content to show, to whom, and in what arrangement. This means that a site that uses templates already has built into it a structure and business logic that greatly facilitate subsequent data analysis.

Templates' advantages in facilitating content management can also be exploited for the deployment of some measurement techniques. For example, adding page tags to thousands of handcrafted HTML pages for tracking and measurement purposes is very laborious. However, adding page tags to 10 templates is very quick and easy and will have improved results.

16.3.3   Design Guidelines

Creating a design guidelines document will help ensure that all development initiatives can be relied upon to follow certain standards, making reporting and analysis significantly less complex. For example, if you know that frames will never be used and you know that the layout of all pages will be governed by a single central style sheet (using cascading style sheets), there will be many fewer trivial exceptions and special cases to deal with when it comes to analysis.

16.3.4 Navigation Guidelines

For more on design guidelines, refer to Section 2.1, Documentation.

If navigation guidelines are not included as part of the design guidelines, you should also create a document that specifies the navigation scheme and the principles to which navigation must adhere: How many levels of navigation are there? What navigation elements are ubiquitous? How will temporary content such as a marketing microsite be incorporated in the navigation? How are navigation elements named? Codifying the navigation in this way further facilitates analysis. For example, if you know how ad hoc promotional microsites will be incorporated and where they will be in the navigation and site hierarchy, it is easier to ensure that they are not overlooked in standard site reporting activity, as might otherwise be the risk for such "floating" content.

16.3.5 Technology Infrastructure

Clearly, the way that the technology infrastructure is set up and maintained greatly affects your reporting and analysis capabilities. Sometimes there may be systems to which you cannot gain access for security reasons, or you will be using external service providers such that data need first to be transferred to you before they can be analyzed. Increasingly, distributed technology infrastructures, multiple Web servers, and complex application architectures all contribute to making accurate analysis much harder. For example, if you have multiple Web servers for a single site (to provide increased capacity and redundancy), then the log files for a unique user's visit may be split across several servers with time stamps that are fractionally out of synch. It is very unlikely that choice of technology infrastructure is going to be dictated by reporting and analysis needs, but it is worth bearing in mind, and improvements can often be made to an existing setup to aid analysis.

16.3.6 Metadata and Tagging

This is covered in more detail in Section 5.6, Metadata, in Chapter 5, Key Concepts and Building Blocks. If you know what data you need to deliver and the reporting you require, you can make sure that all site content elements are described and tagged consistently and according to a schema that gives you a ready-made measurement framework.

16.3.7 URL Policy

Analysis becomes much more complex not only when the technology infrastructure is fragmented but also if multiple URLs are marketed in all sorts of forms (some targeted to subdirectories and some different domains that redirect) and nobody is quite sure who is using what URL and why. There is nothing wrong with using targeted or special URLs (e.g., for a microsite), but to make analysis easier and more accurate, it helps to have a clear URL policy, which should define what URLs can be used and in what way. It should also list which URLs are actually owned by the company, who registered them, when, and through which ISP.

   If you do not have a URL policy, things can quickly become unclear and analysis efforts confused. Imagine an international company has a German office that wants to launch a dedicated recruitment site. Should that be *www.company.de/recruitment*, *www.company.com/germany/recruitment*, or *www.companyrecruitment.de*?

16.3.8 Naming Conventions

Naming things consistently (e.g., files, directories, page titles, keywords) also helps analysis because the protocols you have adhered to make interpretation that much quicker and more accurate.

16.3.9 Logging

Although you must avoid the temptation to try to analyze everything just because you can, you should nonetheless log information that you know will be of future use to you but that you may not have the time or resources in the short term to analyze. For example, you might want to capture all form-submitted information to a database for later analysis even though initially that data will only be sent as an email from the site to the relevant person. Equally, you might want to store what keywords users search your site on to help with optimization efforts at a later stage.

You should also check that logging systems are correctly configured and logging as expected. Web servers, for example, can be configured not to log anything, to log in different formats, and to log to different locations. A simple oversight could mean that when you come to do your analysis, you find you are missing the necessary information.

As you can see, designing for analysis is largely about bringing increased structure, process, and standardization to Web development. Standards are important because they give everyone a frame of reference that reduces complexity and helps ensure consistency of quality and delivery. With technologies like XML becoming the norm and increased use of outsourced service providers (e.g., application service providers), standards will become even more important to ensure efficient communication between disparate parties and the reliable integration and delivery of services. This is not to say that Web development should lose any of its iterative nature or that creativity should be restricted; rather, it is about building solid foundations and frames of reference that can then accommodate the fast pace of change so characteristic of evolving Web sites. The analogy to building a house is often used: You need to get the architecture right, build solid foundations, and make sure all the key services such as heating and water are working properly, but as for the decoration, you can change that often. You can even knock through a wall or two or add an extension if it is in keeping with the rest of the building. Web performance analysis is a key service that relies on solid foundations and a well-designed architecture.

16.4 Choosing a Measurement Tool

The hardest elements in choosing a software solution are understanding what you want and why and then defining your requirements. It is foolhardy to omit these steps and be led purely by technology and promises of features that you must have, which was a common mistake in the hype of the dotcom golden days. Without defined requirements, the choice is too overpowering, and it is difficult to know where to start, meaning you are likely to waste time trying to evaluate every product on the market. Web site measurement tools are many and range in cost from freeware to solutions that cost upward of half a million dollars.

If you want to find out more about particular measurement vendors, you will find a list in the Resources section.

Once you have defined your requirements, you would typically go through a vendor selection process: canvasing and understanding the market and the players, drawing up a short list and sending out an invitation to tender, meeting vendors and following up, further short listing (perhaps to two), commercial negotiations and due diligence, contract and service-level agreement negotiations, and then purchase.

Apart from the quality of the product and the quality of the company behind it, some of the following are likely to feature among your requirements and purchase considerations:

▶ *Cost.* What budget do you have available? What cost can be justified by the benefits the tool will bring? How is the cost worked out—per machine, by seat, or by volume of data? What are the upgrade, support, training, and service costs?

▶ *Existing technology capabilities.* How does what you currently have affect your requirements?

▶ *Resourcing.* Do you have the skills in house to use, maintain, and even enhance the tool? If not, where can you get help, how long would it take, and how much would it cost?

▶ *Support and training.* What levels of support are provided? Twenty-four hours a day? On site, phone, or Web-based? What training can you expect to receive? Are there support communities you can turn to?

▶ *Partnerships.* Who or what else does the software rely on? Does the company have partners and how does the relationship work?

▶ *Scalability.* What is the upgrade path if the solution has to scale? What about multiserver deployment? What are the load issues if the number of users grows considerably or the amount of processing required increases?

▶ *Integration.* How will the tool integrate with other systems? Are there special software hooks or bridges required? Are open standards used? What data formats are employed?

▶ *Intellectual property and legal.* Are there any IP issues you should be aware of? If the solution runs remotely, who owns the data? Who is legally responsible for protecting the data? Do you have access to the raw data if you need it?

▶ *Ease of use.* Is the interface easy to use? Is the tool intuitive? Do you get meaningful and intelligible results out of the tool? What support do you get from the instruction manual or help files? How steep is the learning curve?

▶ *Accreditation and standards compliance.* Does the tool comply with industry standards? Is it accredited by relevant industry bodies?

▶ *Multichannel and multiformat capabilities.* Can the tool deliver results across multiple channels in multiple formats (e.g., HTML, CSV, Word, Excel, streaming media)?

▶ *Security and access.* How secure is the system? Can multiple levels of permission and access be set up for different users? What are the collaborative working or multiuser capabilities of the tool?

▶ *Flexibility.* Can the tool be configured to work in different ways and deliver different results depending on varying end user requirements?

▶ *Out of the box features and functionality.* How much of what you require is already offered by the tool? How much will need to be customized and how will this be done?

▶ *Future releases and patches.* How will you be kept up to date about upgrades, fixes, and new releases? What will these cost?

▶ *Real-time analysis.* Does the tool provide real-time feedback and analysis? On what metrics? What processing implications does this have?

One of the key decisions is whether you want to buy into an analysis service or just a piece of software. Buying a service is likely to be more expensive in the long run, but it takes away a lot of the requirements for trained and experienced staff and software and hardware updates. You should be clear where along the software-services line each potential vendor is and how it sees itself evolving. Software-centric vendors tend to be balanced around 75% software to 25% services, the services element only really there to help get people going and to help sales through some free initial consulting work. If you do not have the in-house resources or you are very new to Web site measurement, it may be preferable to choose a service rather than a tool. After all, the tool is only a means to achieve the results you want, so as long as the service can deliver those results, the tool it uses is less important in the short term.

Increasingly, Web analytics services are being offered by application service providers (ASPs). The ASP hosts the applications required to do the analytics and has the expertise on hand to do the analysis. You effectively rent the service from the ASP. There are many apparent advantages in using an ASP, but there are also considerations that you should be aware of. Table 16.1 summarizes some of the points to bear in mind if you are considering opting for a Web site measurement service provided by an ASP.

Table 16.1 Considerations in opting for an ASP-based measurement solution.

Advantages	
Cost	The ASP can keep costs down because the technical infrastructure is centralized: One infrastructure can service many clients, so the cost is shared. The initial capital outlay could otherwise be prohibitive for just one company. As ASPs hire out their services, costs can be accurately predicted and managed.
Maintenance	Updating software, maintaining the hardware, and ensuring availability and quality of service are the ASP's responsibility, not yours.
Expertise	It is the ASP's job to know their technology back to front and to provide a high quality of service reliably. They can guarantee to have experts on hand and on site very quickly because their operations and the data are consolidated in one place.
Lead times	As the ASP already has everything set up, it is in theory just a matter of switching on the service. In practice, there is more that needs to be done than that, but the service should be faster to get up and running than doing it yourself.
Considerations	
Site speed and performance	You must be absolutely sure that the time incurred in making the remote call to the ASP is not materially affecting your page load times. Even though the ASP may only be serving single pixel GIFs, the volume of requests could build over time, as they take on more clients, to become overwhelming. The ASP must thus be able to guarantee 24×7 operational excellence.
Privacy	For ASPs to remotely collect data attributable to unique users, they have to set a cookie for users who visit your site. There is a fear that they could then violate users' privacy by aggregating this information with data from all their customers' sites. Because of this privacy fear, both Netscape and Microsoft are adding features to their browsers allowing users to be alerted if a third-party Web site is trying to set a cookie. If these features are widely adopted, the reliability of the results of any ASP service risks being greatly compromised, and visitors to your site could be alarmed by such alerts.
Requirement for code tags	For the ASP to be able to log activity, calls need to be made from your site to the ASP via code that is inserted as tags into your Web pages. Depending on how large your site is and how it is set up this could be a daunting task (see Section 15.1.2, Measurement Techniques, Chapter 15, Measurement Approaches and Techniques for more details).
Data integration	As we have seen, the real value of a Web site comes when it is integrated with the core business, and the only way to deliver CRM is to have an integrated view of the customer. This means having your data integrated. If you use an ASP, then either you will need to take the data back from them to integrate it with other enterprise data you have (so why not keep it at your end in the first place?) or you would have to give them all of your private customer data for them to consolidate, a prospect fraught with privacy and security concerns.

16.5   **Report Scheduling and Distribution**

Superior analysis and reports are not of much value if they do not get to the right people at the right time. Just as important as the contents of the report are the business processes that govern who gets what, when, and how. The dynamic and interactive nature of the Web means that time is of even greater importance in good decision making and seizing opportunities or countering problems as they arise.

You will need to talk to all project stakeholders to get their input, understanding, and buy-in when developing the overall measurement framework. Once this is agreed upon, you will need to talk to these same people to gather their measurement and reporting requirements. This must include not only what they would like to know but when and how so that you can build a clearer picture of report scheduling and distribution needs.

To capture scheduling requirements, you need to ask questions about time and frequency of desired reporting: weekly, monthly, real time, ad hoc? To capture distribution requirements, you must ascertain who should have access to what (e.g., permission levels for sensitive information or management summaries), in what format (download file, Web pages, or paper), and through what channel. The process for gathering and auditing these requirements is very similar to that described earlier for capturing the content update needs as part of a content management project.

As the Web is still a comparatively new medium, people are keen to be involved but do not necessarily know what they want. Often when gathering requirements for measurement, the requirement will be "Tell me everything you can" or "I don't know—what can you tell me?" or you will end up with a very wide-ranging and different set of requirements. How do you bring some order, clarity, and direction to something that can otherwise feel like it's out of control? Here are a few pointers:

▶ Use the measurement framework you have developed to give focus and to prioritize requirements. If you have agreed on the measurement framework with senior stakeholders and, even better, agreed which areas of measurement are to be prioritized, then it will be much easier to confidently structure and phase the delivery of disparate requirements.

▶ For those not sure of what they want, it is worth asking what they currently get from other channels and investigating how this might be complemented by the Web or how this measurement approach or metric would translate online. Not only should this be easier to understand, but it is likely to help the Web site's cause because it will be more readily and easily integrated into existing measurement, reporting, and analysis activities. Additional reporting only possible for online channels can then be added later. For example, at a simple level, an offline publisher may think in terms of "circulation" or "readers," which translates to "unique users" online. More advanced interaction reporting, such as path analysis, which is only possible online, can be introduced at a later stage.

▶ Manage expectations. The Web suffers from the perception that everything is possible and you can have it yesterday. Building an effective measurement framework with all the levels of detailed metrics, with all the associated measurement techniques, with all the necessary delivery and people processes, and with all the required technology takes time to do well and it improves over time. You are building a measurement infrastructure with long-term strategic value: Rush it and you will lose out in the long term. Be clear that you intend to review and iterate. Set up review meetings and draw up an evolution plan so that if people feel frustrated that they are not getting all that they want right away, they can at least see what is coming.

16.6   Example Reports

To give you a more concrete idea of how metrics are used to create reports that support different types of e-business, a series of example reports follows. These examples are by no means exhaustive, as these kinds of reports can be very long and detailed, but they contain illustrative metrics, measurement techniques, and data for a range of sites and applications to show how different needs will necessitate different kinds of report focus and measurement approach.

16.6.1   Traffic

Figures 16.3 and 16.4 are examples of reporting that would be typical for a high-volume traffic site, such as a search engine, portal, or directory. As the principal revenue stream is likely to be advertising sold per 1000 page impressions, the metric focus is the number of page impressions and any other elements that combine to help increase the total number of page impressions

	Actual April	Actual May	% change	Actual YTD
Page impressions (PI)	26,133,382	21,211,886	23.2	82,531,179
Visits	3,709,740	3,172,375	16.9	14,209,187
Visitors	1,339,740	1,129,171	18.6	5,056,650
Avg. visits per visitor	2.77	2.81	-1.4	3.12
Avg. pages per visitor	19.5	18.8	3.8	17.87
Avg. pages per visit	7.0	6.7	5.4	5.83
Avg.time spent per visitor *(min/mos)*	26.6	25.5	4.3	28.41
Avg. page impressions per day	871,113	707,063	23.2	2,730,380
Avg. visits per day	123,658	105,746	16.9	469,479

Site sections	26,133,382	21,211,886	23.2	82,531,179
Search	21,977,435	14,508,039	51.5	62,519,139
Shopping	1,579,232	1,483,341	6.5	5,704,229
Auto	5,176	11,446	-54.8	36,806
TV guide	332,403	285,328	16.5	1,324,329
Finance	8,012	18,746	-57.3	52,716
Property	91,643	81,010	13.1	327,599
Travel	143,926	124,331	15.8	472,603
etc.	etc.	etc.	etc.	etc.

Site sections	3,709,740	3,172,375	16.9	14,209,187
Search	1,626,037	1,173,395	38.6	5,237,302
Shopping	478,413	429,462	16.4	1,644,121
Auto	3,560	8,080	-55.9	25,893
TV guide	120,990	101,904	18.7	453,669
Finance	5,138	13,325	-61.4	36,191
Property	47,468	40,483	17.3	165,611
Travel	115,495	16,834	586.1	422,329
etc.	etc.	etc.	etc.	etc.

Traffic by country/organization	PIs	% Chg
Numeric (IP address only)	9,802,051	11.3
United Kingdom (.co.uk)	9,177,648	13.5
Commercial (.com)	7,859,738	9.7
Network (.net)	2,043,247	3.2
France (.fr)	46,877	1.8
Netherlands (.nl)	42,686	34.6
Germany (.de)	37,970	32.4
etc.	etc.	etc.

Top referring pages	Referred PIs	% Chg
Ask Jeeves main follow up	1,181,096	87.9
MSN search results	845,923	18.5
Yahoo UK search	611,696	870.3
Freeserve search	474,930	52.7
BT Openworld	169,725	60.5
Google search	109,586	8.9
Excite search	81,863	30.0
etc.	etc.	etc.

Top pages viewed	PIs	% Chg
Seach (incl. home page)	18,873,154	8.9
TV guide	248,052	13.2
Cinema listings home page	63,560	30.8
Travel weather	61,579	1.7
Shares home page	48,696	11.5
Travel home page	41,936	7.5
Property home page	41,700	2.6
etc.	etc.	etc.

Top entry pages	Site entries	% Chg
Search (incl. home page)	1,610,760	12.1
Competition page	69,778	-15.6
Leisure home page	9,340	3.0
Filmfinder search	8,964	11.1
Filmfinder home page	7,324	3.4
Personal finance home page	7,246	-31.1
etc.	etc.	etc.

Top exit pages	Site exits	% Chg
Search (incl. home page)	2,202,416	11.4
Competition page	253,293	-0.1
Leisure home page	11,702	10.4
Weather page	11,222	134.5
Stocks and shares	9,103	-4.0
Cinema listings	8,476	28.8
Shopping home page	8,404	6.9
Personal finance home page	8,246	283.4
etc.	etc.	etc.

Figure 16.3 Top-line traffic figures.

such as increasing the number of pages viewed per visit, increasing the number of visits per unique user, and increasing the number of unique users.

The measurement technique to arrive at the data for both Figures 16.3 and 16.4 is Web server log file analysis or analysis of logs created by tagged pages. There is no user-centric or path analysis. Figure 16.3 gives top-line traffic figures and an overview of where traffic is coming from, entering, and leaving the site during the month's reporting period. Figure 16.4 is an example graph that

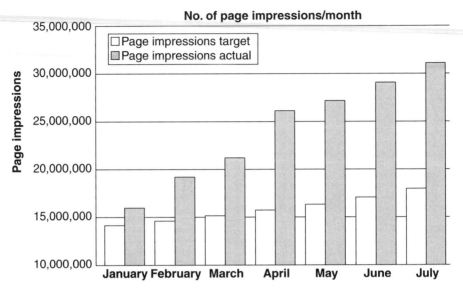

Figure 16.4 Graph of traffic trends.

helps show trends over time. A log file analysis tool typically allows the underlying data to be represented in tables, graphs, and charts of all types that allow easier visual and snapshot insight into trends.

16.6.2   Customer Loyalty

Figure 16.5 shows how you can move beyond straightforward traffic analysis to take a more user-centric view. These data might come from a community Web site, online publication, or niche portal where users register to receive online content, features, and services. Revenue streams most likely come from users paying for premium content and services as well as sponsorship deals. Revenue is less dependent on the volume of traffic and more dependent on the number of registered users and their commitment to the site. Their loyalty will not only indicate the likelihood that they will pay for content and services, but it is also the key selling point of any potential site sponsor.

Although the example data given are for an online publishing venture, it would be just as relevant to measure customer loyalty for an e-commerce operation in a similar way. A publishing venture might describe a loyal user as one who has been registered on the site for more than 3 months, who has visited at least five times, and at least once in the last 4 weeks. An e-tailer, however, might measure loyalty according to RFM (recency of purchase, frequency of pur-

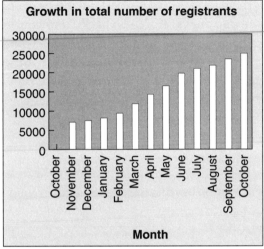

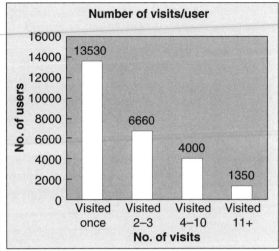

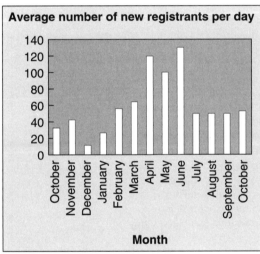

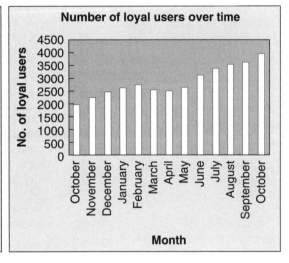

Figure 16.5 Customer loyalty analysis.

chase, monetary value of purchases) metrics. In both cases, the measurement technique is a user profile database that stores customer information given when the customer registers or purchases and subsequent user-centric tracking with the individual user being identified on each subsequent visit either by a cookie or through the user logging on.

Figure 16.5 does not show who these loyal users are. However, the site owner will know this by referring to the user profile database. The obvious next step, having done some initial customer loyalty calculations as in the graphs, would be to analyze the loyal customers' data and try to ascertain what it is about them that makes them loyal. Are they a particular type of person? Is there something on the site that draws all of them back? Your conclusions based on such quantitative data analysis could then be validated with qualitative follow-up: perhaps a few group or one-to-one sessions with selected users. The intelligence gathered should help you acquire and retain more of these valuable loyal users.

16.6.3   E-commerce

Figure 16.6 shows a real example, taken from a major UK e-tailer, of the index of e-commerce reports that they use for measuring the success of their online

Index of Reports

Basic
Visitors by Channel
Customers by Channel
Order Value by Channel
Items Ordered by Channel
Invoicing Value (ex. VAT) by Channel
Invoicing Volume by Channel
Conversion Rate
Discount
Order Value per Visitor
New Visitors by Channel
Visits by Channel
Proportion of Visits by Channel

Customers
New Customers by Channel

Ordering
Basket Value by Channel
Orders by Channel
Proportion of Items Ordered by Channel
Postage by Zone
Orders RRP by Channel
Order Value by Product Type

Invoicing
Invoicing Value by Product Type
Invoicing Value (ex. VAT) by
    Channel (not stacked)

Fulfilment Rates
Ordered vs Invoiced All
Ordered vs Invoiced Ratio All
Ordered vs Invoiced Books
Ordered vs Invoiced Ratio Books
Ordered vs Invoiced Games
Ordered vs Invoiced Ratio Games
Ordered vs Invoiced Magazines
Ordered vs Invoiced Ratio Magazines
Ordered vs Invoiced Music
Ordered vs Invoiced Ratio Music
Ordered vs Invoiced Stationery
Ordered vs Invoiced Ratio Stationery
Ordered vs Invoiced Video
Ordered vs Invoiced Ratio Video

Warehouse
Average Manual Credits
Average UK Postage per Item—Ordered as Invoiced
Average UK Postage per Item—Ordered
Invoice to Sent % at 24 and 48 Hours
Manual Credits as % of Sales
Ordered to Sent % at 2 and 7 Days
Postage as Proportion of Sales
Shipping Efficiency

Figure 16.6 Example e-commerce reports.

selling. This gives you an idea of the wide range of metrics and variables that might be useful for e-commerce reporting and analysis.

Figure 16.7 shows what one of these reports might look like. In this case, the average basket value for the Internet channel is graphed over an eighteen-month period.

16.6.4 Campaigns

The examples given so far have focused on ongoing reporting, but what about analysis for one-off campaigns or a series of campaigns? Following are two simple examples, one for a viral marketing campaign and the other for email marketing.

Viral Marketing

Figure 16.8 shows the sort of report that a small to medium-sized e-commerce operation might use to measure the effectiveness of a viral marketing campaign. For example, a special offer might have been sent to select customers with additional money-off benefits if the offer is passed on to friends. The results show that, depending on profit margins for the sales and the cost of the campaign itself, there could have been a good return on investment for this

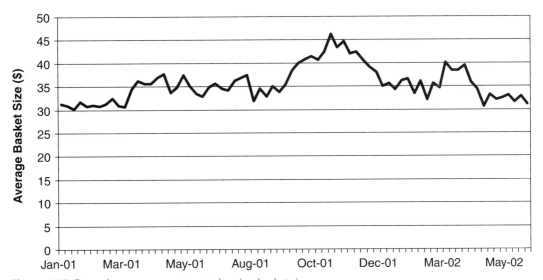

Figure 16.7 Example e-commerce report showing basket size.

Viral campaign	Unique users attracted	No. of users who referred a friend	Total no. referred	Visits following referral	Effectiveness of referral	Viral effect
Description	23,560	1,435	1,941	1,521	78.36%	8.24%

No. click throughs to main site	Click through rate	No. who purchased	Overall conversion	Average purchase value	Total sales
4,673	19.83%	415	1.76%	$75.00	$31,125.00

Figure 16.8 Results from a viral marketing campaign.

campaign. It is also clear that if the viral effect were a little higher, or the click through or conversion rates higher, then the number of sales would quickly increase at no extra cost, significantly improving profitability. Efforts should be focused on improving performance at these points. Also of interest in this example is to see just how powerful customer-to-customer referral is at getting people to visit the site.

The measurement technique used to track these metrics would be tracking URLs plus a database plus cookies. The tracking URLs would log activity related to the campaign to a database, and the cookies would identify those who had come to the site as a result of the campaign. Using the cookies and the user profile database, you would also be able to tell who had purchased as a result of the campaign. This could be important: You might find that the type of people that the campaign has brought in as customers are in fact the sorts who are not valuable to the business in the long term. A high percentage of financial services organizations' customers actually lose them money, for example, so those organizations are particularly interested in ensuring they are attracting more valuable customers.

Email Marketing

Figure 16.9 shows the results from an email marketing campaign, perhaps from a professional services organization such as a management consulting organization or law firm. The organization may have been promoting a particular white paper, report, or piece of research that users could access for free if they registered on the site. Conversion in this example means registration as opposed to purchase. The professional services company leverages the intellectual property value of their white paper, report, or research to acquire

Campaign ID	Date of campaign	Target sites	Position in series	Emails sent out	Cost	Total referrals	Click through rate	Conversion on click through	Total registrants	Total conversion	Acquisition cost
12	08.03.02	e.g. website.com	3	27,500	$1,600.00	1,080	3.93%	24.07%	260	0.95%	$6.15

Creative execution

The message sent out

Registrant details

Name	Company	Position	Country	No. of visits	Date registered	Last visited
Joe Bloggs	Company ABC	Marketing Manager	UK	3	08.03.02	12.03.02
etc.	etc.	etc.	etc.	etc.	etc.	etc.

Figure 16.9 Results from an email marketing campaign.

user data. In doing so, they might ask for permission to send the registrant their monthly newsletter or invite them to a free seminar they are holding. If the company knows from past experience how many of these registrants they are likely to convert to paying customers and what they will be worth to the company in the long term, it is possible to assign an average value to each registered user acquired. If the average acquisition cost per user, as shown in the final column of Figure 16.9, is lower than the average value per user, the campaign is delivering a positive return on investment.

As in previous examples, this report does not show details of who registered. This is valuable information that the company should further analyze. There are other intangible aspects of value that can be realized over and above an average value per customer calculation based on actual future revenue. For example, there may be users acquired who are in a position to inform public or industry opinion.

In this example, the results are for a particular email that forms part of an ongoing campaign. Changing the creative as well as the target sites would be two key variables to play with and compare results in the effort to reduce the final acquisition costs. It would also be important to check whether there was deterioration in response rates as the campaign continued.

How to Improve
a Web Site

Increasingly, the challenge for all Web initiatives is to show that they are delivering value to the business. At the same time, we have come to realize that it is absolutely essential to put customers at the heart of any Web site: Continually improving their experience is the only way to acquire and retain customers who have the luxury and power to go elsewhere if they wish. Optimizing the performance of a site is about improving the customer experience. But with maximum commercial efficiency, it is about doing everything you can to squeeze every last drop of quality out of a site to keep the customers happy and squeezing out every last drop of business value, while maximizing efficiencies to keep the business happy.

The same strategic framework can be used to structure and focus improvement efforts as discussed in Section 16.1, Defining a Measurement Framework. This framework distills what the business is trying to achieve and maps out the business drivers and levers that can be pulled to achieve the end goal. As with any project, measures to improve a site must be carefully planned, measurable goals and targets must be set, performance and results must be measured. As with Web projects in particular, optimization efforts will be ongoing and iterative with continual small steps being taken to improve and fine-tune performance.

There are no one-size-fits-all answers on how to improve Web sites because they have different purposes and different target markets. A large part of site improvement, as with other Web development, will be about tireless testing and experimentation, trial and error, to find out what works best. Of crucial importance is to measure the results of what you do so that none of this invaluable insight is lost. However, experience is increasingly giving us some best practice guidelines to assist our improvement efforts. What follows is a collection of tools, techniques, and approaches that you should consider in your "site improvement mix" as they have been proven to be extremely effective in improving the performance of Web sites. If you are under pressure to improve performance quickly, then you may select a couple of these approaches as tactical measure to get the ball rolling and start seeing results: the infamous "quick wins." You should ensure, however, that time is set aside to create the measurement framework that then becomes the strategic structure around which all efforts can be designed. Only this gives the necessary focus to really drive things forward.

17.1 Get the Basics Really Right

For all that the Web and other digital channels represent something new and exciting, there is no substitute for focusing on getting the basics right. At the most fundamental level, you need to identify and reach your customers efficiently, offer them something that they want, and then deliver on your promise flawlessly.

Too many sites try to run before they can walk. I have spent a lot of time watching real users interacting with real sites, listening to what they say about their experience, and following up with questions. It is abundantly clear that what really annoys users, or impresses them, is how the most basic elements of the site perform. More than anything else, you should concentrate site improvement efforts on the quality of basic operational execution: the speed of the site, ease of navigation, lack of errors, time to respond to inquiries, up-to-date information, and delivery that is on time and accurate, to name just a few key areas.

The golden rule of Web performance improvement, indeed of Web development more generally, is to do a few things really well instead of a lot of things poorly. End users simply will not tolerate poor quality experiences on-line. End users care infinitely less about what they cannot see compared with what they can experience. Managers also should worry less about what they have not delivered and much more about what they have set live to the merciless scrutiny of end users.

From this one golden rule, two other basic recommendations arise. First, do not overexpand your offering if you cannot properly support it, and second, concentrate your efforts on your *existing* customers. It is far preferable to focus your energies on improving the quality of your existing proposition before expanding; it is better to have fewer assets of deep quality than a scattered assortment of broad but thin propositions. Only in this way can you hope to maintain your points of difference and competitive advantage. Focusing on existing customers not only helps you build a long-term, valuable, strategic asset—a loyal customer base—but it also ensures again that you concentrate on understanding and serving those customers really well rather than casting your net too wide and risk trying to be all things to all people.

Another reason that focusing on getting the basics right is so important is that it is easy to say "basics," but actually to deliver these things well on an on-going basis is extremely difficult. For all the grand visions and plans that you, or management, might have for the site, the majority of time is rightly taken up with ensuring that the basics are working well. What little time is left can then be used for advancing a further little step toward the longer term goals. What makes keeping the basics running smoothly such a challenge is that the context often changes: Customer expectations change, the market changes, new channels emerge, new partners need to be integrated, or localized versions in new countries need to be developed.

Hardest of all is when your business model changes—something that has happened unfortunately often as dotcoms struggle to find a way to reach profitability. Changing business model midstride is not only alarming from a business point of view, but it is also very difficult to refocus a site quickly. All the processes that you have fine-tuned and all the time that you have invested in creating valuable intellectual property assets risk being jettisoned. Rarely have such sudden changes in business models worked, and that is partly because a successful, focused, commercial site takes time to deliver, maintain, and evolve. It is better to ensure that the business plan, which is a rather important basic before you even think about Web sites, is solid in the first place.

17.2 A Combined Hard and Soft Approach

Chapter 15, Measurement Approaches and Techniques, deliberately combines a range of quantitative, data-driven, factual approaches with methods that are much more based on subjective judgment, gut feelings, and emotional reactions. After all, Web site users are human, and to understand why things are happening often requires emotional empathy. Equally, in your efforts to improve the performance of your Web site, it is important to combine the "soft" and the "hard" approaches to get the best results. This means involving a range of people in coming up with site enhancement propositions. A creative director is just as likely to come up with an idea that radically improves site performance as a business analyst, although they may approach things from a different angle.

Figure 17.1 shows how the soft and hard approaches combine to produce recommendations that can be executed. The results are then measured to

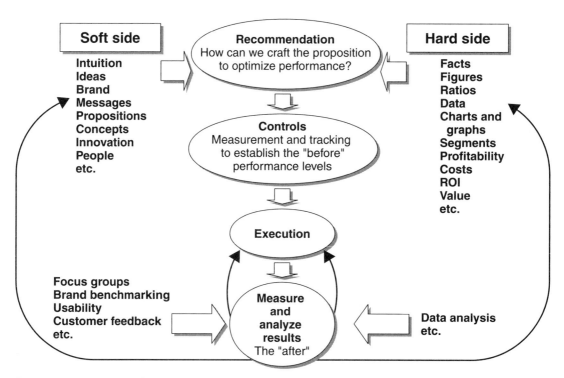

Figure 17.1 Combining soft and hard approaches for site improvements.

show the impact of the recommendation using an appropriate combination of soft and hard measurement practices.

17.3 Content Management

We discussed content management in Part II of the book, but it is worth reiterating just how important effective content management can be in improving a Web site. Measurement is vital because without it you do not know what impact, positive or negative, your efforts are having. But if you really did not have the time or resources to do measurement properly (and sadly, measurement is often the first thing to get dropped as delivery deadlines loom), then concentrating on improving content is guaranteed to deliver results.

Without going too much over ground we have already covered, reflect, for example, on how far effective content management can create efficiencies of time, that most important of assets in today's economy:

▶ With proper versioning and file management through a content repository, you can develop more rapidly, safe in the knowledge that you can fall back on previously known good versions if necessary.
▶ Using notification services within workflow ensures that there is as little lag as possible between task handoffs, maximizing productivity.
▶ Capturing content in a structured way, especially through online forms, ensures minimum further reformatting and tagging work as well as allowing for easy and fast integration and reduced testing time. It also makes it possible to exploit the value of the content asset through personalization, reuse, repackaging, and syndication.
▶ Workflow processes in a larger organization ensure that as little time as possible is spent bringing new team members up to speed as they become involved with the Web project. The structures and processes in place also ensure that work moves through the organization as efficiently as possible.
▶ Using templates makes it much faster to make sitewide updates and changes.
▶ The development of subsites, such as foreign language versions, becomes much quicker.

Clearly, you need to judge each situation, weighing the merits of introducing formal processes and the efficiencies this can bring to a large organization against the informality and simplicity that will allow a smaller team to progress more quickly. Nonetheless, there is no doubt that the need to manage increasingly complex content assets will increase for all sizes of organization as the number of delivery channels increases, the number of required content formats grows, and the need for increased content structuring and metadata becomes more apparent. Even without process elements such as workflow, the requirements for intelligently managing content assets will be such that content management will grow in importance. As it does so, it risks becoming much more costly and is therefore a prime candidate upon which to focus optimization efforts.

17.4   Improving the Moments of Truth

As well as improving production and back-end processes to boost efficiency, you should be obsessive about improving the customer experience. In particular, you should focus on the site's moments of truth. What are these moments of truth? These are the key yes/no or shall I/shan't I decision points in the customer's interaction experience with your site. Typically, these might be the home page, the registration page, or the point of purchase. These are critical points in the customer journey and what happens at these few stages radically affects performance. The smallest of changes can have a huge impact on the bottom line because it can tip the balance one way or another. Most Web users are still a little wary and distrusting of the medium, and they are typically time poor, so the slightest bump in their journey through your site is enough to put them off committing and becoming customers. It is incredibly important to measure abandonment rates at these key points and do all you can to avoid them.

Take legal compliance in the financial services sector as a simple example. Financial services organizations need to be very careful that they comply with laws governing the provision of their services: Giving financial advice, for example, is a very delicate area. How then do financial services organizations design the process users must go through online to ensure compliance? If done poorly, it can have a disastrous impact on the customer experience and hence the bottom line. The compliance screens are a moment of truth for these sites because a customer must go through them to purchase or apply, and yet they can easily put customers off. Perhaps simply by reducing the number of "I accept" screens and placing the "I accept" button clearly at the top of the page, rather than forcing users to scroll past text that they do not read, conversion rates can be drastically improved while staying on the right side of the law. The click stream flow through these pages should be carefully measured and every detail scrutinized to increase the ratio of users who make it all the way through.

Following are examples of the most common moments of truth for customers as they interact with a Web site and some of the things that you can do to improve the effectiveness of your site at these crucial points.

17.4.1   Home Page

When Amazon makes even the tiniest of changes to its home page, there is a big stir among customers and within the digital industry. Why? Because it is recognized what a big difference even the slightest change to the home page can make, and as the world's largest e-tailer, Amazon has a lot to gain or lose through such changes and so invests a large amount of time and money in making sure any improvements they make really do work.

Assuming that you can get customers to your home page in the first place, how can you ensure that they make that all-important next click further into your site? Most sites are dismayed to find that their home page ranks top in their statistics for exit pages and single-page visits. If you can increase the percentage of those who explore just a little bit further by even a few points, you could have a significant effect on overall performance. Users who explore past the home page are like customers who are tempted past the shop window to come into the shop to browse. This step is a prerequisite on the path to purchase.

How you improve your home page will depend on your site and your customers, and the only way to get it really right is to experiment and evolve over time and to measure the results with each iteration. The two most important sensations that your home page must seek to create within the user are a sense of trust and a sense of interest to explore further. Trust is absolutely vital to successful selling online, but you also need some initial hook to get users to make that first tentative step past the home page. Make it easy for them to take this step.

Some common approaches to building trust and interest on the home page are:

▶ Reduce the time it takes for your home page to load. Your home page absolutely must not take too long to load. If it takes longer than 10 seconds, your users will already be thinking of other things and getting increasingly frustrated and ill-disposed toward your site.

▶ Experiment with *reducing* the amount of information on your home page. You may be eager to try and show all you have, but this may overpower and frighten users. Google's stripped down approach as a search engine has proved very popular.

▶ Use real-world events that users can empathize with, such as seasonal festivities, to immediately create a sense of recognition among users, giving them a small shot of confidence.

▶ Experiment with links into the site that appeal to *who* the user is and what their need is rather than just promotions of your content or products. For example, an e-tailer at Christmas might have a link saying "Last minute Christmas shopping?" rather than "Great Christmas bargains!"

▶ Branding, or cobranding, is very powerful online for creating trust. Exploit the power of your brand, or partners' brands, to make users feel confident and at home.

▶ Ensure your navigation and page layout are easy to use. Make sure common elements such as contact, search, checkout, and site map are easy to find. If users feel confident they will be able to navigate the site, they will be more comfortable to dive in past the home page.

▶ Include links to privacy and security policies and guarantees in the footer information of your home page to reassure users that you take these things seriously.

▶ Provide clear contact details—ideally, a contact phone number—prominently on the home page. Companies sometimes claim that encouraging people to phone is defeating the point of having a Web site. However, the reality is that some customers will prefer to phone, and many just want a sense of reassurance that the telephone safety net is there. If it is, they will explore the Web site further and give that a go before resorting to the telephone.

▶ Experiment with humanizing your home page to make it more reassuring. Photos of people, less formal language, and customer testimonials could make your customers more willing to explore online.

▶ Cater to both the new user and the repeat user. You could have a "New to site?" guide for new users if what your site is offering is quite complicated or unusual. Or if you know the visitor is a new user, then you might dynamically show a very tempting promotional offer on the home page. For repeat users, focus on personalizing the experience: Allow users to configure what they see and let them know what is new on the site since their last visit.

▶ Do not radically update the look and feel of your home page too often or you risk alienating repeat visitors who become confused and lose faith or patience in your site.

17.4.2 Site Entry Page

It is not always going to be the home page through which users enter your site. They might enter the site at a different page by following a link from another site through a search engine that has indexed other pages on your site or because you have sent them to a particular page with a targeted URL or special domain for marketing purposes.

The key to improving these pages is to ensure that you match the contents of the page with the expectations of the user who arrives there. There is little you can practically do about third parties who choose to link to you, though you can help ensure that search engine referrals give users what they expect by making sure your page metatagging (in particular, keywords and description) is up to date and accurate and that you help guide search engine spiders to index only those pages that you wish to be indexed. However, if you are promoting a special URL, then you can control the contents of the landing page that users arrive at. This page must clearly connect with the message that you sent out to get users there in the first place; you can then use interactivity to progress to a more enhanced experience, including purchase, building on the initial awareness. A marketing microsite or competition is a typical example where the site entry page may not be the home page. This is still a moment of truth as for many users it will be their all-important first impression of you.

17.4.3 Registration

For some sites, converting a user occurs when he or she registers on the site. Turning a user from an anonymous site visitor into a user with a profile and then, ideally, into a loyal repeat user with configured preferences and interests vastly increases the value of that user to the site owner. Advertisers and sponsors, in particular, will pay a premium to site owners who really know their users and can demonstrate those users' commitment to the site and genuine interest in particular topics.

The registration process is clearly a very important moment of truth for such sites. How do you improve registration conversion rates? These ideas are commonly applied:

- *Focus on privacy.* Web users are understandably wary of submitting their details online. Doing so to purchase an item seems fair enough because the details are required to ship the product and to check credit status. Submitting information for registration purposes, on the other hand, makes users uncomfortable: Why do you want the data? What are you going to do with it? If you do not already have a proper privacy policy, then you must create one. With new browser releases, court cases, and increased user awareness, a privacy policy is a requirement. Display it prominently for users to see. Ideally, you should get a third-party organization to certify your privacy policy to further bolster potential registrants' trust.

- *Let users know where they are in the process.* There is nothing worse than for users not to know how far along a registration process they are. If they fear that there may be many more pages to come, it is likely they will abandon registration. You must clearly manage their expectations by signaling to them how many stages there are, why they are necessary, and at what point they are in the process ("Step 1 of 3: Address Details").

- *Reduce the number of registration steps and/or data required.* The fewer the registration steps and the less personal data that need to be submitted, the higher the registration conversion rate. It is as simple as that. You must think very carefully about balancing your customer data needs with users' dislike of filling in long forms. If at all possible, reduce the number of registration steps required. If data are not absolutely necessary, then consider making them optional for users to fill in. Use drop-downs, radio buttons, or check boxes to make it easy for users to click on answers rather than having to fill them in.

- *"Drip acquire" data.* Rather than requesting all the data you would like at the point of registration, devise means to acquire the less important supplementary data at a later stage when users sign up for newsletters or enter a competition, for example.

▶ *Hook customers' interest with email first.* Along similar lines to the one-click ordering concept, make it really easy for users to sign up to an email newsletter by entering just their email address and clicking Submit. If what you are offering is attractive, then conversion rates will be high because users can still protect their anonymity. You can then use the email newsletter to try to upgrade users to be fully registered over time by persuading them of the additional benefits.

▶ *Keep selling the benefits at each step of registration.* You do not want potential registrants to get cold feet and back out once they have started on the path to registration, so you should make sure that you continue to reaffirm the benefits of registration at east step. Use different techniques: testimonials of existing customers, time-dependent special offers, or perhaps a surprise benefit at the final step as a deal clincher.

17.4.4 Checkout

Obviously, the checkout process is a critical moment of truth for any e-commerce site. As customers become more used to shopping online, e-commerce software becomes more flexible, and protocols become more established, it is easier to create a checkout process that follows best practice. Only in special cases would it be advisable to break with standards that customers know and recognize. If customers have made the decision to purchase and you have all but converted them, the checkout process must be as smooth, efficient, and fast as possible to make sure you lose as few customers as possible.

Optimization approaches are similar to those used for registration:

▶ Only require data to be submitted that are clearly relevant to the purchase in question. Asking for more risks alerting users and making them suspicious, possibly resulting in abandoned purchases.

▶ Reduce the number of steps required to purchase. Amazon has popularized the ultimate extreme in this: one-click ordering.

▶ Make absolutely sure that your e-commerce system is secure and emphasize this to customers. Online fraud is a major concern to most Web shoppers. Give all the reassurance you can. Third-party certification can help.

▶ Provide alternative payment mechanisms. Not everyone wants to pay online. In some countries, notably Germany, there are cultural barriers to online payment.

▶ Guarantees, warrantees, or other such policies help to convince the potential customer that you can be trusted with their business.

▶ Make sure contact details and customer service details are readily available throughout the purchase process. There needs to be a safety net there to reassure the customer and make sure that sales are not lost because a user has given up buying online in frustration and has no other route to turn to.

▶ Avoid nasty surprises at the end of the process. It should be clear, for example, whether additional costs such as packaging and shipping charges are included in the price given or not. If you only deliver to certain geographical areas, let customers know this up front.

▶ Even if customers do not wish to buy right now, set them on the journey to eventual purchase. Just as you might use an email newsletter as a way to eventually persuade a customer to register, use shopping wish lists to get customers in the mind-set that they can one day buy the items. This also has the advantage of giving some insight into what the customer is interested in.

▶ Experiment with cross-selling techniques but be careful: The imperative must be to close the sale that the customer actually wants to make. If you push much else at the user before allowing them to buy what they want, you risk annoying the customer and losing both the sale and, perhaps, the customer for good.

▶ As with registration, make sure the user is clear at what step he or she is in the purchase process. Clearly signposting the steps gives customers confidence and manages their expectations about how much is yet to come, making it more likely that they will successfully see the purchase through.

17.4.5   Search

As the amount and complexity of information available on the Web, as well as on individual Web sites, increase, it becomes ever more important to have a good search function. Just because there is more information out there does not mean that users are any more patient in finding what they want or tolerant of sites that do not get them where they want as quickly as possible. The opposite is true: As Web users become more experienced and are spoiled by their positive experiences on sites with excellent search and personalization features, they become even less patient and tolerant with negative experiences. Using a site's search function is thus a moment of truth. If the user gets relevant and meaningful search results, then this is a great step along the journey toward a user becoming a customer. But if the search function gives poor results, the user is likely to give up and go elsewhere.

How can you improve your search function?

▶ Make it faster. If your search results take ages to appear, the user may not wait for them to load or attempt a second more refined search. Improve the speed at which results are displayed by optimizing your code, your database, and your indexing. Consider how much information to display on any one results page and make sure the file size of this page is not too large. Consider first showing thumbnail graphics rather than larger ones.

▶ Improve the accuracy and relevance of your search results. Migrate your content to be stored in a database. Add descriptive data and keywords to your content. In this way, searches can be faster; they can be confined to relevant database fields, and the results can be weighted for increased relevance. For example, a field that contains human-added search keywords could be weighted higher than a free text search on the body content. Use more advanced features to spot user misspellings and still pick up the correctly spelled versions in search results. In addition, closely associated words such as past tenses of verbs or nouns with their corresponding verb forms can be included as possible matches in results.

▶ Offer an advanced search option for power users. This could include more advanced filtering options as well as support for more sophisticated search phrasing such as Boolean operators (AND, OR, NOT).

▶ Rank results in order or relevance to the keywords or phrase searched on and show what section of the site the search result belongs to. This helps users filter out results that they know will not be relevant. A product name may feature in a press release and in the product section; depending on whether the user was a journalist or a shopper, they would be likely to want to follow different paths.

▶ Include the term(s) searched on with the search results. This reminds users what they searched on and is particularly helpful both in spotting spelling mistakes and further refining a second search.

▶ Log what terms are searched on. This not only helps improve site design by understanding what users are interested in or are finding difficult to locate, but it also tells you what the most popular search terms are. With this insight, you might want to create specially crafted search results pages that can be hard-coded to appear if particular terms are searched on, allowing you to guide customers even more accurately.

17.4.6 Contact

If a customer wants to contact you, this too should be considered a moment of truth. You should aim to design your Web site so that customers have no need to contact you. This is most cost effective. However, some customers may wish to interact with your organization directly via other channels. Improving your online "contact us" facility involves both offering customers a variety of ways to get in touch and yet also trying as hard as possible to ensure that the site itself answers the majority of inquiries with customers servicing themselves.

Here are some approaches to improving your online contact services:

▶ *Offer multiple contact channels.* If possible, you should offer site users a number of ways to contact your organization other than online. In particular, a telephone contact number is important because users are likely to want an answer to their inquiry right away. Experience has shown that prominently displaying a contact telephone number does not overly increase the amount of telephone calls that a site generates, but it does increase users' feeling of confidence and comfort using the site, which in turn enhances performance.

▶ *Capture questions from site users.* However the questions and inquiries come in, via email, phone, or mail, you should capture them and make the answers available to future site users. This could be done by introducing or updating a frequently asked questions (FAQs) section or, going one step further, by building a knowledge base that users can search to find answers to their questions.

▶ *Centralize storage of all communications.* One of the fundamental requirements for customer relationship management (CRM) is the centralization of customer information—the single customer view. If you can pull together all of a customer's contact communications into a single place, you are able to serve and understand that customer in a far superior way. As a first step, you should at least try to store all customer form-submitted data so that you have an audit trail of previous correspondence that can be referred to and analyzed.

For more on effective customer servicing online, refer to Chapter 12, Customer Service, in Part III.

▶ *Route communications efficiently.* You should try to capture the nature of an inquiry at the point of contact if possible. This allows you to route the contact to the right department or person to be dealt with. This minimizes the chance of the communication going astray and improves the speed and efficiency with which a response can be given. It also aids analysis of volume and nature of customer service demand by inquiry type, by time, and even by customer segment, allowing for more efficient future resourcing.

17.5 Usability

One of the simplest and most effective ways to optimize any Web site in a relatively short time, for relatively little cost, is to improve its usability. This means making the site easier to use. Even now that the Web industry has had more time to understand online user behavior, likes, and dislikes, research continues to show that huge amounts of money are being lost because users find Web sites hard to use. The most consistent reason for users to abandon a purchase, or a site, is because they cannot achieve what they want to do because of poor site usability, often the navigation. It is absolutely critical that your site is easy to use, and it remains extremely important that the site downloads quickly. Concentrating on optimizing these two fundamentals can bring enormous improvements to overall Web site performance.

Usability is too large, too important, and too specialized a discipline to do it justice in one section of this book. Some excellent books have been written on this topic, and you can find recommendations for what to read in the Recommended Reading section of Resources. It would have been quite wrong, however, to leave usability out of a section on site improvement because it really can be a surprisingly powerful tool in improving the performance of Web sites.

If there are three key messages that should be remembered about usability in relation to site improvement efforts, they would be:

1. Usability does not have to take much time or expense, but you must do it.
2. You must build usability techniques into your Web development process.
3. You must develop an understanding of usability best practices.

Point 1 is quite self-explanatory, but it is worth remembering that it is infinitely better to conduct any usability testing than none at all, even if your testing takes one day and involves one member of the team sitting down with the site in front of a few friends to see how they manage it. That alone is likely to yield very valuable insight for very little investment.

Points 2 and 3 are covered in more detail later and are about involving users more in your development and building a greater understanding and appreciation of how real users interact with sites.

Following are the most common usability techniques and practices with a brief description of each and how it should be integrated in the Web development process.

17.5.1   Usability Techniques and Practices

Competitor Analysis

When defining what your site is going to do and what features and content it is going to have in the context of your Web strategy, it is likely that you will analyze what your competitors are doing to see what you can offer to improve on their propositions. Usability experts can help at this stage:

▶ *Interpretive analysis.* This type of analysis requires recruiting users to perform common tasks with competitor sites. Each site is tested using natural scenarios aimed to test important common features and afford insight into what works best.

▶ *Predictive analysis.* This evaluation requires expert usability practitioners attempting to place themselves in the role of a less experienced user to spot likely usability problems so that they can be avoided in the development of your own site. This is less costly and faster than interpretive analysis because there is no requirement to recruit actual end users, but it is less comprehensive.

Inquiry

As you begin to develop creative concepts and designs to realize your site's proposition, usability experts can canvas feedback from users through interviews, questionnaires, surveys, and field observation techniques to assess their likes, dislikes, needs, and understanding of the proposed design approach. Although this sounds similar to traditional focus group techniques, the two are not the same. Focus groups would typically be used earlier in the process to gauge reactions to the overall site proposition and brand positioning, whereas usability inquiries are much more functionally and interface focused. As you begin to concretely realize your proposition, it is then that usability can give you feedback on how users are reacting, or are likely to react, to it.

Interface Design and Information Architecture

Once you have progressed your creative concepts and are beginning to define the user interfaces and user-facing elements of the information architecture (principally the site sections and levels that the user navigates around—the site map), it is important to validate your work with real users. Doing this early, even if only on a small scale, avoids costly and time-consuming rework later in the process.

Among other user-centric, collaborative design techniques that usability professionals employ at this stage is card sorting and cluster analysis. This practice presents users with the proposed sections of a Web site, which they then sort into categories meaningful to them. This can be extremely useful in developing, or fine-tuning, a navigation system and information architecture.

Prototyping

During the prototyping phase of development, you can use low-fidelity prototypes with little detail as models to assess concepts, functions, and information architecture.

A paper prototype of the intended design, architecture, and navigation is presented to the user. A few simple tasks and questions are directed at the user, and on the basis of feedback, a modified design can be immediately constructed for further testing.

Once the prototype is iterated and a functional model is created (a high-fidelity prototype), this too should be tested with users in a controlled environment with realistic tasks and scenarios.

Expert Evaluation

An additional or alternative route to testing prototypes with end users is to get an expert evaluation, typically from two or more usability experts, of the functional model to highlight any usability issues. The interface can be reviewed for compliance with common usability heuristics (best practice rules) to flush out potential usability problems.

Contextual Task Analysis

This technique is typically employed with an existing site because it allows an understanding of how to reengineer current usage to create a more efficient user experience. The contextual task analysis approach takes into account a user's current task knowledge as well as human cognitive constraints and capabilities by observing users within their normal usage environment. From these data, a model of a user's goals, actions toward a goal, and decisions made to reach the goal is plotted, allowing an updated, more effective information architecture to be formed.

Soft Launch Usability Evaluation

A usability assessment should take place at the soft launch stage to eradicate any significant but small-scale issues. The evaluation approach would be the same as for the high-fidelity prototype evaluation; that is, the site is tested in a controlled environment with realistic tasks and user scenarios.

Launch Usability Evaluation

Similar to the soft launch evaluation, this is a final check before full launch.

17.5.2   Navigation

Point 3 mentioned in Section 17.5 suggests that you develop an understanding of usability best practices. Note that more important than understanding usability best practices is understanding your users. Best practices are, by necessity, generalized and should act only as a guiding framework and reference point. Ultimately, your site must be developed to meet your users' needs.

For more details on usability best practice, refer to the Resources section.

This section cannot possibly cover all areas of usability best practice, and indeed, these evolve all the time. However, the following usability guidelines on navigation have been included to give you a starting point and because navigation is the one usability area that can deliver the greatest benefits.

A site's navigation should help users understand where they are in the site, where they have been, and where they can go next. It sounds simple, but it is surprisingly hard to get right, which is crucial. Research regarding users' sense of trust when interacting with e-commerce sites, so vital for sales, shows that the feeling of security experienced by a user is determined by his or her feeling of control within the site. Among the aspects contributing to this feeling of control, ease of use, availability of user support, and an effective navigation system are the most influential. Conversely, poor navigation is the top reason for users to leave Web sites due to frustration.

Here are example usability guidelines to help you improve your site's navigation.

Consider Accessibility Issues

How many partially sighted, blind, or disabled site users are you losing through poor accessibility of your site navigation? In the UK, for example, about 3% of the population are partially sighted or blind and more than 10% are disabled. Consider further that the Internet is an ideal potential shopping medium for anyone who is housebound or has difficulty getting to the store.

You should ensure that your navigation system is compliant with accessibility standards:

▶ Ideally, provide a text alternative version if you have graphical navigation.
▶ Use Alt tags for all graphical navigation elements so that users who have text-to-speech systems for Web surfing know where to go.
▶ Use client-side rather than server-side image maps because Alt tags on each of the link options will provide descriptions as the user explores the various options. Users with difficulty moving a mouse will benefit because client-side image maps allow them to move through links with keyboard control.

The importance of hierarchy

Research in cognitive psychology suggests that the structure of human knowledge is hierarchical in nature. As our knowledge is the primary resource used in decision making and problem solving, the presentation of information in hierarchical form will aid a user in completing his or her task within a Web site.

The foundation of almost all good information architectures is based upon a well-designed hierarchy. Your navigation scheme should clearly reflect the hierarchy of information. This helps users immediately understand the site's information architecture and makes them more confident in following quick links to specific content because they will know where they are when they get there. Reducing the number of clicks for a user to get what he or she wants increases performance.

Consider breadth and depth issues: whether to have lots of top-level options with little depth or few options and lots of pages deeper. Research in this area has suggested that navigational breadth produces better performance than depth.

The importance of consistency

Consistency in navigation design helps users gain a sense of control and security that increases the chances they will trust the site. Core navigation elements should appear consistently on all pages, excluding perhaps the home page and forms. Page titles should also be used consistently to give users a visual and semantic anchor on each page and so they can be sure they have arrived where they wished to go.

Help users determine their location

In the real world, to determine our current position, discover our way back, or plan a route, we rely on landmarks, maps, compasses, GPS, and so on. On the Web, you must provide similar sources of information for users to help determine their location:

▶ Breadcrumbs (home > products > mens > shirts)
▶ Color of hypertext link (visited/unvisited)
▶ Site map
▶ Clear information hierarchy
▶ Logical link labels
▶ URLs

It is essential that these elements are designed with care to inform users of their location at all times by providing clear "you are here" information.

▶ Breadcrumbs are effective in providing users with a clear understanding of where they are and where they have been. They also provide a good method of moving back up the hierarchy to higher level categories.
▶ Support users who have jumped into the middle of the site from a search engine or external link. Clear page titles and a clear name or logo for the organization is a simple but effective technique to provide this information.
▶ If you move away from the Web standard of blue underlined text for unvisited hyperlinks and purple for visited links, then ensure your hyperlink styles are consistent and self-evident. This provides users with clear, consistent navigation cues while browsing your site.

Use formatting to aid body text navigation

As people tend to scan pages quickly when searching for information on the Web, it is possible to miss a crucial link if it is embedded within a paragraph.

<u>Consider</u> that overuse of <u>embedded</u> links within a <u>Web page</u> can <u>lead to</u> <u>cluttered</u> and <u>confusing</u> content.

It may be better to present these on a <u>separate line</u> <u>or in a bulleted format</u>

▶ <u>whatever</u>
▶ <u>is</u>
▶ <u>most</u>
▶ <u>appropriate</u>

Help users understand where links will take them

Consider the context in which the link is presented; for example: "My interest in <u>Usability</u> is growing!"

Where will this link take the user? To a definition of usability? Maybe to a usability forum? Or to a book on usability? It is important to attempt to provide users with as much information as possible about where the link will take them:

▶ *Provide more context.* For example, based on the previous example, the links could be arranged to give the user more detail about where it will lead: "My interest in usability is growing! Most of my learning takes place at the <u>usability forum</u>."
▶ *Link labels.* Supported by the latest browsers, you can add a description of where the link will go to your code. Users will see this if they hover over the link.

17.6 Viral Marketing Tools

Viral marketing occurs when an existing site user spreads word of a site to friends, colleagues, and contacts. As they in turn spread the word further, the effect becomes viral. This word of mouth, or perhaps "word of mouse," marketing is clearly a dream for site owners: It is free and it is highly targeted. Existing site users and customers are only likely to refer other people who will have a high tendency to become users and customers themselves. All research and results to date corroborate the power and efficacy of viral marketing. Getting it to actually happen in the first place is the hard part. So what can you do?

There are two elements to successful viral marketing: a good product and the right tools to facilitate the viral effect. The bottom line is that nobody will refer their friends to a bad site however much you encourage them or give them the tools to do so. Viral marketing is hard to control and almost impossible to predict or guarantee. In many ways, the best you can do is focus all your efforts on making your site the best that it can possibly be and let your users take care of any viral marketing themselves.

However, assuming you have a site that users would feel happy referring contacts to, you can help improve customer acquisition by giving users the right viral tools and giving users ample opportunity to use them. Here are some common tools that encourage viral activity.

17.6.1   Send to a Friend

Of course, users can always send friends the URL of any page that they like via email. However, not all users are familiar with copying and pasting URLs, particularly if the URL is extremely long, and in some cases, the URL in the address bar will not take the friend directly to the correct page, which is often the case when frames are used. Users are also busy, often impatient people, so if you can gently remind them that they might want to let their friends know about the site and make it really easy for them to refer friends, then they are more likely to do so. Send to a friend or email a friend functions, which send the contents of a page, or its URL, to the friend, have proved very effective in promoting viral activity, particularly on high traffic, content-rich sites.

E-postcards and e-greeting cards are an extension of this send to a friend function and capitalize more on entertainment value or seasonal and personal events to encourage usage. Christmas or birthday cards are typical examples.

17.6.2   Email Forwarding

Increasingly, people are aware of the power that a simple email signature can have for promoting (or tarnishing in some unfortunate cases) a company or individual. As an email can easily be virally distributed to people who will not otherwise know of its source, the recipients must rely on the contents and will typically look at the bottom of the email for further details that they can follow up on. For example, posting valuable information to a large community site can be extremely effective in driving targeted traffic to your site, but only if you include the necessary footer information for users to follow up.

This principle applies for any emails that you send out from your site, such as newsletters, promotions, forum digests, or alerts. You must assume that these emails might be forwarded and include enough information for any recipient at least to know who you are, what you do, and where to find out more. This can be as simple as a name, proposition statement, and URL.

In addition, you should encourage users to forward emails that you send them, particularly things like special promotions or newsletters. Some users may not be sure whether they are allowed to forward a newsletter, perhaps for fear of copyright infringement.

17.6.3   Print This Page

Where this is a lot of information on a page, many pages for a single piece of content, or the complexity of the information is dense, users may prefer to print the page. They can do this simply by clicking the browser's print button. However, there are potential pitfalls here: If frames are used, the incorrect frame may be printed, or the page formatting may not be suitable for printing. Having a print this page function not only reminds users that they may wish to print the page, but it allows you to format the page so that you can be sure it will print correctly.

From a viral activity point of view, printed pages can be effective as they can be shared among many people offline, photocopied, and circulated. The URL will be on the page, along with the page title, so those that see it offline can come and find the content online. How many times have you gone to the printer to see some Web pages being printed and you think, "Oh, that looks interesting. I think I'll go and have a look at that too"?

17.6.4   Save to Disk

A save to disk function allowing users to save Web content into a file format that they can store on their computers is again not only popular with users, but also can also help encourage viral marketing. Allowing users to store Web content in a file enables them to share that file, make it available on the company network, and email it around the company or to friends. Pages of content can be saved to disk as well as promotional items such as screen savers, wallpaper, music, and video files.

17.6.5 Privacy

Users are increasingly sensitive and aware of their privacy online. They will not give you their details, or enter details of friends, if they are concerned about your privacy practices. Any tool that encourages a user to enter details of friends for referral purposes must very clearly state how the information entered will be used. Given that the friend has not explicitly asked to be contacted, it is advisable only to use email addresses acquired for the purposes of actually sending the email. If you make this clear, then users will feel more comfortable in referring their friends.

You can, of course, create marketing campaigns that are designed to be viral. Rather than being built into the fabric of the site, these are designed to create spikes of interest and, ideally, create a flood of new interest. These campaigns work best either when there is a great promotional offer, so people pass the offer on to friends who can also benefit from it, or when the content of the campaign itself is entertaining. The latter is hard to do because you cannot be sure that people really will find your efforts entertaining. Get it wrong and at best the campaign will go unnoticed and at worst the effects could go virally in the wrong direction. Conversion rates from an entertainment-driven viral campaign are likely to be quite low, unless the entertainment element is also the product (e.g., a film), as the user has primarily come for a bit of fun and not to sign up for something. However, viral campaigns of this sort can be very effective for brand awareness and brand extension purposes.

17.7 E-commerce

All of the traditional elements of successfully selling products apply online: product range, product sourcing and purchasing, pricing, merchandising, promotions, fulfillment, logistics, inventory and stock control, and customer service, to name but a few. Without going into detail on how to improve all these elements, here are a few proven techniques that will help improve your online conversion rates as well as increase the amount of money that a customer spends with you.

17.7.1   Improving Customer Acquisition

▶ *Privacy, usability, search, checkout, home page.* These are all core site elements that have already been addressed in this chapter. Focusing on improving these elements will reap great rewards.

▶ *Make it easy to buy.* This involves not only improving usability and the checkout process, including payment and delivery options, but also experimenting with how much information you display on your pages. Many e-tailers have found that taking information off their home pages has resulted in higher conversion rates and sales: Too much choice can be a bad thing. By restricting users' choice, at least initially, you make it easier for them to decide if and what to buy. The success of this will depend on your product and target market as well as whether the customer is a frequent buyer or not. Typically, the longer the user has been a customer, the broader the product range and site complexity he or she will be open to. Experiment and use personalization to improve the site.

▶ *Product information and photography.* Working with real users, it is amazing to see how important it is to have good quality, up-to-date, and in-depth product information and clear, high-quality accompanying product photos. Apart from navigational problems, users become most frustrated, and are most likely to drop out of a sale, if they cannot properly understand or be fully sure that the product is what they want. It is hardly surprising when you consider that users are expected to buy without actually seeing or touching the product. Everything that you can do to give the customer as full an experience and understanding of the product as possible will help improve sales. Improving the way that products are categorized, indexed, and named, and improving any associated metadata, are extremely important in improving the quality of search results, or allowing users to find products via multiple access points as they wish, for more advanced functions such as filtering, personalization, or product feature comparisons.

17.7.2   Increasing Basket Size and Share of Wallet

▶ *Cross- and up-selling.* Cross-selling involves selling customers products associated with the one they have chosen to buy: the famous "Would you like fries with that, sir?" Up-selling involves selling a higher value item up from the original purchase: Instead of just an armchair, you can persuade the customer to buy a whole suite. If you have well-indexed product information and a suitable content management system or e-commerce engine, it is relatively easy to cross- and up-sell online using business logic to present associated products to users. However, the question is when do you try and cross- or up-sell? Experience has shown that rather than presenting potential purchasers with all that you would like to try and cross- and up-sell them too early in the purchase, it is more effective to wait until the last moment, or even after the sale, to cross-sell and certainly to reserve up-selling until after the sale. You must ensure that you give customers what they came for first and not risk distracting or frustrating them along the way. Once they have what they want, they will be more open to other ideas. It is extremely powerful to use purchase information to customize the posttransaction confirmation page for cross- and up-selling purposes. For example, if a user has come to buy a formal shirt, you might consider offering cuff links or a tie at the point of purchase and then suggesting a range of suits on the posttransaction page.

▶ *Personalization.* Personalization is covered more fully in Part III, Customer Relationship Management, but you should certainly look at personalization as a tool for increasing the amount a customer spends with you. Just as making it easier to buy improves conversion rates for new customers, personalization can make it increasingly easy for a customer to repeat buy: Stored shopping lists and different address, delivery, or payment profiles are good examples. As we have seen, the customer data acquired for personalization are also the platform for increased customer insight and relationship building, helping you make sure that what you offer customers is likely to meet their needs and increase their likelihood of spending.

18

Tackling a Web Site Measurement Project

The preceding chapters explain the background and evolution of Web site measurement as well as the key concepts, metrics, techniques, and approaches. But how do you actually tackle a whole measurement project? What are the key stages and deliverables? In the following sections, I first suggest some smaller, tactical initiatives that you might want to tackle to get the ball rolling before looking in more detail at how you might tackle a full project to implement and integrate a measurement software solution.

18.1 Tactical Initiatives

Starting with a smaller, more tactical project is a good way to flesh out issues and learn in a lower risk environment before moving on to bigger things. Because Web site measurement is still a new discipline, there is a lot of value in experimenting and learning. For management who are wary of large-scale projects that they do not fully understand, or are not convinced will deliver a return on their investment, a smaller project is an attractive proof of concept exercise.

18.1.1   Planning and Education

Following are some planning and education initiatives that will help save you time when you come to larger projects or implementation.

How to approach creating a measurement framework is discussed in Section 16.1, Defining a Measurement Framework.

▶ *Define your measurement framework.* This task requires a lot of careful thought and is likely to need some refinement before it is generally accepted. This is because it represents a strategic blueprint of the business. It maps out the business' end goal and the determining factors in reaching it. Creating this framework is a step that you cannot avoid if your Web site measurement efforts are truly to be of relevance and value. The sooner you can start creating this framework, the better. This work is of great strategic value irrespective of the Web site's role. If this is not within your sphere of influence, then find out who might be able to help. Strategists, business analysts, and senior management are most likely to have this model in their minds, if not already documented.

▶ *Customer and content categorization.* Another piece of work that requires a high degree of commercial, intellectual, and strategic input is the categorization of your company's customers and content. This is addressed in much more detail in Parts II and III of the book, Content Management and Customer Relationship Management, but it has a great bearing on measurement. Your ability to analyze and report on customer segments, for instance, will depend on those segments being clearly defined and your having collected the right data that can be filtered accordingly. If your customer segments are determined primarily by location, you will clearly need to focus your efforts on collecting geographic information from customers. Or if you are expected to report on which customers show interest in a particular product or service on the Web site, then you need to ensure that site content contains information (metadata) describing the product or service that they are relevant to. If you know what slices and axes of customer and content data you will require to do the analysis and reporting you need to deliver, you can work with the Web development team, in particular those responsible for content management, to ensure the site delivers the necessary data. As with the measurement framework, you can begin categorizing your customers and content at any time. The marketing team is the obvious first port of call.

▶ *Management information (MI).* Ultimately, Web site measurement is most powerful if it can be integrated with the rest of the company's management information reporting. The Web is just another channel for doing business that should really be measured according to the value it brings to the overall effort and not be seen in isolation. If you do not already understand what management information is delivered in the company, to whom, and how it is created and delivered, then it is worth finding out. In doing this research, canvas opinions from those you talk to about what additional information of value they would like to see coming from the Web site. Try to map existing offline MI processes and practices to a potential online equivalent. Most reporting translates, and will integrate, directly (e.g., sales information), but other measurements may need further thought: How will you measure customer satisfaction, brand awareness, or customer loyalty online and tie that in with current reporting? Get a feel for what information and metrics people are really interested in, how they like to receive reports, and what they feel is missing.

▶ *Data.* You need data to do any reporting, and once again in the spirit of integrating the Web with the rest of the organization, you should find out what data sources you currently have. Document the data format, gauge its quality and volume, and understand the processes by which it is created, managed, analyzed, and destroyed. Think through the potential value within the data to contribute to Web site measurement. Equally, think how the data you collect online might supplement what already exists offline. Customer information databases are a good example. You might find that a database used for direct marketing contains no customer email information. You could help plug this hole by cross-referencing customer records from your online and offline systems to populate both with more complete customer information.

▶ *Workshops.* Part of the difficulty with Web projects, and certainly Web site measurement, is that general levels of understanding, awareness, and skills in these domains are currently low. This will change as best practices become more established, common processes are put in place, and a common language is spoken. If you can raise levels of awareness of Web site measurement in your company through educational workshops so that there is at least a baseline level of understanding and some common terms, this will greatly help any related project.

18.1.2   Implementation

In terms of smaller, practical steps that you might take, consider the following:

▶ *Online services.* There are many online services that you can try for free, or use for low cost, which will quickly and simply give you a degree of performance reporting. This could be a good introductory step to take. These services are unlikely to give you customer-centric reporting unless you send them data, but they provide basic site-centric measurement and are particularly good if you require technical performance measurement. Apart from their low cost and ease of implementation advantages, many services can also benchmark the performance of your site against peers and provide quite advanced monitoring and alerting services ensuring you are aware of problems as soon as they occur.

▶ *Benchmarking.* Measurement becomes most relevant when you have benchmarks against which to gauge your reports. Often these benchmarks are missing from Web site reports: Documents are printed and given to management, but little analysis is done on variance over time or results in comparison to industry standards. If you do not currently have benchmarks, begin to develop them and include them as a useful diagnostic in current reporting.

Find out more about this in Section 15.2, User-Centric Measurement.

▶ *Identifying individual customers.* As detailed earlier, you must ultimately be able to understand and report on online users at an individual level. Your standard reports may group customers by segments, but if you want to create a custom segment (e.g., to do a special promotion), you need to query individual customer profiles using rules that extract the relevant customers. If you cannot already identify individual customers coming to your site, then it is worth investing the time and effort to do so.

▶ *Improving existing services.* There are no doubt small things that can be done to improve any existing measurement that you do: providing browser-based access to reports; creating an online index and archive of previous reports that can easily be called up online; improving the consistency and quality of the way you capture customer data; improved screening and filtering of extraneous log file data to improve accuracy of reporting; going from common to extended log file format to deepen your level of reporting; importing log files into a database for custom querying; and more consistent file naming and conventions to make analysis more straightforward.

Find out more in Section 17.4, Improving the Moments of Truth.

▶ *Focused inquiry.* Why not start by choosing something very specific to focus your attention on? Perhaps pick one of the moments of truth, such as the home page, and focus all your efforts on really understanding what is happening there. Or you could choose a particular email or other marketing campaign and go to all lengths to understand every element of how it performs. This will expose you to a wide range of techniques and approaches, building valuable experience and insight, at minimal risk and cost.

18.2 Process for Medium to Large Projects

It is possible that you are undertaking a large-scale site redesign, relaunch, or indeed are launching an entirely new site and wish to incorporate Web site measurement into you overall project plan. This is ideal because you can ensure that the measurement elements are built into the architecture of the site itself. However, it is more probable that you have an existing site with some rudimentary reporting and analysis but wish to enhance your site measurement capabilities.

Table 18.1 presents a method for tackling entire Web projects. These four phases and eight work stages constitute the framework for Web project management that I explain in much more detail in my first book, *Web Project Management: Delivering Successful Commercial Web Sites.* I use this same framework to shape how you would tackle a Web site measurement project. This is not to force you to buy my first book, although it will be helpful for anyone familiar with my proposed method to integrate measurement into their project planning, but rather to show how measurement would be tackled as part of an overall Web project life cycle. If your measurement project is a stand-alone one, which is not part of a wider initiative, you can still use this approach, albeit in an accelerated manner.

Table 18.1 The four phases and eight work stages of a typical Web project.

Preproduction			Production			Maintenance	Evaluation
Project clarifi- cation	Solution definition	Project specifi- cation	Content	Design and con- struction	Testing, launch, and handover	Maintenance	Review and evaluation

18.3 Project Clarification

During this work stage, you focus most on really understanding what it is you want to achieve and why.

18.3.1 Project Sponsors

Decide who are going to be the sponsors of your project. Ideally, these should be a combination of people with relevant experience and senior decision-making authority.

18.3.2 Project Team

Identify who will form part of the project team, their level of commitment, their role, and their responsibilities. Identify also broader project stakehold-ers who may not be directly involved in the project.

18.3.3 Project Mission

Briefly articulate the goals and success criteria for the project. This is your mandate to get project buy-in and commitment.

18.3.4 Organization Interaction Plan

It is important that your project gets off to a good start. It is also important that you do not waste the time of members in the organization. Create a plan for how you want to interact with the organization: Who do you need to talk to and why? What are you going to ask them? How much of their time do you need and when? Get your project sponsors to ratify this plan: They will know better which boats not to rock.

18.3.5 Audits

You need to understand what has been achieved so far and the state of readiness within the organization for Web site measurement. You are likely to audit existing systems and processes for the delivery of management information across company as well as existing data sources, formats, and structures. Collect examples of existing or previous work on site measurement.

18.3.6 Customer Insight

It will be very important in developing customer metrics to understand the target customer groups. You need to define the customer segments that you will be measuring and their characteristics. Understanding the customer life cycle and customer decision drivers will also help enormously in defining your measurement framework. This knowledge typically is in the marketing department and has been gained from focus groups, surveys, questionnaires, interviews, panels, or secondary research, but you may find that wider canvasing leads to necessary, and valuable, debate. There is a risk this will slow your process, but it is worth getting right up front.

18.3.7 Requirements Gathering

Talk to all relevant stakeholders to capture their needs and requirements for a measurement system. Do not worry at this stage about prioritizing or limiting the scope of requirements; document them all.

18.3.8 Education

Having spoken to members of the organization about their requirements and your project, you will have a much clearer appreciation of how well Web site measurement is actually understood within the organization. Being a relatively new discipline, there are likely large gaps of knowledge. Ignorance risks damaging the project, whereas if people feel they are learning, you have a greater chance of their commitment. Draw up a suggested education plan giving introductory training in core e-business intelligence and measurement concepts.

18.3.9   Risks and Issues

As you go, keep a list of risks that you fear might impact the project, with suggested ways to avoid the risks, and issues that are already impacting the project and need resolution. You may find this list is very long near the beginning of the project when all sorts of organizational pain bursts to the surface as you talk to more people. Do not bear all this pain yourself: Document it and discuss it with the project sponsors at review meetings.

18.3.10   Initial Project Plan and Budget

Create a Gantt chart with tasks, milestones, timings, dependencies, and resources as far as you can. Also draw up cost estimates. Neither will be comprehensive or fully accurate, especially for later stages of the project, but you will refine the plan as you go. Try to ensure that at least your short-term plan is as accurate as feasible, which should be possible. This will allow senior management to commit to budgetary decisions at least for the initial stages. It will also make people take you, and the project, more seriously.

18.3.11   Deliverables

The deliverables for the project clarification work stage, based on the work described, are as follows:

▶ Project brief (including details of project sponsors, the project team, and project mission)
▶ Organization interaction plan
▶ Customer insight analysis
▶ Web site measurement status report (including audits and readiness assessments)
▶ Requirements document
▶ Education plan
▶ Risks and issues document
▶ Initial project plan and budget

18.4   Solution Definition

This work stage involves thinking through and defining the best solution to your needs

18.4.1   Measurement Framework

For more on defining a measurement framework, see Chapter 16.

Before you define your metrics, you have to know what you need to measure in order to analyze whether your Web site is delivering value against overall business goals.

18.4.2   Metrics

Metrics are covered in Chapter 15.

Using your higher level measurement framework, define what lower level metrics you will require for reporting and analysis.

18.4.3   Data

Once you have your set of metrics, you need to map them to the relevant data sources. If these do not exist, then you must define a data capture strategy to acquire the data. You should define data structures and schemas as well as data cleansing, storage, archiving, and management requirements. Specify how data will be integrated with other enterprises or Web applications. Finally, the legal implications of your usage of data must be addressed.

18.4.4   Reporting

What will your standard reports contain? How often will you deliver them? Who will have access? What format will the reports be delivered in? How will you support reporting?

18.4.5   Analysis

Depending on your metrics and reporting, you will require different forms of analysis and corresponding resources and support. Define the optimal analysis approach and solution.

18.4.6   Technology

Based on the technical requirements you have gathered, define the environment in which your chosen performance management tool must operate: platforms, operating systems, languages, protocols, and network environments. You should define an initial systems architecture and proposed integration and configuration solution but not actually choose your software solution at this stage. Once everything is buttoned down in the project specification, you then have the criteria and requirements you need to go through a vendor selection process.

18.4.7   Testing

How are you going to test your measurement solution once it has been built? You should create a plan that details what process you are going to go through and what sorts of testing you plan to carry out (e.g., user acceptance testing, scenario and load testing, security and penetration attack testing) and create sample test routines and scripts.

18.4.8   Deployment and Rollout

When and how is the system going to become operational and what will then happen to integrate it within the organization? Depending on the size of the project, it is unlikely that everyone who will use the system will immediately be able to do so or that all systems that will eventually integrate with it will simply slot into place. A step at a time, you will need to fully integrate with organizational systems and ensure that all relevant staff can comfortably work with it. This is not just a technical or process challenge but an emotional one: Change must be carefully managed. Documentation, guidelines, and training should form part of the rollout plan.

TIP   **Rollout**

You can choose to stage your rollout a number of ways: by individuals, department, business unit, country, language, or even by digital channel (e.g., mobile or PDA). It is advisable to begin where things will be easiest. Not only will this build your confidence, but it will also give you a more forgiving environment in which to fine-tune your process, training, support, and documentation. Generally, increasing the number of system users creates more work than increasing the complexity of the system: It is easier to deliver an all singing, all dancing system to a few people than a more basic system to many. For this reason, it is often best to roll out as follows: basic features rolled out to a select group; advanced features rolled out to the same select group; basic features rolled out to a wider group; advanced features rolled out to the wider group.

18.4.9   Maintenance

Define the ongoing maintenance requirements for your solution, including your requirements for any service-level agreement (SLA) to be made either with an in-house team or with a third party. This is likely to include contacts, problem escalation procedures, response times, training commitments, monitoring, and alerting services.

18.4.10   Project Documentation

Based on your recommended solutions, you should be able to refine and update your project plan and budget as well as your risks and issues documentation and any other project management documentation you are maintaining. Change control could begin at this stage but is perhaps best commenced after the project specification stage.

18.4.11   Deliverables

The deliverables for the solution definition work stage, based on the work described, are as follows:

- ▶ Measurement framework with metrics
- ▶ Data strategy
- ▶ Reporting and analysis recommendations
- ▶ Systems architecture and technical environment
- ▶ Testing plan
- ▶ Rollout and deployment plan
- ▶ Maintenance plan
- ▶ Updated project documentation

18.5   Project Specification

During this work stage, you will be documenting in detail the specifics of the project and choosing a measurement software solution.

18.5.1   Create the Project Specification

You formally document the solutions that you have defined in the previous work stage. However, you will be going into finer levels of detail and making final iterations. The project specification document you create is the single document that all relevant parties must sign off and agree to. It is often the basis for contractual relationships and will also be used in your vendor selection process (see Section 18.5.3). If you take the time to do the work on the project specification, the subsequent implementation and maintenance work stages will be much easier. You may have taken some time getting to this point, but you are unlikely to have committed large sums of money to the project. Larger capital expenditure and resource costs will, however, be incurred from here on, so it is doubly important that key project stakeholders and sponsors have signed off the project specification.

18.5.2   Buy versus Build

For a fuller examination of the generic buy versus build arguments, refer to Chapter 6, Content Management Systems (CMS), in particular Section 6.2.1, Build versus Buy.

You need to make a decision on whether you are going to build your own measurement tool or whether you are better off buying one. If you examine your needs as detailed in the project specification, then the scale and scope of tool that is required and the measurement approaches that will be used should be clear. It is increasingly likely that you would be better advised to buy a tool that serves your needs rather than build, maintain, and develop one in house. It is likely that even with a purchased tool, you will need to do a reasonable amount of customization and specialized development to get it to do everything you want.

18.5.3   Vendor Selection

Assuming you decide to buy rather than build, the selection of hardware and software often occurs at an earlier point than this in Web development projects. For example, you can select Web server and Web application software during the solution definition work stage once you have defined the technical requirements and technical environment. However, in choosing a measurement tool, it is wise to wait until all other elements have been defined and agreed upon. This is because these tools vary in approach and features to a much wider degree than more basic Web software, such as choice of Web server, and are likely to cost quite a lot more. If you wait until this point to go through a vendor selection process, then you can be absolutely sure of what you require and you can use your project specification to drive the selection process. Use elements from it to create your request for proposal (RFP), selection criteria, and evaluation matrix.

18.5.4   Final Project Plan and Budget

For more about particular measurement vendors, you will find a list in the Resources section. If you are interested in knowing more about a suitable vendor selection process, refer to Chapter 6, Content Management Systems (CMSs), in particular Section 6.2.2, Selection Process.

By now, you should have all the information you need to confidently plan and budget the remainder of the project, including resourcing, time scales, tasks with dependencies, key milestones, and sign-off points. It is quite possible that in putting this together you find that the project is much more expensive and will take much longer than was originally imagined. You will need to confer with the project sponsors and key stakeholders to decide the best path to take: ask for more time and money, reduce the scope of the project, try and negotiate down quoted times and costs, or break the project up into phases. It is rarely a good idea simply to try and force down quoted times and costs because this usually results in poor end quality and results. Asking for more time and money is not always the best way to make friends either. I would favor delivering less but doing it really well either by reducing scope or, perhaps best of all, breaking the project into phases. This ensures people are not disgruntled if they can see their full requirements will eventually be met in later phases, and it gives you a much better chance of actually delivering the first phase on time, to budget, and to a high level of quality. If you can do this, you are much more likely to get the time and money to do the remaining phases, which by that point are likely to have been refined in any case. If you cannot get agreement on scope reduction or phasing, then try at least to build consensus around prioritization of requirements.

18.5.5   Training

Based on the chosen tool (bought or built), you should develop a training plan to familiarize users with it. Different levels of training will be required depending on the types of users and their needs of the system.

18.5.6   Sign-Off and Change Control

Of course, you will be building consensus throughout the project and getting sign-off where appropriate, but the project specification is the most important document to be signed off. You do not want to be the one held responsible for hitting the expensive go button as you enter the production phase of the project. Once the project specification has been signed off, you should begin change control.

18.5.7   Deliverables

The deliverables for the project specification work stage, based on the work described, are as follows:

▶ Project specification, including final project plan and budget as well as updated risks and issues
▶ Vendor selection process, including request for proposal, selection criteria, weighted evaluation matrix, scorecard, and supporting documentation

18.6   Content

In the context of a Web site measurement project, the content work stage is about ensuring that the correct data will be available for processing. Note that this work stage can run in parallel with the following work stage.

18.6.1   Assemble Test Data

Without data, you cannot do any measurement. Furthermore, the quality of any e-business intelligence analysis is dependent on the quality of the data being analyzed. Thus, it is very risky to wait until your system is built and ready to go before ensuring the quality and reliability of your data feeds. At this stage, you should request typical samples of all data that are available that you will be using. Check that these data fit with the formats and structures defined in your data strategy and specified in the project specification.

18.6.2   Test Data Processes

If you need to convert, clean, or otherwise process data—for example, extract, transform, and load (ETL) functions—you should test these. If you can, you should also test that data arrive at the defined time, be it via manual transfer or through automated schedules.

ETL refers to a set of three functions used to manage the transfer of data between databases. The extract function reads a desired subset of data from a source database. The transform function then uses rules, lookup tables, and other predefined instructions to convert the acquired data into the desired state. The load function writes the resultant data to a target database. ETL is used to populate data warehouses and data marts and in moving data between various different types of databases. For example, you might use ETL functions to move data from a database containing customer or transaction information into the data repository that your measurement tool works with.

18.6.3   Deliverables

The deliverables for the content work stage, based on the work described, are as follows:

▶ Sample data
▶ Iteration of data strategy, including updated processes, data flow maps, and conversion and delivery plans as required
▶ Data conversion and processing scripts
▶ Clean data sources and feeds

18.7   Design and Construction

You implement the project specification using your chosen tool.

18.7.1   Project Management

Although this work stage may take the longest and involve more resources than any other work stage, there is little to say about it other than you do what the project specification says. The hard work is in managing all the people involved and in ensuring that good communication continues and that problems are prevented or resolved. Just keeping up to date with progress and project status with regard to the project plan is a large task.

18.7.2   Change Control and Risk Management

Change control and risk management are also likely to feature much more strongly during this work stage as you juggle potential changes to requirements and fend off challenges that might derail the project's progress.

18.7.3   Training and Consulting Services

If you have bought a measurement tool, then there will be some training required, particularly for the development and technical teams that may need support from the vendor.

18.7.4   Deliverables

The deliverables for the design and construction work stage, based on the work described, are as follows:

▶ Project milestones as defined by the project specification
▶ Updated project documentation, including change control, risks and issues, and the project plan

18.8   Testing, Launch, and Handover

You ensure that the system is working as expected before deploying and rolling it out to the organization. *Launch* refers to the deployment of a public-facing Web site with all the attendant fanfare and marketing efforts. *Deployment* is a more standard term for the go live and integration of an enterprise software application.

18.8.1   Testing

Follow the testing plan you created in the solution definition work stage. Web site measurement systems are very rarely available to customers and tend to be used by a relatively small number of people within the organization. This is not an excuse not to do rigorous testing, but it does mean that any problems encountered once the system is live are less critical. The level and complexity of testing will depend most on the level to which the measurement system is integrated with other systems, introducing layers of dependencies. Generally, measurement systems are less complex to test than, say, content management systems because they are less dynamic and integrated. Problems are most often found with the quality and format of data. Resolving user interface and access issues (e.g., remote or mobile access to reports) for end users can also be time consuming.

18.8.2 Deployment and Rollout

Follow the deployment and rollout plan you created in the solution definition work stage. As suggested previously, it is best to concentrate on the few power users who really need the system first before rolling it out more widely.

18.8.3 Internal Marketing

Be wary of overtrumpeting the arrival of your new system as this may then set you up for a fall. At the same time, you should not let your team's efforts go unnoticed, and you will have failed if the system goes unused. You must be the judge of what internal marketing is most appropriate.

18.8.4 Training

Some end users will already be aware of the system and have used it during testing. However, now that you have a fully functioning offering, users are likely to require introductory training and subsequent support.

18.8.5 Documentation

Often as a result of deadline pressures, your documentation and training processes may not be quite as up to date as you had hoped at this stage. If you roll out initially to a few tame users, take this opportunity to get their input and help.

18.8.6   Handover

In your maintenance plan, you should include details of the resources that will be responsible for maintaining the system. This may be a reduced version of the team that developed it or a completely different set of people. Either way, you need to plan a series of handover sessions to facilitate the smooth transition from the initial project team to the maintenance team. Create a handover brief detailing all those things the maintenance team needs to know but which may have escaped other documentation: an external data feed that has been proving unreliable and needs regular checking, for example.

18.8.7   Deliverables

The deliverables for the testing, launch, and handover work stage, based on the work described, are as follows:

▶ Testing documentation and results
▶ Handover briefing
▶ Updated documentation
▶ Training

18.9   Maintenance

Once the system is up and running, it needs to be maintained and refined. Note that this work stage is likely to run in parallel with the following work stage.

18.9.1   Maintenance Plan

Follow and update the maintenance plan that you defined in the solution definition work stage. Make sure that backup, archiving, and data expiration functions are running smoothly. As demands on the system increase, through greater numbers of users and more usage per user, check that the performance of the system is not suffering. Work with the tool vendor to ensure software upgrades occur as necessary. Improve support and service levels, update and refine documentation and guidelines, and provide ongoing training.

18.9.2 Prepare for the Next Phase

If you have phased the implementation of your project, then you will by now already be planning the next phase. You should not miss the review and evaluation work stage that follows, but you should be able to accelerate the project planning work stages that you go back into. As you begin to maintain the phase 1 system, you will learn a lot that is likely to affect your phase 2 planning. Note improvement and enhancements that could be made. Users are likely to give feedback and suggestions. Unless they have spotted critical bugs, which should have been ironed out during testing, resist pressure to make significant changes ad hoc. Instead compile a list of all the little things that need doing and make these part of the phase 2 project or a separate project.

18.9.3 Change Management

For more on change management practices, refer to Part I, Change Management.

During the maintenance work stage, you will receive requests to change and modify the way the system works from end users. For example, users may request new reports or alterations to the formatting or contents of existing reports. Depending on the nature of the change request, you might wish to save it and tackle it as part of a second project or it may need addressing as part of a regular change process. Effective change management during the maintenance work stage helps you keep an audit trail of who requested what and what changes have been made. This is important for effective future planning and ensures that knowledge of what has changed does not reside solely in the head of a single person or scattered around the organization. The system status should reflect system documentation plus subsequent documented changes.

18.9.4 Deliverables

The deliverables for the maintenance work stage, based on the work described, are as follows:

► Updated documentation, including service-level agreements, maintenance and training plans, system documentation, and guidelines
► Wish list of desired improvements, additional features, and functions
► Change management documentation

18.10   Review and Evaluation

You conduct a review of the project and evaluate the results it has achieved against the goals defined at the beginning.

18.10.1   Project Review

Conduct a project review that focuses on assessing how well the project itself was run and how things might be improved in subsequent phases. Elements to address include quality of planning, communication, expectation management, efficiency, team morale, milestone management, budgetary control, key project processes (e.g., reporting, review, and sign-off), and documentation.

18.10.2   Evaluate Results

Refer back to the success criteria defined in the project brief at the beginning of the project to evaluate to what degree the project has underdelivered or exceeded expectations.

18.10.3   Recommendations

Based on your experience, you should make recommendations for what can be done next. If you are going into phase 2 of a large project, then it is highly probable that phase 1 will have taught you some lessons and uncovered requirements that will necessitate some refinement of plans for the coming phases. Actually using the system to measure the Web site's performance will also give you valuable insight that will drive recommendations for site improvements such as content and functionality enhancements, improved customer communications, more accurate lead and revenue forecasting, and better evaluation of the value that partners and third parties are delivering.

18.10.4   Deliverables

The deliverables for the review and evaluation work stage, based on the work described, are as follows:

▶ Project review, including performance against objectives
▶ Recommendations

Summary

We have discussed a wide range of measurement approaches, techniques, and metrics as well as looked at how you might run a Web measurement project. However, as there is increasing focus on this area, the following four points are the most important to remember:

▶ It is very important to understand Web metrics and measurement techniques if you are to use them appropriately and to your advantage. As we have seen, there are all sorts of things you *can* do, but to be sure of success you must understand what is right for your requirements.

▶ You must develop a Web measurement framework that is aligned to your overall business strategy and objectives. Web measurement requires specialist knowledge and practices, but the results it generates must integrate with the core business and add value to it.

▶ You must combine measurement techniques to get an accurate, full picture and intelligence you can rely on. Look at combining online and offline as well as qualitative and quantitative approaches.

▶ Measurement must provide actionable intelligence. Any reporting that cannot be analyzed to come up with actions has little value. What use is it knowing that average users look at six pages per visit? Is that good or bad? What is the resulting action?

Resources

T his part of the book contains resources that will further help you maintain and evolve a successful commercial Web site. There are four sections: details of what is on the companion site to this book; a list of recommended reading to further your knowledge in the key topics addressed in this book; some recommended Web sites; and finally, a list of product vendors, again broken down into the principal areas of content management, customer relationship management, and site measurement.

Companion Site

The companion site to this book can be found at *www.e-consultancy.com*. That is the URL for the home page from which you can explore and take advantage of all the resources available. However, if you want to go to the page that groups the resources directly relevant to this book as detailed in the following, you should visit *www.e-consultancy.com/book2*.

The following table details what resources are available and where you can find them. Not all of the content on the Web site is replicated in the book. For

Location and description of resources that go with the book.

Resource	Description	In book?	On Web site?
Example documentation	Files for download are posted to the Web site. For example, there is a template Web project file that you can use and modify for your own projects.		✓
Table of contents and example chapter	If you have got as far as reading this, you probably will not need these for yourself but might want to pass them on to a colleague.	✓	✓
Buy and comments links	Links to where you can buy the book online and leave your comments for other potential purchasers.		✓
Useful URLs	Recommended sites to help you with your work.	✓	✓
Recommended reading list	A list of books I would recommend on the subject of maintaining and evolving Web sites.	✓	✓
Glossary	A comprehensive database of Internet terms with definitions in case anything you have read in this book is not clear.		✓
Expert forums	Discussion forums where you can ask questions or give advice on the topics covered in the book. If you want to ask me a question, the forums are the place to do it.		✓
White papers, reports, research, case studies	A database of over 500 white papers, reports, research, and case studies covering the topics in this book.		✓
Quiz	A somewhat more fun way to learn. A quiz with questions about the Internet to test your knowledge. Helpful knowledge tips with each answer.		✓

example, the glossary is available on the site but not here because it is much easier to add terms and keep it up to date via the Web. The content that is replicated here, like the reading list and useful URLs, will be kept up to date on the Web site, so it is worth visiting. In particular, the template documents and other files are only available from the site.

NOTE   **Want to Ask My Advice? Want to Ask a Question Related to the Book?**

I am happy to try to answer questions on anything in this book, but I only do so via the e-consultancy forums at *www.e-consultancy.com/forum/* (unless I am being paid to do so otherwise, of course). This is so everyone can join in the discussion, contribute, and share knowledge and experience. I regularly publish my latest thinking to these forums and edit a monthly newsletter that site users can subscribe to. I look forward to "talking" to you there. ∎

Recommended Reading

Rather than give a long list of books, I have debated long and hard and managed to reduce my recommended reading list to just seven books. These are the books that I have learned most from in relation to the topics discussed in this book. As new books come out, they will be added to the *www.e-consultancy.com/book2* site.

Don't Make Me Think: A Common Sense Approach to Web Usability
Steve Krug
Que Publishing
ISBN: 0-7897-2310-7
This relatively short book is a gem of common sense. Krug makes the potentially complex problems of Web site usability accessible and easy to understand. If you have ever wondered what you are doing wasting your time in design meetings discussing what shade of what color a graphic should be, then this book will help you focus on what is really important in improving your site for your users. Everything Krug says seems so obvious and yet revelatory. He speaks with the wisdom of someone who has used a lot of sites himself and has watched a lot of other people using sites. Starting from the premise that "people won't use your Web site if they can't find their way around it," Krug explains how people really use the Web, how to write for the Web, how to design the home page and navigation, and how to do usability testing yourself.

Content Management Bible
Bob Boiko
Hungry Minds
ISBN: 0-7645-4862-X
Unlike Krug's book, this one is long at almost 1000 pages. But then again, content management is a big subject, and Boiko goes into every aspect of it in quite some detail. This is the most comprehensive book dedicated to content management that I have read. Despite its length, and some sections that are quite technical, it remains very readable and contains a good balance between the

practical (processes, deliverables, checklists, forms, etc.) and the more conceptual. The book begins by asking What Is Content? and then What Is Content Management? before moving into the main sections addressing how to do a content management project and how to build a content management system.

Web Content Management: A Collaborative Approach
Russell Nakano
Addison-Wesley
ISBN: 0-201-65782-1
I did not get as much out of this book as I did from Boiko's on content management. However, I did find it particularly strong and interesting when talking about how to organize development teams and development environments to suit the scale of initiative. As the title suggests, there is a focus on how to orchestrate collaborative development work, which is not easy but very important. The sections on workflow, how to handle multiple Web initiatives, and how to approach globalization and localization are particularly good.

CRM at the Speed of Light: Capturing and Keeping
Customers in Internet Real Time
Paul Greenberg
Osborne McGraw-Hill
ISBN: 0-072-12782-1
I have read a lot of books and white papers on CRM and eCRM, but this is the one that stands out for me. A lot of what I have read on CRM comes across as marketing vapor-speak, but Greenberg's book manages to get the core concepts across in a clear and convincing manner. Coming from a background in digital media, I found it particularly useful to hear his take on CRM versus eCRM and how the two have evolved and are coalescing. A reasonable chunk of the book is dedicated to evaluating some of the major CRM players, which though interesting and valuable at the time, risks dating quickly in this rapidly evolving field.

Permission Marketing: Turning Strangers into Friends,
and Friends into Customers
Seth Godin
Simon and Schuster
ISBN: 0-684-85636-0
This book has become quite a cult classic of the Internet age with Godin now heralded as the "father of permission marketing." As with Krug's book on usability, Godin's points are quite straightforward and seemingly obvious, but it al-

ways helps to have someone else say them before they become clear in your own mind. The key message is that interruptive marketing, where you push marketing messages intrusively into people's awareness, is giving way to permission marketing, where the goal is to build a permission-based relationship between company and customer. As you can no doubt tell, permission marketing has a strong affinity to the concepts of CRM and it is particularly well suited to the Web because of its interactive nature, facilitating more involved, two-way dialogues. If you want to improve the performance of your Web site, you would do well to improve the levels of permission you have to talk to your site's users.

Measuring the Success of Your Website: A Customer-Centric Approach to Website Management
Hurol Inan
Prentice-Hall
ISBN: 1-740-09648-7
This is the best book I have so far read on how to understand the success of your Web site. The author spent 11 years at Andersen Consulting and Deloitte Touche Tohmatsu, which helps ensure that the focus is a commercial one and based on a wealth of experience. Furthermore, far from being too "management consulting" to be intelligible and practical, the book addresses operational and implementation issues as well as giving enough technical detail without being overwhelming. Definitely worth a read. The accompanying Web site (see Recommended Sites) is also a good resource.

Web Metrics: Proven Methods for Measuring Web Site Success
Jim Sterne
John Wiley and Sons
ISBN: 0-471-22072-8
Jim Sterne is a leading Internet marketing expert and has already published several books and white papers on online marketing and Web metrics. The book promises to "explain the criteria for building a successful site, surveying the tools, services, techniques, and standards for Web measurement, and fully integrating those metrics with the customer experience." It is certainly comprehensive in the techniques and approaches that are reviewed, and the text is supported by some good case study material and real-world insights. The book takes very much a marketing focus and skirts issues like content management, customer relationship management, or implementation, but if you really want to delve into the world of Web metrics from a business and marketing point of view, there is no better place to start.

Recommended Sites

Here are the sites that I use to keep up to date on the topics discussed in this book.

Customer Relationship Management (CRM)

CRM has been around for quite some time, and there are more sites and trade publications dedicated to it than to many other topics. The industry is already large and projected to grow, so the proliferation of CRM-focused sites is not surprising. Here are the most significant and important of those sites, at least in my view.

CRM search engine
www.searchcrm.com
Part of the techtarget.com family of industry-specific search engines, this is a one-stop shop for CRM needs. It is somewhat more than just a search engine, including a marketplace to buy CRM-related books and a directory of vendors, among other things.

CRMGuru.com
www.CRMguru.com
"Real CRM Gurus. Real Answers." That's the tagline for the site, and it's not an unjustified claim. Apart from some useful white papers, definitions, and news, the real attraction of this site (which had over 175,000 subscribers worldwide at last count) has to be its moderated discussion group CRM. Talk, which has a consistently high level of high-value contributions and contributors.

CRM Project
www.crmproject.com
Published by Montgomery Research and sponsored by Andersen Consulting, CRM Project is a tome of information on CRM and personalization. Particularly useful is the library of white papers from thought leaders in this sphere. Definitely worth a visit.

CRM-forum.com
www.crm-forum.com
"The CRM-Forum is the pre-eminent independent on-line resource centre for CRM professionals working in the business-consumer marketplace. It provides CRM professionals and companies involved in CRM on both the de-

mand and supply side of the industry with a place to keep up-to-date with CRM developments, and to meet, discuss, and contact each other about CRM-related issues." That is what it says on the site, and that is exactly what this site is: a great, deep resource.

CRMcommunity.com
www.crmcommunity.com
This site has a strong white papers section, but its distinguishing feature when compared to the other resources here is its emphasis on community. More of the content on the site is actually generated by users, and the discussion boards are lively and informative as a result.

CRMassist.com
www.crmassist.com
You would be forgiven for thinking this was a Yahoo! site because of its design and navigation. This site is particularly useful for a more technical and vendor skew on CRM: If you're looking for vendor solution white papers, for example, this is definitely the place to come.

European Centre for Customer Strategies
www.eccs.uk.com
Clearly, the European focus is the unique slant to this site. It is a slick site that has a good Advice Centre containing plenty of CRM knowledge resources, a European Directory of CRM solution providers, and a unique Product Finder that, while not bulletproof in its results, could be a useful first stab in any product selection process.

DestinationCRM.com
www.destinationcrm.com
This is the accompanying site to the industry standard magazines *CRM* and *eCRM*. Thus, it gets a lot of attention, users, and traffic. Not surprisingly, good for news and careers as these are the mainstay of the print publications. This site is not quite as compelling as some of the previous sites, but it should be in your CRM bookmarks nonetheless.

Content Management

Content management is only just beginning to catch on in a big way, so expect the number of sites dedicated to it to increase in the same way as they did to cater to the explosion of interest in CRM. In the meantime, the following three sites are my favorites for content management information.

CMSWatch

www.cmswatch.com

CMSWatch bills itself as "an independent source of information, news, opinion, and analysis about Web content management." The site contains news, features, and reports as well as views on trends. The main focus, however, is around research and analysis of the products and vendors themselves. As this is such a fast evolving arena, the site is very useful in staying up to date.

Metatorial

www.metatorial.com

This site is run by Bob Boiko, author of the *Content Management Bible* on the recommended reading list. There is supporting content for the book on the site but also a lot more valuable resources such as presentations, seminars, white papers, discussions, and interviews with experts. Whereas the CMS-Watch site is product-centric, this site is more useful for understanding the discipline, practice, and concepts of content management.

Content-Wire

www.content-wire.com

This site is less specifically about content management and more about online content generally: its creation, production, management, aggregation, publishing, and syndication. Whereas the Metatorial and CMSWatch sites are more about research, analysis, and thinking around content management, this site is more news and features driven, so there is a higher turnover of more lightweight content.

Site Measurement

I am aware of fewer sites that are dedicated to Web site measurement. In most cases, I have pieced together information from various marketing resources that I have come across. If you know of other good sites for this topic, let me know via the e-consultancy site and I will add them to the list on the site.

Various Vendor Lists

I suggest various measurement vendors in the next section, but if you want to find a more comprehensive list, you could try:

▶ Yahoo!
(*dir.yahoo.com/Business_and_Economy/Business_to_Business/ Communications_and_Networking/Internet_and_World_Wide_Web/ Network_Management/Traffic_Management/Log_Analysis_Tools/Titles/*)
▶ HTTPD Log Analyzers
(*www.hypernews.org/HyperNews/get/www/log-analyzers.html*)
▶ Internet.com
(*serverwatch.Internet.com/dtanalysis.html*)

Managing the Digital Enterprise
digitalenterprise.org/metrics/metrics.html
This site was created to be used in conjunction with a graduate-level course taught at North Carolina State University. This page on web metrics is just one topic of the online course by Professor Michael Rappa, and it brings together an excellent collection of resources about key issues in Web site measurement, including research, sites to visit, data sources, webcasts, and online discussion forums.

Measuring the Success of Your Web Site
www.hurolinan.com
This is the accompanying Web site to Hurol Inan's excellent book of the same title. It is one of the few sites that is truly dedicated to providing resources on Web site measurement. Obviously, it encourages you to buy the book, which I think you should do anyway, but there is plenty of useful information there even if you do not purchase his book: a glossary of relevant terms, a list of other good books on the topic, lists and brief reviews of site measurement vendors, and links to relevant articles.

Target Marketing
www.targeting.com
This is the Web site of the company that Jim Sterne, author of one of the books I recommend earlier, is behind. Not surprisingly, the site promotes Target Marketing's professional services as well as Jim's books, but it also contains

some good past articles on Internet marketing and Web metrics. You can also sign up for Jim's "mostly monthly" newsletter, which contains good insight and advice.

CustomerCentric Solutions
www.customercentricsolutions.com
Formerly known as NetGenesis, CustomerCentric Solutions is a product vendor that has done more than most to increase the levels of awareness and knowledge on the topic of Web site measurement. The section on their site dedicated to e-metrics (at *www.netgen.com/index.cfm?section=solutionsand-file=emetrics* the last time I visited) contains some useful resources including a glossary, a recommended reading list, and a good white paper.

CHI-WEB
www.chi-Web.org
If you want to learn more specifically about usability, then CHI-WEB's moderated discussion list "on the human factor aspects of the World Wide Web" is a great resource. It is targeted at, and used by, usability professionals, so the level of contributions is generally high. You can search the list archives to find quickly the information you are after. Past discussions have included log analysis tools and site-centric Web metrics and measurement as well as usability and interface design.

Product Vendors

Following are product vendors for the three main areas addressed in the book: content management, customer relationship management, and site measurement. These lists do not constitute any kind of recommendation or endorsement for these particular products, but at least you will have somewhere to start if you are looking for a solution. I have not included a review of vendors' products because they will no doubt have changed by the time you read this, and the right solution for you will depend very much on your needs and requirements.

Content Management Systems

Here are some of the leading CMS vendors broken down into three broad categories representing the scale and cost of solution. The enterprise solutions typically contain features and capabilities that mean they are not considered only CMSs, but also e-business platforms that incorporate CRM, CMS, measurement, and more.

Enterprise Scale Solutions

Vignette
www.vignette.com

BroadVision
www.broadvision.com

Documentum
www.documentum.com

Interwoven
www.interwoven.com

Mid-Market Solutions

Microsoft—Content Management Server
www.microsoft.com

Obtree
www.obtree.com

Mediasurface
www.mediasurface.com

IBM—Content Manager
www.ibm.com

Lower Price Solutions

Infosquare
www.infosquare.com

Atomz
www.atomz.com

CRM Vendors

Next are the better known CRM vendors broken into two broad categories. You will notice that the likes of Vignette and Broadvision qualify both as CRM and CMS vendors. The likes of BEA, Oracle, and ATG position themselves not only as CRM solutions but also as broader e-business platforms, or suites, that cover all needs. Many of the larger CRM vendors come from an offline heritage (e.g., call centers, ERP, or data mining) and have evolved their products to cater to a multichannel CRM strategy. The more specialized vendors tend to focus either on particular customer contact channels (e.g., online) or are particularly strong in one area of CRM (e.g., analytics or customer service).

Enterprise Class Solutions

BEA
www.bea.com

ATG
www.atg.com

Oracle
www.oracle.com

Vignette
www.vignette.com

BroadVision
www.broadvision.com

Siebel
www.siebel.com

PeopleSoft
www.peoplesoft.com

Amdocs
www.amdocs.com

Onyx
www.onyx.com

MicroStrategy
www.microstrategy.com

Mid-Market or More Specialized Solutions

Pivotal
www.pivotal.com

Kana
www.kana.com

eGain
www.egain.com

e.Piphany
www.epiphany.com

NetPerceptions
www.netperceptions.com

CustomerCentric Solutions
www.customercentricsolutions.com

Site Measurement Tools

Note that the following vendors provide products and services that are based on data analysis. There are plenty of ways to measure the performance of sites by working with users or groups of users, such as usability testing, panels, or focus groups, but this section concentrates on software vendors. There are two broad groups given: enterprise-level system performance measurement and Web site measurement and analysis. The former is for enterprisewide solutions that incorporate the testing and performance management of large-scale Internet applications and architectures. The second group is for vendors providing intelligence on how your Web site is being used and by whom, using log file analysis, page tagging, and other techniques. These tools can also help you assess, monitor, and manage the performance of your Web site, including checking for broken links, monitoring server uptime, checking file sizes, monitoring server response times, and load and stress testing.

Enterprise-Level System Performance Measurement

Segue
www.segue.com

Mercury Interactive Corporation
www.mercuryinteractive.com

Web Site Measurement and Analysis

LiveStats from Deepmetrix
www.deepmetrix.com

WebTrends
www.Webtrends.com

WhiteCross Systems
www.whitecross.com

Nedstat
www.nedstat.com

Hit List from Accrue Software
www.accrue.com

I/PRO Netline from LightSpeed
www.lspeed.com

Hitwise
www.hitwise.com

Index